THE DOMINION OF VOICE

THE DOMINION OF VOICE

Riot, Reason, and Romance
in Antebellum Politics

Kimberly K. Smith

UNIVERSITY PRESS OF KANSAS

© 1999 by the University Press of Kansas
All rights reserved

Published by the University Press of Kansas (Lawrence, Kansas 66049), which was organized by the Kansas Board of Regents and is operated and funded by Emporia State University, Fort Hays State University, Kansas State University, Pittsburg State University,
the University of Kansas, and Wichita State University.

Library of Congress Cataloging-in-Publication Data

Smith, Kimberly K., 1966–
    The dominion of voice : riot, reason, and romance in Antebellum
politics / Kimberly K. Smith.
        p.   cm.
    Includes bibliographical references and index.
    ISBN 0-7006-0957-1 (cloth : alk. paper)
    1. United States—Politics and government—1815–1861. 2. United
States—Intellectual life—1783–1865. 3. Political culture—United
States—History—19th century. 4. Northeastern States—Intellectual
life—19th century. 5. Political culture—Northeastern States—
History—19th century. 6. Riots—Political aspects—United States—
History—19th century. 7. Rhetoric—Political aspects—United
States—History—19th century. 8. Politics and literature—United
States—History—19th century. I. Title.
E415.S65   1999
306.2′ 0973′ 09034—dc21   98-55248

British Library Cataloguing in Publication Data is available.

Printed in the United States of America
10 9 8 7 6 5 4 3 2 1

The paper used in this publication meets the minimum requirements of the American
National Standard for Permanence of Paper for Printed Library Materials Z39.48-1984.

CONTENTS

PREFACE

The American Revolution settled, more or less, the question of *whether* the people should participate in politics. But it left open the question of *how* they should participate. Would democracy turn out to be a series of boisterous public gatherings, parades, and riots—a kind of permanent revolution, or one long Tea Party? Could the energy of the people be disciplined into tamer, more orderly meetings and elections? In short, what would democratic politics look like, on the ground?

The answer was far from obvious. There were few precedents, and the founders were deeply suspicious of many of the practices we now take for granted. Political associations, parties, newspaper editorials, freewheeling public political debate—these were, to most early Americans, sources of anxiety and discord, not the reassuring evidence of a burgeoning civil society we now look for in new democracies. This is a generalization, of course; but as generalizations go, it's accurate enough. Where we see healthy political conflict and an alert, active citizenry, they saw a threat to the republic.

It's hard to know what to make of their concerns. Weren't the founders supposed to be the architects of democracy? Doesn't democracy *imply* free political association, critical public argument, and an informed, reasoning citizenry? The answer, surprisingly, is not necessarily. In fact, when we look back at the turbulent beginnings of mass politics in America, we find a number of different conceptions of democracy in play—not all of which gave rationality and public debate the favored place they now hold in contemporary democratic theory. My goal here is to explore some of these conceptions and to understand how, and to what extent, rational argument became integral to what we mean by "democracy." In other words, I want to understand how Americans answered the question of how the people should participate in politics.

My particular focus is a set of antebellum debates about the question of means: the question of what norms and conventions should govern political action. These debates, I argue, played a critical role in establishing rational argument as a good (perhaps the best) form of political action. Unhappy with the riotous, often violent politics of the era, antebellum Americans suggested that democracy should not be simply another name for mob rule. On the contrary, they insisted, it should mean informed, reasonable people cordially and peacefully debating important issues in the public arena.

But at the same time, antebellum Americans had concerns about whether this ideal should or could be realized. In addition to their arguments for more rational deliberation, we find three major "antideliberative" themes in antebellum discourse: the claim that mob action is an important part of democratic politics, the fear of demagoguery that constantly haunted the practice of public debate, and the abolitionists' argument for a politics of storytelling that would serve as an alternative to rational debate. Understanding these themes is critical to understanding how the ideal of a reasoning republic emerged during the early years of the nation, what that ideal actually meant, and what problems it created—for them and, arguably, for us.

As is customary, I take full responsibility for what is misguided or wrongheaded in this book and credit my friends with all that is smart, well considered, and interesting. I benefited a great deal from the comments and criticisms of my committee: Don Herzog, Doug Dion, Jackie Stevens, and Sue Juster. I also had a lot of help from my friends; Paul Freedman, Maria Bergstrom, Erik McKee, Ted Clayton, Marek Steedman, and Eric Kos were particularly generous with their time, their ideas, and their encouragement. I am grateful to Carey McWilliams for his feedback on the manuscript and to the staff of the University Press of Kansas for their efforts in bringing the book to publication. Fellowship support from the University of Michigan Political Science Department and the Rackham School of Graduate Studies made it possible for me to write the book I wanted to write. But my greatest debt is to my family, who provided (in addition to the usual emotional and financial support) demanding readers, a stimulating intellectual environment, and models of scholarly and professional excellence.

INTRODUCTION

"[W]here all is plain," insisted Frederick Douglass, "there is nothing to be argued." It was 1852, and his subject was abolition. "What point in the anti-slavery creed would you have me argue? On what branch of the subject do the people of this country need light? Must I undertake to prove that the slave is a man? That point is conceded already. Nobody doubts it. . . . Would you have me argue that man is entitled to liberty? . . . Must I argue the wrong-fulness of slavery? Is that a question for Republicans?"[1]

These were rhetorical questions, of course. The audience was meant to nod approvingly, in tacit agreement that the issue was beyond the bounds of legitimate debate. Douglass was simply reminding his audience of the principles they all agreed on. But—and this is what gives the passage its darkly ominous tone—it was notorious that everyone *didn't* agree on the wrongfulness of slavery. And if Douglass refused to argue the point any longer, what did he propose to do about it?

Put it this way: If democratic politics is ideally the realm of reasoned argument, as many theorists would have us believe, then Frederick Douglass's famous rejection of argument sounds like a rejection of politics itself—a call to arms, perhaps, or a prescripton for passivity. Is it? Or did Douglass just have a different answer to the question of how the people could, and should, legitimately participate in politics? What other answers make sense, and in what way, within the limits of American political traditions?

These are the questions I want to answer. Admittedly, at first glance they don't look too promising. After all, it hardly seems necessary to affirm that American political culture supports differing opinions about what kinds of political activities are legitimate and desirable in a democracy. But (more interestingly) such diversity, if it exists in the broader political culture, has not found its way into contemporary democratic theory. Instead, a survey of recent scholarship reveals an almost unchallenged consensus that rational public debate should be the primary means of practicing politics in a liberal democracy. Some go so far as to suggest that a politics of public debate is, or should be, implied by the very concept of democracy. To James Fishkin, for example, deliberation is "an essential part of any adequate theory of democracy"; a political system without deliberation is not, in his view, a democracy. According to David Yankelovich, deliberative democracy is a particular vision

1

of democracy, "one that involves those who wish to be involved and that recognizes that the highest expression of human rationality is . . . ordinary people speaking and reasoning together on issues of common concern." Amy Guttman and Dennis Thompson similarly advocate a "conception of democracy that secures a central place for moral discussion in political life," thus affording the practice of reason giving a special place in democratic politics.[2] The standard bête noire of this camp is the view that democracy is simply a device for aggregating preferences, a conception that puts deal making and interest group bargaining at the center of democratic politics.[3] But they also implicitly reject, or at least devalue, visions of democracy centering on such activities as protest and resistance or storytelling—both of which traditions, I argue, have an important history in American politics. Conceptions of democracy centering on these alternative traditions, and privileging values such as courage or compassion over rationality, bring a richness and complexity to American political thought that contemporary democratic theory lacks; while proponents of "deliberative democracy" may illuminate the role of reason in democratic politics, they tell us little about the role of passion, interest, sympathy, or violence.

Of course, the preference for rational public debate over other forms of political action is nothing new. Americans have been calling for more rational deliberation as long as there has been an American republic—which makes Douglass's rejection of argument all the more striking. But this distrust of argument isn't unusual, either. In fact, Americans' stance toward rational argument has been more complex, and qualified, than the current chorus of enthusiasm would suggest. This value is actually riddled with ambiguity and unresolved tensions that create an ambivalence too often concealed by the rhetoric surrounding it. How often do we assert, without actually believing, that debate will somehow resolve into consensus, that confining politics to public argument will diminish the threat of domination and violence, that truth will eventually prevail? The fact that people can make such claims without being called on to defend them suggests that the value of rational debate is long overdue for a more critical analysis. Thus, instead of calling for more reasoned deliberation or adducing further reasons to encourage it, I ask how this value achieved such a dominant place in our thinking about politics, what it actually commits us to, and what kinds of problems it creates for us.

Of course, anyone who tackles a subject like this has to address the work of Jürgen Habermas, which has inspired much of the recent interest in democratic deliberation and rational public discourse. His historical investigation of the relationship between liberal democracy and the practice of critical public discourse is an important starting point for my study. Habermas argues, cogently and persuasively, that for eighteenth-century philosophes, the practice of critical public debate—a practice suggested by if not fully realized in the institutions of bourgeois coffeehouses, salons, and literary societies—was supposed to embody the rationality and equality considered essential to liberal politics. These architects of liberalism hoped that as a politics of reasoned argument replaced the arbitrary exercise of power, politics would become a domain of rationality rather than force.[4] To put the point a little too simplistically, then, Habermas suggests that coffeehouse debates and similar practices played a central role in constituting "the public" of liberal theory and practice, so that the conventions of public debate developed in those institutions became normative for many liberal conceptions of politics more generally. If he's right, then we should expect that coffeehouses, salons, and debating societies served as important models of democratic politics for early Americans. And to some extent they did. But the story is more complicated than that, and my purpose is to unravel some of the complications.

In fact, the American founders were far from certain about or unanimous on how the people should participate in politics. Voting was widely accepted as the primary means of participation, but beyond that there was surprisingly little consensus on what popular politics should look like. Campaigning was suspect, as were political clubs, and the Sedition Act of 1798 expressed a profound discomfort with newspapers and other forms of public political argument. Gradually, over the course of many decades, government officials grew more comfortable with public debate, but the "question of means" (as the problem was typically glossed) was still a controversial one when Jacksonian democracy and the mass political activism of the antebellum era made it a central focus of political discourse.

This, then, is the period I have chosen to focus on—the years between the election of Andrew Jackson and the Civil War. This was a critical period in the formation of American democracy, witnessing the beginning of mass politics with the creation of mass-based political parties and the mobilization of workers, women, and blacks into the political system. It was also, of course, a particularly turbulent and conflict-ridden period, during which politics was especially salient. For all these reasons, the norms and conventions of democratic political action were the subject of frequent discussion and debate. In fact, it's easy to overlook this theme in antebellum political discourse, precisely because it's so pervasive. Comments and reflections on the question of means punctuate practically every editorial, pamphlet, and letter: "if we look at the matter dispassionately"; "we abhor violence"; "we should strive to avoid heats and animosities"; and so on. Much of this sounds like mere boilerplate, standard throat clearing before the real argument begins. But if a great deal of this discourse *was* boilerplate language, it was there

for a reason. It needed to be said; the ground rules of political action were
not taken for granted. It was *not* obvious, not in the tumultuous decades
preceding the Civil War, that we would be "dispassionate," that "we abhorred
violence" and would avoid "heats and animosities." (Nor, for that matter, was
it obvious who "we" were; the shape and character of the democratic public
were also at stake here.) The proper norms and conventions of democratic
politics were both nonobvious and hotly contested. This chapter in the republic's history therefore makes a good case study of the question of means
in American political thought.

At one level, then, this is a contribution to the field of American political
thought—an exploration of how the problem of participation and political
action was framed, interpreted, and debated during the early years of the
republic and, in particular, a history of the category of rational political argument. But what will this excursion into American history contribute to the
contemporary theoretical debate—or, more properly, nondebate—over the
norms of political action? This is a methodological point, calling for some
discussion of the uses of history in political theory.

Theory and History

If political theory is meant to be the critical examination of abstract, timeless
ideas, then one might expect theorists to use history merely as a source of
interesting problems and illustrations of theoretical points. But because those
ideas are contained in texts, we must also be historians, since interpreting
texts always, to some degree, involves making historical arguments; even the
most abstract of theoretical concepts refers to a background of social practices. Thus, even if our only interest is in ferreting out the author's intended
meaning, we need to consider the text's historical context—a point most an-
tihistoricists usually grant.

But when we begin to interpret texts as interventions in actual political
conflicts, as I do throughout this study, we seem to be moving away from our
initial concern with the unchanging meaning of abstract ideas. Here the his-
toricist would argue that ideas don't have unchanging meanings, that ideas
in fact can't be separated from practices. From this point of view, political
theory begins to look very much like social history, since understanding what
a given idea means involves understanding the particular social practices in
which it is embedded. At times we may even want to reduce ideas to practices, by treating them as abstractions from patterns of discourse that are
themselves social practices. We needn't go so far, of course; but I would sug-

gest that the boundaries between practices, languages, and ideas are primarily a matter of analytic convenience. I may approach the Declaration of Independence, for example, as expressing abstract ideas about liberty and rights, as using a political language in which the words "liberty" and "rights" figure prominently in characteristic ways, or as the product of a complex set of social practices that includes writing documents that refer to "liberty" and "rights." Which approach I take will depend on what I'm trying to explain, to whom, and for what purpose.

In this study I rely primarily on the second and third approaches, focusing on social practices and the public use of language. This choice follows from my pragmatic (as opposed to strictly idealistic or materialistic) reading of history—which is to say that my subjects are people, not ideas (and certainly not *timeless* ideas) or large-scale social forces. It is not that ideas and social forces aren't important in explaining human behavior, but I don't take them as determinative. My subjects, I assume, are neither led by the inescapable logic of ideas nor pushed around by material forces; they are actors responding to specific circumstances in sometimes habitual and sometimes inventive ways—ways that involve changing or clinging to a certain manner of talking about and doing things (in this case, mostly political things). In the words of Don Herzog, "The plight of social actors, or if you like their opportunity, is then clear. They inherit an ongoing ensemble of social practices and concepts and categories: they no more start from scratch here than they do in gaining empirical knowledge. They learn what have already been defined as their problems, and the terms of political debate as they currently stand. And they can expect new problems, thrown up by social change and the development of new arguments. This situation leaves them with plenty of alternatives."[5] Our opportunity, then, is to make sense of the actors' situations, alternatives, and choices.

But this approach begs the question, why would a late-twentieth-century American care about 200-year-old sets of social practices? Surely our practices (ideas, languages) have changed since then. What do these ancient documents have to do with us, if they're not expressing eternal truths? They may, of course, have nothing to do with us, which is in itself a good reason to study them. Exploring how others have responded to a given situation—what concepts and categories they used to make sense of their world—may give us insight into our own responses, if only by contrast. But when we study the history of the nation we live in, we generally expect it to have some connection, however tenuous, with our current situation. For example, we may discover that we're still making the same responses our ancestors did, through habit or because those responses have been institutionalized in some way, even though they may no longer be appropriate. Or we may find that our situation hasn't changed that much and that the older concepts and languages are actually more useful than whatever we've been using recently.[6]

It may be this concern with how useful the concepts and categories under investigation actually are, or were, that separates political theory from intellectual history. More conventionally, what marks this study as political theory rather than history is my focus on canonical texts (or the texts that I think should be canonical). Although I draw extensively on newspapers, novels, and other forms of popular discourse, my primary aim is to illuminate those texts—such as Douglass's Fourth of July speech and *Narrative*, Angelina Grimké's debate with Catharine Beecher, Frances Wright's lectures, and Harriet Beecher Stowe's *Uncle Tom's Cabin*—that reflect and extend, and sometimes take to extremes, the ideas circulating in everyday political argument. Such texts, although not always representative of ordinary political talk, give us insight into the assumptions and meanings behind such talk (besides being interesting and thought provoking in themselves).

In short, I am more of a theorist than a historian. My historical account is intended to provide a better, more insightful reading of certain key texts in the canon of American political thought. Beyond that, it is intended to further a theoretical point: specifically, that the category of "rational public debate"—a concept that plays a central role in our theories of and contemporary discourse about democracy and political action—has a history. It was constructed in the heat of political conflict and in response to real-world situations. Understanding this history gives us better insight into what that category means, what problems it is good for solving, what problems it creates for us, and what alternatives might be available.

The Argument

First, some caveats about the scope and limits of this study. I am interested in the debates surrounding the question of means, as they took shape in the North between (roughly) 1830 and 1850. My focus, then, is northeastern, urban political culture, as reflected in such pervasive and widely read texts as newspapers, pamphlets, speeches, sermons, and novels, as well as less public (or more ambiguously public) documents such as letters and diaries. This broad range of materials should provide a good understanding of the modes of political discourse in play at the time. Of course, my net could have been wider; varieties of public discourse are carried out in popular music and theater, in art and architecture, even in fashion and manners. I excluded these sources simply to keep the scope of my research manageable.

One might object that my choice of sources introduces a class bias into my analysis, because these texts were produced and read (arguably) mostly by the middle and upper classes. I doubt that this is quite accurate; newspapers and political pamphlets, at least, were read and sometimes written by members of the working class. But it is true that I have not attempted to examine the less-accessible public discourse of lower-class communities. Nor do insular ethnic communities (the Irish and Germans, for example) receive much attention. But I am not trying to document the full range of political languages and practices available to antebellum Americans, just a few of the dominant (or hegemonic) ones.

I make the same excuse for limiting my choice of texts by geography. I have focused primarily on Philadelphia, on that city's politics and political activists and the texts produced and read by those activists. Philadelphia is not representative of the whole country, of course, but it had a complex political culture similar (at least in its broad contours) to that of other northeastern cities. In addition, although certainly not the dominant center of politics it was during the eighteenth century, antebellum Philadelphia was still a major center for publishing and for politics, and political activists in Philadelphia were in close contact with their counterparts in other cities. Therefore, the city was both fairly typical of northeastern urban political culture and an important influence on that culture; it reflected and contributed to the major political trends of the times. Thus Philadelphia may be taken as representative of one of the relevant contexts (though certainly not the only one) for interpreting many of the significant political texts of the era. Nevertheless, the narrow scope of my research necessarily qualifies my conclusions, and despite my occasionally sweeping language, I do not intend to make any claims about western, southern, or rural political culture.[7] Simply put, I would like to understand how a politically engaged person in the urban Northeast might have read Frederick Douglass's *Narrative;* I don't expect to provide much insight into how it would have been read by a planter from Alabama or a farmer in Michigan.

With those caveats in mind, the study focuses on three political practices: mob action, public debate, and narrative testimony (storytelling). I'm interested in how these practices were promoted, justified, or condemned—what reasonings and assumptions about politics, political community, and democracy lay behind the norms of political action, and particularly the norms surrounding public debate. I begin with the eighteenth-century tradition of mob action because of the close historical connection between rioting and argument; the genealogy of the value of rational argument in American politics is linked to the suppression of the earlier tradition of mob action. Part I examines this displacement of mob action by argument and the construction of reasoned public debate as a peaceful, orderly alternative to the disorder and violence of the mob.

My goal in Part I is to underscore the contingency and instability of the value of rational argument; it was not the only nor the most obvious answer to the question of means. Part II, in contrast, explores the tensions and fault lines within the concept of rational public argument itself. I focus on two competing models of political debate. The first, drawn from the tradition of neoclassical rhetoric, highlights the problems with using speech as a tool to persuade and motivate the public. The second, rooted in Enlightenment rationalism, abandons this concern with the mechanisms by which we convince and motivate one another through speech, focusing instead on the potential of political debate to promote public rationality. In this part, I try to explain, if not resolve, the incoherence that infects the ideal of democratic deliberation. Where, for example, do interest and passion fit into a deliberative democracy? What is the relationship between the speaker and the audience, and between political debate and truth? The Enlightenment tradition, I argue, has left us with an extraordinarily flat, simplistic conception of political debate that offers unconvincing answers to these key questions.

Part III explores the practice of narrative testimony, exemplified by the abolitionists' use of slave narratives as an alternative to rational debate. I examine the abolitionists' explanation of why rational argument failed to resolve the slavery issue and why they thought testimony would be more effective. Their critique of the politics of rational debate, I suggest, posed a radical challenge to the conception of democracy as a collection of reasonable people reasoning together. Emphasizing the moral complexity of the democratic public—a public that ranges from saints to savages—they made a case for a kind of politics informed more by sympathy than by rationality and aimed at moral reform rather than rational comprehension of the truth.

My historical point is that American political traditions admit of a range of answers to the question of how the people should participate in politics. It is possible, even fairly easy, to make a persuasive case against argument and in favor of storytelling or riotous resistance. Proponents of deliberative democracy have thus far done little to address these arguments. My theoretical point is that they may not be able to, hampered as they are by a deeply problematic ideal of reasoned deliberation—an ideal that, because it was shaped by the specific contexts, problems, and traditions of early American politics, fails to capture the positive role that interest, passion, compassion, or even violence might play in the political life of the nation.

PART ONE
MOB ACTION

1

EIGHTEENTH-CENTURY RIOTS

In 1786, a crew of about 600 Massachusetts farmers stormed the courthouse in Springfield. Led by Daniel Shays, they were part of a general uprising in western Massachusetts aimed at securing relief from taxes and creditors. The militia was called out; skirmishes ensued, and the rebellion was suppressed.

It was a nervous moment for the new nation, but Thomas Jefferson viewed the disturbance with legendary sangfroid: "God forbid we should ever be twenty years without such a rebellion. . . . The people cannot be all, and always, well informed. The part which is wrong will be discontented in proportion to the importance of the facts they misconceive. If they remain quiet under such misconceptions, it is lethargy, the forerunner of death to the public liberty."[1] Compare Philadelphia patriarch Thomas Cope, who just a few years later was complaining that an ill-informed and riotous public would bring on "the speedy introduction of anarchy, riot & confusion & the desolation of the choicest blessings of society [*sic*]." In stark contrast to Jefferson, he condemned mob action as "deluded," even when it was directed against oppressive Old World regimes.[2]

Both of these responses probably seem puzzling to modern readers. Why, under a democratic regime, would rebellions be necessary to preserve liberty? Conversely, why does Cope conclude that mob action even under a non-democratic regime is "deluded" and that popular riotousness would soon result in anarchy? I want to focus on these questions as an entry into the question of means. Complaints and justifications of mob action permeate colonial politics, constituting a central axis of pre-Revolution discourse about citizenship and political action. My purpose in this chapter is to recover the context in which such judgments about mob action made sense and to discover how and why they differ from the more familiar post-Revolution condemnations of mob action. This discussion lays the groundwork for my subsequent examination of the rhetoric surrounding riots and other forms of political action during the antebellum era.

The subject of mobs and riots is, admittedly, well-worn ground for historians of the American Revolution. Most agree with Pauline Maier's conclusion that mobs in the eighteenth century were "quasi-legal" or "quasi-legitimate." "Eighteenth-century Americans," she claims, "accepted the existence of popular uprisings with remarkable ease." This tolerance, the story goes, began a precipitous decline shortly after the Revolution, resulting in our current rejection of mob action as a legitimate form of political action.[3] But this account begs a number of questions. For example, if mobs were tolerable within bounds, as Maier maintains, how does one explain the numerous riot acts enacted throughout the eighteenth century that condemned *all* mob action? Similarly, why (or in what sense) did Americans' alleged tolerance decline after the Revolution? And what is it that distinguishes both Cope's and Jefferson's statements about mob action from modern reactions to popular rioting? Maier's account, which concentrates on the status of mobs in the Whig republican tradition, does not answer these questions. When we adopt a wider focus, we discover that there were in fact *multiple* discourses surrounding mob action during the eighteenth century, each positing a different relationship between riots and social and political order. The status of mob action in the eighteenth century, I argue, cannot be reduced to a single coherent set of norms about popular rioting that suddenly changed after the Revolution. The story is more complicated than that.

To summarize my argument, Cope and Jefferson represent two opposing, but related, eighteenth-century political traditions. Cope's statement represents the language of authority and state power—what may be called the language of governance. This tradition associated rioting (negatively) with certain claims about social order, authority, and hierarchy and the practices of deference related to those claims. The language of governance established a close relationship between riots and the political order, interpreting mob action as a threat to the legitimacy of the regime. But it was the Whig tradition—the language of opposition—that represented rioting as a form of democratic political action, a positive exercise of the people's liberty. This was the tradition that accorded mob action quasi-legal status and that Jefferson and other revolutionary leaders drew on to justify mob action against the British.

Both the language of governance and the language of opposition interpreted riots as acts of resistance, representing popular dissatisfaction with the regime. After the Revolution, however, many of the political elite rejected this interpretation. Seeking to legitimate democratic government by disassociating it from mob rule, they characterized riots not as a form of political action but as a negative model of politics—an example of what democratic politics *is not*. Significantly, this interpretation shifted focus from the rebellious character of rioting to its passionate, violent aspect, thus giving prominence to the interpretive categories of violence and argument (corresponding to the underlying categories of passion and reason) instead of obedience and rebellion. Riots, along with violence and passion, were relegated to the realm of apolitical disturbances, while rational argument took their place as the cornerstone of democratic politics.

This account, I hope, both clarifies and complicates the standard analysis of eighteenth-century riots; but it has broader implications as well. This chapter and the next not only offer a genealogy of modern antiriot rhetoric but also trace the rise of rational argument to its current dominant place in the hierarchy of American political values. This story, too, has already been told, most notably by Jürgen Habermas in *The Structural Transformation of the Public Sphere*. Habermas argues that the importance of reasoned debate to liberal politics can be traced to the practices instituted in eighteenth-century coffeehouses and salons, which provided a model of reasoned interaction that seemed to promise a more rational politics organized around free and open debate among equals.[4] I don't dispute this thesis; the founders were familiar with coffeehouses and salons. But the fact that they continued to discourage popular debate well after the Revolution casts doubt on whether they thought that the coffeehouse was an adequate model for popular politics.[5] I suggest that we can get better insight into the creation of a politics of public debate if we start from the other direction, asking not what was desirable and praiseworthy about rational argument but what was wrong with mob action.

"The Subvertion of All Order"

The Knock-Down Election

Riots had a recognized, if uncertain, place in eighteenth-century politics—as illustrated by the 1742 election riot in Philadelphia. Historians typically explain this riot as resulting from political conflict between the proprietary party and its Quaker rivals, and this does in fact appear to be the immediate cause of the violence.[6] The trouble began the morning of October 1, election day. Rumors that the Quakers were mobilizing a group of unnaturalized Germans to swamp the ballot box were circulating alongside rumors that the proprietary party had brought a group of armed sailors to town to prevent the Quakers from voting. Conflict, then, was anticipated. Unfortunately, election procedures were not conducive to maintaining order. The polling place was the courthouse, located near the inns and taverns and a few blocks from the wharves where the sailors typically congregated. Moreover, the election itself was preceded by the election of inspectors, a disorderly process in which the voters gathered at the polling place and lined up next to their respective candidates when the candidate's name was read. Crowds often grew unruly; the previous year, fistfights had broken out between the contending parties.

On this occasion the Quakers, worried about reports that sailors were gathering in the city, asked the recorder, William Allen (a member of the proprietary party), to take measures to prevent disruption of the election. Allen cautioned a group of unarmed sailors not to interfere with the elections, and the mayor had the sheriff read a proclamation as the polls opened, ordering everyone to keep the peace. But the sailors were already gathering at a local tavern, and soon an argument between their leader and prominent Quaker Israel Pemberton ensued. By ten o'clock, tempers were fraying. When the Quaker candidate Isaac Norris was elected inspector, a group of fifty to seventy sailors, bearing clubs, descended on the courthouse and started swinging at the Quakers and their German supporters. Most of the voters retreated; a few were injured. The sailors had withdrawn by the time Allen arrived, but they soon regrouped and made another attack on the courthouse itself. But this time the Quakers (contrary to their reputation for pacifism) drove the sailors off and proceeded to elect their candidates to the Assembly.[7]

In the subsequent investigation by the (Quaker-dominated) Assembly, William Allen and the other proprietary candidates were accused of having either instigated the riot or at least failed to take measures to prevent it. The testimony against Allen and the others takes up page after page of the legislative record.[8] But the officials' culpability was far from clear; their response to the riot was actually typical of eighteenth-century riot control procedures, which consisted primarily of asking the rioters to stop and jailing those who could be caught.[9] Benjamin Franklin's initial assessment of the riot, recorded in the *Pennsylvania Gazette,* attributed the disorder solely to the sailors (who were subsequently jailed) without suggesting any involvement by Allen. Years later, however, he remembered the "Knock down Election" as an attack on "the Friends of the Constitution, when they in a peacable Manner came to vote." He implied that Allen and his allies were responsible for "encouraging an armed Mob, whom they afterwards, in the Face of the Inhabitants of this City, screen'd from Punishment."[10]

The governor arranged to have the charges against Allen dropped, and the extent of his involvement, or that of the Quaker leadership, remains a mystery. Nevertheless, most historians interpret this riot as relevant primarily to elite factional politics, illustrating the growing friction between the proprietary and Quaker parties.[11] But one might also look at the riot as part of a long-standing tradition of mob action. Citizens of Philadelphia, despite their reputation for peaceableness, were familiar with riots. In 1715, a mob defending a pastor who had been jailed for adultery attacked the prison and the homes of the officials who had arrested him. In 1726, the stocks and pillories were burned by a mob to demonstrate popular support for the election of the democratically inclined Richard Keith to the Assembly.[12] In 1738, another mob rioted against a law banning fish weirs in the Schuylkill River.[13] Nor were the years leading up to the election riot particularly calm. In 1741, Britain was at war with Spain, and the governor was trying to generate some popular support for his defense measures by threatening the citizens with the prospect of an imminent invasion. In addition, the city suffered an unusually cold January, which threatened to produce food shortages. Then an influx of foreign coins unsettled the currency exchange rates, which led the city's bakers to refuse to make any bread until the exchange rates were settled. This provoked a bread riot, resulting in the usual broken windows in the houses of the city's merchants. To make matters worse, yellow fever struck the city in August. The plague was generally attributed to the German immigrants, which suggests some ethnic conflict between the native Philadelphians and the German "Palatines." By 1742, then, the people might have been expected to express their dissatisfaction with things in general in some manner—such as erecting a gallows along the highway where departing proprietor Thomas Penn was passing.[14] Against this background, the election riot looks less like an offshoot of elite politics and more like a typical example of eighteenth-century mob action—a traditional, highly conventional, and well-recognized way of expressing popular discontent.[15]

But typical does not mean unproblematic. The riot was considered serious enough to prompt a months-long investigation by the Assembly, which condemned it as "manifestly destructive of our Liberties, and subversive of our Constitution."[16] And the scandal nearly destroyed the career of William Allen, who was unable to win reelection to the Assembly for fourteen years after the incident. In fact, the reaction to the riot was, if anything, *too* extreme; after all, eighteenth-century elections were often "mobbish"—the previous elections in Philadephia had also been disturbed by fighting—and mobs were generally not very disruptive. On the contrary, riots were usually fairly orderly events, causing little property damage or physical violence (at least compared with twentieth-century riots). Colonial mobs, by all accounts, were both deliberate and discriminating, focusing on specific targets that they attacked with considerable restraint.[17] Even the 1742 election riot, the worst of Philadelphia's uprisings prior to the Stamp Act, resulted in only a few injuries. But it would be misleading to suggest that riots were for this reason quasi-legitimate. As we shall see, the Whig tradition did provide grounds for legitimating mob action, but official public discourse—the language of governance—did not accord them *any* legitimacy. The Assembly's condemnation of the 1742 riot was not idiosyncratic; it echoed a standard eighteenth-century interpretation of riots as serious threats to social and political order.

Consider Pennsylvania governor Patrick Gordon's response to the 1726 attack on the stocks and pillories: "The Growth of [such] Practices . . . tend[s] not only to the Corruption of Youth, and the Encouragement of Vice and Immorality, but more directly to the Subvertion of all Order, and the Introducing of the utmost Confusion amongst us, [and] May therefore if not timely prevented, Provoke the Divine Being to withdraw the Signal Blessings, with which he has been Graciously Pleased to Favour this Province, and in Lieu thereof to pour down his just Wrath upon an Ungrateful People."[18] The move from riots to "the subvertion of all order" and the withdrawal of divine favor looks like a pretty big leap, but this close symbolic and rhetorical relationship between riots and social disorder was common in eighteenth-century public discourse. "Riot," defined in English law as the forcible doing of an unlawful act by three or more persons gathered for that purpose, had broad connotations. It could refer to such diverse mob actions as revelers breaking a few windows to a full-scale rebellion like the Paxton uprisings in Pennsylvania.[19] On a rhetorical level, "riot" served as a metonym for disorder and anarchy, in particular the breakdown of political order. Riots were often linked to rebellion and were portrayed as attacks on authority and government; officials condemned riots as "setting at nought the just powers of Government," an "attack upon the bounds of order and decency" showing "Contempt of his Majesty's Authority."[20] Moreover, this association of riots with social disorder went deeper than rhetorical flourishes, or so I want to argue. Gordon's uncompromising condemnation of mobs was part of a discourse of political legitimacy in which legitimacy was intimately associated with the maintenance of social order. Riots were central to this discourse because they represented the breakdown of order caused by the failure of deference, and therefore threatened the legitimacy of the regime.

Hierarchy, Deference, and Authority

Before the revolutionary period, the language of governance in colonial America—the official language of public discourse represented in laws, speeches, and sermons—postulated a close relationship among social order, hierarchy, and authority. "[T]he various Ranks and degrees of men," explained William Burnham, "are for the advantage and benefit of mankind in General, in as much as without this variety, and if all mens Conditions were alike, . . . there could be no such thing as Government." And without government, the world "would soon become a heap of Confusion, a stage of mournful Tragedies, a Theater of woful [*sic*] Spectacle."[21] As stated in John

Winthrop's "A Modell of Christian Charity," social order is a function of social hierarchy: "God almighty in his most holy and wise providence hath so disposed of the Condition of mankind, as in all times some must be rich some poor, some high and eminent in power and dignity; others mean and in subjection." This God-given hierarchy, according to Winthrop, "order[s] all these differences for the preservation and good of the whole" and ensures that "every man might have need of other, and from hence they might be all knit more nearly together in the bond of brotherly affection." Hierarchy, then, ensures social order. In addition, it structures political relationships by defining the moral obligations of each class: "the rich and mighty should not eat up the poor, nor the poor, and despised rise up against their superiors."[22] Political subordination of the poor is legitimated by this moral obligation of deference, the obligation not to "rise up" against one's social superiors. Such an uprising would violate the natural (divinely mandated) order. But the superiors have duties as well: to rule wisely and responsibly, and to serve as moral examples that will influence the character of the lower orders toward obedience and deference. As Timothy Cutler admonished his congregation, "The Wisdom, Gravity, Integrity, Fidelity and Shining Examples of Rulers do much Tend to Command [deference] from a people."[23] Deference relationships united political and social power in a single hierarchical order; political power was legitimated as resulting from the people's moral duty to defer to their social (and moral) superiors, which in turn was justified as in keeping with God's plan. The "model of a happy state," then, was one in which "rulers are wise and good, and the people are quiet and submissive," obeying their rulers "without murmuring or opposition."[24]

The model, of course, leaves open crucial details. Importantly, what sort of deference were the people supposed to show? After all, there are any number of ways to justify political subordination of the lower classes, each suggesting a different relationship between the lower orders and the elite. J. G. A. Pocock, for example, describes "classical" deference as a kind of rational obedience, the sensible decision by the masses to let people with superior abilities (presumably the social elite?) conceive and debate policies—retaining, however, the ultimate power not only to choose their leaders but also to decide which policies to adopt. Under this reading, deference describes the kind of mass-elite relations we typically find in modern representative democracies—not, one suspects, what John Winthrop had in mind. And (to quibble a bit) what makes this version of deference "classical"? Pocock finds it in James Harrington's *Oceana* (1656), a Whig standard.[25] But Whig ideology could support other accounts of deference, such as the claim that, since government was instituted to protect property (a familiar Whig tenet), the rich had a greater right (or perhaps just a greater capacity?) to rule.[26] This also could

lead to a kind of rational obedience, based on respect for the principles justifying government by the wealthy. Or, alternatively, consider the explanation
of deference relations we find in *Cato's Letters* (an important source for eighteenth-century revolutionary ideology):

> Now it is most certain, that the first principle of all power is property;
> and every man will have his share of it in proportion as he enjoys prop-
> erty. . . . Men will ever govern or influence those whom they employ,
> feed, and clothe, and who cannot get the same necessary means of sub-
> sistence upon as advantageous terms elsewhere. This is natural power,
> and will govern and constitute the political. . . . [F]or, it is foolish to
> think, that men of fortunes will be governed by those who have none,
> and be plundered to make such whom they despise. . . . And, on the
> other hand, men will contentedly submit to be governed by those who
> have large possessions, and from whom they receive protection and sup-
> port, whilst they will yet always emulate their equals.[27]

This version of deference has the lower orders rationally calculating their
costs and benefits and "contentedly submitting" to the highest bidder.
     Even less flattering to the lower orders—and more consistent with the
practices of aristocratic status display—is the notion of deference as a fawn-
ing or cringing servility, produced by nothing more substantial than the
masses' tendency to be dazzled by "the theatrical show of society."[28] This sort
of deference, historians emphatically (and rather tendentiously) insist, was
not typical of eighteenth-century colonial society.[29] But servility isn't the only
alternative to a Whiggish notion of rational obedience. The constant references in elite discourse to God's will, divinely ordained subordination, and
the penalties God would exact upon an ungrateful people suggest a different
perspective on deference, one owing more to traditional Christianity than to
Whig ideology: Christian morality emphasized submission as a spiritual discipline necessary for salvation, regardless of its utility for more earthly ends.
Sometimes (as a testy John Winthrop reminded his fractious subordinates in
1645) rulers make mistakes; as long as they are at least plausibly acting in
good faith, the people should bear these troubles as they would any other trial
sent by God. Or, as William Penn put it, the ruler is "the minister of God to
thee for good.—Wherefore ye must needs be subject, not only for wrath but
for conscience sake."[30] Importantly, under this interpretation, deference does
not require the suspension of one's critical faculties; indeed, it is precisely
the lower orders' recognition of their rulers' faults that makes submission
to them virtuous.[31] Submissiveness, then, isn't necessarily irrational. It could
be a Christian virtue. Deference might diminish the political agency of the
lower orders, but it was supposed to enhance their spiritual agency.

Under this reading, the celebration of deference had an impressive moral tradition behind it. Nevertheless, the language of social hierarchy and quiet submission did not go unchallenged. Winthrop himself gave the claims of Christian egalitarianism their due, moderating his model of hierarchy by emphasizing community and spiritual brotherhood; some, such as Benjamin Franklin and Roger Williams, went much further, seeing in America the potential for a more democratic mode of government than Winthrop could have tolerated.[32] But the leveling impulse was not particularly strong in the colonies. While the equality of man in nature was a well-accepted starting point for theorizing about social relationships, this equality of original condition implied nothing in particular about the structure of civil society. In general, American colonists were torn between acceptance of social hierarchy and a distaste for aristocracy, with its corrupting wealth and love of luxury. This tension was resolved in the notion of a natural aristocracy: social rank shouldn't be eliminated, but it should be distributed through (shades of Harrington?) popular recognition of merit and talent rather than through the king's favor. A rough equality of condition (such as already prevailed in the colonies) would facilitate the emergence of this natural hierarchy, which would in turn legitimate the association of social rank and political power and maintain social order. However, the assumption that social order required hierarchy of some sort was generally taken for granted—at least by those at the top of the hierarchy.[33]

This begs the question, to what extent does this elite discourse reflect popular attitudes? There is some debate whether hierarchical relations were accepted willingly or only under compulsion, but for my purposes, the question is irrelevant. My focus is on the public use of language, not on attitudes. And whether or not the lower orders developed a counterhegemonic discourse, the relationship among social order, hierarchy, and authority was a significant aspect of the reality within which they lived.[34] As the eighteenth century advanced, the Puritan community of saints increasingly resembled England's aristocratic society, complete with social inequality and a growing concern with social status. By the late eighteenth century, social status was easily identifiable, being displayed in one's dress and language.[35] And political relations reflected the emerging social inequalities. As the crown expanded its control of the colonies in the early 1700s, colonists found their political world more overtly structured by hierarchical relations of dependence, or patronage. A patronage society, in theory, unites social, political, and economic power in a hierarchy that extends from the king to the ordinary freeholding voter, with each subordinate link in the chain receiving protection from its superior. In return, the subordinates owe allegiance and deference to their patrons. The unity of interest resulting from this arrangement was supposed to guarantee social harmony.[36] In practice, of course, hierarchical relationships were problematic and failed to guarantee harmony, especially in colonial America. The unusually large body of freeholders in the colonies weakened patronage relationships, while democratic institutions and relative freedom from British interference were prevalent enough to encourage a strong republican ethos among the colonists.[37] Thus, the ties of dependence that encouraged deference probably fell most heavily on the upper and lower ends of the social spectrum: the wealthy still needed patronage from superiors for social advancement, and the poor had to display deferential attitudes to benefit from charity. The large middling class had sufficient independent means and little enough political ambition to gain some freedom from such dependence. Nevertheless, deference to social superiors was preached as a norm and seldom challenged as a basic principle of political relations until the late eighteenth century.[38]

The link between deference and social order gave prominence in public discourse to the virtues of obedience and submissiveness. Election sermons repeatedly exhorted the people to "be subject to the higher powers," lest they provoke God's displeasure. The common good shall flourish, declared Gurdon Saltonstall, "when there is a Spirit of Wisdom, Prudence & Judgment in those that rule, & Subjection in others." (Note that the subjects apparently don't need judgment or wisdom; so much for Harringtonian rational obedience.) But "if there be an Ungrateful, Murmuring, Proud Spirit, a Mutinous, Envious and Rebellious Spirit . . . Prevailing among a People; it is not all the Counsels of the Wisest, nor Understanding of the Prudent, nor Conduct of the most Sufficient men, that can keep off Ruin from them."[39] God is "highly displeased" with "Murmuring and Faction" and can "easily make us know it." The people should remember that "the condition of persons, as well as State of Affairs here below, won't admit of Perfection; and should consider that the Ablest Rulers on Earth are men of many Infirmities. . . . If they miss it in some things, yet in the main they are right, we have reason to bless God for it; and not to be dissatisfied."[40] Although most clerics allowed for resistance to earthly authority in the name of divine law, this theme was not prominent in the language of governance; in general, political virtue was supposed to lie in honoring rulers and tolerating their imperfections—in submission and obedience rather than dissent.

Riots and Deference

If the language of governance celebrated submissiveness as a political virtue, it equally condemned riotousness as a political vice. Riots were "outrages and enormities" threatening the "honour and dignity" of government. The Philadelphia mob that attacked the stocks and pillories in 1726 was denounced as having committed an "audacious" act, to the "great Terror of the Sober and Peacable Inhabitants, the Scandal and Reproach of Government, and the Dishonour of God and all Religion." Rioters aroused "Heats and Animosities amongst the Inhabitants" instead of "that mutual Love and Benevolence" that contribute to the "good Order, Peace and Unanimity," the foundation and glory of all civil society. Thus the Pennsylvania colonial assembly was moved to express its "Abhorrence of all such Riotous and Tumultuous Attempts" and its "Resentment against all Persons, who shall be discovered to be the Authors or Promoters of such Tumults."[41]

This concern over the effects of riots on social and political order stems less from their inherent disruptiveness (as mentioned earlier, eighteenth-century riots were not particularly disruptive) than from their relationship to the practices of deference politics. This relationship is easily misunderstood; some historians have suggested that crowd action revealed a submerged strain of popular egalitarianism and radicalism that aimed at undermining the dominant ideology of social hierarchy.[42] But the evidence suggests that the crowd, up until the late eighteenth century, did not challenge social and political hierarchy per se; rather, it enforced the traditional moral order by punishing those (including public officials) who violated community norms. In other words, the traditional mob might object to particular exercises of authority, but not to the idea that public authority should be held by the social elite. Its aim was at most the moral reform of existing authority structures, not their elimination or transformation.[43] This generalization holds true for the American colonies. There is little evidence of popular resistance to the aristocracy or monarchy expressed through crowd action in the colonial period; the instrumental aims of the mobs were not radical constitutional changes. Riots erupted over things such as food shortages, religious conflict, and resistance to impressment gangs—all standard examples of popular resistance to attacks on traditional practices or norms.[44] The first workers' strike, in contrast, did not occur until after the Revolution, and even in Philadelphia, the most radical of colonial cities, demands by the lower classes for more political power emerged out of the Revolution rather than leading into it. In sum, colonial riots closely resembled the eighteenth-century English country riots described by George Rudé, which were oriented toward the defense of customary rights and norms.[45]

But this does not mean that riots posed no threat to the regime. In the context of eighteenth-century deference politics, popular resistance, even in defense of the constitutional order, could have serious implications for political legitimacy. Government officials typically viewed riots as challenges to their authority—a refusal to defer to those with a legitimate claim to deference. In other words, the system of deference relations provided the context that made these specific refusals of deference meaningful, in the same way that the rule of law makes civil disobedience meaningful. Mob actions against public officials were symbolic insults, mocking the forms of public punishment meted out to ordinary criminals: burning effigies, pillorying, and tarring and feathering. In this respect they resembled the carnival, a form of folk celebration in which the normal rules of social interaction—hierarchical rank, privileges, prohibitions—are temporarily suspended or inverted.[46] But the mob's aims were not just celebratory; they were clearly punitive. For example, in 1769, mobs of sailors protested the collection of duties by a customs informer. This attack was unusually brutal for a Philadelphia mob, but it drew on the traditional forms and rituals of eighteenth-century riots. The sailors first tarred and feathered the victim, John Keats. Then they put him in a cart with a rope around his neck and paraded him through town. Keats, however, wouldn't cooperate with the ritual; he did not stand up properly in the cart and show himself to the crowd, so the sailors abandoned the cart and made him walk, dragging him down the street when he refused. Then they put him in the pillory and threw mud and stones at him, finally driving him down the street to the customhouse. In case the message wasn't clear, someone wrote "Woe be to the Collector" on the walls of the customhouse later in the day. Clearly, the attack was aimed not only at punishing Keats but also at showing contempt for those public officials he worked for. In 1770, the same fate befell a customs official and his son who angered sailors by seizing smuggled goods. They were beaten, tarred and feathered, put in the pillory, and then ducked in the Delaware.[47] Such punishments were not simply acts of violence; they elaborately expressed disrespect for the public officials they targeted. Persons who would ordinarily be entitled to deference were mocked and humiliated. Mob action, then, was the other side of the culture of deference; it replaced the forms and conventions of deference with ritualized insults.[48]

Official discourses surrounding riots suggest that public officials were at least as concerned about the failure of deference represented by riots as they were about economic loss or physical damage. Mob action, as John Adams noted, was typically denounced as "insolent, and disorderly, impudent, and abusive." Officials attempting to put down the Paxton rebellion complained about the "impudence" of the mob and seemed particularly disturbed by an advertisement, apparently posted by the rebels, mocking the institutions of government and religion.[49] Similarly, after a Boston mob attacked the property of certain officials in 1765, the governor was urged to seek compensation from the Assembly, to secure those persons from "any further insult," and to "take Care by [his] Example and Influence, that they may be treated with that respect to their Persons and the Justice in regard to all their Pretensions, which their Merits and Sufferings undoubtedly claim."[50] The disrespect shown to the officers appears to be at least as disturbing as the economic loss.

The government response to riots is best explained by this interpretation of riots as ritualized refusals of deference. Eighteenth-century officials in the colonies were reluctant to rely on force to put down rioters, a fact historians usually explain by pointing to the lack of a trained, professional police force.[51] But why didn't colonial officials seek to create a more effective police force (modeled perhaps on the militia) to control rioting? To be sure, colonists expressed a deep hostility to "standing armies," which a police force might resemble. But I would suggest that the idea that standing armies aren't appropriate under a free government is simply another expression of the conviction that the government shouldn't use force to maintain social order—a legitimate government could rely on deference. In short, the colonists didn't consider creating a police force because they interpreted riots as a failure of deference, to be cured by restoring the proper moral relations between the people and the rulers through rituals of authority and deference. The usual practice for subduing rioters was for an official—a magistrate or sheriff—to confront the rioters in person, bearing the symbols of authority, and enact a drama centered on the reading of the riot act. Officials were instructed to "make, or cause to be made, Proclamation in these Words, or like in Effect: OUR Sovereign Lord the King chargeth and commendeth all Persons being assembled, immediately to disperse themselves, and peacably to depart to their Habitations, or to their lawful Business, upon the Pains contained in the Act of the General Assembly of this Province."[52] The threat of "pains," which legally could amount to death, was in practice an empty one since the officials lacked the means to carry it out. Ideally, the rioters were supposed to be impressed with the authority of the official and acknowledge it by dispersing. This would complete the ritual of deference to authority.[53]

For example, on the morning of the 1742 election riot, Philadelphia magistrates responded to the threat of violence by drawing up a proclamation directing all persons to keep the peace and having the sheriff perform a public reading. In addition, the sheriff, mayor, recorder, and alderman (without any additional support) confronted the sailors and attempted to persuade them to remain peaceful. Later, another alderman, by himself, tried the same tactic. In each case the sailors deferred to the show of authority by proclaiming themselves to be peaceable and orderly, interested only in enjoying their holiday. When fighting did break out, the sheriff could not persuade anyone to help him suppress the rioters. Therefore (the mayor explained), the sheriff "went singly among the Sailors, and told them they were a Parcel of Villains, and ask'd them how they dare act in such a Manner? One of them speaking to the rest in the Sailor-language, to give him a Huzza; he told them he wanted none of their Huzzas, but abhorred them and their Practices, and bid them depart from the Place immediately."[54] The sailors ignored him. But what is significant about these events is the extent to which the magistrates sought to rely solely on a show of authority to control the mob. This approach is consistent with the interpretation of riots as failures of deference: if riots represent a refusal to defer to the authorities, then the only way to quell riotousness in the long run is to restore to the rioters a proper deferential attitude.

Riots, then, took on political meaning by virtue of their relationship to the practices of deference. Far from challenging deference relations, the mob assumed a system of deference and hierarchy that would make its refusal to show respect for authority meaningful. But this doesn't mean that Governor Gordon was completely off the mark when he complained that riots would "Introduce the utmost Confusion amongst us." After all, repeated riots could undermine deference, thereby threatening the whole political order—just as repeated instances of civil disobedience could undermine the rule of law. Widespread rioting could be taken as evidence of a more general failure of deference, perhaps a systematic problem in the relations between the rulers and the ruled. From this point of view, Gordon's leap from riots to "the subvertion of all order" looks less improbable. If order depends on deference and obedience, and "mobs and tumults" represent the breakdown of deference relations, then riots could very well be the critical link between disobedience and anarchy.

Rioting, in sum, could potentially call into question the legitimacy of the regime: if the rulers could not maintain the people's deference, then they could not maintain order, and their right to rule was suspect. The leaders of the Revolution were quick to exploit this point. As one patriotic preacher argued, "The righteous Lord . . . will support and succeed rulers [who employ their authority and influence to advance the common interest]. . . . The natural effect of this is quietness and peace, as showers upon the tender grass, and clear shining after rain. In this case a loyal people must be happy, . . . while they find their persons in safety, their liberties preserved, their property defended, and their confidence in their rulers entire."[55] On the other hand, "[f]rom the unregarded grievances of the people, and their intollerable want of the necessaries of life, what dreadful commotions may we not fear?"[56] The clear implication, happily drawn by revolutionary leaders, is that the occurrence of riots is evidence of injustice by the rulers. The breakdown of social order during the Revolution became in itself an indictment of the regime: "The calamities of the multitude," charged one correspondent to the *Pennsylvania Packet*, "is always owing to those that govern."[57] But note that this tradition speaks in terms of cause and effect, rather than right. It predicts that riots will result from tyranny, but it does not justify them. But the rhetoric of resistance—the language of opposition—went beyond this understanding of riots, creating a place for mob action as a regular part of constitutional politics, a legitimate form of democratic political action.

Riots and Resistance

The representations of riots examined so far have been unqualifiedly negative, according them no legitimate role in the political system. Against this official discourse, though, we find another strain of rhetoric, such as Jefferson's optimistic evaluation of Shays's Rebellion, according riots a more positive value. Historians have generally pointed to the Whig belief in the right of resistance as a sufficient explanation for such defenses of mob action.[58] But this explanation begs the question, how is it that riots came to be perceived, discussed, and practiced as instances of the right of resistance? And how do we reach Jefferson's position that riots might be not symptomatic of the breakdown of the constitutional order but evidence of its vitality?

The Right of Resistance

That the people have the right to resist unjust rulers was always an element of Whig ideology. John Locke's justification of resistance is well known. The people, he argued, may resort to force when the government "acts against the trust reposed in them" by invading the property or "making themselves or any part of the community masters or arbitrary disposers of the lives, liberties, or fortunes of the people." Under such conditions, the people "are absolved from any further obedience, and are left to the common refuge which God hath provided for all men against force and violence."[59] As preached from the revolutionary pulpit, this right even became a sacred obligation: "The people forfeit the rank they hold in God's creation when they silently yield this important point, and sordidly, like Issachar, crouch under every burden wantonly laid upon them."[60] But what exactly is this right, and how is it related to mob action? In the first place, the right of resistance, as it appeared in the rhetoric of the Revolution, was not an individual or minority right. Although there are strains of Whig political theory that support the notion of individual natural rights that may be exercised against the government, the right of resistance typically was not one of them.[61] In fact, it was more a duty than a right, and it was held by the majority, not the individual.

The Whig justification for resistance started from the contract model of government: government authority is granted by the people for a particular purpose, and if the government fails to perform, it reverts to the people (the communty as a whole). Jonathan Mayhew, for example, argued that the duty of submission to rulers applies only to those who "*actually* perform the duty of rulers by exercising a reasonable and just authority for the good of human society." That is, only a government that performs its proper duties by seeking the good of society is really a government. He concluded from this that the duty to obey government *requires* resistance to those who do not truly govern.[62] John Adams, relying heavily on the Whig tradition, spelled out the nature of the right of resistance in a pamphlet aimed at legitimating mob action. Quoting Grotius, he argued that when the magistrate fails to enforce the law, the right (or duty) to do so reverts to the community at large: "If the law of God and man are therefore of no effect when the magistracy is left at liberty to break them, and if the lusts of those who are too strong for the tribunals of justice, cannot otherwise be restrained than by sedition, tumults and war; those seditions, tumults and wars, are justified by the laws of God and man."[63] He then concluded that the magistrate, in refusing to enforce the law properly, becomes an outlaw. "[A] legal magistrate who takes upon him to exercise a power which the law does not give . . . [is] in that respect . . . a private man . . . and may be restrained as well as any other." Therefore, the community may—in fact, must—act against a magistrate who breaks the law, just as it must act against a common criminal whom the law cannot otherwise reach. The responsibility for enforcing the law and maintaining order falls, ultimately, on the community.[64] Thus, rather than representing riots as the breakdown of social order, the language of resistance justifies them in the name of maintaining order. Under this view, even though it is the people who are rioting, it is the magistrates who are the true rebels: "those, whoever they be, *who by force break through, and by force justify the violation of them, are truly and properly rebels.*"[65]

The right of resistance, then, is the right of the community as a whole to take over the functions of government when the regular government fails, justified by the general mandate to maintain social order. Coupled with the usual pessimistic assumption by Whigs that the magistrates are always trying to overstep their authority, the right of resistance turns the community into a kind of shadow government with an ongoing duty to monitor and correct the regular government. This duty was commonly glossed in revolutionary rhetoric as the people's liberty, or "active" liberty. Samuel Cooke, for example, called the people's right to examine and criticize the government their "decent liberty," "without which their obedience is rendered merely passive."[66] Passive liberty is the mere enjoyment of one's rights under the government; active liberty refers to this ongoing duty to further the ends of government, in particular, maintaining the laws under which rights are protected. This is the duty embodied in the right of resistance.

But what does this right of resistance have to do with mobs? Much of the Whig-inspired rhetoric implied that it had nothing to do with mobs at all. Whig theorists typically insisted that private individuals and minorities did not have the right to try to overturn the government, which follows from the understanding of the right of resistance as a right of the community as a whole.[67] Even John Adams decried "private mobs." In "Novanglus," he quoted Grotius again, declaring: "When we speak of a tyrant that may lawfully be dethroned by the people, we do not mean by the word people, the vile populace or rabble of the country, nor the cabal of a small number of factious persons, but the greater and more judicious part of the subjects, of all ranks."[68] This sounds like a condemnation of mob action—*but it is not.* This pamphlet was written in *defense* of the Stamp Act mobs and tea riots. Somehow, Adams assumed that these mobs represented "the greater and more judicious part of the subjects." Where does this assumption come from? The answer is not to be found in the pamphlet, nor in Whig political theory. Rather, the representative character of the mob was part of the background of meanings and practices that informed revolutionary rhetoric.

Mobs and the People

To read mob action as the exercise of the community's right to take over the functions of government, we must be able to see mobs as the quasi-official representative of "the people," the democratic element of the constitutional order. The mob's status as the representative of the community is not theorized in the Whig tradition; rather, it is an assumption borrowed from the rhetorical representations of mobs circulating in official public discourse. Although riots were often attributed to outsiders of some sort—foreigners or disaffected troublemakers—they were also commonly represented, by defenders and opponents alike, as expressions of community sentiment. One newspaper characterized the Stamp Act mobs as "a People . . . justly sensible of the Injury that such a detestable Wretch (meaning the victim) must be to the Traders of this place." Similarly, the British Admiralty complained about colonial governors' failure to defend captains from the "rage and Insults of the People," meaning mobs aroused against impressment gangs.[69] One of the more interesting examples of this assumption is the case of the 1765 riot against the lieutenant governor of Massachusetts. The lieutenant governor suffered considerable property damage, and he asked the Assembly to compensate him. His point was that the mob represented the "Madness of the People," so the damage was chargeable to the whole community.[70]

It's unclear how mobs came to acquire their representative status. Eighteenth-century discourse about mobs contains little in the way of arguments about their representativeness. Dismissive references to mobs as composed of "boys and Negroes" or sailors suggest that the social composition had some relevance to their ability to represent the community at large. However, mobs, especially in the colonies, often drew from a range of social classes. Mobs resisting impressment gangs were composed mainly of sailors; bread riot mobs were often made up largely of women; men of "property and standing" participated in many riots, along with the rabble.[71] All these types of mobs were commonly characterized as "the people."

The mob's ability to represent community sentiment may reflect the perception, still common in the eighteenth century, that communities were relatively homogeneous, so that any large crowd probably expressed common sentiments. But it can also be traced to the traditional status of the *posse comitatus,* a legitimate means for enforcing the law in communities with little or no formal means of doing so. English common law afforded sheriffs and constables the power to call up a posse to enforce the law, which made the posse a legal institution assumed to be capable of acting for and exercising the authority of the community. As Pauline Maier has demonstrated, the distinction between the illegal mob and the official posse was obscure, especially because the people who made up posses were generally the same people who made up (illegal) mobs.[72] Thus, illegal mobs might plausibly share the representative character of the posse.

The representative status of mobs was so well established in public discourse that few on either side of the debate sought to challenge the notion that the mob was actually "the people" (not, at any rate, until after the Revolution). This rhetoric assumed that the mob was authorized to act on behalf of the community; it attributed to the mob a type of political agency. It was therefore a fairly straightforward move to use the language of Whig political theory to grant the mob the right to act against any perceived injustice by the authorities. In fact, such language was so common that even Thomas Hutchinson, who was no friend of the mob, admitted that "a sort of them at least are constitutional."[73] Such admissions made it relatively easy for revolutionary leaders to justify the use of mobs against the British authorities. If mobs represented the people, then they might legitimately exercise the right of resistance, which, as we have seen, was an ongoing duty to monitor the government and correct injustices. Mobs were thus institutionalized, at least in the language of opposition, as the vehicle for expressing the people's liberty—that is, their right to govern when the regular government fails.

Mobs and Passion

The Whig tradition, then, provided grounds for legitimating mob action. But even within this tradition, the status of mobs was complicated by their association with passion and licentiousness. Whigs as well as Tories often described mobs as "deaf to the Voice of Reason," representing the "rage" of the people—a "turbulent and unruly spirit" rather than calm, quiet deliberation.[74] Consider this defense of a Boston mob formed to resist an impressment gang: "I don't in the least Wonder, at the People's running together for their mutual Defense; and had they gone no further they could not justly have been blam'd: For when they are suddenly attack'd, without the least Warning, and by they know not whom; I think they are treated as in a State of Nature, and have a natural Right, to treat their Oppressors, as under such Circumstances."[75] The author interprets the mob's actions as an expression of the people's right of resistance. But the remainder of the argument makes clear that the mob, exercising this right, is not acting out of rational calculation: "[I]t is not at all surprizing, that their Resentment grew up into Rage, and Madness, which soon, for Want of a proper Check, or Diversion, vented it self, in an indecent, illegal, and riotous Manner, upon the Government. . . . [T]here could not be a prudent, thinking Man among them."[76] The mob acts out of passion (rage or madness) rather than reason, which is why it can be driven, imprudently, to attack the government itself.

This characterization of mobs as creatures of passion was problematic because it brought into play the opposition of reason and passion, a basic element in eighteenth-century moral philosophy. According to a tradition stretching back to the ancient Greeks, passion (described by one philosopher as an "agitation of the mind" similar to a storm or tempest)[77] was morally suspect; a will undisciplined by reason and driven solely by passion was wayward, ungovernable, and potentially destructive—or, in the parlance of the day, licentious. As David Hume put it, "Nothing is more usual in philosophy, and even in common life, than to talk of the combat of passion and reason, to give the preference to reason, and to assert that men are only so far virtuous as they conform themselves to its dictates."[78] Hume, of course, took issue with this denigration of passion, but the superiority of reason was still the prevailing view during the latter half of the eighteenth century. As Samuel West reminded his congregation, "The most perfect freedom consists in obeying the dictates of right reason. . . . When a man goes beyond or contrary to the law of nature and reason, he becomes the slave of base passions and vile lusts; he introduces confusion and disorder into society, and brings misery and destruction upon himself."[79] To the extent mobs were creatures of passion and not reason, they could be considered a dangerous influence in politics. "[V]icious, hot-headed and inconsiderate" (in the words of Gouverneur Morris), there is no ruling them—or, as Benjamin Franklin put it, "The Mob's a Monster; Heads enough, but no Brains."[80]

Those who undertook to defend mob action thus found themselves

challenging received wisdom by insisting that passion had a positive role
to play in politics. As Jefferson argued on behalf of the Shaysites, "[W]hat
country can preserve it's [*sic*] liberties if their rulers are not warned from time
to time that their people preserve the spirit of resistance?" The fact that passion might lead to "a little tempest now and then, or even . . . a little blood,"
was no more than a minor inconvenience. "The tree of liberty must be re-
freshed from time to time with the blood of patriots and tyrants." It is, after all, lethargy, not passion, that is "the forerunner of death to the public
liberty."[81] In fact, according to Samuel West, "It would be highly criminal
not to feel a due resentment" against tyranny. Patriots, he insisted, should
be "animated with a noble zeal for the sacred cause of liberty." Jonathan
Mayhew similarly exhorted his congregation to cherish the "chaste and virtuous passion" for liberty, and John Hurt praised the love of country as "that
elevated passion, of all others the most necessary, as well as most becoming,
to mankind."[82]

Under this view, passion, in the form of love of liberty, resentment against
injustice, and love of country, is essential to the preservation of a free government. On the one hand, those attempting to raise up a mob could lend
their actions some legitimacy by appealing to the people's zeal for justice and
their rightful resentment against "Evil Doers, Infamous informers and Tide
Waiters."[83] On the other hand, appealing to the people's passions could be
dangerous. Mayhew warned against the "evil passions," such as lust for power
or wealth, that are "inimical to a free, righteous government." Even "love of
country," warned Hurt, "may be so conducted as to become a very criminal
passion," leading to "the high fanaticism of distinction and empire" and a
"feverish fondness for dominion and renown."[84] And passion should always
be accompanied by prudence, the ability to "weigh consequences, and to deliberate fully upon the probable means of obtaining public ends." Colonists
were thus informed that "measures determined on by integrity and prudence,
are most likely to be carried into execution." But prudence can be carried too
far as well; Nathaniel Whitaker warned against the "overprudent," who will
"waste away days, yea months, to consider; and are ever full of their wise
cautions, but never zealous to execute any important project."[85] The goal was
prudent yet spirited action. Reason, in the form of prudence, should merely
guide and instruct passion, not diminish it.

Passion, in sum, was potentially destructive but nevertheless indispensable,
since it provided the impetus to resist tyranny—and, as John Adams pointed
out, tyranny is a greater threat than a little licentiousness: "Shall We submit
to Parliamentary Taxation, to avoid Mobs? Will not Parliamentary Taxation
if established, occasion Vices, Crimes and Follies, infinitely more numerous,
dangerous and fatal to the Community?"[86] But the problem with passion was

not simply that it might lead to licentiousness; it also, according to the prevailing theories of moral philosophy, impaired the judgment. The standard interpretation of the relationship between passion and judgment was stated succinctly by Scottish philosopher Thomas Reid: Only when "there is a calm in the mind from the gales of passion or appetite," he explained, can a man "calmly weigh goods and evils" and judge "what is best upon the whole, without feeling any bias drawing him to one side."[87] Thus John Dickinson, worried about the riotousness occasioned by the Stamp Act, warned that resentment against injustice could cause "too great a transport of zeal. . . . These emotions blind the understanding; they weaken the judgment."[88] Similarly, Mayhew worried that passion could take the form of "a sort of consternation, not unlike to a frenzy occasioned by a raging fever," so that the afflicted would be "ready to do any thing or every thing, to obtain relief; but yet, unhappily, not [know] what, when, where, how; nor [have] any two rational and consistent ideas about the matter."[89]

The charge that passion impairs judgment, rendering the mob "deaf to reason," threatened to undermine the whole theory of resistance: if the mob represents the people politically mobilized, and the mob is incapable of sound judgment, then the Whig tenet that "the whole People, who are the Publick, are the best Judges, whether things go ill or well with the public" is questionable at best.[90] Moreover, these doubts about the mob's ability to reason were reinforced by the complaint, commonly voiced by Whigs as well as Tories, that the people are easily confused by appearances and the rhetoric of demagogues. "[P]eople are generally more influenced by their eyes and ears, than by their reason," acknowledged Dickinson. Such concerns gave rise to the Tory concern that "ill affected and factious men" would "spread among the people, and make them believe that the prince or legislative act contrary to their trust, when they only make use of their due prerogative."[91] But the problem worried some Whigs as well; a mob driven by passion and manipulated by the "Encouragement of some Dissatisfied Persons" or, in George Washington's memorable words, the "arts of self-interested designing disaffected and desperate characters" hardly seems like a fit guardian for the people's liberties.[92]

Defenders of mob action argued that such concerns were misguided. Although the people may be easily confused by demagogic rhetoric, this hardly matters, because abstract argument alone is not enough to motivate action. The people, after all, are not generally disposed to rebel. John Adams, quoting Locke, reminded his readers that "[g]reat mistakes in the ruling part, many wrong and inconvenient laws, and all the slips of human frailty will be borne by the people without mutiny and murmur." As Samuel Cooke explained, "The body of people are disposed to lead quiet and peaceable lives.

. . . They retain a reverence for their superiors, and seldom foresee or suspect danger till they *feel* their burdens."[93] The people will rebel only when their concrete interests are damaged, when they actually feel the tyranny affecting their lives. Moreover, this feeling of injustice is reliable precisely *because* it isn't the result of argument but of direct experience. After all, "[m]en cannot but perceive when they enjoy their rights and privileges; when they sit at quiet under their own vines and fig-trees, and there is none to make them afraid." Similarly, "[i]t is as impossible for a governor, if he really means the good of the people, and the preservation of them and the laws together, not to make them see and feel it, as it is for the father of a family not to let his children see he loves and takes care of them."[94] According to this reasoning, not only is the people's judgment generally reliable, but a sudden outburst of passion is better evidence of injustice than calm, deliberate reasoning. Injustice is something one can't help but feel; it should not take argument or deliberation to recognize it. Thus, a spontaneous uprising prompted by some concrete grievance (such as a riot), rather than a carefully planned and organized movement guided by some abstract principle, has the best claim to legitimacy.

Of course, the revolutionaries undoubtedly recognized the weakness of such reasoning—surely there is some room for interpretation, and therefore poor judgment, in deciding whether a particular government action is unjust. And are feelings any more reliable than reasoning? What if the people are oversensitive or simply mistaken about their feelings? But the argument is worth noting, because it offers an alternative to the equation of popular political action with licentiousness. In this rhetoric, judgment (the ability to recognize injustice) and agency (the ability to act) are inextricably linked, and both are functions of passion—in particular, the love of liberty and the anger or resentment one feels when one's rights are invaded. Since the feeling of oppression is the most certain evidence of injustice, the people may safely rely on their feelings in making political decisions. This reasoning thus gives passion a positive valence and, at the same time, tends to devalue argument as a tool of politics.

I do not mean to suggest that the revolutionary leaders had a deep commitment to passion as an element of politics. On the contrary, their endorsement of passion was probably mostly strategic, designed to counter Tory complaints about the licentiousness of democracy and to lend legitimacy to Whig-led mobs. It was also qualified; a competing motif in Whig discourse expressed a profound discomfort with passion, rebelliousness, and mob action. The following sections explore how these reservations, initially a minor theme prompted by the "spirited" resistance to the Stamp Act, eventually came to form the basis of a distinctive pro-democratic, antiriot rhetoric after the Revolution.

Beyond Obedience and Rebellion

Both the language of governance and the language of opposition discussed riots in terms of the categories of obedience and rebellion: riots were either rebellious resistance to lawful authority or legitimate resistance to rebellious magistrates. But not all the colonists were comfortable with these alternatives; neither seemed suitable for describing legitimate dissent. In searching for some middle ground between passive submission and riotous rebellion, they began to elaborate a different framework for interpreting riots and their relation to the political system, structured less by the opposition between obedience and rebellion than by the opposition between orderly political action and riotousness. This theme emerged in public discourse in the 1760s, as the colonists began to take serious action against the British government.

The conflict that erupted between the American colonies and the British Parliament over the 1765 Stamp Act was not confined to North America. Mobs in St. Christopher and Nevis in the West Indies also rioted against the act, burning all the stamped paper on the islands and even forcing the resignation of customhouse officers. Barbados, however, remained quiet—but not content. Instead of raising mobs, the Barbadians expressed their opposition to the tax in a widely published letter from the colonial legislature to their agent in London, asking him to petition the king for relief.[95] Putting their dissatisfaction in writing forced the Barbadians to confront the rhetorical problem that plagued all of the colonists' initial attempts to oppose the tax: how does a subject express dissent without sounding rebellious?

The Barbadians' letter moved uneasily between the conventional rhetoric of obedience and submissiveness and a more rebellious tone of resentment: "We have, indeed, submitted, with all obedience, to the act of parliament; yet our submission has by no means, arisen from any consciousness of our ability to bear the burden of these taxes, or from the want of a due sense of the oppressive weight of them in all its parts, but from a principle of loyalty to our king and mother country."[96] The committee described the taxes as a "new and extraordinary burden" and an "oppression beyond measure grievous," threatening not only trade and justice but also the colonists' civil rights and liberties. But the Barbadians emphasized that, despite this oppression, they remained obedient. The committee directed the agent to avoid anything in "the stile [sic] and substance of that representation, as might give offence to those from whom only our redress can come, our appeal being to the very powers by whom we think ourselves oppressed." It further warned that "tho' we may remonstrate to them with justice, we cannot reproach them without danger." The agent was thus to give the complaint "the complexion of our conduct, shewing an humble submission to authority, even under the most painful heart burnings of our community, at its severe decrees." In order to highlight their submissiveness even further, the letter compared their own conduct with that of their sister colonies: "[I]f we have suffered without resistance, we have learnt by it to complain with reason; and *since we have raised no clamours from our own fears,* we must surely have the better title to remonstrate from our feelings." In case the allusion to the riotousness of the other colonies wasn't clear, the letter went on to refer to the "REBELLIOUS opposition given to authority, by our fellow-subjects on the northern continent."[97]

It was apparently this reference to rebellion, coupled with the obsequious tone of the Barbadians, that incensed John Dickinson. In 1766 he published a scathing response that set out the colonists' case for resistance: that the act imposed an unconstitutional tax, violating the basic rights of Englishmen. But the theoretical justification for resistance was not the pamphlet's main focus; Dickinson's central concern was with how that resistance was being *described.* He made his point clear on the frontispiece, where he quoted Shakespeare: "This word, REBELLION, hath froze them up like fish in a pond." In the preface, he specifically objected to the Barbadians' accusation of rebelliousness, particularly their reference to the "violent spirit raised in the North-American colonies," which they had applied to all colonists and not just "those few of the lower rank, who disturbed us with two or three mobs in some of the provinces."[98] Dickinson's complaint, then, was that the term "rebellion" was being used to describe *all* the agitation over the Stamp Act in the North American colonies—most of which, according to him, was not riotous.

Certainly, Dickinson did not mean to suggest that the colonists were obedient subjects like the Barbadians. On the contrary, he went on to quote the Barbadian petition in full, italicizing those very phrases (such as "humble submission to authority," "obedience to the laws of our mother country," and "oppressive weight") that contrasted the Barbadians' obedience with the severity of the injustice they were tolerating. Dickinson found no virtue in such "humble submission" (a phrase he quoted repeatedly throughout the pamphlet). He accused the Barbadians of "unmanly timidity" and "irretrievable depravity," suggesting that they were wanting in "understanding, resolution, and integrity." They were, he asserted scornfully, "ignorant of the rights of British subjects, and . . . insensible of all concern on the invasion of those rights"—unlike their northern counterparts.[99]

The North Americans, then, were not submissive; but neither were they rebellious. To call the behavior of the colonies a "REBELLIOUS OPPOSITION given to authority," Dickinson insisted, was an "unjustifiable aspersion." Surely the Barbadians did not mean that the oppressed must content themselves with "PALE petitions—and that *all other* opposition is 'rebellious'?"[100] He was, he claimed, loyal to Great Britain: "I am devoted to my gracious sovereign, and his truly royal house, by principle and affection." But the British prefer "to hear their children speaking the plain language of freemen, than muttering the timid murmurs of slaves."[101] Of course, the colonists had done more than speak; they had also stopped the importation of goods from Great Britain and rioted against stamp distributors and customhouse officers.[102] Dickinson defended the nonimportation agreements as evidence of "industry and frugality," but his attitude toward the mobs was more cautious: "It was indeed a very improper way of acting; but may not these agonies of minds *not quite so polished as your own,* be in some measure excused?" He concluded, somewhat opaquely, that none of the mob actions constituted rebellion.[103]

Dickinson's reluctance to use the term "rebellion" was not idiosyncratic. As late as 1781, Americans were objecting to being termed rebels. As one defender of the colonists insisted, "who in their senses, unawed by power, and interested only in truth, will presume to stigmatize a repulsion of force by force, under an invasion, with the spiteful name of rebellion?" Another asked rhetorically, "When the illustrious Hampden resisted the lawful sovereign's demand of an unlawful tax, was he too guilty of rebellion?"[104] This claim that resistance to tyranny is not properly termed "rebellion" is, of course, a familiar theme in the rhetoric of resistance; Adams, as discussed earlier, drew on Locke to make the case that "seditions and tumults" were not rebellions if they were directed against unlawful actions of the magistrates. According to this line of reasoning, the legitimacy of riots depended on determining who the true rebels were. But Dickinson, interestingly, did not explicitly rely on this argument. Instead of debating who the true rebels were, he focused on how the colonists had *behaved:* all they had done, he pointed out, was to speak the "plain language of freemen" (and show their "industry and frugality"). He dismissed the riots—there had been only a few, and only among the "lower orders." His interpretation of the resistance thus downplayed both the riots that had occurred and the rebelliousness they implied.

But if the colonists' opposition was neither riotous nor rebellious, what was it? In the third of "The Farmer's Letters," Dickinson tried to answer that question. Abandoning the categories of obedience and rebellion, he focused on the orderliness and peacefulness of the colonists' resistance, compared with the disorder and violence of riots. Responding to complaints that resistance to the Stamp Act would result in "riots and tumults," he argued that "[t]o talk of 'defending' [rights], as if they could be no otherwise 'defended' than by arms, is as much out of the way, as if a man, having a choice of several roads to reach his journey's end, should prefer the worst, for no other reason, but because it *is* the worst."[105] Rather, he merely wanted to persuade the colonists "immediately, vigorously, and unanimously, to exert themselves, in the most firm, but most peacable manner, for obtaining relief." Calling for a "sedate, yet fervent spirit," he abjured "hot, rash, disorderly proceedings," but acknowledged that resistance might ultimately result in the use of force.[106]

This masterpiece of ambiguity was occasioned by the virtual identification, in the language of governance, of political protest with social disorder. Deference politics, as discussed earlier, made social order dependent on popular obedience and submission. Dickinson was trying to break that connection, legitimating protest by (re)describing it as disobedient but orderly, rather than riotous. He accomplished this, in turn, by reinterpreting "orderliness," linking it to peacefulness and deliberateness (resistance should be "sedate") rather than obedience. Protest could indeed be orderly, if "orderly" simply means peaceful and organized, and a peaceful, orderly resistance, according to Dickinson, should not be called a "rebellion."

Emphasizing the peaceful and orderly character of legitimate resistance, Dickinson highlighted a new set of political virtues to be exhibited by the colonists—not the patriotic zealousness suggested by Whig pro-riot rhetoric, but "prudence, justice, modesty, bravery, humanity and magnanimity" (not coincidentally, the virtues usually attributed to *rulers* in conventional election sermons).[107] Colonists were to be neither riotous nor submissive; rather, they were to behave in a manner befitting freemen—and the gendered term is appropriate here. Attempts to legitimate resistance typically relied heavily on the masculine and (as war became imminent) martial virtues. Firmness, fortitude, and courage replaced submissiveness; colonists were exhorted to act with "the temper and dignity of freemen, undaunted and firm, but without wrath or vengeance."[108] One instructive editorial celebrated the virtues of the "staunch Whigs," who were "undismayed with misfortunes," but not "unusually elated with trifling advantages over our enemies," and were "friends to order and good government." "Furious Whigs," in contrast, "injure the cause of liberty as much by their violence as the timid Whigs do by their fears."[109] Such language counters the picture of a populace that remains quiet and submissive until a long train of abuses prompts them to a violent outburst. Freemen (as Dickinson might argue) don't act that way; they are more temperate, more orderly, and more dignified.

So how do freemen respond to injustice? In 1766, Jonathan Mayhew reflected that the Stamp Act crisis had taught the colonists "how to act, in order to obtain the redress of grievances"—by a "joint, manly and spirited, but yet respectful and loyal petitioning, setting aside some excesses and outrages, which all sober men join in condemning."[110] But it was far from clear that petitioning was what Dickinson had in mind. What about his scorching essays and his approval of the nonimportation agreements? Or perhaps he was thinking of public meetings, such as the one that took place in Philadelphia in October 1765, in which thousands of people gathered to force the resignation of stamp officer John Hughes; no violence actually occurred, so the defenders of the action claimed that Hughes was persuaded in a peaceful and orderly fashion to resign.[111] And what about the groups of citizens who marched through the streets carrying effigies of stamp men—orderly resistance or a riotous mob? Of course, these questions would not arise if one viewed such events from the perspective of John Winthrop or Patrick Gordon; they would have seen even the most well-organized and restrained mob action as rebellious and disorderly, a clear refusal of deference and obedience to those who deserved it. When Dickinson refused to grant the point that subjects must be either obedient or rebellious, he opened up a complicated set of questions about how they *should* act: what counts as "violent," "peaceful," "orderly"? (We might also ask what counts as "moderate." Could that term be applied to Dickinson's reply to the Barbadians? Might they not have preferred a little tar and feathers to being publicly accused of unmanly timidity and irretrievable depravity?)

In short, the Stamp Act crisis may not have settled the question of how the colonists should *act*. Against a background of mob action, "orderly" resistance could mean a lot of things: peaceful, moderate, and dispassionate, or just organized. But at least the crisis taught the colonists how to *talk* about their actions. Specifically, they learned to contrast their acts of resistance with riotousness—to disavow the rioting (the "excesses and outrages") that accompanied resistance and focus instead on peaceful, orderly (but spirited and manly) behavior. This strategy of bolstering the legitimacy of popular politics by contrasting it with riots created a kind of counterpoint to the Whig justification of mob action. On the one hand, revolutionary leaders claimed that mobs and tumults were evidence of the oppression of the British regime and were justified as the expression of the people's liberty; on the other hand, they denied that the people were really riotous. A defense of committees and irregular assemblies, for example, contrasted them with the "[u]niversal tumults, and all the irregularities and violence of mobbish factions, [that] naturally arise when legal authority ceases."[112] Committees, by implication, were legitimate forms of political action because they were not disorderly, like mobs. A 1775 debate in Philadelphia over the legitimacy of these committees similarly centered on their resemblance to mob action. The Quakers

responded to a proposal to abolish the regular Assembly by declaring themselves against "all combinations, insurrections, conspiracies and illegal assemblies," implying that the only alternative to the Assembly was some form of
mob rule. Some of the denomination, though, claimed that they objected
only to riotous behavior, not orderly political action. This claim was met by
a response in the *Pennsylvania Journal* arguing that committees could not be
considered riotous because such meetings were legal and peaceful (the definition of riot, recall, is forcible doing of an unlawful act by three or more
persons gathered for that purpose).[113] Of course, whether or not committees were legal depended largely on whether they were peaceful, which is precisely the point at issue: are such meetings riotous or orderly? Legitimating
the type of activity in question meant showing that it was orderly—that is,
not riotous.

Thus the key point is not that the colonists' resistance became more orderly
after the Stamp Act crisis, but that orderliness took on a new and more central significance in discourse about political action as the colonists attempted
to legitimate their resistance. Initially, this focus on the difference between
orderly and riotous political action was aimed simply at legitimating dissent,
as in Dickinson's address to the Barbadians. But as Americans moved toward
independence, the contrast between riots and legitimate popular politics took
on a deeper significance. Consider Thomas Paine's defense of the liberal suffrage provisions of the Pennsylvania Constitution of 1776. Against the claim
that such widespread suffrage would subject the state to mob rule, he argued:
"The cry of being elected by a mob is idle and frivolous. It is a nick name
which all parties give to each other. It means no *particular* class of men,
but *any class* or number of men acting irregularly and against the peace, and
cannot be applied in any case to a legal rightful election."[114] His point here is
not that elections, like committees, are a legitimate form of political action; elections had been a regular and well-accepted practice for centuries.
Rather, Paine objected to the fact that legal, rightful elections were often
characterized as mobbish, particularly when they were "carried by a Levelling spirit."[115] Such characterizations were, in fact, part of a familiar critique of democracy: that it was equivalent to mob rule. Paine's distinction
between elections and riots was aimed not simply at redescribing dissent but
at redescribing *democracy.*

This defense of democracy reflects the direction in which antiriot rhetoric
would develop after the Revolution. As worries about the legitimacy of dissent faded (at least temporarily), public discourse about popular political action increasingly revolved around Paine's problem: the association of democracy with mob rule. As a result, the debate over what sort of political action is
truly riotous—the distinction between riots and legitimate politics—became

even more salient after the Revolution, taking center stage in the founders' struggle to legitimate the new democratic regime.

The Eclipse of Passion

In 1777, a Philadelphian who was worried about the conflict over the new state constitution suggested that "serious and candid inquiry into the reason and relation of things, and a dispassionate resolution," should take the place of this "noisy and ill natured wrangling" that would only "injure and disgrace us."[116] The complaint suggests a new problem with riotousness, created by the establishment of democracy: whereas before the Revolution, riots might indicate a breakdown in deference relations, after the Revolution, riots tended to call into question the ability of the people to rule themselves. In the context of a democratic regime, riots represented not the dangers of government tyranny but the dangers of democratic politics—namely, its tendency to degenerate into mob rule. It was this problem that led the founders to abandon the pre-Revolution interpretation of rioting as a form of popular politics.

Rescuing Democracy from the Mob

The revolutionary leaders, when they set about creating a new government, faced two problems. First, they had to legitimate democracy, which in the 1780s was still typically a term of opprobrium.[117] Second, they had to decide how the people would participate in government, which was not at all self-evident. As it turned out, these were actually the same problem. The chief objection to democracies, according to Whig theory, was their susceptibility to faction and instability.[118] Whatever these defects might have meant in ancient Athens or Rome, in the wake of the Revolution, factions and instability were intimately associated with mob rule. Revolutionary rhetoric and practice had established the connection between the people, the exercise of liberty, and riots. As argued earlier, the mob had been virtually institutionalized as "the people" exercising governmental authority. The founders thus confronted an unhappy chain of associations: democracy, mobs, disorder, anarchy.

To fully appreciate this problem, we have to examine more closely the meaning of "democracy" to eighteenth-century Americans. As explained in Regina Morantz's classic study, during the eighteenth century, "democracy" typically designated a form of government in which the people, as opposed to a king or aristocracy, exercised sovereignty by making and executing laws. Most Americans had ancient Greek democracy in mind when they used the word, so clearly what made a government democratic was not universal participation. Rather, "the people" meant the body of citizens who were not members of an aristocratic class; Federalists could thus argue that the American Constitution was democratic not because it allowed everyone to participate in government but simply because it did not lodge political power in any formal aristocracy or monarchy.[119] Nor did democracy necessarily mean liberty or the rule of law; those characteristics were more closely associated with the term "republic," which meant a good government, one that exists for the good of the whole community and protects the citizens' liberties. By the time the Constitution was being debated, there was a fairly strong consensus that what was wanted was a republican government, and that kings and aristocrats could not be trusted to maintain a republic. But it was hardly self-evident that the demos could be trusted either; "republican" thus implied "democratic," but not vice versa.[120]

Given this understanding of democracy, the Constitution created a democracy simply by abolishing the aristocracy and monarchy. By doing so, it created a popular government, "sometimes termed Democracy, Republick, or Commonwealth," as one Philadelphia newspaper explained, "the plan of civil society wherein the community at large take the care of its own welfare."[121] There was, in fact, no element of the Constitution that was not democratic, a point Fisher Ames used to counter the charge that the Federalists were elitist: "Indeed it is notorious, that there was scarcely an advocate for the federal Constitution who was not anxious, from the first, to hazard the experiment of an unprecedented, and almost unqualified proportion of democracy. . . . The truth is, the American nation, with ideas and prejudices wholly democratic, undertook to frame, and expected tranquilly and with energy and success to administer, a republican government."[122] But Ames did not intend by this assertion to endorse democracy. On the contrary, the democratic nature of the Constitution was precisely its weakness: "The danger obviously was, that a species of government in which the people choose all the rulers . . . would be found on trial *no better than a turbulent, licentious democracy.*"[123] As this quotation illustrates, democracy was not necessarily any more legitimate than aristocracy or monarchy. In fact, a letter in the *Federal Gazette* declared that "when we consider the consequences of the late revolution, some of its best friends are almost induced to lament its success." The new regime, the writer complained, left government to the "wantonness and prodigality in the character of the many-headed monster." Democracy was hardly better than monarchy, he pointed out, since the mob was susceptible to "that power, which intrudes itself through the channel for popular deceit and low cunning"—the tyrant who "lurks under the disguise of republican zeal."[124]

To its critics, democracy was simply another name for mob rule, an interpretation strengthened by the practice of democracy during the Revolution. Revolutionary government proceeded largely through "popular assemblies," committees, and conventions, which were typically no more than informal and often spontaneous mass meetings of the citizenry. Such meetings drew huge crowds and proceeded with little attention to the formalities of parliamentary procedure—the participants would shout down unpopular speakers and threaten them with sticks and clubs, or even take to the streets in search of miscreants. To many, this is what democracy meant. Colonial government had been turned over to "Committees and mobs," complained one loyalist. Gouverneur Morris worried that this government by committee would so arouse the people ("Poor reptiles!") that they would destroy the aristocracy, and then the colonies would be left under "the domination of a riotous mob."[125] But while Tories and conservatives played on this identification of mobs and democracy in order to delegitimate democracy as no better than mob rule, Whigs also identified mobs with democracy in order to legitimate mob action as the expression of the right of resistance. Thus, while Morris contemptuously characterized committees of correspondence, popular assemblies, and public debate as the actions of the "mobility" (the mob), John Adams announced that the destruction of a stamp office by a mob "was thought an honorable and glorious act" of the people.[126]

The association of democracy with mob rule continued after the Revolution. The adoption of the radically democratic 1776 Pennsylvania Constitution, for example, prompted complaints about "mob government" and "execrable democracy."[127] The campaign of Democrat Israel Israel for the Pennsylvania state legislature in 1798 similarly filled Philadelphia presses with antidemocratic rhetoric. An Israel election, warned the Federalists, would allow the "lawless sons of anarchy and misrule" to plunder the citizens' property. "Our government and laws totter under the unremitting exertions of ruffians panting for tumult, plunder and bloodshed."[128] Clearly, a primary concern was Israel's appeal to the poor, but this appeal to class was couched in antidemocratic language: allowing the poor to exercise political power was equivalent to giving over the reins of government to a lawless mob. When Israel won, the Federalists used the victory to demonstrate the dangers of democracy. As one Israel opponent remarked, it was appropriate that working classes should elect a "Jewish Tavern Keeper": "The *sovereign people*," he declared, "never speaks his mind right freely, except when he's half drunk."[129] (The state was spared the consequences of popular sovereignty, however; the Senate declared the election fraudulent and refused to seat Israel.)

The French Revolution dramatically reinforced the interpretation of democracy as mob rule. Initially hailed as a victory for reason and the rights of man, it soon became a symbol of the dangers of unrestrained democracy:

atheism, anarchy, and bloodshed. Even more disturbing, enthusiasm for the Revolution seemed to be encouraging a kind of riotous democracy in the United States. William Cobbett, for example, complained about the democratic enthusiasm expressed for Citizen Genet, which included an address by the "sovereign citizens" of Philadelphia, a *republican* dinner (including even sailors!), and other "nonsensical, stupid, unmeaning, childish entertainments, as never were heard or thought of, till Frenchmen took it into their heads to gabble about liberty."[130] Concerns about the influence of French democracy combined with fears about the influence of secret societies (the Illuminati in particular) that were popularly thought to be conspiring against law, order, and Christianity. To many, the ultrarational doctrines of the Illuminati sounded suspiciously like the doctrines behind the French Revolution and promoted by the proliferating democratic societies—a worry that found support in John Robison's newly published *Proofs of a Conspiracy against All Religions and Government of Europe Carried on in the Secret Meetings of the Free Masons, Illuminati, and Reading Societies.* Robison charged that French Freemasonry had spawned a general conspiracy "for the express purpose of ROOTING OUT ALL THE RELIGIOUS ESTABLISHMENTS, AND OVERTURNING ALL THE EXISTING GOVERNMENT OF EUROPE," and that the "most active leaders in the French Revolution . . . conducted their first movements according to its principles, and by means of its instructions and assistance." Robison's theories enjoyed wide circulation, due to their propagation by Boston minister Jedidiah Morse.[131] In sum, by the 1790s, democracy implied (at least to a growing body of Federalists) not only riotousness but also active conspiracy against all government.

Such negative evaluations of democracy made defending the legitimacy of the regime problematic. On the one hand, there was no real public support for an aristocracy or a monarchy; as John Adams observed optimistically, by 1776 "[i]dolatry to Monarchs, and servility to Aristocratical Pride" were eradicated.[132] On the other hand, to declare that the Constitution set up a democracy was to invite the charge that it simply handed over political power to the mob. This was precisely the dilemma that had given rise to *Federalist* 10's awkward attempt to characterize the Constitution as republican but not democratic, first by confining "democracy" to direct democracies and then by redefining "republic" as "a government in which the scheme of representation takes place" (rather than a government devoted to the public good, its usual meaning).[133] This was somewhat idiosyncratic; as Thomas Paine later pointed out, the term "republic" was *not* typically confined to representative governments. He justified conflating the two by arguing that only a representative government could be a republic, because only a representative government could be trusted to devote itself wholly to the public good.[134]

But ultimately Paine, like most other defenders of democracy, rejected

Madison's distinction between a representative and a democratic government. The American government, he concluded, was both republican and democratic or, more specifically, "representation engrafted on democracy."[135] For those, like Paine, for whom the word "democracy" held some positive connotations, the favored response to the legitimacy problem was not to deny that the Constitution was democratic but to challenge the association of democracy with mob rule—to argue that, contrary to conventional wisdom, mobs had no place in a democracy.

This position departs dramatically from the pre-Revolution tradition of resistance, represented by Jefferson's claim that a healthy constitution could tolerate a certain degree of chaos. Most supporters of the democratic regime argued on the contrary that democracy had to be defended *against* mobs, that the legitimacy of democracy depended on the ability of the people to participate in politics in an orderly fashion. "Mobs are a reproach to Free Governments," worried one Philadelphia correspondent. Another argued that while "riots and bloodshed" might characterize popular elections in "the old world," Americans "ought to guard against the inroads of such improper practices" so as to preserve the "order, freedom, and regularity" of elections. This would guarantee that election results would be "conformable to the *general will*" and beyond contention.[136]

Fisher Ames elaborated this argument in a series of essays defending the government's right to use force to put down Shays's Rebellion. Ames was not usually enthusiastic about democracy, but he could hardly hope to convince the Shaysites to renounce mob action by attacking popular sovereignty itself. (By 1786 it was generally agreed that popular sovereignty was what the Revolution had been fought for.) Instead, he began from the principle that all lawful authority derives from the people. Immediately switching to a more conservative note, he then insisted that once the people have consented to a form of government, they have no right to disobey it: "Every man knows that contract shall bind the contracting parties." This wasn't particularly novel; Benjamin Rush, for example, similarly argued that the people possess power "only on the days of their elections. After this, it is the property of their rulers, nor can they exercise or resume it." But Rush added the familiar Whig caveat, "*unless it is abused.*"[137] This caveat implicitly opens the door for mob action against government tyranny, even in a democracy.

Ames closed this door. A government established by consent may abuse its power, he conceded; nevertheless, mob action is illegitimate when the people have the right to vote and instruct their representatives: "But as public trust may be abused, what security have the people against it? The right of annual elections, and instruction. Will a man, in one year, set up a tyranny, which, in the following, another may exercise over himself?"[138] A popularly elected government, he asserted, is not likely to misuse its authority, and if it does, it can be corrected in the next election. Thus, rebellion is illegitimate. The argument neatly undermines the whole set of ideas on which the Whig justification of mob action rested: that the government must always be monitored, that only the energy of the people's passion can resist the encroachments of authority, and that riots are the ultimate expression of the people's liberty. For Ames, the people's liberty depended on the rather prosaic act of voting, rather than the possibility of resistance.[139]

This claim that voting, not rioting, is the proper expression of the people's liberty was a standard response to the riotousness of democratic politics. Noah Webster, for example, argued that assuming that the people may exercise their sovereign power in any way other than voting had led to the "rebellion, tumult and disorder in several of the American States."[140] These worries about disorder led him to reject not only mob action but also popular conventions and the practice of giving representatives binding instructions; vesting authority in *any* institution other than the legislature would undermine law and order by making the people the "*masters* of their *rulers,* and their power paramount to the laws." He even went so far as to deny that the people are the best protectors of their liberties. They tend to be lethargic, he reminded his audience, while "a Legislature, which is always watching the public safety, will more early discover the approaches of disorders, and more speedily apply a remedy."[141] The argument was not confined to conservatives; Samuel Adams took the same line. Although he insisted to Webster that popular vigilance was "the Peoples [*sic*] great Security," he agreed that conventions and popular committees were at best useless: "[A]ll our Men in Authority depend upon the annual & free Elections of the People." If they prove dishonest or inept, "Due Circumspection & Wisdom at the next Elections will set all right." Stated even more succinctly by Thomas Paine, "[T]he republican form and principle leaves no room for insurrection, because it provides and establishes a rightful means in its stead."[142]

According to this reasoning, then, the Whig justification for rioting doesn't apply in a democratic regime because elections are an adequate substitute for riots as a means of preventing government oppression. Clearly, such arguments express a distaste for riots and popular disorder typical of antidemocratic rhetoric. But they also imply, in a more democratic fashion, that elections (unlike riots) are perfectly respectable, occasions for "due circumspection and wisdom" and not the riotous, mobbish affairs that opponents of democracy typically described. Such pro-democratic condemnations of riots, then, attacked not only the Whig justification for mob action but also the antidemocratic complaint that all democratic politics is mobbish; they focus not just on the dangers of mob action but on the *difference* between riots and legitimate forms of popular political action, such as elections. Riots are em-

bedded in this pro-democratic, antimob discourse, not as failures of deference or expressions of liberty but as a negative model of politics—an example
of what legitimate politics *is not*.

But what is it that distinguishes legitimate political action from riots? This
question leads us to the criteria for determining the legitimacy of political
action—criteria that depart from the models of deference and "active liberty"
and reflect an important transition in the relative positions of riots and argument in public discourse. Central to the rejection of mob action was the
reformulation of popular politics around the practice, and ideal, of reasoned
debate.

Reason and Passion

The claim that mob action wasn't legitimate, that it was in fact the very
model of illegitimate action, didn't need much theoretical justification. The
actual experience of mob rule during the Revolution, coupled with the connection between legitimacy and social order inherited from the eighteenth-
century language of governance, was apparently adequate grounds for rejecting it. In fact, some critics of mob action, such as Noah Webster, simply
reverted to the categories of obedience and rebellion, condemning mobs for
their rebelliousness: "[P]opular commotions and rebellions," he complained,
showed a "contempt" for the laws, which could in turn be attributed to the
"vulgar maxim" that the rulers are the servants of the people. Order can be
maintained, he insisted, only if the people exhibit the proper obedience and
submission to those in authority.[143]

But Fisher Ames, concerned that the riotousness of the French Revolution was infecting American politics, developed a different line of reasoning
against mobs. Ames's argument did not focus on their rebelliousness but on
the opposition (already a familiar theme in Whig rhetoric) between reason
and passion. He began with the traditional association of mobs with passion
but did not attribute to passion any positive role in politics: "Is there any one
man without passions, and when these domineer, is that man's will a proper
rule even for the government of his own conduct? . . . Would it not then be
absurd beyond measure, to pretend that a million of men, in a transport of
fury, can do no wrong?"[144] The revolutionary leaders, of course, had never
claimed that the mob could do no wrong, only that it was more likely to be
right. But Ames insisted that passion is no basis for judgment at all. Whereas
Whig defenses of mob action emphasized the force and energy of passion,
which make it a suitable weapon against the power of the rulers, Ames emphasized its irrationality. "The man who expects to disperse a mob of a thousand men, by ten thousand arguments, has certainly never been in one."

Mobs are outside the realm of rationality and argument. They also lack independent judgment: "A rabble animated by praise as heroes and reformers, delighted with scenes in which all is bustle, and all shifting, . . . are the instruments of revolution, the more formidable for being *blind* and *passive*.[145]

This characterization of mobs as both blind and passive reorganized the interpretive framework in which the Whig defense of mob action had placed riots, depriving mobs of the judgment they were accorded in revolutionary rhetoric (they are "blind"), along with their agency (they are "passive"). According to the defenders of mobs, both agency and judgment were functions of passion; Ames, in contrast, challenged the reliability of the people's judgment by making judgment contingent on access to reasoned argument, and he reformulated the concept of agency by detaching it from passion and linking it to rationality. He thus obscured the role of passion and motivation in politics. If passion actually diminishes agency and judgment, what justification can there be for emotional appeals to the people? Perhaps none at all; as Thomas Cope declared in 1801 (sounding very much like John Dickinson in 1766), republican government requires virtue, temperate and dispassionate conduct, prudence, moderation, and disinterestedness—not zeal, passion, or emotional commitment. Similarly, a correspondent in the *Philadelphia Gazette* objected to passion in politics on the grounds that "the medium of passion is too dense to give a lucid view of the object, it is only in the serene air of philosophic calmness that the light of reason can exert its influence."[146] In contrast, Ames himself recognized a legitimate role for passion in politics, in another context. In addressing the House of Representatives on the Jay Treaty, which had occasioned a prolonged and heated debate, Ames commented on the salutary effects of such "warm feelings": "The public sensibility and our own, had sharpened the spirit of inquiry, and given an animation to the debate. The public attention has been quickened to mark the progress of the discussion, and its judgment, often hasty and erroneous on first impressions, has become solid and enlightened at last."[147] So even Ames could entertain the possibility that passion might serve as an aid to public rationality. But if republican politics need not entail the wholesale rejection of passion, the popular tendency to riot clearly drove the political elite in that direction: "Politics should have no passions."[148]

This rejection of passion does not just undermine the legitimacy of mob action; it also influences in critical ways the concept of rationality offered as the appropriate criterion of legitimate action. The distinction Ames drew between rationality and riotousness privileged a particular kind of rationality. After all, mobs typically displayed, and were recognized as displaying, an undeniable instrumental rationality. The descriptions of riots found in prerevolutionary discourse invariably characterized riots as being directed toward some end: punishing miscreants, correcting an injustice, and so forth. More-over, patriots were regularly praised for the "prudence" with which they ex-hibited their "unremitted zeal"; in the rhetoric of resistance, passion and in-strumental rationality were not necessarily incompatible.[149] But this means/ends type of rationality is not what Ames offered as the criterion of legitimate political action. The problem with mobs is not that they don't choose effec-tive means to serve their ends; rather, they are not capable of engaging in rational argument. They lack discursive rationality—the ability to argue, to give and evaluate reasons.

These distinctions—passion versus reason, instrumental versus discursive rationality—supported the opposition between violence and argument that increasingly pervaded discourse on political action. Elections, for example, were regularly accompanied by warnings in the press against the ill effects of passion on the discursive rationality that should prevail in politics: "Every attempt to heat the passions or blind the judgment is wrong—Peacably to assemble, and discuss the merits of public candidates is not only judicious, but seems to be an implied duty of our government—but for the friend of one party to intrude upon or molest the deliberations of another, is an act of indecorum and impropriety, and is especially calculated to introduce anarchy, and thereby sap the foundations of our national institutions."[150] Passion leads to violence (and the inevitable slide to anarchy), whereas reason is expressed solely in peaceful argument. The two are not, presumably, compatible. Op-ponents of the 1789 Constitution complained that "while every measure was taken to intimidate the people against opposing [a convention to ratify the Constitution], the public papers teemed with the most violent threats against those who should dare to think for themselves, and *tar and feathers* were liberally promised to all those who would not immediately join in supporting the proposed government be it what it would."[151] Tar and feathers were, in the revolutionary tradition, a perfectly legitimate political means, the expres-sion of patriotic sentiment and revolutionary fervor. The complaint voiced here suggests that such "violent" behavior may inhibit rational decision mak-ing by preventing people from thinking for themselves. This rhetoric opposes the purely instrumental rationality displayed by the Federalists (who, after all, did choose effective means to accomplish their purposes) with a politics of discursive rationality.

This concern over the effects of passion—particularly its tendency to degenerate into violence—lay behind the emphasis on dispassionate delibera-tion permeating post-Revolution rhetoric. *The Federalist Papers,* for example, began with a long discourse on the norms that should govern public debate on the adoption of the Constitution: "Happy will it be if our choice should be directed by a judicious estimate of our true interests, unperplexed and unbiased by considerations not connected with the public good." The author worried that various "views, passions, and prejudices" might bias the public judgment, but that was not his only concern; he also warned that "we are not always sure that those who advocate the truth are influenced by purer principles than their antagonists. Ambition, avarice, personal animosity, party opposition . . . are apt to operate as well upon those who support as those who oppose the right side of a question." It is not just that passions and biases might lead us to make poor decisions, then; there was also a danger that the "intolerant spirit which has at all times characterized political parties" would release a "torrent of angry and malignant passions"—in other words, debate might degenerate into riotousness.[152]

Writings on both sides of the debate over the Constitution expressed this fear of passionate and potentially violent conflict. The Federalists informed readers that the plan was recommended to "sedate and candid consideration" but that "it is more to be wished than expected that it may be so considered." Similarly, the Anti-Federalists insisted that the plan "ought to be dispassionately and deliberately examined" rather than approved in a "frenzy of enthusiasm." Both sides accused the other of "alarming [the people's] passions"; the Federalists even cited the "danger of disturbing the public tranquility by interesting too strongly the public passions" as a reason to avoid frequent constitutional conventions.[153] Perhaps Madison's plan to "refine and enlarge" the public views—to mitigate the influence of factions—through representation should also be read against this background. The problem with factions, after all, is that they bring "injustice, instability and confusion" to public counsels; in other words, they make politics riotous.[154] These nervous admonitions thus offered deliberation and reasoned argument as an alternative to the violence, passion, and general riotousness that seemed constantly to threaten democratic politics.

Of course, these worries that passion might distort judgment and lead to violence weren't novel; as discussed earlier, Whig theorists had relied on such arguments to limit the right of resistance to extreme cases of governmental abuse. In this respect, Ames and other critics of mobs were simply turning back to a more conventional, negative evaluation of the role of passion in politics. But, in contrast to the language of opposition, this rhetoric was aimed not at limiting the people's influence in government but at determining how that influence should be exercised *on a regular basis.* Reason, under this view, should not simply moderate political action that is motivated by zeal; rather, it should be the entire ground and substance of political action. Thus, argument should replace mob action as the paradigmatic form of democratic political action—not just any kind of argument, however, but dispassionate, deliberate, sedate, candid, temperate, impartial, disinterested, moderate, cool, firm, and manly argument.[155] Of course, we could read this list as expressing (to put it anachronistically) a Habermasian ideal of rational deliberation. (But then why "firm" and "manly"?) I would instead point to its resemblance to the kind of action Dickinson was trying to describe in 1765: active rather than passive and submissive, but also restrained, temperate, and dignified. The category of reasoned argument, I would suggest, took over Dickinson's middle ground between obedience and rebellion, taking shape as both the opposite of and a substitute for mob action.

To put the point more concisely: the founders did not reject mob action simply because they were committed to a preexisting conception of a popular politics of rational argument. This conception, in important ways, *grew out* of the rejection of mob action, for which they had other reasons—namely, the problems that the politics of mob action posed for the legitimacy of the regime and, in particular, the desire to get beyond the categories of passive submission and active rebellion to some understanding of democratic citizenship that preserved the subject's agency without undermining the ruler's legitimacy. These concerns about legitimacy, social order, and agency— concerns ultimately rooted in the traditions of deference and active liberty— are as integral to the value of rational debate as rationality itself. In short, if the founders valued argument because it brought rationality to politics, they valued it equally because it was neither (or at least to the extent it was neither) passive and submissive nor rebellious and riotous.

Conclusion

In 1784, Thomas Tucker declared that "tumultuous proceedings are as unnecessary as they would be improper and ineffectual. Other means are in our hands, as much preferable as good order is to confusion, as peace to discord, as efficacy and security to disappointment and ruin."[156] His statement echoes both of the prerevolutionary traditions: In declaring that mob action is no longer necessary, Tucker alludes to the right of resistance by implying that mob action may be justified under a regime that is not responsive to the people. But he sounds more like Patrick Gordon in his assumption that "tumultuous proceedings" would lead to confusion, discord, and ruin. What sets Tucker's statement apart from both these traditions, however, is its emphasis on "other means." He advocates neither deference nor passion-driven resistance. The people, he insists, have the power to engage in far-reaching political action, even changing the Constitution itself, "without the smallest disturbance"—that is, through some orderly, nonriotous form of political action.

After the Revolution, this contrast between riots and legitimate politics—between violence and argument—became a central element of public discourse about political action. It was hardly the only element, of course; the models of deference and active liberty did not disappear overnight. Rather, I suggest that this new language became available, along with the older rhetorics, as a way to discuss and deal with the problem of popular political action. Thus, even after the Revolution we find Jefferson celebrating mob action as an expression of the people's liberty and Cope characterizing it as "deluded" and the forerunner to anarchy, confusion, and desolation. Eventually, though, Ames's interpretation of riots as representing the dangers of passion and violence inherent in democratic politics displaced the eighteenth-century traditions of deference and active liberty; the discourse of violence and argument superseded the discourse of submission and rebellion.

In sum, the picture of peaceful, orderly, dispassionate argument familiar from postrevolutionary discourse evolved out of and against a background of mob action: an amorphous combination of reasoning, ritual, and resistance that confounded distinctions between violence and argument. Thus the colonists were not faced with a simple choice between the violence of riots and the rationality of argument; rather, they were faced with the disorder of mob action or the passivity of submission and constructed a third alternative—not just public debate, but a particular conception of public debate—that would not threaten social order and hence political legitimacy. At the same time, they relegated mob action to the category of violence (irrational, passionate, and "blind"), thus obscuring both the expressive and instrumental dimensions of riots and the role of passion and violence in politics. In short, the rejection of mob action was part of a thorough reorganization of the conceptual scheme Americans used to interpret political action. It is not just that the political elite became less tolerant of mobs after the Revolution; the significant change was not in Americans' willingness to tolerate riots but in their interpretations of what a riot is, what politics is, and how they relate to each other.

What finally emerged out of the Revolution was an affirmative vision of democratic politics as a realm of nonviolent, rational interaction represented by the practice of public argument as opposed to riots. But so far, this was only a vision. The suppression of popular rioting and the establishment of the value of rational argument were long-term projects that extended well into the nineteenth century. The next chapter follows this story into the antebellum era, exploring how the opposition of riots and politics took shape in discourse and in practice.

2

RIOTING IN THE ANTEBELLUM ERA

"The world is now witnessing," claimed one mechanic in 1829, "the novel spectacle of the laborious class of citizens seeking their rights, not by mobs and riots, but from reason, justice, and constitutional means."[1] Perhaps; but it was also witnessing what was probably the highest incidence of urban rioting in the history of the United States. Charles Godfrey Leland predicted that "[w]hoever shall write a history of Philadelphia from the Thirties to the era of the Fifties will record a popular period of turbulence and outrages so extensive as to now appear almost incredible."[2] He was prophetic. Histories of antebellum Philadelphia document one riot after another: race riots in 1834, abolition riots in 1838 and 1842, a nativist riot in 1844, and a host of election riots. And Philadelphia was not exceptional. According to Michael Feldberg, 70 percent of large cities had at least one riot between 1830 and 1865.[3] Leonard Richards similarly documents a sharp increase in rioting in the 1830s—from 28 riots between 1812 and 1829 to 179 between 1830 and 1849.[4] Nevertheless, the antebellum period proved to be the end of the era of traditional popular rioting. After the Civil War, the character of rioting changed, becoming more violent and less controlled by traditional conventions such as effigy burning, tarring and feathering, and mock punishments. At the same time, the frequency of rioting in the urban Northeast *declined* dramatically; certainly by the twentieth century, the claim that mob action is not constitutional sounds more like a simple descriptive statement and less like the contestable proposition it still was during the antebellum period.[5]

Standard explanations of why a norm of nonviolence replaced the tradition of mob action point to the developing middle class's growing intolerance of riots and rejection of the plebeian values with which rioting was associated. This "growing intolerance" is usually explained by the assertion that the middle class was becoming increasingly concerned with property rights, or with the disciplining of the lower class to facilitate the creation of a new industrial economic order.[6] But this explanation is unsatisfactory. First, the value system associated with the rejection of rioting does not map neatly onto class divisions. Many "gentlemen of property and standing" participated in riots, and some working-class communities adopted the values of self-reliance and moral reform usually attributed to the middle class.[7] Second, the class argument doesn't explain how rioting came to be represented as something that

51

decent middle-class citizens would never engage in. After all, the concern with property rights and disciplining the lower orders was not new; what was new was the belief that mob action was not an appropriate method to defend property rights or punish those who violated social conventions. This change in norms, then, is not an explanation but the phenomenon to be explained.

This chapter argues that the rejection of mob action resulted from a self-conscious and determined effort by political leaders to discourage social and political disorder in order to preserve the legitimacy of democracy. In other words, the antebellum era did not mark a sudden change in Americans' attitudes toward rioting but was the culmination of an effort that had begun with the Revolution itself, brought to a head by the upsurge of rioting in the 1830s. The antebellum era did, however, mark an important change in the context of riots, stemming from the rapid absorption of Jacksonian democracy into mainstream political culture. The egalitarian ethos promoted by the Jacksonians altered the ways in which social order was conceptualized and political legitimacy defended. This evolving set of discourses about social order and legitimacy, as they related to riots, is the focus of the first half of this chapter. The second half examines the antebellum efforts to institute norms of political action in response to the continued persistence of popular rioting, concentrating on the opposition of violence and argument in political rhetoric and the development of state institutions to enforce that opposition.

Democracy and Social Order

Robert Collyer, recording his experiences traveling in Philadelphia and other American cities in the 1830s, concluded that "the great experiment whether a Republic can stand through the severe trials incident to human infirmity has been long and patiently tried," and the result has disproved the hypothesis that America's "promised glory, based upon a Republic, would be but transitory."[8] His optimism about democracy was not widely shared, however. On the contrary, persistent criticism of American riotousness from European travelers such as Thomas Brothers, Edward Abdy, and Charles Dickens indicated that riots continued to threaten the legitimacy of democracy.[9] The editor of *Niles' Register* worried that riots subjected the country to "the contempt and scorn of the old world," and his fears were constantly confirmed by comments such as the following in the British press: "[T]he most prejudiced democrat of the British isles must agree with us in ascribing these awful displays of popular violence [referring to American riots] to the inevitable action of democratic principles on human nature." Niles responded by scolding his readers: "The American people are responsible for the cause of republican-

ism. Whatever irregularities and excesses they commit must injure not only
their own character, but the interest of freedom universally." This theme pervaded political discourse in the 1830s. Mob action was denounced as not
only destructive but also traitorous; the suppression of riots was widely urged
as "involving not only [our] lives and property, but as vital to the preservation
of our republican institutions."[10]

This rhetoric still echoes eighteenth-century patterns of political discourse,
which linked political legitimacy to social order. At the same time, however,
the eighteenth-century conception of social and political order on which that
connection was based was eroding, problematizing the relationship between
riots and politics. Riots had fit neatly (or not so neatly) into eighteenth-
century politics as representing the failure of deference. Antebellum complaints about riots, in contrast, frequently reflected uncertainty about the origins of social disorder: "From whence arises this baneful spirit," asked one
editor, "bringing society back to its pristine state of barbarism, and which, if
not suppressed, must sooner or later lead to the annihilation of all that is
worth possessing? . . . Is it to be found in the freedom of our institutions?"[11]

That was, of course, the central question. If riots are not to be interpreted
as failures of deference occasioned by some (real or imagined) abuse of
authority, then what are they? Do they stem from democratic political institutions—an inevitable concomitant of mass-based political conflict or the
"action of democratic principles on human nature"—or is the culprit some
other characteristic of American society, something that could be changed
without threatening democracy? Much of antebellum antiriot rhetoric favored the second option, usually locating the source of riots in the rioters'
character defects. This strategy focused the discourse of political legitimacy
on the character of the citizen rather than on political institutions. In doing
so, it not only shielded democracy from criticism but also offered a picture of
the relationship between politics and social order that challenged the eighteenth-century claim that order depended on maintaining a unified social-
political hierarchy.

Social Order

Alexis de Tocqueville considered democracy to be "the most striking feature" of Americans' social condition. With the Revolution (according to Tocqueville), Americans had rejected hierarchy as the organizing principle of
a unified social-political order.[12] Americans, by and large, agreed. As one editor insisted, "Here we have no aristocracy, no privileged persons. Here the
interest of no class is fostered at the expense of another. And this is civil
and political independence."[13] Politics in this democratic nation was to be

governed by the norms of independence and equality, rather than deference and hierarchy; there were not supposed to be different classes of citizens. But Tocqueville's claim that this principle of equality governed *all* areas of social life is too strong. Consider the story with which Teresa Murphy opens her study of antebellum working-class politics: Paulina Brown, a sixteen-year-old factory worker, was harshly disciplined by her supervisor for a minor error. Her father charged the supervisor with trespass, assault, and battery, arguing that he had usurped the father's authority over the girl by inflicting corporal punishment. The supervisor argued that the factory was essentially a kind of household; Paulina was a servant who could be disciplined like any member of the family. The jury agreed with the father and awarded Paulina substantial damages. The conflict here was not between the principles of hierarchy and equality; no one disputed the idea that someone had authority to discipline the girl. The conflict arose because the supervisor's paternalistic authority conflicted with the father's. As Murphy notes, this case reflects the separation of social life into distinct spheres. Although both institutions were hierarchical, the factory was in some respect distinct from the family.[14]

In retrospect, this separation of social life into distinct spheres is a more prominent feature of antebellum society than the application of equality to all relationships. In fact, the emphasis on political equality actually differentiated politics (centering on elections, parties, and lawmaking) from most other areas of social life, where hierarchy and deference still prevailed.[15] I don't mean to overstate the differentiation; that political activity affected and was affected by other institutions was well recognized. The relationship between the family and politics, for example, received considerable attention during this period.[16] Rather, political equality meant that social and political relationships were not incorporated into one overarching hierarchy governed by a single principle of deference to superiors; the family, the workplace, the church, and other institutions were conceptually distinct from, if intimately related to, the political arena.

This principle of political equality must be carefully qualified. It did not necessarily mean that social status—particularly race and gender hierarchies—should have no relevance to political status. In fact, during this period, race and gender became central to determining citizenship.[17] But this trend was actually one expression of the dominant conception of politics as incompatible with deference relations: one could plausibly argue that maintaining political equality meant excluding from participation those who were, in most dimensions of social life, subordinate. Of course, this reasoning was hotly contested by activists representing women, blacks, and immigrants. But despite their disagreements about the proper bounds of citizenship, the majority of political activists (at least in the north) were united in their hostility to the norm of humble submission to social superiors advocated by eighteenth-century colonial leaders. Their goal was to replace the personal and divinely mandated moral hierarchy that structured colonial society with an impersonal legal order applying equally to all citizens. Thus, where eighteenth-century officials had seen in riots the failure of deference to superiors, antebellum commentators saw simply a failure to respect the laws of the republic. The prevalence of mobs showed that "[b]rute force has superseded the law"; riots "strike not merely at individual rights, but at the law itself" and "set legal restraints at defiance." Citizens were constantly urged to "rally round the standard of law."[18] No references to God's will and divinely mandated hierarchy shored up these calls for obedience; respect for law and for republican institutions, rather than unquestioning submission to God's ministers on earth, was supposed to guarantee political order.

That democratic politics requires impersonal legal and political relations to replace personal ties of deference has become a well-accepted principle of democratic theory. Egalitarian political relations may not require that social inequalities be eliminated, but such inequalities must not infect the political sphere.[19] According to this standard, the antebellum era was the first truly democratic period in American politics. Deference relations continued to structure politics until the age of Jackson. By the 1830s, though, at least in the Northeast, deference to social superiors in politics was idealized only by the increasingly isolated upper class.[20] The forces undermining the culture of deference are complex, but a critical element was the loss of the revolutionary generation (which had served as a type of aristocracy with a plausible right to deference) and the resulting fragmentation of local elites, giving rise to greater electoral competition.[21] This general trend received dramatic reinforcement from the election of Andrew Jackson in 1828, which was interpreted as a victory for a populist sort of democracy at odds with the culture of deference. Thus, although local elites continued to exercise a disproportionate political influence, the language of egalitarianism—the assumption that social privilege shouldn't translate into political privilege—was a standard feature of antebellum politics.[22]

This is not to suggest that elitism didn't persist. The diary of Sidney George Fisher testifies to the continued viability of the ideology of social and political hierarchy. Fisher, a minor scion of the Philadelphia gentry, detested the lower orders and complained of "the horrid, vulgar" crowd whenever he was forced to rub shoulders with them.[23] Echoing the antidemocratic rhetoric of the Revolution, he portrayed popular politics as mob rule. Giving political power to the majority was equivalent to handing it over to the crowd, "a canaille population, without property, without education, utterly degraded and anxious to promote disturbance and revolution"—hence "riots, political judges, judicial demagogues, electioneering, office-holders, etc, and the host of abuses with which the country is filled."[24] But such rhetoric provoked a swift rebuttal when uttered in public. For example, a newspaper editorial that casually referred to a senator as "the Ohio ostler" brought on the following response: "What *was* the president of the United States? What *Greene,* the right arm of Washington, what *Franklin,* what *Sherman*—what *Clay,* what *Webster,* with thousands others, the ornaments of the past age, and *markers* of the present?"[25] Nor was this egalitarian rhetoric confined to Democrats. Abolitionists, for example, legitimated their cause by insisting that their ranks were filled with "the middling interest men—the mechanics, farmers, and laboring classes" and that "the Aristocracy of the North" was against them. And the Whigs and other anti-Jackson parties delighted in accusing Jackson of monarchical pretensions that were at odds with democratic values.[26] The contrast between Fisher's private elitism and this public endorsement of equality suggests that the anxiety over the legitimacy of democracy was not misplaced; some people, at least, still wanted an aristocracy. But Fisher correctly recognized that the weight of public opinion was against him and (like most of the Philadelphia elite) withdrew from politics rather than attempting to counter the democratic ethos of the day.

Ridiculing rhetoric like Fisher's helped to insulate political from social relations by making it difficult to suggest that social standing conferred some special qualification for political office. Along with devices such as the elimination of property requirements for voting, this egalitarian discourse created an at least conceptual separation between the (supposedly egalitarian) political order and the (often hierarchical) social order. This separation necessarily altered the relationship among riots, politics, and social order. Eighteenth-century antiriot rhetoric represented social disorder (riots) as the result of a breakdown in social-political relations, interpreted as the failure of deference. But if deference no longer governed political relations, to what could we attribute riotousness? Why would citizens fail to respect the laws that they themselves had enacted?

Sources of Disorder

Some, like Fisher, located the sources of riots in the political sphere, in the actual operation of democratic politics; democracy itself, in his view, was to blame for social disorder. Riots are the work of "the democratic spirit" and evidence that "[d]emocracy is indeed triumphing," he insisted. Recurrent elections are the chief cause of "party spirit, bad passions, demagogism, idleness, drunkenness, mobs & riots."[27] To Fisher, riots were simply a way—and to the vulgar, the preferred way—to practice democratic politics. This view was undoubtedly supported by the fact that many antebellum riots took place between competing political groups—nativists and immigrants, abolitionists and their opponents, Democrats and Whigs—so that they looked very much like a disorderly sort of politics. But Fisher's complaint was not just that democracy increased the salience of politics among the masses, giving them more things to fight about. The people who hold political power in a democracy, he worried, were more inclined to riot than were the elite; they were ignorant, and their "standard of excellence in government, in morals, and in social life is low." They *prefer* social turmoil, he claimed, because "scenes of violence afford opportunities for the gratification of their brutal passions." Democracy, then, fosters a "wild, radical, agrarian spirit" that the "incendiary presses" and those notorious "designing demagogues" are constantly fanning.[28]

Supporters of democracy countered this view, not necessarily by disputing the tendency of the lower orders to riot but by exploring the causes of riotousness in institutions other than those of democratic politics. For example, consider an anonymous pamphlet entitled *The Life and Adventures of Charles Anderson Chester* that appeared in Philadelphia in 1850.[29] The pamphlet tells a story, a kind of republican morality play, about the Philadelphia election riots of 1849. The hero, Charles Anderson Chester, was a dissolute youth cast off by his wealthy father, Jacob, after Charles's mother ran off with another man: "You comprehend Charles? You are not my son. The conduct of your mother breaks all ties between us." Twice abandoned, Charles steals a few thousand dollars from his erstwhile father and heads for Havana.

Three years later, Jacob becomes enamored of an innocent young actress, Ophelia, and concocts a plot to abduct her on election night, with the help of a Negro bartender, "Black Herkles." Unbeknownst to Jacob, Dick Hellfire, leader of the Killers (Philadelphia's most notorious street gang) is also making plans for election night, which include a little rioting and relieving Jacob of his extra cash. So the stage is set; the unfortunate parties come together in the midst of the election night riot of 1849. Ophelia is chloroformed, and unwittingly killed in the process, by Black Herkles. She is removed to a room above the bar where Jacob waits. Below in the bar, Dick Hellfire arrives with his motley crew, knocks out poor Herkles, and finds Jacob. He then reveals that he is, of course, the hapless Charles, returned from Havana. He takes Jacob's money belt and goes down to the bar, where his gang has started a brawl. The ensuing conflict leaves Charles dead and Jacob mortally wounded. Only Herkles escapes.

The elements of the story are standard fare in antebellum literature: the Gothic story line, the stereotypical characters, the theme of corruption and innocence. But the centerpiece of the story is the connection between the breakdown of the Chester family at the beginning, represented by the faith-lessness of Charles's mother, and the breakdown of social order at the end, represented by the riot instigated by Dick and his crew. To be sure, class snobbery like Fisher's figures into this account of social disorder; the rioters are primarily criminals and other social rabble. But the fact that the lower classes are always ripe for riots isn't really the point. Rather, the story uses the riot of 1849 to explore how disorder within the family—a problem for the indigent Ophelia, whose unscrupulous mother tries to prostitute her, as well as for the wealthy Chesters—tends to undermine social order generally.

Clearly, this approach to social (dis)order is not the same as that found in eighteenth-century antiriot rhetoric. Compare the Chester story with this Revolution-era story (from the *Pennsylvania Packet*) about politics and social order: The hero is Behram, king of Persia, who succeeded his father at "an age more proper to be under control, than to govern his species." He therefore left the government to his prime minister, who "shamelessly abused the power delegated to him, as did all the subordinate officers under his direction . . . so that they all thought only of their own profit, without any regard to the public." As a result, the troops became negligent, order broke down, and the people became seditious. One day, while reflecting on his troubles, the king met with a shepherd who was in the process of hanging his dog. The king asked how the dog had earned this punishment, and the shepherd explained that it had not defended the flock from the wolves. Therefore, the shepherd concluded, the dog was responsible for the calamities the wolves inflicted on the sheep. The king took this lesson to heart and condemned his prime min-ister to the same punishment—whereupon "good order was established in Persia."[30]

The differences between the two stories reflect the different political agen-das animating eighteenth- and nineteenth-century interpretations of riots. The story of Behram was directed against the British monarchy, while the Chester story was a lesson in republican morality, addressed to the "youth of our land."[31] But they also reflect differing accounts of the sources of social disorder. In the story of Behram, social disorder stems from the disorder in-fecting the relationship between the rulers and the ruled. The author of the Chester pamphlet, in contrast, was more concerned about the character of the republic's citizens than about the possible political origins of the riot (which was, after all, an election riot). This points toward a characteristic antebellum concern about social order. Whereas the story of Behram links social disorder directly to poor government, in the Chester story, social dis-order ripples out from the family in concentric rings of corruption, beginning with the mother. Charles's mother lacks virtue to begin with and conceives an illegitimate child. This act corrupts both the husband and the son, whose bad character in turn corrupts society and, finally, disrupts the political sphere. The Chester story thus locates the source of social disorder in what was typically considered the most private of relationships—those between wife and husband and between mother and son.[32] The chief threat to social order here is not a breakdown in the hierarchical relations between the rulers and the ruled but the spread of corruption from one individual through the whole society.

This kind of complaint was a prominent feature of antiriot rhetoric in the antebellum era; apparently, riots stemmed not from poor government but from the rioters' lack of character, which in turn resulted from the operation of forces that lay outside the realm of actual political conflict. Although character, in the sense of Christian virtue, was a theme in early-eighteenth-century antiriot rhetoric, it was submerged in the greater anxiety about the political implications of riots—namely, their disruption of the divinely mandated social-political order. In contrast, by the antebellum era, the rhetoric pervading public discourse displayed an almost obsessive concern with character as the source of riotousness. Rioters were "brutish," constituting a "body of men ripe and ready for scenes of riot" who "neither know nor care for causes or consequences."[33] The editor of *Niles' Register* concluded from the frequent riots that "the character of our people has suffered a considerable change for the worse. . . . We fear that the moral sense of right and wrong has been rendered less sensitive than it was."[34] Another editor warned that "[e]very individual is a component part of the whole, and the slightest deviation of that individual from rectitude of thought or action, throws more or less disorder into the whole frame of society."[35] Implicit in such complaints is the assumption that democracy will not produce riots if the social sources of poor character can be corrected; if Fisher is right that the poor are always inclined to riot, the answer is to improve their character, not to reject democracy. This approach thus deflects criticism away from democratic political institutions and toward other features of American society such as gender relations, race relations, ethnic heterogeneity, and class structure. Riots could be (and were) attributed to the influx of immigrants, prejudice against blacks, the increasing class of urban poor—everything except "the inevitable action of democratic principles on human nature."

Of course, this strategy of attributing social disorder to the character of the citizen echoes an old theme in American republican thought, which emphasizes the importance of civic virtue to the stability of a republic. As Gordon Wood put it, the founders considered that "[f]rugality, industry, temperance, and simplicity . . . were the stuff that made a society strong. The virile martial qualities—the scorn of ease, the contempt of danger, the love of valor—were what made a nation great." The chief danger to social order in a republic, according to this perspective, was a corrupting love of luxury, which tended to enervate the citizens, leaving them more concerned with private affairs than with public measures.[36] This is a simplification, naturally; as argued in Chapter 1, eighteenth-century Americans were familiar with a range of political virtues besides those of classical republicanism. My point, however, is that the understanding of civic virtue animating antebellum antiriot rhetoric departed in some important respects from this classical framework. Most notably, it did not center on zealous attention to the public good and spirited resistance to oppression, nor on the danger that private vices would lead to public passivity. (Antebellum rioters, after all, often appeared all too spirited and overly attentive to public affairs.) In the Chester narrative, for example, it is not public-spiritedness but sexual virtue that is singled out; without sexual virtue, the family structure breaks down and the children are abandoned to malign influences and their worst impulses—an analysis that suggests that attention to private affairs is at least as important to political stability as attention to the public good. Similarly, one antimob diatribe worried that "idleness and dissipation," along with "vulgarity and lawlessness," would lead not to a general inattention to public affairs but to a politics of mob action: "The character of the town when it becomes a multitudinous city will be, in a measure, what we make it now. The time will come when there will not want materials for a mob of the most destructive character. And even now, by considerable fostering, by those means and appliances which demagogues and bad men know how to use, it is not impossible to excite such a riot."[37] The political significance of idleness and, prominently, intemperance was not that they distracted citizens from public concerns but that they caused riots—which in turn threatened the legitimacy of democracy. Thus, despite their political effects and often explicitly political motivations, the source of riots actually lies in the private sphere, in the form of such vices as intemperance, idleness, or unchastity.

This focus on the private sphere was, however, only one dimension of antebellum antiriot rhetoric. The relationship between riotousness and individual character also showed up in discourses about citizenship—the major debates over citizenship during the antebellum period referred constantly to the danger of riots—but these debates also brought antiriot rhetoric back to a concern with how politics affects social order. The rhetoric surrounding citizenship is interesting for another reason as well, however. It reveals a change in the context of antiriot discourse: the elevation of democracy from a problematic and contested value to an ultimate end whose desirability is beyond debate. The change is a subtle but important one. In the arguments over citizenship, riots were presented as threatening not the desirability of democracy but actual democratic institutions.

Citizenship

Riots threatened politics, as the Chester narrative suggests, by disrupting political activities such as elections. But riots were not simply like natural catastrophes, which might also disrupt politics. To many observers, riots seemed to result from the failure of specifically political virtues: respect for law, self-control, tolerance, and open-mindedness. To call these "political virtues," of course, is to assume what I am trying to show: that antebellum antiriot rhetoric was rooted in a picture of democratic politics as *properly* the domain of rational and temperate debate. Sidney George Fisher, for example, would not consider tolerance and respect for law to be integral to democratic politics. That others did is suggested by the frequent use of rioters as models against which to define the proper content of the citizen's character and, in turn, the proper bounds of the political community.

Consider, for example, the debates surrounding the nativist anti-Catholic riot in Philadelphia in 1844.[38] The causes of the riot are disputed, but a central element was a conflict between the Irish Catholics and the Native American Party (a nativist, not an American Indian, faction) over the public schools' use of a version of the Bible not authorized by the Catholic Church. A defender of the Irish participants blamed the riot on the fanaticism and bigotry of the Native Americans. He wrote his book, he claimed, in order to "warn the brethren of the same family and citizens of the same country, against that spirit of licentiousness and sectarian intolerance, which will be satisfied only with . . . the final ruin of all our blessed civil establishments." More specifically, he charged that the Protestant press had started the trouble with its "inflammatory works and impassioned harangues." The riot, then, resulted from the failure of tolerance and reason and, significantly, from the misuse of the republican institution of the free press.[39] The nativists responded that the riot was not caused by the Native Americans, who were orderly and peace loving. Rather, it was the foreigners (the Irish) who lacked the qualities necessary for self-government, being inherently violent. Eschewing the proper means of politics—reason, discussion, and argument—they used brute force to disrupt meetings. The problem with foreigners, they complained, was that Europe sent only its worst citizens: "a would-be regicide," for example, and "that class who, discontented and oppressed at home, leave

there, filled with all the requisite materials to spread among our citizens anarchy, radicalism, and rebellion."⁴⁰ These characteristics, they asserted, make
foreigners unfit for republican politics.

Most political activists would probably agree that "would-be regicides"
were unfit for republican politics, but they were also aware that this conviction struck uncomfortably close to the revolutionary tradition. After all,
aren't "would-be regicides" precisely the type of people who fomented the
American Revolution? Those concerned about riotousness countered this objection with the claim that the qualities needed to obtain liberty and those
needed to preserve it are different. Or so Abraham Lincoln, for one, believed.
The temperament of revolution, he declared, the "principles of hate, and the
powerful motive of revenge" must fade now that the revolutionary generation
is passing away: "Passion has helped us; but can do so no more. It will in the
future be our enemy. Reason, cold, calculating, unimpassioned reason, must
furnish all the materials for our future support and defence. Let those materials be moulded into general intelligence, sound morality and, in particular, a reverence for the constitution and laws."⁴¹ The rhetoric used to reject
the revolutionary tradition is familiar by now: Citizens must be rational
and law-abiding, not passionate and rebellious. Passion leads to violence, and
on down the slippery slope to anarchy. So *Niles' Register* explained a riot by
Irish immigrants by arguing that they had been "made mad by oppression
at home." Now that they were in America, they would have to "learn to
reason—if disposed to listen to its dictates."⁴² Becoming a citizen is a process
of learning to reason and listening to its dictates. The angry mob is the foil
for the virtuous, temperate, dispassionate citizen; the citizen is defined in
contrast to the member of the mob.⁴³

The construction of citizenship against the mob provided a standard for
determining the bounds of the political community, particularly in the context of the suffrage debates that took place in many northern cities during
the 1830s and 1840s. These debates were driven, in large part, by the concern
over rioting. Consider, for example, this statement from a grand jury in New
York, issued after indicting a number of people for rioting during an election:

> While a proper zeal in conducting our elections is commendable, it is
> desirable that it be so attempted as not to inflame the citizens or inter-
> rupt the free exercise of their civic rights. And on the occurrence of
> scenes like those brought to the cognizance of this jury, it is all impor-
> tant they should be checked in their incipiency.
>
> In reference to this . . . they are fully of the opinion that the plan now
> in agitation, of registering the names of voters prior to every election, is

best calculated to avert the recurrence of so lamentable an evil as that alluded to.[44]

This reasoning is a little puzzling; how is voter registration, usually aimed at preventing unqualified people from voting, supposed to reduce riotousness? The implicit argument here is that people who are not qualified to vote (foreigners) are coming to the polls in large numbers, and they, not the natives and long-term residents, are responsible for the violence—presumably because they lack the habits of civic virtue produced by an upbringing in the United States. As one concerned citizen worried, "Scenes of violence, disorder, and riot have taught us in this city that universal suffrage will not do for large communities. It works better in the country, where a large proportion of the voters are Americans, born and brought up on the spot."[45] The introduction of this foreign element into politics was creating the disorder that suffrage restrictions were supposed to fix.

This was a familiar argument in political discourse during the 1830s, as northern cities experienced the first large influx of immigrants to the United States. A disproportionate number of riots took place among these immigrant groups (particularly the Irish),[46] and political leaders hastened to use this fact to insulate democracy from charges of licentiousness. Since so many of the rioters are foreigners, they argued, it must be European tyranny, rather than democracy, that produces these disorders—or, more properly, the transition from tyranny to democracy. According to an article in the *North American Review,* the character of the immigrants had been shaped by the prejudices of the "altogether differently constituted societies of Europe." They had been "demoralized by the arbitrary and capricious exactions of the governments under which they . . . lived." The Irish, for example, were "betrayed by the ardor of their temperament, and the recklessness of their habits."[47] Others were more concerned about the Germans, who suffered from "rationalism and infidelity" (a reference to German radicalism), which "will not fail to sow the seeds of anarchy and bloodshed."[48]

These complaints do not simply echo the familiar Whig claim that tyranny causes riots by making the people unhappy—a claim that still animated some of the debates on citizenship. For example, consider Thomas Earle's arguments against property restrictions on voting during the 1838 Pennsylvania Constitutional Convention: Excluding people from the political community, he claimed, simply creates a set of men within the republic who are disposed to riot. "Treat a man as an outcast, and he becomes an outcast in fact, and he is ready to aid any set of men who desire to destroy your Government."[49] Debates over race-based voting restrictions sounded a similar theme. Denying blacks the vote, argued one opponent of restrictions, is "the same thing as if their abode were transferred to the dominions of the Russian Autocrat, or of the Grand Turk."[50] If you give the black man his rights, "you may make him a contented, and perhaps a useful citizen; but take away from him those rights which belong to him, and his bosom will rankle with hate, and discontent will prevail among them."[51] Here the standard claim that tyranny causes riots is being leveled against the undemocratic aspects of American government.

In contrast, opponents of immigration claimed that immigrants, who were not riotous at home because they were too demoralized to resist tyranny, would become riotous once they experienced political freedom. For example, one editor warned immigrants that their sudden freedom from the "disabilities which have . . . [hovered] over [them]" might lead them to "extravagances of thought and action" that would threaten the "institution, the good order, the peace, the happiness of society." He continued, "You are now, for the first time perhaps, in the strict sense of the word, FREEMEN! No haughty lord—no unrelenting taskmaster, will here assume a dictatorship on your person, your conversation, or your conduct;—but beware that you use not your liberty as a cloak for licentiousness." Instead, they should "study to be quiet, and mind [their] own business."[52] The immigrant, warned another, has been "suddenly transferred from a land where he possessed no interest in the conduct of [the government], to one where every barrier is thrown down. . . . Under such circumstances, it cannot be a matter of surprise, if the emigrant, unfortunate alike in his previous disqualification and in his sudden investiture with new and untried privileges, be found sometimes to add his weight to that portion of society which is most susceptible of partial impressions, and most exposed to violent and hurtful impulses."[53] To reduce the threat of riots, then, immigrants should be restricted from participating in politics altogether, at least until they have been in the country long enough to form an attachment to the country and "arrive at a just understanding and appreciation of the character and institutions of the republic." Otherwise, the "admixture of all the prejudices, interests and passions of the known world" would "corrupt the sources of liberty."[54] As in the Chester narrative, the threat to social order is not the abuse of power but corruption of the body politic by persons of poor character.

The arguments directed against immigrants, then, linked riotousness to certain disfavored social groups. Against the association of the mob with the people typically found in eighteenth-century rhetoric (and in the complaints of elitists such as Sidney George Fisher), this rhetoric echoes Fisher Ames's insistence that the mob is made up of people who aren't actually part of the social order: the "offscourings of society" rather than common working people.[55] The presence of foreigners among the rioters reinforced this view; the mob, it seemed, was made up of "the others" (Irish, Germans, and so forth), those who were different in critical respects from real Americans. Even immigrants from British countries "are essentially different from us," claimed one nativist: "Though they may use the same words that we use; though they express the same abhorrence of tyranny and oppression, yet liberty, considered as a creature of the mind is with them a different thing, from what it is with us. . . . From their infancy, they have associated with government and law the idea of tyranny and injustice, and with liberty, a state of society as unrestrained, as a state of nature."[56] The immigrant therefore "declaims against oppression, flames with zeal for liberty, and seldom fails to be at the head or tail of innovation and reform, perhaps of insurrection."[57] (Notice how these qualities are presented as political *vices*.) To call such "naturalized foreigners" citizens is a contradiction, like "foreign natives" or "hostile friends," insisted one concerned (not to say paranoid) native. Unlike the immigrants who first settled the country—"the real lovers of liberty"—the current "invasion" consisted of those "selected for a service to their tyrants, and by their tyrants; not for their affinity to liberty, but for their mental servitude, and their docility in obeying the orders of their priests."[58] (This picture, incidentally, contrasts with the common complaint among Europeans that only "the honest, the industrious, the independent, are quitting us.")[59] The problem with immigration, then, is that unless the newcomers "are more civilized and more virtuous, and have at the same time, the same ideas and feeling about government," they will corrupt American political institutions.[60]

These concerns about how the differently formed character of immigrants would affect political stability laid the groundwork for race- and ethnicity-based exclusions that have structured American immigration and citizenship laws ever since this period; character, and particularly character for riotousness, served as a standard by which to evaluate who was or was not worthy of citizenship. But the above arguments suggest a more complicated relationship among laws, social institutions, and civic virtue than the simpler (and increasingly more popular) racial theories. They tended to locate the sources of social order in the influence of tyranny on one's character. In doing so, they went beyond the careful distinction we found in the Chester narrative between the social origins and the political effects of riots. The arguments against immigrant suffrage reflected both the characteristic antebellum focus on character and the older tendency to trace riotousness to political arrangements, namely, tyranny. They thus directed attention back to the political causes of riots—but in a way that continued to insulate democracy from criticism. It is not democracy that is at fault here, but the influence of foreign tyranny, carried over and spread among the population by immigrants. Lurking behind this discourse, of course, is the assumption, or hope, that people who were brought up under a democratic government would have the proper character for self-government. The threat of riots, in short, is not an argument against democracy but an argument for it.

The suffrage debate thus undermined the neat distinction between the social causes and the political effects of riots, even while it continued to deny the connection between democracy and licentiousness. But perhaps more significantly, these debates tended to displace the question of the legitimacy of democracy altogether. The suffrage debates were animated less by a concern with reducing social disorder in order to preserve the legitimacy of democracy than by a concern with protecting democracy from social disorder. When the New York grand jury recommended restricting suffrage to prevent rioting, its primary concern was not to prevent rioting per se but to prevent riots from disrupting elections. Similarly, proponents of immigration restrictions argued that immigration was a danger to the "political condition of the state" through the "*corruption* by the undue accession of unassimilating elements."[61] Such arguments elide the question of whether the political condition of the state is worth preserving, of whether democracy is a legitimate form of government. Democracy is not treated as a regime whose legitimacy is debatable, but as an ultimate value.

The citizenship debates, then, reveal a change in the rhetoric of political legitimacy: the question of the legitimacy of democracy was becoming obsolete. Although one strand of antiriot rhetoric still focused on the relative virtues of democracy and monarchy, other closely related discourses were using democracy as an ultimate value to determine citizenship and establish the boundaries of the political community. But if the battle to legitimate democracy was being won (at least in the cosmopolitan north), riots were still a problem. After all, riots undermined law and security, returning society to its "original elements" where the "law of force must govern." If they continued, "social security and order would wither under the heated atmosphere of passion." Since republican institutions are based, as one editor put it, "upon foundations, recognizing . . . obedience to all wise and just regulations," riots would eventually lead to the "annihilation of all that is worth possessing," including democracy itself. "When the Greeks began to trample underfoot the supremacy of laws," reminded another, "their republics, though based upon the soundest wisdom, were changed for the despotic government of the Roman Legions or the tender mercies of the Macedonian Phalanx. . . . We must not flatter ourselves that similar causes will not produce similar effects."[62] Riots, then, threaten not only the legitimacy of democracy but democratic institutions themselves. For the sake of law, order, and democracy, riots must be suppressed.

Force and Reason

Readers of *Niles' Register* in September 1829 were treated to the following vignette:

> A fracas occurred in New Orleans on the 20th ult. between the edi-tors of the Argus and Courier, in consequence of an electioneering para-graph, published by the latter. The editor of the Courier . . . gives the following account of the affair.
>
> "The traitor came yesterday to Hewlett's coffee house, where I was seated . . . and after having walked several times around me . . . without daring to attack me, and after having rallied, a few assassin-like wretches of his species, he gave me from behind, a blow with his fist in the face. . . . I rushed upon him, and striking him with the end of my umbrella in the stomach, I made him lose his equilibrium, and abandoning my umbrella, I jumped upon him, seized him by the throat with my two hands, and dragged or rather carried him to the reading table. . . . [S]ee-ing that the rascal would not give up his soul; I let my right hand loose to take my penknife and open his guts."[63]

Fortunately, the affray was broken up by the crowd before the editorial may-hem went any further.

Niles was characteristically shocked by this incident, as was the editor of the *Pennsylvanian:* "According to our notions, quill driving is, beyond the use of words, essentially pacific, and these bloody encounters between scribblers, even in the west, sound as strangely as it would be to see our contemporaries of the Sentinel and Poulson's Advertiser, dodging, and firing at each other in the street."[64] But in fact such events were common during the antebellum era, and not only in the West. In 1831, New Yorker Philip Hone recorded a simi-lar altercation between the editors of the *Evening Post* and the *Commercial Advertiser,* in which William Cullen Bryant whipped William Stone with a cowskin. And Philadelphia editor Joseph Chandler complained in 1837 that "Bowie knives, dirks and pistols are worn, shown and used in Philadelphia as well, if not as much as they are in Mobile."[65] Political conflict regularly took the form of fistfights, canings, duels, lynchings, assassinations, and, of course, old-fashioned riots.[66] Although most people condemned these prac-tices (at least publicly), suppressing them turned out to be a fairly compli-cated project. Instituting a norm of nonviolence in politics required, at a minimum, making such riotous behavior look less like a normal concomitant of popular politics and more like an aberration from legitimate and normal political behavior. And this project, in turn, rested critically on the distinction (dubious as it might have seemed to the editors of the *Argus* and *Courier*) between violence and argument.

Chapter 1 identified the opposition of force and argument, based on the reason-passion distinction, as the central axis of post-Revolution antiriot rhetoric. This opposition continued to structure the discourse surrounding riots in the antebellum era, serving as the basis of the norm of nonviolence: One should use argument, not force, to achieve one's political goals. The proper weapon of the political editor is the pen, not the penknife. The rule seems simple enough, a self-evident metanorm that promises to contain and order political activity. But the career of the force versus argument distinction in antebellum politics suggests that it is *not* a self-evident "natural fact" that lies outside the bounds of political controversy. On the contrary, the more people relied on this distinction, the more it revealed its constructed, and deeply contestable, character.

For abolitionists, the difference between violence and argument was dramatically illustrated by such events as the burning of Pennsylvania Hall by a mob in 1838. The riot resembled in many respects the 1742 election riot described in Chapter 1, except that the abolitionists, unlike the Quakers, refused to fight back. The hall had been built to house abolition meetings, and it immediately became a target for the antiabolitionists. The trouble began the day after the hall's official dedication. First, notices appeared around the city exhorting "citizens who respect the right of property" to interfere with the scheduled meeting. Only a few people showed up the next day, but in the evening, a group of antiabolitionists gathered outside the hall and disrupted speeches by Maria Chapman and Angelina Grimké by yelling and throwing bricks. The next morning, the abolitionists found the hall surrounded by a mob but were subjected to nothing worse than insults. But the hall's managers were concerned about the threat of violence, so they asked the mayor and sheriff to protect them. The mayor, pointing out that he commanded a force of only three persons, said that all he could do was speak to the mob and try to discourage the rioters. (The abolitionists later argued that he could have called on the militia or raised a posse.) The mayor took the keys of the building and informed the mob that the hall would remain under his protection for the night. The mob cheered but did not disperse. The mayor withdrew, and the rioters, "passion-maddened, and doubtless rum-inflamed," set the hall on fire. The sheriff tried to restore order by calling on various members of the crowd for assistance, but he was ignored. Nor were the fire companies of any use, since the mob prevented them from putting out the fire.

The abolitionists (like the Quakers a century earlier, and with just as little evidence) blamed the officials for not preventing the riot and accused them of sympathizing with the mob. But, unlike the eighteenth-century Quakers, the abolitionists didn't control the legislature, and the public outcry was confined to the usual pro forma condemnations of mob action in the press. The comments of the editor of the *Pennsylvanian* were typical: "Granting all to be correct that is urged against the frequenters of Pennsylvania Hall—that they were guilty of braving public opinion in a gross manner, and that sentiments were uttered at their meetings well calculated to awaken popular excitement, we contend that violence was neither a proper nor an effectual remedy."[67] But the riot, if not proper, *was* fairly effective; the hall was not rebuilt, and the Grimké sisters, among Philadelphia's most eloquent opponents of slavery, retired from public speaking soon after the incident.[68]

Abolitionists interpreted the burning of Pennsylvania Hall as evidence of the antagonistic relationship between riots and politics. The hall, they declared, was "dedicated to free discussion"; it would confront the enemy of human rights with "a barrier which he cannot pass . . . by the consecration of a spot where all his pretensions may be fully and fairly discussed." But the mob, by destroying the hall, had "trodden under foot the glorious principles of democracy."[69] The violence of the mob threatened the very structure of the political sphere by destroying a building whose only purpose was to house peaceful debates about political issues. Nor was the burning of Pennsylvania Hall atypical. Mobs frequently targeted the means of political activity, including buildings where meetings were held, printing presses, and public gatherings. In Philadelphia, for example, rioters targeted churches (July 1834), meetinghouses (1838), elections and political meetings (October 1834, 1844, 1849), and parades (1842).[70]

Such attacks prompted comments on the opposition between argument and violence, and the exclusion of violence, as the basic organizing principle of republican politics: "Surely every sect or party, religious or political, may assemble together for the better support or further extension of their own particular opinions—and, if persons holding different opinions attend . . . every principle of common sense, and of respect for themselves, should induce them to remain peaceable. Without the exercise of such mutual regard, our churches, as well as primary assemblies of the people, must be rendered places for battle. . . . [V]iolence beget[s] a spirit of violence, and the end is anarchy unrestrained."[71] These exhortations did not necessarily condemn the political aims of mobs—on the contrary, the preceding quotation referred to a riot against abolitionists, who were generally conceded to be crazy and dangerous. But, as *Niles' Register* insisted: "Although none disapprove more decidedly than we have done, the course of Mr. Tappan, and his professors, in relation to the subject of abolition, yet we condemn most unqualifiedly the attack made last night upon his premise. We profess to live in a government

under laws."[72] The problem with mobs is not their aims but their antipoliti-
cal means. They threaten politics itself by undermining the means of legitimate, republican politics—namely, argument. Edward Abdy, describing an
antiabolition mob in New York, complained that "all were animated by a
spirit from which neither freedom of discussion, nor personal safety of their
opponents, could be expected." They "substitute physical force for argument,
and subject freedom of debate to the will of a lawless mob"[73]—an interesting
reversal of the post-Revolution picture of *argument* as a substitute for mob
action.

This opposition between force and argument, mirroring the opposition
between riots and legitimate political activity, is familiar from post-Revolution antiriot rhetoric. Here, it supports the claim that popular political
action is "normally" carried out through argument, not violence; that is, nonviolence is the norm in politics (or it should be—claims about norms notoriously conflate the normative and the descriptive). At any rate, this norm
depends on the distinction between argument and force. But how stable
is this distinction? George Simmons addressed this question in a sermon
prompted by the Thompson antiabolitionist riots in New York in 1851.
Sounding much like an earlier Fisher Ames, he claimed: "[T]he whole proceedings are in general so brutish and violent, that it is not to be regarded as
an *expression of opinion* even on the part of those who compose it, but is a
mad and blind affair, in which the last appeal is made from reason to passion,
from the calm judgments of men to their ignorant prejudices, from the enlightened and the conscientious to the blindest and most abandoned class."[74]
Far from being an expression of opinion, the mob "very often has no opinions; and if it have any, they are as discordant as the noises and shouts they
make."[75] In fact, however, antebellum riots were frequently orderly and deliberate. For example, in 1834 a New York "mob" (as it was termed in the
Pennsylvanian) attacked the local abolitionists by gathering at a chapel where
an abolition meeting was scheduled. When the meeting failed to occur, the
mob entered the chapel and held its own meeting, appointing the mayor
(who was probably there at least ostensibly to prevent disorder) to preside.
After adjourning this meeting, they proceeded to the Bowery Theater. There
they interrupted a play by occupying the stage and demanding that an actor
who had made some uncomplimentary comments about Americans be fired.
They concluded the evening by proceeding to Arthur Tappan's house (he was
not home) and destroying much of his furniture.[76] Was this a "brutal and
violent" mob? (Is destroying property "violence"?) We might ask the same
question about the "attack" on Cassius Clay's printing offices in 1845. After
a lengthy meeting on the Cincinnati courthouse lawn, a "mob" of antiabolitionists passed a resolution (observing all the parliamentary formalities) to

shut down Clay's press. They then converged on the office—Clay put up no resistance—and carefully (instructed by professional advisers) packed his equipment and shipped it to Cincinnati. According to some abolitionists, at least, this was a murderous mob.[77]

And maybe it was; maybe if Clay had put up more resistance, the anti-abolitionists would have become violent. Nevertheless, neither of the mobs described above bears much resemblance to the "wild and awful force" Simmons described—"a *thing,* under the guidance of no soul, having even no intelligent instincts, monstrous in its form, and ferocious in its purposes."[78] On the contrary, both argument and force seem to be integral to these mob actions; after all, the mob had to debate what to do and how to do it. Simmons's point, however, was that mobs are *essentially* creatures of passion, that passion is what motivates and guides them. Therefore, mob action should not be confused with argument. It belongs in the category of violence, even if (like the Thompson riots) it was clearly animated by political convictions and seldom resulted in actual physical violence.

Simmons seems to have a point here. It is not hard to see an antiabolition mob, however restrained, as a creature of passion. However, it is hard to see why such mob action shouldn't be read as an expression of opinion as well. The fact that Simmons felt compelled to *argue* the point is suggestive; the distinctions on which the definition of legitimate political action rested were not as stable as they appeared. Certainly the *rhetorical* distinction between argument and violence was vulnerable to all sorts of manipulation. If violence was the opposite of politics, it was also the model of politics; political activity, particularly debate, was regularly characterized as a war of words. Editorials reported these verbal jousts using unabashedly martial metaphors. Political arguments were "totally demolished," "torn to atoms, and scattered to the winds," and victims were left to make an "inglorious retreat." Victors in such contests proudly declared themselves unswayed by their opponents' argument and boasted of the numbers supporting their cause.[79] (I investigate the origins of this picture of political debate in Chapter 3; it contrasts strikingly with the image of dispassionate deliberation that the founders advocated.) Moreover, while political argument was characterized as riotous, riots were often characterized as politics. *Niles' Register,* for example, ironically reported a "treaty of peace" between two feuding groups of Irishmen, describing their rioting as a "civil war" motivated by partisanship.[80]

Of course, such rhetorical play alone does not necessarily destabilize the distinction between argument and violence; rather, the distinction is what makes the rhetorical mechanism work. But sometimes the distinction between argument and violence broke down altogether. For example, John Hancock Lee, attributing the nativist riots of 1844 to their opponents, the

Irish, recounted the following incident at a public meeting to debate suffrage restrictions:

> [S]everal blustering and exceedingly noisy Irishmen were permitted to take the stand and address the assembly. . . . The violence of these speakers was a subject for regret and censure by the more reflecting and sober-minded of all parties. One of these men, who had been but a short time in our country, in the midst of the most inflammatory speech to which we ever listened, loudly and ferociously declared, that if the native Americans persisted in their determination to deprive foreigners of any rights which they claimed for themselves, they (the Irishmen) *would with bowie knife and rifle demand and maintain those rights!!*[81]

Into which category does this Irishman's speech fall—argument or violence? (What if he had brandished a knife while making it? What if his audience had consisted solely of other Irishmen?) Scenes like this illustrate why the distinction between rational debate and violence is not always easy to draw; the categories of argument and violence do not map perfectly onto the underlying categories of reason and passion. If mob action sometimes looks like the expression of opinion, it is also the case that argument does not always rely on discursive rationality to persuade. It can stir the passions as well.

The fact that political speech did not always exhibit the features of discursive rationality, and that mob action sometimes did, made determining the proper limits of political action problematic. The neat distinction between argument and violence crumbled in the face of the murky distinction between, for example, a legal meeting and a mob. Judge King's handling of this problem after the Philadelphia nativist riots of 1844 is instructive. The riots grew directly out of a series of mass rallies by the Native American Party to protest the attempts of the Catholics to eliminate Bible reading in the public schools. Some of these rallies were held in Irish Catholic neighborhoods, where they were received with a resistance that soon turned violent; the ensuing riots continued until the governor finally brought in the militia to suppress them.[82] Judge King opened the grand jury investigation of the riots by observing that "[r]iotous and tumultuous popular assemblages associated for the purpose of destroying property or life, strike . . . at the law itself." The problem with such assemblages is not necessarily their ends: "Even where tumultuous public assemblies are associated for the accomplishment by force of objects, much more plausible and defencible than those apparently moving the recent riots, it perpetually happens that the counsels of the violent and irresponsible, prevail over those of the more cautious and respectable." The argument thus tracks closely the post-Revolution arguments against mobs explored in Chapter 1, explicitly rejecting the Whig tradition of mob action as a vehicle for defending rights.

But where politics and riots are so closely intertwined, how do we untangle them? King's rather elaborate definition of a riot should help: "every tumultuous disturbance of the public peace by three or more assembling together of their own authority, with an intent mutually to assist one another against any who shall oppose them in the execution of some private object, and afterwards executing the same in a violent and turbulent manner to the terror of the people, *whether* the *act* intended is *lawful* or *unlawful,* is a riot."[83] This seems clear enough, if we can be sure that we know what a "violent manner" is. But in *Commonwealth v. Daley,* a murder case connected to the riots, King was faced with following facts: On the third of May, a meeting of about 300 native Americans was held in Kensington, a mostly Irish neighborhood. The meeting was disrupted by a group of Irish Catholics, including the defendant, John Daley. They proceeded to dismantle the stage, possibly threatening the crowd with firearms (the evidence was uncertain). The meeting was adjourned, but another, prompted by the killing on the previous day of a native American, was held in Independence Square on May 7. The participants at this meeting decided to move the meeting to Kensington. Whether the participants were armed was again disputed, but both sides agreed that they carried an American flag bearing the inscription: "This is the flag that was trampled on by the Irish papists." The Irish met the approaching Native Americans with firearms. It's unclear who started firing, but the result was a "bloody combat" between the two parties. According to the prosecution, it was during this combat that the victim (Matthew Hammit) was shot by someone in the group of Irish with whom John Daley was acting.[84]

The question of guilt turned on whether the Irish had intended to attack the native Americans all along, or whether the riot was simply "unlawful mutual combat," in which both parties were at fault (which would make the charge manslaughter instead of first-degree murder). The jury apparently wasn't sure; they split the difference and returned a verdict of second-degree murder. But King's instructions included this interesting analysis: Any body of citizens, he explained, "having in view a constitutional and legal purpose, have the right, peaceably and quietly to assemble for its consideration and discussion." However, a public meeting "otherwise legal, may, from the manner, place, and circumstances of its organization, become an unlawful and even a riotous assembly." If the participants came to the meeting armed, marched to "a place principally inhabited by citizens notoriously opposed to its objects; openly exhibiting arms, and displaying banners containing inscriptions lacerating to the feelings of such citizens," then the assembly was not the exercise of a constitutional right but a "mere riot." Thus the adjourn-

ment of the meeting to Kensington was illegal.[85] Note that it was not necessary for participants to actually use force to be guilty of rioting—or more
accurately, to King, the display of weapons and "inscriptions lacerating to the
feelings" *did* amount to the use of force.

Clearly, under this reasoning there can be no simple set of criteria for
determining what counts as a riot. A Fourth of July militia parade might
include the exhibition of arms and the display of "inscriptions lacerating to
the feelings" without being termed a riot. But when the Philadelphia black
community organized a parade celebrating West Indian emancipation in
1842, a grand jury concluded that it had caused the subsequent race riot.
Apparently, the flag showing a slave in broken fetters against a rising sun (or
a burning slave ship?) was considered by some white onlookers as an incitement to southern slaves to rebel.[86] In short, what counted as a riot depended
less on whether the participants were speaking or shooting than on whether
what they were doing was likely to arouse passion and lead to violence.

Did these people just misunderstand what seems to late-twentieth-century
Americans like an obvious distinction between speech and violence? (Or is it
obvious? Is flag burning speech or violence?) If it seems that Philadelphia
grand juries were too quick to condemn what looks to us like peaceful expression, we should remember what they were dealing with: a long-standing
tradition of mob action and the revolutionary experience of politics out-of-
doors. Traditional mobs did not look all that different from rallies and parades; it's hardly surprising that the attempt to suppress the former cast doubt
on the legitimacy of the latter. These forms of political action, in the context
of antebellum politics, didn't fit neatly into the force-argument framework.
On the contrary, they threatened to undermine it altogether.

Consider inflammatory speech, such as the oration of Lee's impassioned
Irishman: conflating argument and violence, such exhibitions underscored
the contestability of the distinction. The most notorious example is the debate over abolitionism following the 1835 postal campaign. The American
Anti-Slavery Society flooded the South with cheap, mass-produced antislavery propaganda, distributing over one million pieces of literature.[87] Southern
reaction to these "inflammatory" pamphlets was extreme. Some newspapers
recommended making the very discussion of slavery illegal: "Let the declaration, that '*discussions, which, from their nature, tend to inflame the public mind,*
and PUT IN JEOPARDY THE LIVES AND PROPERTY OF OUR FELLOW CITIZENS,
ARE AT WAR WITH EVERY RULE OF MORAL DUTY AND EVERY SUGGESTION
OF HUMANITY,' be only embodied in some legislative act with appropriate
penalties."[88] The mere discussion of slavery was represented as riotous, threatening the Union and the Constitution. Abolitionists were accordingly incen-
diaries with "murderous designs" to arouse a slave rebellion.[89] And this char-

acterization was not confined to literature that explicitly called on slaves to "wash their hands in the blood of whites"; southerners saw incitement to rebellion even in the woodcut ornamenting much abolitionist propaganda, showing a kneeling slave in chains and captioned, "Am I Not a Man and a Brother?" Pennsylvania governor Johnston was accused of inciting the bloody Christiana race riot in 1852 simply because he had publicly expressed some cautious criticisms of the Compromise of 1850, which strengthened the Fugitive Slave Law. Johnston's criticism, complained one editor, "operates on the slaves like an appeal to violence. It is the voice of command calling upon those who are at home to cut the throats of their master."[90] Abolitionists, in contrast, declared themselves vigorous champions of free speech, comparing their dedication to free discussion with that of their opponents, who substituted "[t]he Bowie-knife and the pistol" for "reason and argument" and waged war against freedom of speech.[91] The sense that the two sides were talking past each other comes from their disagreement over the line separating violence from argument; the issue was not so much whether political argument should be protected and violence discouraged as what counted as "argument" and "violence."[92]

The distinction between argument and violence, then, was not an a priori principle but a contested issue asking for some sort of authoritative resolution. The attempts to differentiate between argument and violence therefore drew the state into partisan debates over the proper content of political argument. Ironically, the efforts to establish argument as the primary means of practicing politics resulted in a host of government-imposed restrictions on political argument. The federal House of Representatives, for example, instituted a "gag rule" preventing the discussion of slavery, and the federal postmaster intercepted abolitionist literature on the grounds that it was not legitimate political speech. The Pennsylvania legislature even prohibited the circulation of "any pictorial representation, or any written, pamphlet, handbill, or other paper printed or written, of an inflammatory character"—a law prompted by the abolition debate but technically not limited to abolitionist literature. It outlawed *all* "inflammatory" literature.[93] Abolitionists did not hesitate to characterize these actions as illegitimate intrusions by the state into the sphere of politics. But they, too, sometimes asked the state to intervene, forcibly if necessary, on their behalf, arguing that "those who rely on the civil or military power for the protection of their own rights, would be guilty of a neglect of duty, were they to withhold that protection from the innocent, when they were in danger of suffering from Lynch Law."[94] In order to protect the abolitionists' right to free speech, of course, the state would have to decide what counted as orderly, constitutional speech and what was illegitimate violence. The state was thus called upon to settle authoritatively the distinction between violence and argument in order to protect the politics of argument from the intrusion of violence.

This ultimate resort to the state to maintain the distinction between argument and violence importantly qualifies the norm of nonviolence. It was less a rejection than an organization of force, defining its proper limits and functions in the political system. In contrast to the absolute ethic of nonviolence that led some abolitionists to forswear participation in politics altogether,[95] antiriot rhetoric advocated that violence be confined to the state and be used to maintain the boundaries of legitimate politics, including shoring up the violence-argument distinction on which the norm of nonviolence depended. The state, then, and particularly the local state, was an active partner in controlling and maintaining politics as a sphere of rational, nonviolent interaction.

The State

The abandonment of rioting was not a natural and obvious result of the inevitable triumph of middle-class values.[96] Simply establishing a distinction between violence and argument took active state intervention; convincing the public (both the lower classes and the "gentlemen of property and standing") to abide by the distinction was even more difficult. The persistence of rioting into the antebellum era, particularly in the urban Northeast, indicates how deeply wedded Americans were to mob action. But the rioters were not unconcerned about the future of democracy; they simply had different ideas about how to preserve it—or, perhaps, different ideas about what democracy actually meant and whether mob action had a place in it. Polemics against riots implicitly recognized that the rioters had some justification for their behavior, albeit largely unarticulated. As already suggested, this justification was drawn from the tradition of mob action inherited from the eighteenth century.

Riots were generally justified, if at all, by reference to the eighteenth-century tradition of active liberty, in which the mob represented the people politically mobilized, a kind of shadow government responsible for enforcing the law. For example, opponents of abolition in Philadelphia urged mob action against abolitionists in order to preserve law and order: "Whereas a convention for the avowed purpose of effecting the immediate abolition of slavery in the Union is now in session in this city, it behooves all citizens, who entertain a proper respect for the right of property, and the preservation of the Constitution of the United States, to interfere, *forcibly*, if they *must*, and prevent the violation of these pledges, heretofore held sacred."[97] Abolitionists, then, were the outlaws, and the rioters were simply protecting property rights. Another complaint about abolitionists accused *them* of using the language of resistance to raise a mob, quoting this abolitionist handbill prompted by a pending court decision regarding a runaway slave: "Will men who love LIBERTY, and believe that *innocent men* have a right to it, tamely see such villainy perpetrated *by law* in this city?"[98] Similar language appeared in an exhortation to mob action against bank owners in Baltimore: "[R]ally around the free and unbiass'd judge Lynch who will be place upon the seat of justice and the people enmasse will be the members of the Bar, and these lions of the law shall be made to know that the people will rise in their majesty and redress their own grievances."[99] Again, mob action is justified as necessary to preserve law and order from the "lions of the law."

Arguments against mob action targeted this tradition of mob justice. To return to Judge King's instructions to the grand jury in 1844: When the mob's aims are of a "general and public nature," he insisted, such as preventing the execution of a law, attempting to coerce the repeal of a law, or attacking some class of people "under colour of reforming a public grievance," the rioters have left the realm of politics and are liable for "high treason."[100] (Compare this rhetoric with John Adams's conclusion that private mobs posed a greater threat than public mobs.) King also attacked the eighteenth-century assumption that the mob has authority to act for the people. The mob, he emphasized, is not the people, but an "unauthorized multitude" that has illegitimately assumed "the authority to redress supposed wrongs."[101]

But King confused the issue by asserting the duty of every citizen to assist the authorities in enforcing the laws. "Their vindication and maintenance is the first duty of patriotism. . . . [E]very citizen should regard their infraction as an outrage on himself, and be ready, prompt and eager, to sustain and support them."[102] The problem with this position is that mobs typically defended themselves on the grounds that they *were* helping the authorities by enforcing the laws. As pointed out in Chapter 1, the line between a legitimate *posse comitatus* and an illegal mob was obscure. The judge's charge therefore perpetuated the eighteenth-century confusion between posses and mobs that tended to legitimate mob action. When the *Pennsylvanian* declared that, "[s]hould these tumults continue, it will be necessary for the citizens to organize themselves, and by the most forcible and decisive means, make such an example of the disorderly as may strike them with terror," was it advocating or objecting to mob action?[103]

A more radical attack on the tradition of active liberty came in the form of calls for a professional police force. Philadelphians began discussing police reform in the early 1830s, but it was the riots of the late 1840s that provided the most effective impetus for the creation of a modern police force for the city. A committee appointed in 1842 recommended the creation of a police force of 200 men to be on call for riot control when needed, and its suggestion was supported by the editors of the *Public Ledger* and the *Pennsylvania Freeman*.[104] On the face of it, of course, it's not clear why the increase in riots should have produced this response; after all, riots were perceived as a serious problem in the post-Revolution period, but the anxiety over riots at that time did not result in police reform. The conventional explanation is that antebellum Americans created police forces because, in the increasingly urban and heterogeneous world of the 1830s, the use of personal authority and posses was less effective at riot control than it had been in the eighteenth century.[105] But America was *always* "increasingly urban and heterogeneous," and if "effective" means actually preventing riots, there is no evidence that eighteenth-century methods of riot control had *ever* been effective.[106] So why did Americans wait so long to begin creating local police forces?

No doubt the reasons for this development are complex, and I don't intend to investigate them all here. My goal is not so much accounting for the creation of police forces but accounting for this change in ideas about how to deal with riots. I suggest that the decline of personal authority as a means of riot control should be seen as part of the general rejection of deferential political relations in the antebellum era, at least in the more urban areas in the north. What is striking about antebellum responses to riot control in northern cities, compared with earlier responses, is the lack of concern over the rioters' nondeferential attitude—the problem is not that they aren't sufficiently submissive but that they aren't sufficiently orderly. This change is evidenced by the general clamor in favor of using force to put down the rioters. The mob "is influenced chiefly by the presence of a power able and willing to punish offences against the law," insisted Hezekiah Niles. Newspaper editorials often took a decidedly bloodthirsty tone, advocating that the authorities refuse to "repeat the idle pageant of a military procession" and "add to the confidence of the rioters by an empty, ineffectual display of unused weapons." Thus, the tools of deference politics—the display of the tokens of authority—are scornfully rejected. Rather, "[l]et them be fired upon. . . . Let those who make the first movement towards sedition, be shot down like dogs—and thus teach to their infatuated followers a lesson which no milder course seems sufficient to inculcate. . . . We would recommend that the whole military force of the city be called out."[107] Gone is the eighteenth-century scruple against using force against one's own citizens; absent is any suggestion that the people be restored to a more deferential attitude. By the 1830s, the themes of deference and the moral authority of superiors had been replaced by the themes of respect for law and the legitimate use of force.

But if force was becoming the preferred method of riot control, what accounts for the eventual replacement of posses with professional police? Again, further study might uncover other causes for the creation of a professional police force. But even if a professional police force was desirable for other reasons, why ask it to take on the task of suppressing riots? True, the complaint that officials lacked any other means to respond to riots was an old one—it was, for example, the chief defense of William Allen against the charge that he had failed to prevent the election riot of 1742.[108] But posses were not necessarily inadequate at suppressing riots once they began. During the riotous summer of 1844, Philadelphia's local officials relied on a posse of several hundred citizens, along with the militia. These armed forces responded quickly to reports of violence and dispersed a number of crowds. The official responses to the race riots of 1834 and 1838 in Philadelphia were similar, as were responses to riots in other cities. In New York, for example, an antiabolition mob was promptly put down by a combination of the militia and a citizen posse, organized by the mayor.[109] It's hard to see why a professional police force would be more effective than these traditional forms of riot control.

Of course, a professional police force had one important advantage over a posse: its presence could undermine the traditional justification for rioting—that the citizens were ultimately responsible for enforcing the law. A professional police force would make such mob action unnecessary by relieving the general public of the responsibility for enforcing laws themselves. There is some evidence that officials had this problem in mind. Judge King, for example, insisted that "rights are not to be asserted, nor laws vindicated by a tumultuous mob," and that citizens should not attempt to avenge the laws themselves; injured parties should appeal to the courts for justice and protection. According to the *New York Evening Post,* "there can be no excuse for men's taking the most solemn duty of the Courts upon themselves. . . . Once admit that a mob has, in any case, a right to take the law into its hand, and there is no predicting the nature or extent of the outrages against the institutions of society and the rights of its members."[110] As long as the state was protecting rights and shielding the political sphere from riotous behavior, citizens had no justification for using violence themselves.

The dangers of lynch law were well recognized and probably contributed to the acceptance of a professional police force. This was not, however, the dominant theme in the debates over police reform. They reflect not so much the rejection of the posse but the acceptance of the new model of social order, described earlier: disorder is due to the breakdown of private, or at least nonpolitical, relationships between citizens, rather than the breakdown of hierarchical deference relations between the people and the rulers. This model suggests that social order can be maintained by identifying the seeds of disorder and suppressing or containing them. Thus, in the proposals for police reform, the efficient, almost surgical application of force replaced the general system of deference through which eighteenth-century officials hoped to maintain social order. Proponents envisioned a new type of police, a "preventive police" that would regularly patrol the city, collect detailed information, and respond to problems before they grew into major disturbances. "Judicious organization" of the police would provide "effective control" so that the force would act as a single, powerful unit. The force should "admit of prompt and rapid concentration upon any point or in any emergency . . . so that every movement may be certain, successful and overpowering." Such a police force could quickly identify the point at which disorder was brewing and mobilize efficiently to concentrate an "irresistible force" at that point. It would maintain public order, not through better riot control but by suppressing small disorders before they grew into riots.[111]

This system of police would, ideally, make posses obsolete. Some proponents of reform were even hostile to volunteer law enforcement: "When the public and private occupation are thus intermingled, the mind and feelings will be enlisted for one, while the mere physical powers are devoted to the other; and there will be a constant tendency on the part of the officer to do as much as possible for himself and as little as possible for the public."[112] Others were more optimistic that volunteers could exercise the proper discipline and civic virtue to render them "prudently defensive or effectually offensive, on any occasion."[113] But posses were problematic under this scheme of policing, precisely because it made the use of force, rather than the rituals of deference, central to the maintenance of order. In order to claim that the state could use force to enforce the law *and* that citizens should not use force to pursue politics—both of which were central to the overall goal of reducing riotousness—the state had to maintain its neutrality among contending political parties so that it would not appear to be using force to help one party over another. The problem with posses was that they were generally organized along political lines. For example, the posse called up in 1844 was composed mainly of the Native Americans, who were the initial target and arguably the instigators of violence. During the election riots of 1834 in Philadelphia, the opposing Whigs and Jacksonians acted as posses, taking upon themselves responsibility for defending their neighborhoods from the opposing party. In fact, when the mob gathered to attack Pennsylvania Hall in 1838, the sheriff recommended that the abolitionists form their own posse to defend it.[114]

Since posses organized themselves by party, calling up a posse generally required the official (either the mayor or the sheriff, both of whom were elected) to align himself with one of the parties involved. Sidney George Fisher analyzed the problem thus: "[A] magistrate is placed in a most delicate position & subjected to immense responsibility. If a mob occurs & is successful in its attempts, he is blamed by all. If he resists by military force & life is sacrificed, he is sure of encountering the most furious persecution from the party of rioters, their friends and adherents."[115] When officials failed to use force against mobs, they were similarly accused of favoring the mob for partisan reasons. The alleged lack of official response to the 1838 antiabolitionist riot in Philadelphia, for example, was attributed to the "timid subserviency of the magistrates—beaten and disgraced by those whom they had flattered and strengthened with evil."[116] According to the *Pennsylvania Freeman,* "Men high in authority have manifested an unholy sympathy with the prejudices and passions of the mob—the chosen guardians of the public peace, have manifestly yielded to the popular clamor."[117]

Unfortunately for public officials, to the extent that calling up a posse appeared to be a partisan and therefore political act, it contrasted uncomfortably with the official rejection, in antiriot rhetoric, of violence as a legitimate tool of politics. If the mayor was using his office to further his party's goals through the use of violence, weren't his political opponents equally justified in resorting to violence? Using force to quell a partisan conflict might therefore simply instigate more partisan violence—unless the state could plausibly maintain its neutrality among parties. And a professional police force had a better claim to neutrality than a posse. Uniforms and badges, the day-to-day performance of standardized policing activities, and the bureaucratization of law enforcement—all recommended by proponents of reform—separated the police from the community and created the impression that the police suppressed disorder simply because it was their job, not out of partisan considerations. Given a choice between a professional police force and a posse, local officials had every incentive to favor the police.

The plans for police reform, then, promised to create a particular relationship among the state, politics, and society: In regard to society, the state's role would be to maintain order by monitoring and regulating the minute interactions and relationships that constitute social life through the judicious application of force. In relation to politics, its proper position was neutrality among political groups and the maintenance of the conditions of politics—namely, social order. The new police, a well-organized and bureaucratized instrument of violence, represents this conception of the state. In addition—and possibly unintentionally—the state's monopoly on violence, represented by the replacement of the posse with the police, helped to redefine republican citizenship by taking responsibility for enforcing the law out of the hands of citizens, leaving them only argument and reason with which to practice politics.

In sum, the turn to professional police forces as a means of riot control

was more than a suddenly self-evident response to the increase in riots. At
the very least, it reflected the rejection of hierarchy and deference, which left
force as the only weapon the authorities could use to maintain order. Profes-
sionalization of the police function, in turn, allowed popularly elected officials to use force against (riotous) political groups, while at the same time
maintaining that force should never intrude on politics. In addition, an effective professional police force, by establishing a monopoly on the legitimate
use of force, could remove the central justification for mob action—namely,
the citizens' duty to enforce the law.

But if a professional police force was supposed to maintain the distinction
between force and argument by suppressing political violence, its neutrality
also depended on that very distinction. Only if the police could plausibly
claim that mob action was itself a *nonpolitical* act would its suppression of
that activity also look like a nonpolitical act. In other words, if rioting was
an accepted, regular part of politics—if there was no strong distinction between rioting and arguing—then suppressing riots (even if done evenhand-
edly) would look like an illegitimate intrusion of the state into the political
sphere, just as suppressing political newspapers would. It was acceptable
for the state to suppress riots only because, or to the extent that, riots fell
into the category of violence. The development of a norm of nonviolence in
politics and the creation of a professional police force, then, were two inter-
dependent aspects of the same project: getting rid of riots required that violence be both excluded from the sphere of legitimate politics and lodged in
some politically neutral branch of the state.

Conclusion

An editor in 1836 warned that if the "outbreaks of popular fury" were not
checked, they would "overturn, and scatter, and destroy the whole fabric of
our free government. . . . *There is but a single step from our present position to
a state of anarchy,* the boundaries of which are the confines of despotism."[118]
Where Jefferson once saw the symptoms of a healthy and free constitution,
antebellum political leaders saw the destruction of the regime and, more importantly, the failure of America's unique destiny as the universal guardian of
liberty. The legitimacy of democracy and the future of freedom depended
critically on the people's ability to participate in politics without sparking
riots. The history of this changing discourse about riots and legitimacy is
therefore a genealogy of a rhetoric of popular political action. Against the
tradition of mob action, the founders attempted to make the ideal of discursive rationality, the exclusion of passion, and the opposition of argument and

violence central to the norms governing political action. Democratic politics (they insisted) should ideally consist of peaceful, rational argument instead of violent, impassioned mobbings. Antebellum debates on citizenship took this ideal as a standard, maintaining that citizenship should be conferred based on the citizen's ability to engage in rational discourse. The state's responsibility in this scheme is to protect the political sphere from social disorder through its monopoly on violence, while maintaining a careful neutrality among contending political groups. Even the content and manner of political argument should be regulated to prevent it from disintegrating into riot and anarchy.

As this chapter has shown, these norms gained considerable hegemony during the antebellum period, having the desired effect of making mob action increasingly difficult to defend. But what about the alternative? What did the politics of rational argument look like, and how was it defended? Haunted by the specter of riots, antebellum Americans imagined public debate as an arena of discursive rationality where argument and reason would prevail over violence and passion. At the same time, however, they knew from their practical experience with public debate that passion was not so easily eliminated—nor was anarchy the only danger inherent in democratic politics. The politics of public debate raised its own set of problems, revolving around the relationships between the speaker and the audience, parties and the press, and truth and persuasion.

PART TWO
PUBLIC DEBATE

3

NEOCLASSICAL RHETORIC AND POLITICAL ORATORY

Public debate was supposed to be an improvement over mob action; reason, discussion, and argument were "more reputable weapons" than violence.[1] According to antebellum antiriot rhetoric, a politics of public argument would be orderly and rational; it would escape the turbulence and licentiousness that was supposed to plague democracies. But would it? Charles Brockden Brown raised that disturbing question in his 1798 novel *Wieland,* which revolves around the mysterious and potentially destructive power of the spoken word. Brown explicitly highlights the political implications of this theme.

The novel opens with Clara Wieland's account of the death of her father in a temple he used for religious devotion. After his death, Clara and her brother converted the temple to a summerhouse and installed in it a bust of Cicero. The choice of Cicero was deliberate; Clara's brother idolized and emulated the Roman orator: "He was never tired of conning and rehearsing his productions. To understand them was not sufficient. He was anxious to discover the gestures and cadences with which they ought to be delivered. He was very scrupulous in selecting a true scheme of pronunciation for the Latin tongue, and in adapting it to the words of his darling writer. His favourite occupation consisted in embellishing his rhetoric with all the proprieties of gesticulation and utterance."[2]

This reference to Cicero points toward the connection between the events at Wieland and the fate of the republic. Brown's novel was inspired by what he considered to be the dangers facing the United States after the Revolution; the orphans' experiences may be read as an allegory of republican politics.[3] For Brown, as for anyone schooled in the classics, Cicero represented the dominance of the spoken word and argument, rather than force and blind obedience, in a republican regime. And the Wieland children were model republicans: civil, rational, and egalitarian. For example, when Wieland's friend tried to persuade him to move his family to Germany, against the wishes of his sister and wife, Wieland interpreted his duty in terms culled from the recent republican revolution: "It is not my custom to exact sacrifices of this kind. I live to be their protector and friend, and not their tyrant and foe. If my wife shall deem her happiness and that of her children most consulted by remaining where she is, here she shall remain." Nor would his wife and sister "model themselves by his will"; as his equals, they would make their decisions independently of his desires.[4] Command and obedience had no place in this republic. The only weapon available to influence one another was Ciceronian eloquence.

But installing Cicero in their temple did not usher in an era of peace and good order. Instead, the orphans suffered a nightmarish string of events, all resulting from the influence of the spoken word. The problems began when a malignant stranger entered their society. Clara Wieland was immediately impressed with the stranger's voice: "I cannot pretend to communicate the impression that was made upon me by these accents, or to depict the degree in which force and sweetness were blended in them. . . . The voice was not only mellifluent and clear, but the emphasis was so just, and the modulation so impassioned, that it seemed as if a heart of stone could not fail of being moved by it. It imparted to me an emotion altogether involuntary and incontrollable."[5] Clara's momentary loss of control presaged the stranger's effect on her small community. Unbeknownst to the Wielands, the stranger was an accomplished ventriloquist and mimic, and soon Clara and her friends were hearing strange warnings and threats from disembodied voices. Using his vocal tricks to manipulate the Wielands, the stranger generated fear, jealousy, and religious mania until the community finally disintegrated in violence and death: Clara's brother, obeying unseen voices, murdered his wife and children and nearly Clara herself. In Brown's unhappy scenario, then, the dominion of voice did not guarantee the rule of reason; instead, the power of the spoken word turned out to be a serious threat to social order.

Brown's anxieties about the power of the voice seem out of place in 1798, when most Americans (such as fellow Philadelphian Fisher Ames) were proposing argument as an alternative to rioting. But by the 1830s, both the centrality of public speaking to politics and the problems attendant on a politics of public argument were prominent themes in political discourse, especially in Brown's native Philadelphia. This chapter first examines the increasingly important role of public speaking in the popular politics of the antebellum era, as political debate took over the definitive role once occupied by mob action in democratic politics. Then I consider the pervasive anxiety about the influence of the spoken word in politics, locating its roots in the tradition of neoclassical rhetoric and its distinctive—and highly problematic—model of public debate. The neoclassical tradition added an important dimension to the category of rational public deliberation, by highlighting the tension between the concept of public speech as a tool to influence and motivate political action and the ideals of political rationality, equality, and order that a politics of public debate was supposed to realize.

Frances Wright

On June 26, 1830, handbills throughout Philadelphia announced that Frances Wright would deliver her farewell address at the Arch Street theater. Philadelphians were familiar with the notorious Scottish freethinker; she had given lectures there the previous summer. This performance drew a large crowd, including an unusually large number of women—possibly, as Frances Trollope remarked, because "they were admitted gratis." Here is Trollope's description of the lecture: "Miss Wright came on the stage surrounded by a body guard of Quaker ladies, in the full costume of their sect. She was, as she always is, startling in her theories, but powerfully eloquent, and, on the whole, was much applauded."[6] The *Saturday Bulletin* offered a more critical review:

> [V]ery soon a motley crew of Miss Fanny's friends, to the number of near eighty, marched across the stage led by their queen. They looked and acted much like the witches in Macbeth, and after toiling round and round in search of seats, the priestess *took off her hat.* This was listened to with profound attention, and the lengthened operation of adjusting her curls having been minutely examined with a silence bordering on veneration, after a survey of the audience, and a shake of the head to every individual present, we were entertained with a tissue of nonsense and a farrago of wild assertion.[7]

The woman they observed was tall (five feet ten inches), slender, and graceful; she wore her curly chestnut hair short and often appeared hatless, in defiance of convention. Her dress was even more unconventional: she typically wore trousers, a riding habit, or even a "garment of plain white muslin, which hung around her in folds that recalled the drapery of a Grecian statue."[8] But the most striking thing about Frances Wright, by all accounts, was her eloquence. Trollope described her "extraordinary gift of eloquence, her almost unequalled command of words, and the wonderful power of her rich and thrilling voice."[9] She was praised for her "free, flowing, and ornate style," her "fine, rich musical voice, highly cultivated and possessing great power," her perfect enunciation, her emphasis and pauses, her appropriate and graceful gestures, and her well-chosen language.[10] Her opponents as well as her friends admired her oratory; Lyman Beecher, who dubbed her "the female apostle of atheistic liberty," attributed her success in gaining converts "among females of education and refinement" to her "spirit-stirring eloquence."[11]

But to return to the lecture: It was entitled "Review of the Times," and she promoted it as an "answer to the cry of 'Infidelity' " that the press had leveled at her. She began by predicting "a future big with important changes in the condition of man and the policy of nations," to be accomplished by "the great work of reform." She then praised the American spirit of liberty, which "whenever or however exerted . . . has been successful"—in colonization, revolution, and war. But the same spirit, she went on, "has sufficed when ill directed for their [Americans'] ruin." She went on to attack her two favorite targets, "the religious mania, which has made the land groan beneath the weight of churches, and the more onerous burden of priests," and banks, which have "converted trade into gambling." Fortunately, "[t]he American people (praise be to their political institutions!) have within them a store of good sense, ever equal to discriminate truth from falsehood, reason from declamation." She proceeded to direct their good sense and energy against "freedom's worst enemy," the clergy.[12]

By this point she had apparently antagonized the audience. According to one review, "several interruptions of claps and hisses obliged the lady to sit down."[13] But Wright was not easily intimidated; her lectures had been disrupted before. On one occasion, someone lit a barrel of oil and sent smoke into the crowded lecture hall; on another, someone turned off the gas, but Wright found some candles and finished the lecture.[14] On this occasion, she continued her lecture with the assertion that her views were in accordance with those of George Washington:

> Washington! ever cautiously silent or evasive through life, firmly refused in death the aid and services of men who would fain have engraven upon his tomb, "Washington, the Christian apostle!" instead of "Washington, the patriot hero!"
>
> [I]t is important that we now hold, upon the authority of Jefferson, what was always surmised by the more intelligent portion of the public, and asserted privately by the surviving confidential intimates of the father of his country. *Washington was not a Christian*—that is: he believed not in the priest's God, nor in the divine authority of the priest's book.[15]

This was met by "violent hisses." Wright responded, "I beg the audience to give way to the opposition—let them hiss—it does not proceed from Americans, but from foreigners." At that point a voice called out, "Washington was a Christian." According to Trollope, the hissing was "triumphantly clapped down."[16] The remainder of the lecture defended Wright's attack on religion as necessary to "awaken the people's attention . . . to the affairs of earth" by drawing their attention "from the clouds." She concluded by comparing herself with Thomas Jefferson, who was also accused of infidelity.

This was a typical Wright lecture—theatrical, well attended, and controversial. On previous occasions, for example, she had advocated the establishment of a national system of public education, in which children would be placed in public nurseries at some point between the age of two and six. This institution would raise and educate all the children in the same manner, so as to eliminate inequality of condition.[17] She also advocated amalgamation of the races and free love, which hardly helped her reputation with the American public.[18]

Not surprisingly, Wright generated considerable opposition. On one occasion the proprietor of the hall where she was to speak was threatened with riots and persecution; she had to ask people to assemble in the streets so that she could address them.[19] Newspaper reviews called her crazy, "publicly and ostentatiously proclaiming doctrines of atheistical fanaticism, and even the most abandoned lewdness."[20] She was attacked for her irreligion and character, as well as her doctrines: "She comes amongst us in the character of a bold blasphemer, and a voluptuous preacher of licentiousness. . . . Casting off all restraint, she would break down all the barriers to virtue." William Cullen Bryant frankly told her to go back to Scotland.[21] And, of course, she was criticized for "[leaping] over the boundary of feminine modesty, and [laying] hold upon the avocations of man." She was vilified as a "female monster" and a "bold lady-man."[22]

In contrast, Wright drew enormous crowds and won the admiration of people such as Robert Dale Owen, Frances Trollope, Jeremy Bentham, Walt Whitman, and the Marquis de Lafayette. According to Whitman, "we all loved her, fell down before her; her very appearance seemed to enthrall us." One Philadelphian heard her speech on national public education and declared that hundreds would "date their conversion" from that day.[23] Even her enemies grudgingly accorded her praise for the power of her eloquence and her influence, often comparing her with Thomas Paine.

The comparison was apt. Like Paine, Wright represented the awesome and potentially disruptive power of public speech. As one reviewer complained, this "bold and eloquent woman lays siege to the very foundations of society—inflames and excites the public mind—declaims with vehemence against everything religious and orderly."[24] Yet her eloquence was universally admired. This ambivalent reception of the Scottish orator, I would suggest, was not simply an idiosyncratic reaction to the unfamiliar experience of hearing a woman speak in public. It reflected a deeper ambivalence running through antebellum discourse about public debate: the simultaneous celebration and distrust of the dominion of voice.

The Dominion of Voice

If there was ever a time in American history to worry about the power of the spoken word, the antebellum era was that time. During the 1830s and 1840s, northern states witnessed a remarkable growth in public oratory like Wright's lectures. Credit for the spread of the popular lecture is usually given to Josiah Holbrook, who founded the American lyceum system in the 1820s. Inspired by British mechanics' institutes, associations organized for the education of the working class, Holbrook recommended that American communities form similar associations "for the general diffusion of knowledge, and for raising the moral and intellectual taste of our countrymen."[25] Lyceums spread quickly; by 1831, there were between 800 and 1,000 town lyceums (mostly in the North). By the 1840s, a lecture circuit had developed that boasted orators who could draw audiences of 1,500 to 3,000, such as Edward Everett Hale, Henry Ward Beecher, Raph Waldo Emerson, Theodore Parker, and Horace Greeley.[26]

Lyceums were not the only venue for speech giving, though; the practice was also institutionalized in the debating, literary, political, trade, and moral reform societies that proliferated during this period. Philadelphia, for example, organized only a few lyceums (such as the Franklin Institute, the Athenian Institute, the Mercantile Library Company, the Germantown Lyceum, and the Marshall Institute)[27] but produced a vast array of societies, including the Society of Free Enquirers, the Society of Free People of Color, the American Anti-Slavery Society and its numerous offspring (the Philadelphia Young Men's Anti-Slavery Society, the Philadelphia Female Anti-Slavery Society, the Leavitt Anti-Slavery Society), and the General Trades Union (encompassing forty-eight individual trade societies)—all of which were established in the early 1830s.[28] Meetings of these societies regularly included public speaking, in the form of formal addresses to or debates among the members. Providing an opportunity for public debate was, in fact, one of their primary purposes. The trade unions, for example, intructed their members to "[g]ive freely to each other your views. . . . Agitate the question in all places, that every side may be exhibited, and a perfect system adopted."[29] And if the lyceums and societies did not satisfy Philadelphians' appetite for public speaking, they could hear speeches at political rallies and conventions, both of which became popular during this era.[30]

It would be hard to overestimate the political importance of this proliferation of venues for public speaking. Whereas mob action had come to define democratic politics during the Revolution, public speaking took on an equally definitive role in antebellum politics. In the first place, speech giving provided an important entry into politics for aspiring statesmen (such as Abraham Lincoln and Davy Crockett), who exploited the prestige of public speaking by using the lecture circuit to establish themselves with the public.[31] Even the snobbish Sidney George Fisher, a mostly contemptuous observer of elections, parades, rallies, and riots, appreciated political oratory enough to involve himself in politics through speech making. But Fisher's case reveals a deeper relationship between oratory and politics: for Fisher, public speaking was not only an entry into politics; it defined what politics, in essence, *was.*

In 1834, Fisher made a rare foray into national politics by delivering a speech to a meeting of the Young Men of the City of Philadelphia, challenging Andrew Jackson's policies regarding the Bank of the United States. He took pride in his performance, commenting that the speech "suited the temper of the audience & of the hour & was successful." It was so successful, in fact, that he was asked to present the resolutions of the meeting to Congress. Public speaking, then, provided him an avenue into national politics and the opportunity to meet the leading politicians of the day. Beyond that, however, it served as Fisher's primary criterion for evaluating the politicians he encountered. For example, on meeting Henry Clay, he observed that Clay was a "veteran intriguer and political charlatan. . . . He is incapable of very profound reasoning, depth of thought or extensive & original views." But "[h]e is a keen debater, and it is said that on sudden occasions he utters bursts of declamatory eloquence which are very effective." John C. Calhoun, in contrast, "is honest and sincere, and no plotting politician but a chivalrous enthusiastic champion of the peculiar and unfortunate doctrines which he has undertaken to defend." He has "[r]easoning powers of great force, warmed by feeling and passion." Unfortunately, "his delivery is bad." Of Daniel Webster: He had "an intellect at once clear & logical stored with knowledge. . . . In his oratory there is nothing dazzling or brilliant, but its character is elevated, severe, sober and argumentative." Senator Preston he characterized as "the crack orator of the opposition" with a "very rich & vivid imagination" and a "fluent, passionate and striking style of oratory full of fine tropes, & harmonious sentences."[32] This preoccupation with oratorical ability contrasts with his lack of interest in those aspects of politics that occupy political reporting today, such as electioneering, coalition building, and deal making. He mentioned these activities only to dismiss them as "intrigue" and "plotting." For Fisher, public speaking was what politicians *did,* or at least the only thing they did that was worth commenting on.

This attention to political oratory was not peculiar to Fisher. Newspapers also approached politics as though it were primarily an arena for public speaking, filling their columns with extensive coverage of political speeches given at public meetings and in legislatures. They detailed not only who spoke and on what issues but also the size of the audience, the quality of the performance, and the reception of the speeches. For example, in January 1839, readers of the *United States Gazette* and the *National Gazette* learned that "a respectable assemblage" gathered at the Franklin Institute to consider Jackson's policies toward the Cherokees. They were further informed that the "venerable and respected Bishop White was called to the chair by unanimous acclamation," and that his eloquent opening comments, reported almost verbatim, were received with applause. The accounts faithfully reported the motions made and carried, as well as summarizing the other major speeches.[33] This level of coverage gave aspiring civic leaders an incentive to participate in public meetings, since they could be confident that their speeches would be immortalized and further disseminated in print. In fact, by 1840, such public meetings called primarily for the purpose of speech making had become so popular that "An Observer" was moved to complain to the *Public Ledger*, "Is a meeting called for political . . . purposes; Col. S—, Col. T—, Col. P—, or some other modest political distingue, is by previous concert uproariously called to preside. . . . The business of the meeting is then of course most forcibly, eloquently and enchantingly discoursed by some patent, voluble, modern Cicero or Demosthenes, whose address with slight variations would answer either assembly, and be equally germane to the subject."[34] But the *Public Ledger* gave cautious approval to popular public debate: "If the subject should not be found too exciting and the argument should be conducted with propriety, and with the design of convincing each other by the force of facts and reason, these debates may prove both interesting and instructive."[35]

In general, newspapers encouraged these modern Ciceros. In fact, the leading papers in Philadelphia tended to evaluate political speeches more as oratorical performances than as statements of policies or positions. The *National Gazette*'s report of the 1830 Webster-Hayne debate on public lands is typical. The paper omitted most of the content of the debate (although it printed Webster's celebrated reply to Hayne in full). But it informed the readers that Webster was "solid" and "cogent" and was "heard with universal admiration." It further noted that Webster's reply to Hayne contained "much sound doctrine, ably, resolutely, and temperately expressed." Others admired Hayne's "force, eloquence and effect," even insisting that "[n]o report of these speeches can do them justice." But Rhode Island's Senator Burgess received a less favorable evaluation: his "colossal harangue," we are told, "contains some good argument and some very bad rhetoric."[36] Politics, in these accounts, looks like a contest of oratorical skills.

But if politics looked like an arena for oratory to men like Fisher, what did it look like to the multitude of urban residents—blacks, women, the working class—who were conventionally excluded from public speaking? Members of these groups often approached the podium with considerable trepidation. For example, the abolitionist Angelina Grimké complained, "I can truly say that the day I hav [sic] to speak is always a day of suffering." Her sister Sarah also declared that she was "not very comfortable in the performance of those duties to which I have been calld [sic]."[37] Their discomfort is hardly surprising; the world of oratory was unfamiliar and hostile territory to women, as it was to blacks. Attempting to speak in public could have disastrous results, as it did for the black preacher who tried to address a white congregation in Newark: "The bravado had the result which was to be anticipated in the present state of public opinion. The Church was attacked, the windows broken, and the interior of the building destroyed."[38] Blacks and women were not only denied access to the public podium; they often found themselves excluded from audiences as well. One of the more famous examples is the expulsion of the female delegates, led by Lucretia Mott, from the General Anti-Slavery Conference in England in 1840,[39] but such incidents were not confined to England. Black activists Thomas Butler, John Barr, and James Forten suffered a similar humiliation when they were forcibly ejected from the Constitutional Convention meeting in Philadelphia in 1838.[40] Abolitionists' "promiscuous" meetings (including blacks and whites, and/or men and women) prompted indignant complaints, such as the heavily sarcastic description of a meeting that presented (according to one observer) "a beautiful specimen of Mosaic work, composed of all colors and shades, from the hue of the lily to that of coal. . . . Clear red and white were placed in unctious [sic] communion with dingy black, and the rose of the West, and the coal black rose of Congo, bloomed side by side, mingling their mutual sweets. There was no wasting of fragrance on the desert air, for the delicate aroma was inhaled by hundreds."[41] The convention against promiscuous meetings was so strong that it sometimes led to mob action, such as the burning of Pennsylvania Hall in 1838.[42] But race and gender weren't the only barriers. Even white men, if they belonged to the working class, had trouble gaining access to the podium, since they usually lacked the education or standing in the community that led to invitations to give speeches or chair meetings. As one text on rhetoric noted, public speaking is necessary to hold "a respectable rank in well-bred society," but "the multitude"—women and most men—are not called to the podium.[43] When Frances Wright delivered her lectures in 1828, public speaking was still very much the domain of wealthy white males.

How, then, did members of the excluded groups view the political arena? Since they faced significant barriers to the public podium, one might expect that they would have developed some alternative view of politics, perhaps resorting to the eighteenth-century conception of politics as an arena for mob action. The politics of mob action, after all, had included all these groups, as well as "gentlemen of property and standing," in an unproblematic way. Rioters did not try to exclude disfavored groups from their mobs, and, as discussed in Chapter 1, the mob's status as representative of "the people" did not depend on what sort of people participated in it. But in fact, the groups that were disadvantaged at the podium were the very groups that most eagerly embraced public speaking as a mode of political action. Most of the organizations discussed above—the abolition and trade societies in particular—were organized by blacks, women, and the working class, often expressly to provide them opportunities for public speaking.[44] Public speaking, unlike mob action, offered these groups the opportunity to enhance their political status, in part because public speaking was highly respected, but also—ironically—*because* the conventions of public speaking implicated race, gender, and class.

Participating in eighteenth-century riots may have been patriotic, but it had not appreciably enhanced the political status of disadvantaged groups, because characteristics such as race, class, and gender were lost in the amorphousness of the mob. Thus, although women (for example) might have participated in bread riots, it was "the people" in general, not women in particular, who were recognized as the actors.[45] In contrast, the spectacle of a black person, a woman, or a common mechanic appearing at the podium was recognized as a challenge to conventional notions about who was capable of public speaking (and therefore political action). Bruce Laurie, for example, reports that the eloquence of William English, a trade union organizer, "dazzled the most skeptical and astonished Trades' Union critics." Women speakers provoked similar reactions. The *Boston Morning Post*'s report on Angelina Grimké's 1838 speech before the Massachusetts legislature is typical. It noted that the "immense crowd" was drawn by the "extraordinary phenomenon of a woman talking" and went on to emphasize her gender by paying close attention to her physical appearance. Fanny Wright, as we have seen, attracted the same sort of attention.[46] Constructing popular politics around public speaking created an arena in which race, gender, and class were noticeable and a context in which to debate their relevance to one's status as a political actor.[47] Perhaps for this reason, activists who were interested in expanding political participation did not *resist* the hegemony of public speaking in politics but actively *promoted* it. Further, they used the practice as a lens through which to explore the general relationship between social and political status. Public speaking therefore held a pivotal place in both political practice and political theory. Consider, for example, Philadelphia activists William Heighton, Angelina Grimké, and Samuel Cornish; each used public speaking as a theoretical, as well as a practical, entry into antebellum politics.

William Heighton, editor of the *Mechanics' Free Press* in Philadelphia in the 1830s, took the inability of the working class to speak in public as one of his central themes, arguing that their disability prevented them from constituting themselves as political actors. He explained, "[I]t is a fact too well known for me to dwell on, that we as a class have never yet acquired sufficient intelligence to possess [a public] opinion; and if we did, it is doubtful whether there are at present any facilities existing, through which the expression of it would be allowed to reach our legislative assemblies."[48] Heighton's solution to this problem was the establishment of a newspaper and a library in which workers might participate in public debates. Then, "[i]n their public assemblies they would learn to *speak for themselves;* . . . [they] would soon begin to nominate candidates for public office, *from among themselves.*"[49] By learning to speak in public, they would constitute themselves as a public with a public opinion. This, in turn, would allow them to practice politics themselves, rather than relying on representatives who were not members of the working class to protect their interests. Public argument, under this view, is a particularly empowering kind of political action, enhancing the agency of workers as a class.[50]

Heighton's perception that the degraded political status of mechanics was related to their inability to speak in public was not original. By the 1790s, it was already a familiar complaint that ordinary farmers were unable to match the eloquence of the lawyers and merchants who dominated the legislatures.[51] Most mechanics had difficulty speaking in public, not because they faced legal or even strong conventional barriers, but because they typically did not have the training in rhetoric that the elite received in college. Public speaking was governed by stylistic conventions that called for an educated, refined language; to speak in public in the vulgar dialects was to face ridicule, at least. As one mechanic complained, "Must my inquiries be held up to public contempt, because [my reader] finds some 'little petit defects in . . . [my] sintactical [*sic*] composition?' "[52] Poor speaking was a favorite topic of satire. Readers apparently enjoyed such examples of mangled English as the following: "Mr. Chairman, . . . I say motto . . . to that. To abuse a setaphor, I consider this town and the circumambient country in the light of a burning glass. The bridges are so many revenues of light, diverging into one grand pocus. I heartily say motto to the gentleman who spoke last."[53] Moreover, comic literature of the early nineteenth century reveals a profound awareness that speech reflected class, and that the inability to master a style appropriate to the occasion constituted a barrier to social mobility. The attempts of mechanics to participate in public debate raised images of the social climber whose imperfect grasp of polite language reveals, hilariously, his common origins.[54]

Not surprisingly, then, Heighton's entry into politics was marked by an extraordinary self-consciousness about his lack of an education appropriate to a legitimate participant in public debate. For example, one of his first publications was a well-written piece signed "An Unlettered Mechanic," an ironic comment on the usual association of the ability to speak well with upper-class status.[55] The irony was even more pronounced in his response to a complaint about a grammatical error in his newspaper: "It is certainly laughable enough, that we mechanics should blunder so gregariously [sic] in grammar, when we have such correct examples before our eyes, in presidents, congressmen, judges, lawyers, squires and even some preachers."[56] But even while he challenged (rather unsuccessfully, in this case) the assumption that the ability to speak well follows class lines, he emphasized the importance of public speaking to politics by arguing that the inability to speak in public constituted a barrier to political action.

Angelina Grimké, an advocate for abolition and women's rights, found the reverse dynamic at work: her degraded political status was a barrier to public speaking. Grimké, one of the first American women to take the public podium, considered the opportunity to argue her position before public assemblies critical to her efforts to end slavery by influencing public opinion. The problem she faced was not lack of training in oratory but the conventional exclusion of women from any public activities, including politics. Like Frances Wright, she was harshly criticized for giving public lectures, particularly to audiences including men.[57] Catharine Beecher, for example, considered Grimké's public lectures improper because they subjected her (Grimké) to "sneers and ridicule in public places" and led her into "the arena of political collision . . . as [a] combatant."[58] But the problem was not just that speaking in public was unpleasant for women. The conventions excluding women from public activities effectively disabled women from engaging in rational public debate—or so Beecher argued. (Beecher's criticisms, it should be noted, were written in a private letter to Grimké and later published.)

Beecher's critique of Grimké's activities began from the observation that the act of speaking was surrounded by conventions governing who might speak, in what context, and to whom. Violating those conventions angered people, arousing their passions rather than engaging their reason. She criticized the abolitionists, for example, because they have "[thrown] the minds of men . . . into a ferment, and excited those passions which blind the reason, and warp the moral sense"—in sum, they did not argue but instituted a "system of *coercion* by public opinion."[59] She was not just referring to the abolitionists' combative style; her point was that it was not the *place* of northern abolitionists to remonstrate southerners. "There are cases . . . where differences in age, and station, and character, forbid all interference to modify the conduct and character of others."[60] Southerners would not take reproof from northerners, who were strangers to the South's way of life, any more than the master of a household would take reproof from a nursery maid. Similarly, according to Beecher, men would not take reproof from women. Women were divinely appointed to be subordinate to men. Challenging men directly in public debate, and particularly political debate, would be to leave their appointed sphere and would therefore "be deemed obtrusive, indecorous, and unwise"—just as northerners criticizing southerners would be deemed unwise and inappropriate.[61] Beecher's point, then, was that violating the convention against women speaking in public would not foster rational discussion. Women were effectively disabled from speaking in public because they would not be listened to rationally and dispassionately.

Grimké was not persuaded, perhaps because people *did* come to her lectures and listen to her; despite the public attacks, her audiences were large and often appreciative.[62] Grimké's disagreement with Beecher rested in large part on Grimké's understanding of the role of passion in public debate. Beecher saw debate as ideally dispassionate and rational but considered the public arena, and particularly the political arena, as the last place one would find such dispassionate argument. Grimké agreed with Beecher that public debate was typically combative, but unlike Beecher, she considered passion and confrontation appropriate for her purposes. Public debate, for Grimké, was a way to wield the "sledge hammer of truth" against "the rock of prejudice."[63] Her aim was moral reform. Making people angry was acceptable; all reformers, she pointed out, have produced "recriminations and angry passions" from the people they sought to reform.[64] Therefore, she did not need to respect the social conventions that governed public speaking. In fact, it might be better not to—after all, the convention that prevented the nursery maid from reproving the master "robs the nursery maid of her responsibility, and shields the master from reproof."[65]

But Grimké did not stop with challenging the wisdom of observing the conventions of public speech; she attacked the convention against women speaking in public itself. Disagreeing with Beecher's position that women's subordination to men was divinely ordained, she argued that women and men held equal status as moral beings, and therefore "whatever it is morally right for man to do, it is morally right for woman to do."[66] Speaking against

slavery was a moral duty for all Christians, and women were not to be si-
lenced by their conventional exclusion from politics. Grimké refused to con-
cede "that because this is a *political subject* women ought to fold their hands
in idleness."[67] Her argument thus led her from the right to speak in public,
grounded in a Christian conception of universal moral duties, to the political status of women. She concluded her response to Beecher by defending
women's right to petition Congress on the grounds that women are citizens
and deserve to have a voice in the laws by which they are governed.[68] But her
interest in the political rights of women was secondary. From Grimké's point
of view, the problem with excluding women from politics was that it undermined their ability to speak in public, which was a religious obligation. She
was led to assert women's status as citizens in order to secure their ability to
witness against slavery. Thus, even though she was primarily concerned with
public speaking as a religious act, she ended up addressing the relationship
between public speaking and political status because of the centrality of public speaking to the practice of politics. Thus for Grimké as for Heighton, the
act of speaking had a special connection with political agency.

For many in the black community, the connection between public speaking and one's status as a political actor was even more direct, as we can see
in Samuel Cornish's argument in favor of a black press. Cornish was a leading
voice in the black community in Philadelphia and New York, and in 1837 he
became the editor of the *Colored American*.[69] As Heighton had argued on
behalf of the working class, Cornish argued that the political status of the
black community depended on its ability to speak for itself (through an independent black press). The *Colored American* was intended to constitute the
community both spiritually and politically: it would "carry to [every black
man] lessons of instruction on religion and morals, lessons of industry and
economy—until our entire people are of one heart and of one mind, in all the
means of their salvation, both spiritual and temporal."[70] But while Heighton
rested his argument on the proposition that only the working class could be
trusted to represent its own interests, Cornish emphasized the importance of
speaking as a way to demonstrate to the white community that blacks were
legitimate political actors: "When did Greece and Poland win the sympathy
of the world; after they had published their wrongs, asserted their rights and
sued for freedom at the hands of their oppressors. Then, and only, then were
they worthy to be freemen, nor should *we* expect the *boon,* until we feel its
importance and pray for its possession."[71] Cornish was concerned not simply
with developing a black public but with constituting the black community
as a public *in the eyes of the white community*. By speaking or, more specifically, by complaining about their lack of freedom, they would prove themselves "worthy to be freemen."

In making this argument, Cornish interpreted the practice of public speaking in light of two separate political traditions. First, the conception of citizenship as something one must prove oneself worthy of placed Cornish in the camp of the moral reform movement. The logic behind moral reform as a way to improve the status of blacks rested on the proposition that their current status resulted from the white community's perception that blacks were morally inferior. This perception supported "the strongest arguments, with which to oppose the emancipation of the slave, and to hinder the elevation of the free."[72] The way to combat this prejudice, according to Cornish, was to confront whites with evidence that their perceptions were false. Public speaking, an activity thought to be beyond the abilities of morally and intellectually inferior people, constituted a direct refutation of the claim that blacks were inferior. But Cornish's treatment of public speech also reflects the eighteenth-century language of resistance. By comparing blacks with the revolutionaries in Greece and Poland (who were often compared, in turn, with the American revolutionaries), the passage presents the act of speaking as an act of resistance similar to the founders' resistance to British tyranny. The reference to *feeling* also echoes the Whig language of resistance: according to the (eighteenth-century) Whigs, the feeling of oppression is what prompts the oppressed to acts of resistance (riots).[73] Cornish simply replaced mob action with the act of speaking, suggesting that public speaking, like mob action in an earlier time, could show the white community that blacks were sufficiently protective of their rights to be freemen. In other words, for Cornish, public speaking (like mob action) could be an act of resistance that demonstrated one to be a legitimate political actor.[74]

The conception of politics as an arena for public speaking is particularly pronounced in Cornish's argument because he is using this conception to displace the competing conception of politics as an arena for mob action (as in the Whig tradition).[75] But the idea that politics is, and should be, an arena for public speech is integral to each of these activists' arguments. Despite the barriers they faced—or *because* of the barriers they faced—they did not challenge the centrality of public speaking to politics. On the contrary, they agreed that public speaking was a core political practice. That is precisely why it was important to understand how the practice mediated the relationship between social and political status, and how it could change that relationship. For these activists, as for Fisher, politics was, in important respects, the practice of public speaking.

But despite the widespread acceptance of public speaking as a (if not the) definitive form of political action, its appropriateness to democratic politics remained a subject of anxiety and occasional debate. One dimension of this debate, the struggles to reform public and particularly political speech, has been explored in depth by Kenneth Cmiel.[76] The concern with preserving or transforming public language was as old as the republic, or at least as old as Noah Webster's attempts to standardize American English.[77] While nationalism was an important dimension of the movement to create a genuine "American" language, Cmiel argues that language reformers were also motivated by democratic values. Specifically, they were sensitive to the fact that speech served as a marker of class, so that using speech as a vehicle for politics might create the sort of barriers that William Heighton encountered. Their goal was to create a "middling" style of public speech, in which the speaker's class origins would not be apparent—thus disassociating the rule of reason from the rule of the upper class.

But antebellum fears about public speaking went beyond this concern about the impression of class on speech; they were prompted also by the problematic relationship between public speaking and rational argument. As argued in Chapter 1, antiriot rhetoric characterized speech as the opposite of rioting: peaceful and rational instead of violent and passionate. Unfortunately, political speech was not always a vehicle for rational argument. Grimké, for example, approached her lectures more as sermons—impassioned, confrontational sermons—than as arguments, and Cornish characterized public speaking as an act of resistance parallel to, rather than opposed to, rioting. Moreover, even when political speech was characterized as debate, it did not necessarily correspond to the peaceful, dispassionate practice suggested by antiriot rhetoric. For Beecher, political debate was a "collision of intellects" where "combatants . . . cheer up and carry forward the measures of strife."[78] Privileging public speaking as a mode of political action, then, simply raised questions about whether and how public speaking could serve as a vehicle for rational argument. The following section brings these questions into focus by exploring one influential explanation of the relationship between rational argument and political speech—the neoclassical model of political argument.

The Neoclassical Model of Political Debate

The tradition of neoclassical rhetoric is an obvious place to look for clues to how antebellum Americans understood political argument. Rhetoric, variously defined as the art of speaking well, the art of persuasive speaking, or even the art "by which the discourse is adapted to its end," was a comprehensive discipline, purporting to cover all forms of public speaking and public writing.[79] In practice, it focused primarily on three "theaters" for public speaking: the pulpit, the bar, and the senate. Accordingly, it developed a model of political speech as oratory, that is, a formal address to an audience.

The neoclassical model had a profound but ambivalent influence on antebellum interpretations of political argument. Rhetoric was a core element of the American college curriculum in the early part of the nineteenth century. Every well-bred gentleman was expected to master its principles, as laid out in the basic texts: Hugh Blair's *Lectures on Rhetoric and Belles Lettres,* George Campbell's *Philosophy of Rhetoric,* and Richard Whately's *Elements of Rhetoric.* These eighteenth-century British texts were used in most colleges in the United States, where they were supplemented by lectures from American rhetoricians such as John Quincy Adams and Edward Channing.[80] Although the leading texts developed rhetorical theory in different directions, they all assumed essentially the same model of political speech. But despite its widespread diffusion among the elite, this model was problematic. Specifically, it conflicted with the ideal of free, independent, and rational political actors—a conflict most evident in the neoclassical model's treatment of self-presentation and agency in political oratory.

Self-Presentation, Glory, and Ethos

Neoclassical rhetoric defined political speech as public arguments for or against some public measure, a definition clearly derived from the traditional venues of political oratory: the senate or popular assembly.[81] It treated political oratory as a performance aimed at influencing political decision making and, in the process, winning immortal fame for the orator. The performative dimension of public speaking was central to both these goals: how the speaker presented himself (the orator was invariably male) affected both his likelihood of persuading the audience and his ability to win its admiration. The neoclassical tradition not only recognized but celebrated this element of self-display, both as an end in itself and as an indispensable part of the orator's arsenal of persuasive techniques.

Self-display was an end in itself to the extent oratory served as an avenue to personal glory. According to the neoclassical tradition, the primary goal of the orator was to be seen and admired by the public for his virtuousity. One studied rhetoric so that one would "enjoy a larger share of reputation" than one's colleagues. For Blair, the spur to eloquence was to "attract the admiration of ages," a goal he considered noble, since the love of glory was as much a virtue as "public spirit," "contempt of external fortune," and "the admiration of what is truly illustrious and great." John Quincy Adams similarly represented oratory as heroic, the path to honor and fame for those who

"burn with the fires of honorable ambition," like Demosthenes and Cicero.
He analogized the orator to a soldier and oratory itself to a battle; the study
of oratory gave one "a spear for the conflict of judicial war in the public
tribunals; a sword for the field of religious and moral victory in the pulpit."[82]
The analogy is telling; the neoclassical tradition valued conflict and argument in much the same way as a soldier might value war, as an opportunity
to win glory. Similarly, the pursuit of personal glory by the orator, like the
soldier's quest for fame, was not supposed to be at odds with his duty to serve
the public good. One earned the public's admiration by serving its interests;
the orator "aspires to immortalize his name by the extent and importance of
his services to his country."[83] The orator's dependence on the public for its
esteem thus served to harmonize his personal interests with the public good.

To win glory as an orator, of course, one needs opportunities to perform
before appreciative audiences, and politics provided those opportunities.
Meetings of legislatures, conventions, or societies were stages, complete with
audiences, for the aspiring orator. Thus, one rhetorician described the British House of Commons as a "theatre . . . favourable for the exertion of eloquence" and the politician as an actor seeking the opportunity to "display his
talents" through speech making.[84] Democracy, under this theory, was the regime type most conducive to oratory because it provided the most opportunities for public speaking. Thus, oratory flourished in ancient Athens and
republican Rome, when "all political measures were debated in popular assemblies."[85] As Adams explained, in a democracy, "every citizen has a deep
interest in the affairs of the nation, and, in some form of public assembly or
other, has the means and opportunity of delivering his opinions, and of communicating his sentiments by speech."[86] In other words, democracy made
every (male) citizen a potential orator and, by implication, gave every (male)
citizen the opportunity to seek glory through politics. Self-display was therefore the hallmark of democratic politics.

If self-display was an end in itself, though, it was also critical to the orator's
short-term goal of persuading the audience. Rhetoric addressed the persuasive value of self-display under the topic of ethos, or ethical appeals.[87] Everyone agreed that the ability to present to the audience a good moral character
made a speaker more persuasive. Blair insisted that nothing "contribute[d]
more to persuasion, than the opinion which we entertain of the probity, disinterestedness, candour, and other good moral qualities of the person who
endeavours to persuade." Whately agreed that "good Sense, good Principle,
and Good-will, constitute the character which the speaker ought to establish of himself."[88] Campbell explained the influence of character on belief by
drawing on the principle of sympathy; he argued that the audience would feel
greater sympathy with a man of good character, and this sympathy would

make it easier for the speaker to manipulate the audience's passions.[89] But ethos did not just make the audience more attuned to the speaker's emotional state; it helped the speaker convince his audience's understanding. Although good character did not exactly constitute a reason to accept one's argument, it did constitute a reason to suspend one's rational faculty. Campbell characterized the audience's response to ethical appeals as "blindly [submitting] to the guidance" of the orator, "adopting implicitly his opinions, and accompanying him in all his passionate excursions."[90] In other words, if the audience liked the speaker, it would simply adopt his opinions without subjecting them to critical examination.

Far from criticizing ethical appeals, neoclassical rhetoric taught that one's character *should* have weight in public deliberation. Blair commented approvingly on the force of virtue in argument: "To find any such connexion between virtue and one of the highest liberal arts, must give pleasure." He considered that "the connexion here alleged, is undoubtedly founded in truth and reason." Campbell agreed, noting that "[t]his preference [for speakers of good character] . . . arising purely from the original frame of the mind, reason, or the knowledge of mankind acquired by experience, instead of weakening, seems afterwards to corroborate." Ethos thus "has a foundation in human nature."[91]

This endorsement of ethos was, in effect, an endorsement of the element of self-display in oratory. If one is supposed to use one's character to persuade audiences, then one must take care to present oneself in a positive light. Of course, ethos also explains, and justifies, ad hominem attacks. As Whately argued, "[S]urely it is not in itself an unfair topic of argument . . . to urge that one party deserves the hearers' confidence, or that the other is justly an object of their distrust."[92] If the speaker is permitted to use his sterling character to induce the audience to adopt his views, his opponents must be able to attack his character as well. But why was this attention to the speaker's character more than simply a matter of prudence? Why were ethical appeals not only wise but also desirable?

Of the three leading authorities, only Whately attempted a sustained defense of ethical appeals. His argument is worth examining in depth, because it points toward the assumptions about the social context of political argument that inform neoclassical rhetoric. Whately acknowledged that if a course of action is a good one, it will not become less good because it is proposed by a bad person. However, he pointed out that usually it's not certain whether a measure is good or bad. "It is only in matters of strict science, and that too, in arguing to scientific men, that the character of the advocates . . . should be wholly put out of the question."[93] Politics, then, is not a matter of strict science (a point that opponents of the neoclassical tradition would contest, as we shall see in the next chapter). But why should character carry any weight, even in matters not admitting of certainty? Whately first suggested that the speaker can serve as a kind of witness to his cause. But in what sense? If the speaker is intelligent and sincere, the fact that he believes that he is right may give the audience a reason to consider his argument, but why should it constitute an independent reason to adopt his opinions, which is what Whately was proposing?[94]

Whately's defense actually relied on a series of analogies. First, he suggested that the audience's deference to a good man is like a layman's deference to an astronomer on the proposition that the earth revolves around the sun. The analogy is imperfect, though; one does not defer to the astronomer because he's a good man but because he's an expert. The other analogies were more revealing. First, Whately explicitly equated the audience to "the great *mass* of the people" (as opposed to the "higher orders"). Then he suggested that the masses defer to a good man as a child defers to a parent, or as a Christian defers to God. Of course, the child defers to the parent not because the parent is a good person but because the parent is an authority figure, just as the Christian defers to God because of God's absolute authority. His defense of ethical appeals, in other words, came down to a claim that the audience should defer to morally superior persons because such persons should have authority over the masses, just as parents should have authority over their children.[95]

This claim is consistent with the ideology of moral hierarchy that legitimated deference relations in eighteenth-century British and colonial society.[96] Central to this ideology was the principle that the imitation of morally superior persons is the path to virtue. As explained in a 1731 election sermon by Samuel Whittelsey, "Man was made for *Imitation;* When the *Sacred Three* entred [*sic*] into Consultation to give an *Epitome* of both Worlds in one Creature, Saying, *Let us make man,* it was concluded to cast him in such a Mould that Superior example should have an attractive influence upon him."[97] The imitation of Christ as an element of submission to God is a conventional theme in Protestantism: man assimilates to his maker through a "willing and studied Conformity to him in Spirit and Practice." But Whittelsey suggested that the same dynamic should take place between the people and the elite. The elite should be like "the Generous Sun" and "extend [their] good Influence to all within [their] Circumference."[98] The oft-noted tendency of the lower orders to imitate their superiors was thus a commendable quality, since it allowed the elite to spread their good influence through society and "gradually train the people around [them] to a love of order and subordination."[99]

Ethos worked on the same principle. For Blair, public speaking was one way in which persons of superior character influenced the masses. Drawing on the principle of moral influence, he asserted that "nothing has so great and universal a command over the minds of men as virtue. No kind of language is so generally understood, and so powerfully felt, as the native language of worthy and virtuous feelings."[100] Lurking behind this statement is the assumption that the audience will seek to imitate a virtuous speaker by adopting his opinions. In Campbell's words, ethical appeals allow the speaker to "insinuate himself into [the audience's] favour, and thereby imperceptibly . . . transfuse his sentiments and passions into their minds."[101] In other words, ethical appeals worked because the audience would tend to imitate persons of superior moral character, a tendency that was considered a virtue because it allowed noble characters to spread their influence throughout society. Neoclassical rhetoric thus cast the orator as a member of the elite, whose role was to improve the character of the lower orders through moral influence.[102] In short, the principle of moral influence through imitation justified deference in public argument just as it justified deference in other arenas.

Of course, superior moral character does not have to be linked to social class; noble characters might arise in any walk of life. Thus the neoclassical model does not necessarily depend on an elitist conception of social order, although the classic texts did take elitism for granted. (But as we shall see, antebellum Americans worried about the potentially inegalitarian effects of ethical arguments on other grounds.)

So far, the neoclassical model of politics appears to be an agon where oratorical gladiators compete to impress the audience with their talents and noble characters. But there is more to this model of political speech than self-display. The distinctive characteristic of political oratory is that it is aimed at persuading the audience to action. Political oratory, according to Blair, is that "by which we are not only convinced, but are interested, agitated, and carried along with the speaker . . . and are prompted to resolve, or to act, with vigour and warmth."[103] This connection between speech and action is the second axis of the neoclassical model. To make the connection, though, we have to turn again to the reason-passion distinction, this time placing it in the context of eighteenth- and nineteenth-century psychology.

Reason, Passion, and Agency

As discussed in Chapter 1, the reason-passion dichotomy was a basic element of eighteenth-century moral philosophy. It received the stamp of authority from faculty psychology, the reigning theory of psychology in the eighteenth and early nineteenth centuries in the United States.[104] Faculty psychology treated human nature as composed of various faculties, or powers. These were arranged in elaborate taxonomies in the treatises on moral philosophy, but the classic treatments began by dividing the faculties into the rational and active, or reason and will, with the passions (what we now call the emotions) subsumed under the will. Rational faculties (memory, perception, imagination, and so forth) were passive. Reason, in theory, could change one's understanding but could not move the will as the passions could.[105]

Neoclassical rhetoric drew heavily on faculty psychology, particularly the reason-passion dichotomy and the function of the passions as the most direct link to the will. But the reason-passion opposition played out differently here than it did in antiriot discourse, where reason was associated with argument and passion with violence. In neoclassical rhetoric, speech was often contrasted with violence (as in Adams's statement that in a republic, the government has no arms but those of persuasion),[106] but reason and passion were both associated with speech. Oratory was the vehicle of reason, operating on the audience's understanding, as well as the vehicle of passion, operating on the audience's will. Political oratory, because it is designed to influence the audience's conduct, must include appeals to passion. As Blair explained, "In all that relates to practice, there is no man who seriously means to persuade another, but addresses himself to his passions more or less; for this plain reason, that passions are the great springs of human action."[107] Similarly, Campbell insisted, "To make me believe it is enough to show me that things are so; to make me act, it is necessary to show that the action will answer some end. That can never be an end to me which gratifies no passion or affection in my nature."[108]

Judging from the defensive tone of the discussions, the endorsement of appeals to passion was even more problematic than the endorsement of ethos. Campbell was ambivalent about pathetic appeals. On the one hand, he claimed that "address to the passions . . . never fails to disturb the operation of the intellectual faculty." On the other hand, appeals to passion can ensure that the audience will pay attention and remember one's arguments; thus, "they are not the supplanters of reason, or even rivals in her sway; they are her handmaids, by whose ministry she is enabled to usher truth into the heart."[109] This inconsistency reflects the tension between eighteenth-century rationalism and the (much older) discipline of rhetoric. Campbell, usually a thoroughgoing rationalist, had little choice but to find some justification for appeals to passion, since the art of arousing the passions constituted the major part of what neoclassical rhetoric had to teach. Logical arguments were thought to have no need of figurative language, "the bolder and more striking figures" that "excite admiration."[110] As Blair explained, it was in the pathetic part of the oration that "eloquence reigns, and exerts its power."[111] Fortunately, the connection between passion and the will gave passion, and therefore eloquence, a legitimate role in political argument.

The defense of pathos as necessary to move the will was the core of the theory of agency informing neoclassical rhetoric. Although ultimately it is the audience that takes action, neoclassical rhetoric attributed agency to the speaker, whose eloquence gave him control over the will of the audience. By arousing the audience's passions, the skillful orator could procure "an irresistable [*sic*] power over the thoughts and purposes of his audience." Adams, for example, insisted that rhetoric could "penetrate to the secret chambers of the heart." An effective speaker exercised "magical powers" that could "stem the torrent of human passions, and calm the raging waves of human vice and folly," even "control the course of nature herself" and "arrest the luminaries of wisdom and virtue in their rapid revolutions."[112] When Adams referred to the "dominion of voice," he meant it quite literally: Speaking was an exercise of power.

But the audience, if passive, was not pliable. The orator's task, and the truest test of his art, was overcoming the audience's resistance to his influence. The audience played a critical part in rhetorical theory, because the audience's resistance was the problem rhetoricians claimed to be able to solve. As Blair explained, the public ear "will not easily bear what is slovenly and incorrect" in one's address; an orator will be "neglected and despised" if he fails to master the art of rhetoric.[113] The audience's duty, then, was to resist the speaker's efforts to sway it through mere artfulness, and allow itself to be influenced only by true beauty or eloquence: "[I]t is . . . requisite to attain the power of distinguishing false ornament from true, in order to prevent our being carried away by that torrent of false and frivolous taste, which never fails, when it is prevalent, to sweep along with it the raw and the ignorant."[114] The neoclassical tradition offered the audience two resources with which to defend itself from the speaker's influence: taste and reason. Blair developed the concept of taste, a nonrational faculty defined as the power of receiving pleasure from the beauties of nature and art.[115] Taste allowed the audience to recognize and respond to true eloquence, which was a combination of noble sentiments and sound reasoning. Campbell relied more explicitly on reason, as in his claim that an ignorant crowd was more susceptible to passionate appeals than an educated and hence more rational one. Unfortunately, the masses were assumed to be deficient in both these faculties, which is why democracy was likely to give rise to demagogues; "the rabble," declared Campbell, "are ever the prey of quacks and impudent pretenders."[116] Thus, as a regime becomes more democratic, political discourse becomes less rational and the relationship between the speaker and the audience—the central political relationship—less equal.

According to the neoclassical model, then, political speech was an agonistic activity directed at establishing one's status and dominance by influencing both the will and the character of the audience. This task called for a combination of rational, pathetic, and ethical appeals, and rational argument was not necessarily the most important. As Campbell insisted, "When the hearers are rude and ignorant, nothing is more necessary in the speaker than to inflame the passions."[117] The posited relationship between political speech and rational argument, in sum, was somewhat tenuous, particularly in a democracy where audiences were likely to be deficient in taste and reason.

Reception of the Neoclassical Model

How influential was the neoclassical model of political argument in the urban Northeast? The standard account is that the elites, represented by the Whigs, accepted this model while the Democrats rejected it. Daniel Howe has found evidence of a basically neoclassical perspective among leading Whigs, such as their belief that it was the role of political leaders to mold the character of the masses and their faith in the power of eloquence to do so. The focus on oratory and eloquence in political discourse was strongest in Whig journals and newspapers; the Whig *North American Review,* for example, devoted forty pages to a review of the level of eloquence in Congress.[118] The neoclassical perspective is evident in passages such as the following description of a speech by Calhoun: "[H]is generous spirit expands itself through the vast auditory. . . . They see the grandeur in his eye, and before a word has escaped his lips, they are struck with an irresistible sympathy with the man. Then, he speaks. When he says 'fellow-citizens,' they believe him, and at once, from a tumultuous herd, they are converted into men—into a nation, for the time being."[119] Philadelphia's Whiggish *United States Gazette* used similar language, as in this description of a dinner speech given to the city's Young Men's Society: "The closing of the speech . . . had a thrilling and electric influence on the audience. . . . The deafening applause, and the general cheerings, showed that Mr. *Southard* had reached the heart of his auditors; they felt the influence of a master hand, and they responded like men and patriots."[120]

In contrast, Christine Oravec argues that Democratic journals such as the *Democratic Review* and the *Plaindealer* were more critical of the classical style of oratory, particularly its emphasis on style and delivery over substance.[121] Oravec accurately identifies an ambivalence toward the neoclassical model in these journals, but both she and Howe overstate the partisan dichotomy. Whig journals, for example, did not always embrace the neoclassical endorsement of conflict, nor its elitism. The *North American Review* expressed dismay at the combative element of debate ("that uncompromising spirit of urgency or resistance") and applauded a congressman who deflated his colleague's pretentious oratory, peppered with Latin phrases, by opening his speech with "a sentence in low Dutch."[122] And Democratic journals often drew on the neoclassical understanding of sympathy. The *Democratic Review,* for example, praised an orator who "enchained a vast city in admiration . . . and drew shouts of responsive enthusiasm from the largest assembly it ever saw."[123] In fact, pace Oravec, the influence of the neoclassical model extended well beyond Whig journals. For example, the Quaker paper *The Friend* echoed Hugh Blair in its desire to influence "the formation of the judgment and taste," and the *Pennsylvania Freeman* did not hesitate to praise "the beauty and energy" of Angelina Grimké's eloquence.[124]

Nevertheless, Oravec's point that the neoclassical model was not embraced by everyone is well taken. The neoclassical model was perhaps most influential as a negative model of public debate, capturing precisely what was wrong with political oratory. It lent support to the perception that political oratory did not rely heavily on rational argument, since a skillful speaker could (in theory) produce action through passionate and ethical appeals. The *Public Ledger* made this point in a satire of 1840 campaign rhetoric:

> *Keep it before the People!* Awaken the echoes in the farthest corners of the Union, and thrill the nation with the loud reverberation. Fellow countrymen, unborn millions are yet to pronounce upon our acts, so just look out what you are about. We are just stepping over the first stumbling block in the way of republicanism, and if you are not cautious you will bark your shins, sprain your ankles, or fall upon your noses. . . .
>
> Only *keep it before the people,* because, although the people don't care two pins about it, yet, if you make a noise on the subject, it will appear very clear to them that the thing is of some consequence.[125]

The fact that oratory like this could move people despite its complete lack of rational content raised the uncomfortable suspicion that a politics of public speech might not be any more rational and orderly than a politics of mob action.

For example, abolitionists and others involved in Christian-based moral reform movements worried about the elements of passion and conflict inherent in the neoclassical model. Catharine Beecher's attack on Grimké reflects this concern; she characterized political argument as combative, a struggle for dominance, and therefore unchristian and basically immoral. Against this masculine approach to influencing the public she contrasted a "feminine" approach: "maintaining [one's] place as dependent and defenceless, and making no claims" but extending one's influence subtly, by "making [one-self] . . . respected, esteemed and loved." Similarly, James Forten praised the Philadelphia Female Anti-Slavery Society because, composed entirely of women, it "stands aloof from the storms of passion and political tumult."[126] Implicit in this type of criticism, of course, is recognition of the gendered—in fact, frankly sexual—dimension of the neoclassical model: the speaker is cast in the role of the lover who must defeat his rival in order to dominate the passive but resisting love object (the audience). Because the neoclassical model so explicitly gendered public debate as masculine, it was open to criti-cism from promoters of the cult of domesticity (such as Beecher and Forten), who considered the feminine virtues more suitable to Christians than the masculine ones. Thus, to some, the antagonistic and gendered dimension of the neoclassical model seemed to conflict with Christian ethics; political ac-tion replaced "the prayer of the humble heart" and "the disinterested and self-sacrificing labor of those whose only aim is the good of their fellow men" with "the falsehood and ferocity of a political canvass."[127]

The endorsement of passion and conflict was hardly the most problematic feature of the neoclassical model, though. The ability of one person to estab-lish dominance over the will of another through speech was both fascinating and revolting to the antebellum public, as is illustrated by their reaction to mesmerism (hypnotism). Mesmerism began as a healing practice based on the theories of Viennese physician Franz Anton Mesmer, who postulated that the human body was permeated by an invisible fluidlike energy—a universal etheric medium that conducted light, heat, electricity, and magnetism. Ill-ness occurred, he suggested, when this substance was out of equilibrium; the treatment he devised was based on the idea that the body could be "remag-netized." Mesmeric healing thus included passing magnets, rods, or simply one's hands over the patient. Whether or not this actually resulted in a cure, it often induced a somnambulistic state during which patients exhibited odd behavior—in particular, they became acutely lucid and suggestible. By the time mesmerism was introduced in the United States by Frenchman Charles Poyen in 1836, this psychological effect, the strange rapport that developed between the healer and the patient, had become the focus of scientific inter-est. As mesmerism was popularized on the lecture circuit, however, its sig-nificance to the developing field of psychology received less attention than its theatrical potential. While its devotees were conducting carefully reported experiments, enterprising showmen were staging the kind of exhibitions now associated with hypnotism: an audience member was put into a hypnotic trance and induced to do things he or she would not ordinarily do, at the command of the hypnotist. The demonstrations thus soon became exercises in establishing verbal dominance over the subject.[128]

Mesmerism proved to be disturbingly persuasive evidence that the power of speech could give one person mental sway over the will of another. According to Philadelphia doctor Charles Caldwell, the practice allows one person "completely to identify another with himself—sense with sense—sentiment with sentiment—thought with thought—movement with movement—will with will—and I was near to saying existence with existence." In short, "the perfect *identity* of *feeling* of the mesmeriser and the mesmerised" accounts for the "entire control which the will of the former has over that of the latter."[129] The analogy to the powers claimed for oratory was obvious, particularly since mesmerists usually referred to this identity of feeling as sympathy—the same sympathy achieved by a skilled orator.[130] Caldwell insisted that oratory and mesmerism established mental sympathy through the same means: through some "subtle, invisible, and active intervening medium," one person can produce in another "impressions so vivid and powerful, as to create joy and sorrow, anger, hope, veneration, benevolence, and fear."[131]

Mesmerism was considered dangerous because it undermined the subject's rational agency. Nathaniel Hawthorne's critique of the practice in *The Blithedale Romance* is well known: "Human character was but soft wax in [the mesmerist's] hands; and guilt or virtue only the forms into which he should see fit to mold it." Hawthorne's hero reacted to this idea with "horror and disgust," fearing that "if these things were to be believed, the individual soul was virtually annihilated, and all that is sweet and pure, in our present life, debased." Ralph Waldo Emerson similarly worried that "men are not good enough to be trusted with such power." Such criticisms were so common that treatises on the subject typically began with long apologies defending mesmerism from the "satire and shafts of the malevolent."[132] Mesmerism was associated with sexual immorality and black magic, not to mention sheer humbuggery and fanaticism. One critic even put mesmerism in the same category as such despised doctrines as ultra-temperance, ultra-abolitionism, and Fanny Wrightism.[133]

The negative reaction to mesmerism shows that the power of speech to impair the hearer's rational independence was considered a significant moral problem. But the comparable power of political oratory to impair the public's rational independence was a moral problem with special political implications. Oratory was, in some sense, undemocratic. As many historians have noted, oratory had a persistent association with elitism, which accounts for its decline in the latter half of the nineteenth century.[134] This elitism, however, was not just a matter of casual references to "the rabble" scattered through the texts on rhetoric or the use of high-flown language that revealed the speaker's elite education. It was also intimately connected to the supposed power of oratory over the rational agency of the audience. As the preceding analysis of the neoclassical model demonstrates, it conceptualized public speaking as a vehicle for sustaining deference relations in politics. Its emphasis on self-display and its endorsement of ethos and pathos created what antebellum democrats considered to be an unequal relationship between the speaker and the audience, in which the audience allowed itself to be dominated by the speaker.

This concern is illustrated in a complaint by a mechanic about the manipulative dimension of political oratory:

> True, we assemble on the 4th of July and mingle our shouts or approbation as we hear the invaluable Declaration of Independence read—we may join in the multitude in paying fulsome adulation to some popular orator, as he discants on the many blessings we enjoy in the land of Liberty, and flatter ourselves for the time, that what he says is true . . . : but, when we leave the festive board, and return to our humble homes; when the thrilling accents of eloquence have ceased to vibrate on the ear, and sober reason resumes her sway—then, fellow-mechanics, do we awake to the sad reality of our condition.[135]

The mechanic thus attributes social inequality to the power of oratory to interfere with the audience's "sober reason": the thrilling accents of oratory rob the workers of their political agency by degrading their ability to think for themselves.

This formula echoes a familiar Enlightenment understanding of the relationship between rational independence and political equality, in which the loss of rational independence was the central ingredient in maintaining deference relations. Consider, for example, Adam Smith's analysis of deference. Instead of beginning from the traditional moral-religous framework in which deference to morally superior persons was justified as a spiritual discipline calculated to develop Christian virtue, Smith drew on faculty psychology to characterize deference relations as fundamentally irrational. He attributed the lower classes' tendency to defer to the great to the nonrational faculty of sympathy, which disposes mankind to "go along with all the passions of the rich and the powerful." Moreover, he maintained that "our obsequiousness to our superiors more frequently arises from our admiration for the advantages of their situation, than from any private expectations of benefit from their good-will." Thus, "[e]ven when the order of society seems to require that we should oppose them, we can hardly bring ourselves to do it. . . . To treat them in any respect as men, to reason and dispute with them upon ordinary occasions, requires such resolution, that there are few men whose magnanimity can support them in it."[136] Under this view, sympathy—the same sympathy to which George Campbell attributed the speaker's power over the audience—maintains inequality by preventing the people from rationally calculating the benefits that might accrue to them from refusing to defer to the elite.[137]

Of course, sympathy was only one explanation of why the lower classes defer to the upper classes; other favorite explanations were ignorance and prejudice. William Heighton, for example, attributed the situation of workingmen to a "General want of Intelligence among the great mass of the people," rather than the effects of sympathy.[138] But whatever its cause, this intellectual deference played a leading role in the traditional Enlightenment story about the march of reason furthering political freedom: if intellectual deference maintained a regime in which the citizens were denied their rights, then undermining deference by restoring the people's rational independence was essential to winning political freedom. Thus, Fanny Wright could characterize the American Revolution as a conquest of "knowledge over ignorance, willing co-operation over blind obedience, opinion over prejudice."[139] This formula was prominent in antebellum political discourse, particularly in working-class radicalism. As Heighton put it, ignorance, prejudice, and superstition have "led men to blindly . . . surrender up their rights." But now "the light of reason has burst from the thralldom of ignorance, and has begun to scatter its rays on the minds of freemen!"[140] By teaching people how to exercise their reason, one can free them from the influence of the elite.

In the Enlightenment tradition, then, preservation of citizens' rational independence (conceived as the opposite of intellectual deference) was critical to maintaining political equality and liberty.[141] This understanding of the political implications of deference accounts for the pervasive antebellum anxiety about institutions and practices that might degrade rational independence. The anxiety was most prominent, of course, in the profound distrust of hierarchical organizations, from the Catholic Church to political parties, that were perceived as requiring mental conformity from their members.[142] In the words of William Channing, the problem with such associations was that they tended to "impair or repress the free and full action of men's powers"; too many were designed "to depress the human intellect, to make it dependent and servile."[143] But oratory could have the same effect, as suggested by this passage from a Native American paper, criticizing a sermon by the archbishop of New York that condemned the Italian republicans: "As he preaches to teach, of course we infer that he wishes to *indoctrinate* his audience with opinions favorable to arbitrary power over both mind and body; and as such opinions are injurious to all that our fathers contended for, we have inherited and thus far preserved, we feel bound by duty to oppose them."[144] In accusing the archbishop of indoctrinating his audience, the editor implies that the archbishop's sermon exerted the same "arbitrary power over mind" that the tyrannical Austrian empire exercised. Oratory, the Catholic Church, and tyranny are bound up together in a common conspiracy to undermine rational independence. Clearly, to the extent speech had the power to exert "an irresistible power over the thoughts and purposes of [the] audience," it threatened rational independence in the same way that hierarchical organizations such as the Catholic Church did. Therefore, if the neoclassical model of political debate accurately described the power of political oratory, a politics of public debate would tend to degrade the citizens' rational independence and foster political inequality.

This concern with the political effects of oratory shows up on both ends of the political spectrum. Democrats worried that "[t]he glittering spray of oratory, the vexed foam of declamation, the dashing waves of personal abuse" kept the people in a "constant state of delusion and mystification" that served the interests of the aristocracy of wealth that was considered to be the guiding force behind the Whigs. Workingmen's advocate William Heighton consistently attacked the "false reasonings and artful persuasions" of politicians that kept the working class subservient (even while encouraging the working class to master those same rhetorical skills).[145] But Whigs also worried about the effects of oratory on citizens' rational independence, a concern usually expressed in their condemnation of demagogues. Sidney Fisher, for example, complained of the Democrats' use of oratory to appeal to "the mob." The majority, he claimed, are "ever liable to lead on to anarchy & revolution by designing and artful demagogues."[146] Both complaints stem from the same basic problem with oratory: it prevents audiences from exercising their reason, so that they cannot act for themselves—they simply become the tools of demagogues or the elite. A politics of oratory, then, would not necessarily foster rationality, political equality, or public order. It would simply create an aristocracy of eloquence, dominating a passive, manipulable public through constant appeals to their passions.

Conclusion

Neoclassical rhetoric offered a deeply problematic model of political argument. Although it was considered a plausible description of the power of the voice, it conflicted with the ideal of a dispassionate, orderly politics that would respect the citizens' rational independence. As much as antebellum Americans valued oratory, they were ambivalent about its place in popular politics—an ambivalence that was reflected, for example, in the public reaction to Fanny Wright. She provoked anxiety not only because of her doctrines but also because her "spirit-stirring eloquence" was such that "[s]he made her converts, and that, too, not among the low and vicious alone."[147] Given the neoclassical model of public argument, a popular politics of oratory threatened to create not a reasoning public but a captive one, enthralled by a legion of Fanny Wrights.

Thus, if the politics of mob action posed the threat of social disorder and the loss of political legitimacy, the politics of public debate was not necessarily the solution. According to the dominant theories of political psychology, reason is inoperative without the assistance of pathos and ethos; it may convince the understanding, but it cannot move the will. Thus, confining popular politics to public debate did not guarantee a politics of reason. On the contrary, such a politics may be indistinguishable from mob action; under the neoclassical model, the skillful demagogue and the passion-driven mob are simply two sides of the same disheartening democratic spectacle. And if public debate did not guarantee political rationality and order, neither did it guarantee political agency. After all, how does one preserve the rational independence of the citizens when their primary responsibility is to serve as an audience for articulate political orators?

This analysis suggests a tension within the category of rational debate itself, between the concept of speech as a tool to persuade and motivate the public and the concept of rational independence that was central to political rationality and equality. But the picture of public debate outlined here was not the only available model. The next chapter explores a competing conception, rooted in the Enlightenment tradition. This tradition, or at least one strand of it, characterized public argument not as a vehicle for mental domination and personal self-glorification but as a potentially transparent medium for truth and reason. At the same time, however, it uncovered a host of new threats to political rationality created by, and perhaps endemic to, democratic politics.

4

ENLIGHTENMENT RATIONALISM
AND POLITICAL DEBATE

Historian Richard John argues that the development of an efficient and low-cost postal system worked an important change on the character of congressional oratory. By 1830, congressmen were able to deluge their constituents through the mail with newspaper reports, pamphlets, and other printed accounts of congressional proceedings. As a result, legislators began to give speeches intended "less as verbal performances for their Washington colleagues than as published texts for their constituents back home."[1] In other words, political debate (at least at the national level) was increasingly printed, rather than spoken. One might worry that substituting speeches for the give-and-take of argument would diminish the quality of legislative deliberation, but some antebellum observers thought that the transition from oral to written speech would *improve* the rationality of political debate. Henry Tappan, for example, argued that written speech is qualitatively different from oral communication, because written words can transmit only the trains of thought that the passions arouse. It is the *sound* of speech that communicates the energy of the passions. The perfect communication of sentiment, then, is possible only through the music of speech—through its strength, tone, and pitch.[2] Written speech is therefore less effective at arousing the passions than oral speech. Antislavery advocate Hinton Helper similarly concluded that conducting political debate in the press could mitigate the passion of politics by allowing one to remove deliberation from "the platforms of public debate, where the exercise of eloquence is too often characterized by violent passion and subterfuge," to one's "own private apartments."[3]

These reactions to the movement from spoken to written argument point toward a different picture of political debate than the one considered in the previous chapter: not a contest of oratorical skills, but a collection of written arguments, made public through the press only to be removed from the frenzy of partisan conflict and mulled over, quietly, in private. If the goal is to find a type of public debate that simply transmits information, allowing citizens to make informed decisions without being manipulated by demagogues, then the written word might seem a better medium than oratory—less conducive to arousing the passions through rhetorical tricks and strategies, and more conducive to dispassionate argument.

In fact, however, antebellum commentators derisively labeled congressional speeches directed at constituents "bunkum," recognizing that written discourse was not necessarily any more substantive or rational than oratory.[4] Teachers of neoclassical rhetoric scoffed at the premise that public discourse could be made more rational by purging it of rhetorical "tricks" such as tone and inflection. Eloquence, noted Richard Whately, belonged as much to the writer as to the speaker, and the rules of rhetoric apply even to philosophical works.[5] Rational argument (even written argument) is not outside the domain of rhetoric; reasoned arguments are simply one way to persuade an audience, and probably an ineffective way if one fails to address the passions as well.

Critics of the neoclassical school might grant this point, but they had a point as well: to the extent that the neoclassical school took persuasion as the primary goal of public speech, it granted rational, pathetic, and ethical appeals the same status, because all these kinds of appeals may be needed to persuade the audience. But what would the discipline of rhetoric look like if it took not persuasion but public rationality as its primary goal? According to one Philadelphia editor, it might look something like Locke's *Essay Concerning Human Understanding*, "which should rather have been called Locke on the Abuse of Language; and the Diversions of Purley."[6] To read Locke's major philosophical treatise as a text on rhetoric isn't as strange as it may appear; after all, neoclassical rhetoric was in large part an attempt to synthesize Lockean psychology and classical rhetoric.[7] But the synthesis wasn't entirely successful. It's hard to escape the conclusion that Locke's rationalism calls for a very different approach to public speech than the traditional focus on persuasion. If (as Locke himself argued) persuasion requires appeals to the passions, and passion interferes with the rational faculty, then persuasive speech is hardly a suitable vehicle for a politics of reason. George Campbell's uneasy endorsement of appeals to passion—as "handmaids" to reason that nevertheless "never fail to disturb the operation of the intellectual faculty"[8]— reflects this basic tension between rhetoric and rationalism, or at least between classical rhetoric and a particular kind of rationalism most closely associated with Enlightenment theorists such as Locke. A model of public debate that privileged rational appeals, even at the expense of persuasiveness, would constitute a major break with, and challenge to, traditional theories of rhetoric. And this is what observers such as Helper were getting at when they talked about the transition from spoken to written political discourse, from the classical arena of oratory to the modern institution of the press: the replacement of the dominion of voice with the rule of reason.

This chapter begins by tracing the roots of this Enlightenment vision of democratic politics—democracy as the rule of reason—in Habermas's notorious eighteenth-century coffeehouses, salons, and newspapers. I then explore in detail the model of public debate this vision implied for antebellum Americans: a dispassionate, disinterested kind of debate aimed at preserving and enhancing public rationality. Although this type of debate seems to promise a more rational politics than the neoclassical model, I want to highlight its weaknesses as both a theoretical model of and a practical guide to democratic politics. Briefly, this model, as it took shape in popular public discourse, was too simplistic to resolve the tension discussed in Chapter 3 between persuasive speech and rational independence. Instead, it elided the problem by attributing to truth itself the power to persuade and motivate the public. This solution obscured the problems of conviction and motivation, leaving us with an impoverished vision of democratic politics that failed to accommodate either interest or passion.

The Rule of Reason

Horace Greeley's *New York Tribune* "has done more for human freedom than any other publication in history," declared Charles Leland, editor of the *Philadelphia Evening Bulletin*.[9] Greeley might have demurred at such effusive praise, but he would have understood the compliment; he used similar language to introduce his 1848 compilation of the writings of Cassius Clay. "The Liberty of the Press," he began, "is the palladium of all true liberty; with it despotism is impossible; without it, inevitable." He continued: "Where all subjects may be freely discussed, all wrongs and abuses fearlessly exposed, it is morally certain that the Right must soon prevail. . . . That a majority should persist in perpetuating injustice, after full and free discussion, is scarcely tolerable as a hypothesis, and wholly unjustified by facts. . . . Unawed discussion would gradually make plain to the general understanding that servility corrupts the few while it debases the many, and that the enduring welfare of each demands security and justice for all." Thus, "whenever, in the clear daylight of intelligence, any claim, usage, or institution, repels public scrutiny, shrinks from the ordeal of the general reason, and to argument and criticism opposes the torch and the axe, be sure the knell of that institution has sounded."[10]

Greeley's paean to liberty of the press captures the basic elements of a model of political debate rooted in the complex set of concerns, conflicts, and debates that constituted the Enlightenment. Its essential features are shaped by the traditional Enlightenment preoccupation with rationality, publicity, and liberty: specifically, political debate should be rational, public, "unawed," addressed to "the general understanding," and aimed at exposing abuses of power with the intention of preventing despotism. This seems straight-forward—but it does beg a few important questions. For example, how will simply discussing wrongs and abuses eliminate them? What is the "ordeal of general reason," and why must claims and institutions face it? And what does any of this have to do with the press?

There is no single text, or collection of texts, that gives systematic answers to these questions, as there is for the neoclassical model of public debate. Instead, one has to comb through scattered passages, particularly in and about the press, to piece together the background assumptions and commitments that make sense of these assertions about politics and public argument. But first I want to orient this inquiry by examining the roots of this understanding of public debate in Enlightenment political thought. Jürgen Habermas's study *The Structural Transformation of the Public Sphere* is helpful in this respect. Habermas rightly identifies the practice of public debate (as opposed to voting or rioting, for example) as central to an important theme in Enlightenment political thought: a commitment to a more rational politics organized around, in particular, a free press.

Why the press? This question is the best entry into Habermas's analysis. The Enlightenment model of political argument was closely associated with the press—not (pace Tappan) because written discourse is inherently more rational than spoken discourse, but because of the historical interdependence of the press and the public sphere, a central category in Enlightenment political thought. Habermas argues that the press developed during the eighteenth century (in Europe and Great Britain) into an integral part of the bourgeois public sphere: a set of practices and conventions through which bourgeois citizens could come together and engage in public discourse as equals. Institutions constituting the public sphere include coffeehouses in England (and in the American colonies), salons in France, and literary societies in Germany, as well as the press.[11] The bourgeoisie congregated in these arenas to discuss matters of public interest: business, politics, literature, art. The style of discourse was distinctive—what Habermas calls rational-critical public debate, an exercise in the public use of reason. Participants were to disregard rank and status, so that the only authority would be the authority of the better argument. In other words, the rules of deference (in particular, intellectual deference) were supposed to be suspended.

Charles Brockden Brown described this type of conversation in his 1798 work *Alcuin: A Dialogue*. The book recounts a conversation carried on during the narrator's visits to a salon organized by a Mrs. Carter in Philadelphia. The narrator (supposedly Brown himself) is a poor schoolteacher, while most of the salon's guests have wealth and position. Brown's participation in the discussion as an equal therefore signals the suspension of deference, a fact

Brown comments on by describing the "embarrassments and awkwardness"
of socializing with his superiors in this manner.[12] But Brown takes the rule
of equality even further by opening a conversation with the hostess, asking
her whether she is a Federalist. This prompts an extended debate on the political and social position of women. A short passage illustrates the tone and
style of the conversation:

> If I understand you rightly (said the lady), you are of opinion that the
> sexes are essentially equal.
> It appears to me (answered I), that human beings are moulded by the
> circumstances in which they are placed. In this they are all alike. The
> differences that flow from the sexual distinction, are as nothing in the
> balance.
> And yet women are often reminded that none of their sex are to be
> found among the formers of States, and the instructors of mankind—
> that Pythagoras, Lycurgus, and Socrates, Newton, and Locke, were not
> women.
> True; nor were they mountain savages, nor helots, nor shoemakers.[13]

So it continues, through arguments and counterarguments addressed to the
"general understanding," exploring the possible differences between men and
women as grounds for excluding women from various occupations and from
politics. What is distinctive about this practice, according to Habermas, is
that the participants have no legitimate means of influencing one another
except through rational arguments governed by universal rules. Brown is not
to defer to Mrs. Carter because she is wealthy, and she is not to defer to
Brown because he is a man. The results of such debate therefore "lay claim
to being in accord with reason."[14]

Whether public discourse in reality ever achieved this fictionalized ideal is
a moot point; Habermas contends that the ideal did at least inform the practice—Brown knew what rational-critical debate was *supposed* to look like,
even if the practice only occasionally and imperfectly realized the standards
of universal rationality.[15] In any case, these norms, whether practiced or not,
were incorporated into the political thought that grew out of the tradition
of Enlightenment rationalism, as represented in Habermas's study by Kant,
Marx, Hegel, Mill, and Tocqueville.

The political significance of the public sphere is that the state's regula-
tion of civil society was a principal topic of rational-critical debate. This,
Habermas argues, constituted a critical change in the relationship between
the state and the citizens. State activities were traditionally shrouded in secrecy; the prince had no obligation to justify himself to the people. The

eighteenth-century bourgeoisie rejected this principle, challenging the secrecy and arbitrariness of state power by subjecting it to critical scrutiny in a public arena. (In Brown's dialogue, for example, the conversants considered whether the laws governing marriage, education, and employment treated women fairly and rationally.)[16] This critical scrutiny, in turn, was supposed to produce a public opinion on the state's activities, which was supposed to be the proper basis for law. Basing law on public opinion formed through rational debate would, in theory, bring law under the control of reason (with public opinion representing reason).[17] As Habermas puts it, rational-critical public debate "undercut the principle on which existing rule was based. The principle of control that the bourgeois public opposed to the latter—namely, publicity—was intended to change domination as such" by subjecting it to standards of reason and the forms of law. In this way, the arbitrary commands by which the state traditionally exercised its power would be replaced by the rule of reason.[18]

This understanding of the relationship between the public and the state gained currency in Great Britain during the eighteenth century, shaping the British press's understanding of its role in the political system. Under the Enlightenment model, the press is a central institution structuring the public sphere; it is the primary forum in which the public subjects the activities of the state to rational-critical debate (Greeley's "ordeal of general reason").[19] The model thus conceptualizes the press as independent of, and in tension with, the state. Its function in the political system is to expose to public view the secret operations of the state and to evaluate their rationality. Habermas points to *The Letters of Junius,* published between 1768 and 1772, as examples of this form of political journalism. The letters accused the king, his ministers, certain millitary leaders, and jurists of "political machinations" and thereby uncovered (in Habermas's words) "secret connections of political significance." This type of exposé journalism evolved into a systematic opposition by which the press informed the public about Parliament's arcane political controversies.[20] This opposition between the press and the state was slow to gain legitimacy, but it was a conventional theme in British political discourse by the nineteenth century. The press was the "palladium of all liberties," the forum in which the citizens compelled public authority to legitimate itself before public opinion.[21]

The American press embraced this tradition more cautiously than the British press. Colonial printers were familiar with the concept of a "free press," a press that published criticisms of the government; they sometimes defended their liberty to publish opposition views on the grounds that the press should serve as a free channel for the communication of opinion and a forum for "every Man to communicate his Sentiments freely to the Publick, upon

Political or Religious Points." But they even more frequently defended their
right to refuse to criticize the government, on the grounds that, "as Printer to
the Public," it was their duty "studiously to avoid giving Offence to the Legislature."[22] As a practical matter, though, printers could seldom refuse trade
on political grounds; there was not enough business from either the government or the opposition to support a partisan press in most towns. Nor could
they easily open their presses to both sides; neither the government nor the
public was tolerant of such neutrality, even though printers typically maintained that it was strictly a matter of economic necessity. As one printer argued after printing a controversial sermon, "I printed Mr. *Wesley's* Sermon,
not because I liked it, but because several Gentlemen of Learning and good
Sense . . . desired to have it printed, and I had a prospect of getting a Penny
by it, as I have by all that I print."[23] Most printers took this line, attempting
to avoid political controversy by downplaying their political role, avoiding
the more inflammatory political material and focusing on reporting news
(preferably uncontroversial news from distant places). The colonial press,
then, fell far short of the Enlightenment ideal of an open forum for critical
public opinion, at least until the Revolution. And even after the Revolution
the press was slow to challenge the secrecy of the state. Until the 1800s, for
example, reporters were often unwelcome in the House and barred from the
Senate.[24]

But by the antebellum era this timidity had vanished. The press had become a major presence on the political landscape and was widely acknowledged to be the primary organ of public opinion and vehicle for political
argument. Impressed with the power of the press, the *Christian Chronicle*
claimed that it "moulds and prepares a vast mass of mind which it can afterwards urge with a terrible momentum against any institution. . . . The political champion, bent on lifting his favorite candidate to a seat of honor, or on
securing the dominancy of his own political principles, spares no expense to
put in operation this mighty engine."[25] A more critical evaluation of the liberty of the press complained that "[i]t furnishes a wide field for every Tyro,
who can raise money enough to pay for three cases of type, and impudence
or brass enough to get trusted for paper, rent and labor, to start a new paper,
devoted to certain new principles, dedicated to some particular cause or sect
of people, and thus rigged out, raised in his own estimation to a higher sphere
of ambition than ever Alexander was in all his glory, he is at liberty with his
press to libel, slander, lie, and in every way abuse with his crude thoughts
every one he, in his wisdom, thinks fit."[26]

This complaint does not greatly exaggerate the proliferation of political
newspapers during the first half of the nineteenth century, particularly in the
North. The number of newspapers in the United States increased steadily

from 1800 on; there were 512 in existence by 1820, 1,404 by 1840, and 2,302 by 1850. These 2,302 papers served a nation whose total (free) population was 19,987,356—about one newspaper for every 8,700 free persons. The average circulation of daily and Sunday papers increased as well, from 800 in 1820 to 2,986 in 1850, and between 1820 and 1840, the number of newspapers transmitted through the mail rose from 6 million to 39 million.[27]

These increases reflect the falling price of newspapers after 1830, when technological improvements made printing cheaper. Before 1830, the average annual subscription rate for a newspaper was $8 to $10, over a week's wages for most workers; after 1830, many Philadelphia papers were selling for $2 to $5 per year.[28] But prices and circulation figures probably underestimate how accessible newspapers actually were, especially in cities. Prices were not prohibitive, since publishers typically extended credit, and it was common for families to pool their resources to subscribe to a newspaper. In addition, taverns and reading rooms made newspapers accessible to the working class.[29] Thus, newspaper reading crossed class lines, and even the Whiggish *National Gazette* thought that this influence on the working class could be beneficial: "It would be to their mind as food is to the body—as the free circulation of the blood is to the health of the body. . . . It would place [the workingman] on nearly an equal footing in point of useful knowledge with the scholar."[30] In fact, Americans' devotion to newspaper reading was a subject of constant comment by visiting Europeans, who noted with surprise that Americans depended heavily on newspapers in managing their private and public affairs.[31]

Unlike the colonial papers, antebellum papers were overwhelmingly political. Of course, not all of them carried Habermasian political debate. The commercial and penny press (cheap dailies aimed at the mass public) were devoted more to news than to political argument and usually professed to be politically neutral. But true political neutrality was fairly rare; the 1850 census reported that only 5 percent of newspapers were independent of parties.[32] And even these papers seldom avoided politics altogether—being neutral was not the same as being nonpolitical. For example, the *Philadelphia Evening Bulletin* purported to be a commercial and family journal, in contrast to the city's other "political" papers. But it regularly addressed political issues and started promoting Zachary Taylor for the presidency almost as soon as it was established.[33] Even religious newpapers such as the Baptist *Christian Chronicle* addressed political issues regularly, from a professedly nonpartisan standpoint.[34]

In general, antebellum journalism was devoted not to "the news"—objective facts of general interest—but to politics. Most newspapers were party papers: openly partisan, supported by parties, and devoted primarily to supporting or opposing policies and candidates. They were understood to be vehicles for political debate. But what did this debate look like? A number of historians have discounted the rational content of political debate during this era, suggesting that politics consisted of campaign hoopla more than serious discussion.[35] But the variety and sophistication of antebellum political discourse suggest otherwise; political economy and class relations, women's rights, and racism were only some of the subjects that received extensive and subtle analysis in antebellum newspapers by figures such as William Lloyd Garrison, Matthew Carey, and Orestes Brownson. Party papers served as a clearinghouse for political argument, filling their columns with letters, editorials, speeches, and even selections from journals and books. Certainly, some of these debates were mundane, such as an 1830 discussion in the *United States Gazette* on the proposed route of the Philadelphia and Columbia Railroad. Apparently, the subject interested Philadelphians, though; the paper printed the full report to the canal commissioners on the subject, along with a series of letters between "Civis" and "Simplex" debating the conclusions of the report.[36] But more significant topics were also debated in the *Gazette* in January 1830, including Jackson's nomination, the debate on the sale of public lands in the West, the tariff, and the effects of the city's poor relief on the interests of the working class.[37]

Of course, editors did not consistently view their papers as forums for airing both sides of a subject; more frequently, they presented only one point of view. To get both sides, one would have to read the opposing party's paper as well, and there's little evidence that this was a common practice. The editors, however, certainly read their opponents' editorials and responded to them. (At least they usually responded; the *American Banner* once complained that the political papers in Philadelphia were trying to defeat the nativist cause by ignoring its editorials instead of answering them.)[38] Thus, even if political activists (such as editors) were the primary participants, the debate carried on in the papers did in fact resemble the rational-critical public debate that it was, in theory, supposed to be.

I do not mean to suggest that rational-critical public debate was the only or even the most important element of citizenship in the antebellum era. Just how attentive the public was to political debate is a moot issue. Lewis Saum, for example, found little evidence in the personal writings of antebellum actors that politics was central to their lives, and William Gienapp suggests that participation in partisan pageantry was more central to citizenship than was debate.[39] However, the prevalence and popularity of political newspapers— not to mention political oratory—suggest that political debate did absorb a significant amount of attention. But for my purposes it is enough to show that Habermas's description of rational-critical public debate corresponded, at least roughly, to antebellum political argument as carried on in the press.

(It's useful to remember that, according to Habermas, rational-critical debate is best exemplified by *The Letters of Junius,* which were characterized more by vituperation and accusation than careful, substantive argument.)[40]

Nevertheless, this model, as elaborated in antebellum public discourse, proved to be too simplistic to explain the complex interactions of truth, interest, passion, and reason in political debate. The following analysis explores how this particular instantiation of Enlightenment thought took shape in antebellum discourse about politics and the press, highlighting both its strengths and its weaknesses as a guide to popular political action.

An Enlightenment Model of Public Debate

Newspapers were, among other things, a forum for readers to air their views and opinions. But writing for newspapers was a relatively new practice in the 1830s, and readers apparently needed some instruction. Editors obliged, as with the following advice:

How to Write for Newspapers.

I. Have something to write about.
II. Write plain; dot your i's; cross your t's; point your sentences; begin with capitals.
III. Write short; to the point; stop when you are done.
IV. Write only on one side of the leaf.
V. Read it over, abridge and correct it, until you get it into the smallest possible compass.
VI. Pay the postage.[41]

Apparently, writing for newspapers was much easier than engaging in political oratory; one need only follow these six simple rules, rather than poring through tomes on rhetoric and elocution. This view that writing for newspapers was fairly easy, something that anyone could do without any special training, reflects the rationale and epistemological premises of the Enlightenment model of public debate: the purpose of political debate is to discover the truth, and political truth is objective, uncomplicated, and accessible to any reasonably intelligent person.[42]

Political Truth

The Enlightenment model of political argument was based on a model of scientific debate derived largely from the conventions of civil conversation that governed polite society in England in the sixteenth and seventeenth centuries. Steven Shapin's research into the development of early English scientific culture traces this conjunction of scientific inquiry and civil discourse. The guiding norms of scientific debate in Enlightenment thought were, of course, free inquiry and a strict refusal to rely on authority—norms that do not necessarily entail civility. But the gentlemen scientists of the Royal Academy, attempting to dissociate themselves from the contentiousness and pedantry of the medieval Scholastics, developed conventions of debate that would moderate conflict and maintain the scientific enterprise as civil and humane, a suitable pursuit for gentlemen. Enlightenment truth, as Shapin explains, "was to be sought by selfless selves, seeking not celebrity or private advantage but the civic good."[43] Scientific debate should follow the same rules as polite conversation: "Be not magisterial in your dictate; nor contend pertinaceously in ordinary discourse for your opinion, nor for a truth of small consequence. Declare your reasons, if they be not accepted, let them alone; assure your self that you are not obliged to convert the whole world. It is also an uncivil thing . . . to confute every thing we think is false."[44] Scientists should be humble and modest, always willing to reconsider their views, and disinterested in anything but the truth.

The influence of this model on the conventions of political debate is evident in the rhetoric of antebellum newspaper editors. They informed their readers that the proper attitude toward political argument was "humility and love of truth," which would induce readers "to hear with patience, and impartially to weigh what they hear, in order that they may the better judge." One should consider both sides of the issue, and "address should be made to the reason and judgment," not the "passions and prejudices of men."[45] Public debate should not be a combat but a civil, restrained meeting of minds: "Why should men, because they differ in opinion, fall to beating each other, and 'unpack their heart with words,' as if none could be wise or honest but themselves, and the exercise of independent thought was a privilege secured to them alone? . . . And if it be even possible that our opponents may be correct, why, not merely common charity, but common justice requires that we should yield to them the same courtesy that we demand for ourselves."[46] Political debate therefore demands a proper disposition, advised a correspondent to the *Mechanics' Free Press*. Discussants should ask themselves, "Have you been discussing the subject dispassionately—each endeavouring to promote in himself, a willingness to perceive more truth in the views of the other than he had been accustomed to do? and to impute to them pure motives for holding those views to be correct?—If you have not, and instead of cherishing a desire to arrive at truth, you have each been labouring to obtain a victory—in other words, to perplex and defeat each other, it is not wonderful that you have not agreed."[47] In sum, political argument should be a "temperate discussion of principles and a candid exposition of facts," not a struggle for verbal dominance.[48]

This flat rejection of passion, conflict, and glory signals the Enlightenment model's departure from the conception of politics informing neoclassical rhetoric. The ideal political speaker, under the Enlightenment model, was not an orator but a scientist: dispassionate, rational, and animated solely by the desire to discover the truth. The conflict between the two models is highlighted in this review of a lecture by Robert Dale Owen:

> When Mr. Owen arrived, a few days ago, . . . the feelings of the public in opposition to him and his plans were of a very strong character. He met them fairly and openly, yet with his usual quiet dignity of manner. . . . [H]e fairly conquered [their] prejudices by a simple statement of facts. . . . He courted objections from his hearers, and he seemed most ready to give every explanation required, but he appears to have fortified his system, too deeply in the laws of our nature to be assailed with success. The foundation of his system . . . is founded on a rock, and . . . immoveable by force, cunning or deception.[49]

Owen, then, was no orator. He simply stated the facts, while his opponents (not having truth on their side) relied on prejudice, force, cunning, and deception. Thus he countered the tricks and strategies of the orator with the simple, candid style of one who is interested only in discovering the truth. Similarly, it was not modesty but a commitment to Enlightenment rationalism that made Owen's friend Frances Wright disavow her reputation as an orator. Downplaying the persuasive element of her lectures, she insisted that she merely wanted to "inform the human mind." Her admirers might celebrate her eloquence, but she characterized her lectures as fairly tedious expositions aimed solely at discovering the truth: "to proceed step by step—to trace the outline and consider the details—to substantiate first principles, and then to trace them out in their various applications."[50]

But what kind of truth did one discover through this kind of discourse? According to Wright, "All truth is simple, for truth is only fact. The means of attaining truth are equally simple. We have but to seek and we shall find; to open our eyes and our ears; without prejudice to observe; without fear to listen, and dispassionately to examine, compare, and draw conclusions."[51] Wright included political and moral truth in "all truth," drawing on utilitarianism to give such truths a material basis amenable to empirical investigation: "That is good which produces good; that evil, which produces evil; and, where [sic] our sense different from what they are, our virtue and our vice

would be different also."⁵² Under this view, politics is, or at least might become, a science. As an advertisement for *The Library of Political Knowledge*
put it, "The branch of Politics that regards the nature and organization of
Government, has not as yet been reduced into any thing like a regular science. . . . We merely call for an attempt to bring such information as may be
possessed on this matter, into a regular body of doctrines, with an appropriate
nomenclature, so that it may receive those gradual improvements by which
every science advances."⁵³ Political knowledge, then, could be conceived as a
set of objectively verifiable principles, just like chemistry or physics. The science of politics included "the causes of the mutations and accidents in the
forms of government and of laws—and of the rise and fall of nations, with
regard to their strength, civilization, and prosperity, both of its individuals
and of the body politic." Such knowledge, happily, "will at all times prevent
much impropriety of conduct."⁵⁴

This concept of the kind of truth that was relevant to politics found its
best expression in the discipline of political economy, which took a prominent place in structuring political discourse during this period. An early example is Matthew Carey's *Essays on Political Economy,* subtitled "The Most
Certain Means of Promoting the Wealth, Power, Resources and Happiness
of States."⁵⁵ Carey explained his purpose in speaking and writing on political economy in terms culled directly from the Enlightenment tradition. Dis-
avowing the tradition of neoclassical oratory, he declared that his arguments
"shall be addressed to your reason and understanding, without any attempt
to bias your feelings by declamation." His subject, he explained, was political
economy, "the 'science of promoting human happiness'; than which a more
noble subject cannot occupy that attention of men endowed with enlarged
minds, or inspired by public spirit." He went on to express the Enlightenment
faith that political truth is simple and easily accessible: "[I]ts leading principles, calculated to conduct nations safely to the important and beneficial results, which are its ultimate object, are plain and clear; and, to be distinctly
comprehended, and faithfully carried into effect, require no higher endow-
ments than good sound sense and rectitude of intentions."⁵⁶ Carey did not
hesitate to embrace the democratic implications of this understanding of
truth, which challenged the neoclassical assumption that rational arguments
about politics may be beyond the intellectual capacities of the lower classes.
For Carey, all that was needed to understand political economy was "good
sound sense" and "rectitude of intentions," both of which the lower classes
should have in abundance. Thus, it did not worry him that "so many of our
citizens may aspire to the character of legislators and statesmen." Even
though "numberless instances are to be found in history, in which single errors of negotiators and legislators have entailed full as much . . . than the wild

and destructive ambitions of conquerors," the demos could avoid such ruinous mistakes simply by mastering the principles of political economy.[57]

Carey's interests as a political economist lay primarily in the area of developing industry through protective tariffs, but the idea that political debate must be grounded in a scientific understanding of the world spread well beyond the traditional concerns of economic development. For example, Louis Gerteis has demonstrated how political economy was taken up and applied to the slavery issue by abolitionists after 1840, in an effort to forge a political alliance with northern workers. By the 1850s, free labor Republicans, self-consciously rejecting moral arguments against slavery, were using statistical analyses of population, property values, manufacturing, agriculture, and commerce to demonstrate slavery's failure to meet the test of economic efficiency.[58] This reliance on facts and figures represented a general trend in political discourse, fostered by the development of sociology and statistics. Not coincidentally, this period—more specifically, the 1840s—is generally considered to be the inaugural decade of both these sciences in the United States. Both were promoted as vital to political decision making; they were supposed to form the basis for legislation and social policy. In the words of Francis Lieber, "[T]he strictly scientific portion of that great family of civilized nations . . . has acknowledged the great importance to the legislator, and every one else who occupies himself with the welfare of his species, of statistical inquiries."[59] Thus, when Philadelphian George Tucker proposed the formation of a general statistical society, his supporters immediately pointed out the utility of statistics for settling the "great questions that now agitate the public mind."[60] Using statistics, it was argued, would promote the advancement of truth by replacing the "figures of rhetoric" with the "figures of arithmetic." For example, statistics could help the public decide whether the death penalty should be allowed: "It is either right or wrong to take the life of a fellow-being for crime; and it is of infinite importance that the right and wrong be known. Why is there not more unanimity in this matter? . . . Is it not because of the want of exact practical knowledge of the operation of this Sampson of the Criminal Code? Statistical facts are needed which bear upon this subject in every point of view."[61] The author of this remarkable proposition suggested that facts should be collected concerning the proportion of executions to population, the intellectual and moral standing of every people, the efficacy of capital punishment in preventing crime, the condition of the culprit from infancy, and "whether the expense of crime would not, if properly applied, furnish the means of education to every child of man, so that all will become virtuous and happy." His utilitarian assumptions turned the question of whether it is right to take the life of a criminal into a strictly factual question—and the right facts "would forever put at rest the discussion, and settle the punitory policy on such a basis, as will best subserve the public good."[62] Under this view, arguments about the moral worth of the individual, the virtue of compassion and forgiveness, and the justice of retribution—arguments in which rhetorical figures would have a prominent place—should give way to arguments about facts and numbers.

The use of dry sociological and statistical studies in political debate made sense under the Enlightenment model, in which the touchstone of debate was (scientific, objective) truth—not, as in the neoclassical model, persuasion. In fact, the Enlightenment model tended to devalue persuasion, argument, and words in general. Wright, for example, insisted that "all real knowledge is derived from positive sensation," as opposed to being told about things. Her point was that speech cannot communicate knowledge: what we only hear we may believe, but we cannot know. In fact, words "seem at present contrived rather for the purpose of confusing our ideas, than administering to their distinctness and arrangement."[63] Words, in her view, are mere shadows, and eloquence, rather than aiding understanding (as in the neoclassical tradition), inhibits it. Not surprisingly, Wright was even more hostile to argument; she advised her audience to "curb that futile curiousity, which . . . is ever winging the human imagination beyond what the eye hath seen, the touch examined, and the judgment compared. Let us unite on the safe and sure ground of fact and experiment, and we can never err; *yet better, we can never differ.*"[64] This was in fact her goal—to end "unnecessary" political argument, which for Wright seemed to include any argument not aimed at discovering or clarifying the truth. This distinction between substantive and "empty" argument is a standard theme in Enlightenment rationalism, as in Locke's *Essay Concerning Human Understanding:* "[W]here men have got such *determined* ideas of all that they reason, inquire, or argue about, they will find a great part of their doubts and disputes at an end: the greatest part of the questions and controversies that perplex mankind depending on the doubtful and uncertain use of words."[65] Locke set "the discovery of truth" and the "advancement of knowledge" against "artificial argumentation" and "conviction," clearly taking aim at the discipline of rhetoric and its valuation of "unnecessary" argument, both as an end in itself and as a means of obtaining personal glory and power.[66]

The sole purpose of political argument, in the Enlightenment model, is to find the truth. The press took this point to heart. Sounding very much like Locke and Wright in his desire to avoid unnecessary argument, the editor of the *American Advocate* declared, "An editor should . . . pay the same regard to truth in the columns of his papers, as he would in a court of justice; his readers would then be correctly informed, and place confidence in his assertions, and a great deal of dissatisfaction and strife avoided."[67] Similarly, the editor of *The Friend,* a Quaker newspaper, committed himself to "appearing on the side of truth when occasion calls for it, and *exposing error* under all its disguises." The paper, he declared, "has enabled truth for once to out-travel falsehood."[68] James Forten used similar language in characterizing the purpose of Garrison's *Liberator* as "exposing, more and more, the odious system of Slavery." Samuel Cornish echoed this view in calling the *Colored American* "a journal of facts and instruction" that will "bring to light many hidden things."[69]

Political activists not only appreciated the principle that public debate was supposed to discover the truth; they understood the political significance of this inquiry. Nicholas Biddle, for example, defended his decision to use the press in his battle with Andrew Jackson over the Bank of the United States in strictly Enlightenment terms. The press, he wrote, was the natural vehicle for "the free circulation of plain honest truths" about the bank: "When the Bank was denounced by the President, & all the influences of his patronage arrayed against it, it was an obvious duty not to suffer the institution to be crushed by the weight of power—but to appeal directly to the country—and as the whole channel through which the understandings of the community could be reached was the press, we strove to disseminate widely correct information in regard to the Bank."[70] This explanation reflects the Enlightenment conviction that revealing the truth will counter the arbitrary exercise of state power. Consistent with Habermas's thesis, antebellum rationalists incorporated the search for truth into the political system by putting the truth-seeking press in tension with the power-wielding state.

In fact, this opposition between the press and the state (replacing the opposition between speakers assumed by the neoclassical model) was central to antebellum discourse about political debate, perhaps because it answered one of the basic questions raised by the Enlightenment model: if the truth is so plain, why has it taken so long for people to discover it? The political importance of the search for truth rests on the assumption that the truth has been hidden by those in power, in order to maintain their hegemony. Frances Wright, for example, accused the church, "the guardians of religion," of concealing the truth by preventing free inquiry. "Inquiry, it seems, suits not them. They have drawn the line, beyond which human reason shall not pass." But the church was itself constrained by the politically powerful, "because they command the wealth of the country." The church and the state were united in a conspiracy to prevent free inquiry. Thus the conflict between truth and power, embodied by the opposition between the press and the state, underwrote the claim that freedom of discussion constituted "the vital principle of American liberty."[71] A free press was supposed to subject such matters as the utility of a national bank to the forum of public debate, which would (in theory) produce true information and rational opinion. Public sentiment, thus informed, would then be a weapon "constituting a fearful offset to . . . tyranny and persecution." Under this view, public argument was not, as in the neoclassical model, a way to dominate the public; it was a way to bring the exercise of power under the rule of truth and reason.

Personality

The contrast between the Enlightenment and neoclassical models is even more striking in their respective treatments of the role of personality in politics. The Enlightenment tradition is generally hostile to ethical appeals; one of the most common tropes in newspaper editorials was the claim that "we shall prefer principles to men."[72] Personality had no place in political discussion, as the *Christian Chronicle* explained: "Let the discussion be confined to principles, avoiding all personalities, especially in a public discussion; for it is the *truth,* and not the combatants, in which the public has an interest."[73] In other words, "Whoever the author be is of no importance, for our business is with . . . with his doctrines, and not his identity."[74]

The neoclassical model assumed that the public *did* have an interest in the combatants; after all, the public was supposed to surrender its will to the speaker who wins its sympathy, and the speaker's ethos (character and reputation) was the primary means of establishing sympathy. The Enlightenment tradition rejected ethos out of hand, in large part out of a concern that personal attacks would arouse the passions and thus diminish the rationality of debate. The problem was explored in a fictional debate in the *Mechanics' Free Press* between "Federalistus" and "Democritus": Puzzled as to why they could not agree, the Federalist admitted, "I believe we have not been sufficiently careful.—I confess I felt hurt with some remarks of [Democritus] in the early part of the discussion, . . . I am aware, though probably not to the full extent, that I pursued a retaliatory course." Differences of opinion, the writer admonished, should not be taken personally: "[T]hough it is a misfortune, to hold a wrong opinion, it is not censureable—and though there is an advantage in having right opinion, there is no merit in it—right or wrong, they are the result of what is taken for evidence, and are consequently involuntary— hence neither of you, could, with propriety, praise his favourite, or blame his opposer for honest difference of opinion."[75] This position begs some questions, of course. For example, what if one's difference of opinion *isn't* honest? Is it true that opinions are involuntary? What if one's opponent seems to be deliberately refusing to listen to reason? In fact, if the goal of debate is to discover the truth, character may well be a problem—the speaker's passions and interests might prevent him or her from recognizing the truth. Under this model, however, to attack an opponent as irrational is not an argument; it effectually ends the debate, since one cannot conduct a rational inquiry with an irrational person.

There is even less justification for appealing to a speaker's good character. As explained in Chapter 3, such appeals made sense under the neoclassical model because it endorsed intellectual deference to one's social, or at least moral, superiors; the Enlightenment model did not. As Matthew Carey insisted, it is never appropriate for citizens to "surrender their reason into the guidance of any authority whatever. When a position is presented to the mind, the question ought to be, not who delivered it, but what is its nature?" The "reckless boldness of democratic free inquiry" (in the words of the *Democratic Review*) simply isn't consistent with the "humble deference" and "blind veneration and submission" produced through ethical appeals.[76] In short, since the only goal of political debate is the truth, and the speaker's personality is completely irrelevant to the question of whether his or her position is true (even rhetoricians such as George Campbell did not deny this), personality is irrelevant to political discourse.

This norm of impersonality is best illustrated by the common practice of using pseudonyms, particularly in pamphlets and letters to newspaper editors. The convention constituted an implicit rejection of intellectual deference, since it prevented theories from being "propped up by a bead-roll of great names."[77] If the readers didn't know who was writing, their assent to the argument could not be based on their opinion of the author. At the same time, the use of pseudonyms symbolized the rejection of personal self-glorification as a goal of political debate, since it prevented the author from winning personal recognition for his or her efforts. To use a pseudonym, then, was to reject two fundamental features of the neoclassical model: the use of speech to win the audience's submission, and the use of speech to win personal glory. Under the Enlightenment model, debate was not supposed to be instrumental to any goal but revealing the truth, and impersonality was considered critical to obtaining this ideal. The use of pseudonyms therefore expressed the basic orientation of the Enlightenment model away from personality and toward objective truth.

But the use of pseudonyms did not only make political debate less personal. Speakers typically used pseudonyms (such as "Civis," "Hamilton," "Sydney," or "1776") to identify themselves with the revolutionary heritage that defined the political community. These references to the Revolution and republicanism were more than sentimental patriotism; they importantly qualify the norm of impersonality. Although personal characteristics were not supposed to play any role in political debate, this rule did not vitiate the assumption that participants in public debate all adhered to a common set of values and beliefs stemming from the Revolution. Reflecting this assumption, political argument typically started from the premise that the audience "regards with patriotic love the welfare of our country and its sacred institutions."[78] The editor of the *Public Ledger* declared that, "In a republic, a political teacher [referring to newspaper editors] should be well instructed in rights and duties" because "the object of a republican government is to protect rights and duties."[79] The idea that a political teacher might *challenge* the principles of a republican government was not even considered. In the same vein, the *Philadelphia Evening Bulletin* declared that it would "advocate only what is patriotic and right," thus casually ruling out the possibility that what is patriotic might not be right.[80] William Heighton similarly worried that "some of our friends will think it little short of high treason to speak against the laws of our country, which they say are as free as the air we breathe."[81] And even though he criticized American laws, he did so on the grounds that they were not sufficiently republican. The range of legitimate political dissent was quite narrow. Most topics were open to debate in the pages of Philadelphia newspapers, but the desirability of republican government was not. After all, "one half century has conclusively proved the basis of all former theories of government to be false." As the editor of the *United States Gazette* declared, "We cannot believe that there are many citizens of our country who are not at heart, as well as in word, republicans." The *Philadelphia Evening Bulletin* shared this view, estimating that four-fifths of the country was truly democratic.[82]

If political debate is aimed at finding out the truth, and the truth about the desirability of republican institutions is beyond dispute, then there is no need to listen to arguments from persons still harboring aristocratic sentiments, those "kingly fibres" that "yet enlace and poison this commonwealth."[83] This is, of course, an ad hominen argument, but one that carried weight. One all-too-common explanation for political conflict was the belief that dissenting opinions sprang from that disaffected one-fifth alluded to by the *Evening Bulletin*—those who were not, after all, true republicans. For example, in a debate with the *Washington Globe,* the editor of *Niles' Register* found himself defending not only his opinions but also his patriotism. The *Globe,* after castigating Niles for his views, concluded that "he is not an American by birth. He has not the heart of an American." Niles responded that he did indeed have an American heart, being a third-generation Philadelphian whose family had fought in the Revolution.[84] The question of whether Niles's views had a legitimate place in political debate collapsed into the question of whether Niles himself had a legitimate place in political debate.

This assumption that only committed republicans should have a voice in public debate was most evident when the speaker's commitment was questionable. It showed up, for example, in Frances Wright's efforts to establish her credentials to address the American public. Wright was aware that her republicanism was open to challenge, since she was an immigrant who had been raised among European aristocrats. Her enemies did not hesitate to remind her that she wasn't a native American; they implored her to go back to Scotland and "reform [her] native country first."[85] Her response to this problem is interesting, because it contrasts with her response to similar attacks on her religious commitments. When charged with infidelity, Wright simply invoked the norm against ethical arguments, insisting that "[i]n opinions there are but the true and the false," and the public should be concerned only with truth of her beliefs.[86] She might have made a similar answer to charges that she lacked patriotism, arguing that the public should concern itself solely with whether her arguments were correct, not whether she was devoted to American institutions. Instead, she responded to the ethical attack with her own ethical argument, developed in the introduction to her "Course of Popular Lectures." In explaining her motives for addressing the public, she went beyond her usual insistence that she was simply serving the cause of universal truth and justice; she also took pains to establish her Americanism. She described her conversion to American republicanism in terms similar to those typically used to describe a religious conversion: "I first accidentally opened the page of America's national history. . . . [F]rom that moment my attention became rivetted on this country, as on the theatre where man might first awake to the full knowledge and the full exercise of his powers. I immediately collected every work which promised to throw any light on the institutions, character, and condition of the American people."[87] She went on to assert that "the great principles laid down in American government" had "so warmed [her] own feelings" that she saw and heard the Declaration of Independence everywhere.[88] This account explicitly drew on the conventional language of patriotism, such as this description of the republican spirit of a free black man: "He bears upon his person the scar of wounds received in his country's service. He owns a farm which his own hands have cleared—pays his taxes and supports a large and intelligent family, and justly enjoys the respect and confidence of those around him. When the subject of the Revolution is mentioned in his presence, the old man's heart grows warm."[89] Although Wright could not claim battle scars—or, for that matter, a farm or a large and intelligent family—she could, and did, claim that she had an American heart. But what is interesting about her narrative is not the way she defended her patriotism, but simply the fact that she did. It suggests that Wright, like her audience, believed that the public had a legitimate interest in her commitment to American republicanism.

What are we to make of this public interest in the political commitments of speakers? Was this an exception to the general rule against ethos, or simply a mistake—an illegitimate resort to personality? Since ethical appeals were both common and widely condemned, it's difficult to gauge whether some of these appeals were considered more legitimate than others. But I suggest that this category of ethical argument could be justified without departing completely from Enlightenment principles, because confining debate to true republicans was actually supposed to *limit* the influence of personality in public debate, and thereby preserve its rationality. To be a republican was, in essence, to be devoted to the public good instead of private interests; as one editor observed, "the predominance of personal interests and feelings" is inconsistent with the concept of republicanism."[90] More specifically, speakers' common devotion to the revolutionary tradition and American institutions gave content to the concept of "the public good," which in turn informed the ground rules that contained political debate.

Speakers were regularly instructed that when they engaged in debate, they should subordinate their private ends to the public good. In the words of the editor of the *National Gazette,* "[E]ach citizen at a public meeting enjoys a peculiar trust and dignity above and beyond his distinguished position as a freeman. His voice there having potentiality for public good or evil, his place should be likened unto that of a representative of the people. . . . A sense of individual ennoblement thus specially conferred, would have the tendency to antagonize the ordinary evils of popular assemblies, resulting from intemperate fervor, party rancor and riotous dispositions."[91] By acting as representatives of the public, participants would ensure that debate would have that temperate, orderly character conducive to discovering the truth and reaching consensus. For example, one Philadelphian criticized participants in a debate over the location of a city market for being "influenced more by personal convenience or interest, than from motives of public good, (at least a majority)." He recommended that participants act as representatives of the city as a whole; they should "divest [themselves], as far as possible, of personal motives, and consider the citizens of each and every section of [their] city, and adjoining districts, equally entitled to the advantages and conveniences (if any) arising from our public arrangements."[92] If all the participants followed these instructions, the problem of locating the market would become a simple matter of determining population and distances, and thus would be amenable to the type of objective, scientific—and orderly—investigation promoted by the Enlightenment model. In this way, the participants' shared commitment to (a particular conception of) the public good would prevent debate from degenerating under the influence of individual interests; it would preserve the impersonality, and therefore the rationality, of the debate. The requirement that participants be good republicans, then, was simply the other side of the norm of impersonality: engaging in public debate in an impersonal manner meant engaging in debate from the standpoint of a committed republican.

Limiting participation to republicans can be justified without departing from Enlightenment principles because, under the Enlightenment model, debate was not an end in itself (as in the neoclassical model) but a means to an end, namely, finding the truth. Since the goal of debate was to find the truth, it was acceptable to exclude people whose participation would impair the rationality of the debate. Of course, this reasoning could be mobilized to exclude whole classes of people, such as women, blacks, or immigrants, who might be considered incapable of the type of rationality and/or civility that public debate called for. But if the Enlightenment model is not inherently inclusive, neither is it inherently exclusive; rationality could serve as a reason to include previously excluded voices as well. Recall, for example, Angelina Grimké's debate with Catharine Beecher. Beecher argued that the participation of women would degrade the quality of public debate about slavery, not because they were incapable of rational debate (a proposition Beecher would never have affirmed) but because men would not take the norm of impersonality so far as to engage in rational debate with women—the master would not take reproof from the nursery maid. Grimké responded that women, and by implication blacks, must participate, because only they knew the truth about the harms of slavery—only the nursery maid was in a position to reprove the master.[93] Truth, then, was a two-edged sword: it included the epistemically privileged, but excluded the civically impaired.

In sum, the norm of impersonality was supposed to contribute to truth and rationality, as well as equality. It undermined the intellectual deference and personal self-glorification that characterized political debate under the neoclassical model, but it also encouraged participants to approach debate from the point of view of the public good (defined by the shared belief in republican values). This, in turn, was supposed to prevent the predominance of personal interests and feelings that could lead to irresolvable conflict. The norm of impersonality therefore diminished the potential for inequality, disorder, and conflict inherent in political argument. If citizens put the good of the whole community before their personal interests, then "blind veneration," "party rancor," and riotousness should be avoided, and the truth should emerge.

So far, the Enlightenment model of political debate seems to promise a rational, egalitarian, and orderly popular politics, in contrast to the neoclassical model. But it does so by ruling out both the legitimacy of political conflict arising out of disagreement about values and the possibility that the truth might not be easily accessible. And we haven't yet considered the most troublesome aspect of the model: how exactly does it work? That is, how does temperate, objective political debate translate into rational policy? On this point the antebellum version of the Enlightenment model differs importantly from Habermas's description. In Habermas's account, rational debate is supposed to move from the public sphere into the legislature, where it will be carried on by politicians seeking the advancement of their own or their party's fortunes; this legislative debate will then result in rational policy—at least in the sense that policy will be supported by reasons, and presumably good reasons (though that is hardly assured in Habermas's model).[94] But according to the rhetoric permeating antebellum political discourse, Americans wanted not simply policy that is supported by reasons, but policy based on *truth*. Unfortunately, it is much harder to explain how public debate will produce truth—or, more precisely, it is hard to explain why the public would be convinced by the truth rather than by the incorrect arguments that the truth must contend against, and why they would be moved to act on the truth once they understood it.

Conviction and Motivation

Judging from much of the rhetoric about political debate, truth is supposed to vanquish error automatically. In the words of Benjamin Franklin, "when Truth has fair Play, it will always prevail over Falsehood."[95] What gives the truth this advantage? According to Nicholas Biddle, truth has an "irresistible power." Wright agreed: "Could truth only be heard, the conversion of the ignorant were easy."[96] Workingmen's advocate John Ferral thought that the success of the 1835 general strike in Philadelphia constituted good evidence of this principle. The Philadelphia strike was part of a general ten-hour movement that swept through the northern states in the summer of 1835, beginning in Boston and spreading as far south as Baltimore. Whereas the Boston strike was confined mainly to the building trades and was soon defeated, the Philadelphia strike was joined by most mechanics and received support from the city council and even the professional classes. The workers prevailed; by the end of June, most trades in Philadelphia had adopted the ten-hour policy. Ferral attributed this success to the power of truth. In his account, the Philadelphia strike was prompted by a circular issued by the Boston workingmen's organization explaining their reasons for striking in favor of a ten-hour day. The circular, wrote Ferral, "plucked the veil from off the eyes of the industrious portion of the community," revealing the "duplicity of all the party press in Philadelphia," which (he claimed) had hidden the truth about the circumstances of the Boston strike. Once the workers read the circular, a successful strike was inevitable: "[O]ur weapons were reason and truth, which sooner or later must triumph wherever they are wielded."[97]

Conspicuously absent from this rhetoric is any mention of persuasion or motivation; Ferral accepted as a matter of course that once the people were exposed to the correct ideas, they would recognize their errors and act accordingly. This lacuna is not an oversight. Ferral's faith in the automatic effect of truth on public opinion was based not on a theoretical account of the connection between speech and action, such as that which informs neoclassical rhetoric, but on a historical account of the relationship between truth and liberty—on the claim that truth historically *had* conquered error and, at the same time, injustice. As Heighton put it: "From the remote ages of antiquity, down to the present period, a large majority of the human family in all civilized nations, have been kept in a state of degradation and poverty. . . . Where then has justice slept? Or in what chains has it been confined, that it has not arisen in its power . . . ? It is the trifold band of ignorance, prejudice, and superstition, which has, for so many ages, held justice an unresisting captive."[98] Heighton argued that "the want of information relative to their rights and powers" had allowed the working class to be controlled by their superiors.[99] Under this view, the diffusion of the truth robbed the powerful of their chief means of controlling the people (disinformation), and thus automatically undermined their despotism. How exactly did disinformation allow the rulers to control the masses? Modern readers may read into this account some notion of ideology, but in fact the arguments circulating through conventional antebellum politics did not typically draw on any such sophisticated theoretical concepts. Instead, writers and speakers simply gestured toward the widely known narratives about the authorities persecuting those who challenged orthodoxy (Galileo, Martin Luther, and so forth). Apparently, these stories of official persecution constituted sufficient evidence that truth was inimical to power. The precise connection between truth and liberty remained somewhat mysterious.

Of course, to the extent that publishing the truth is a *component* of freedom, the connection between truth and liberty is clear. One important strain of Enlightenment rhetoric defended freedom of speech on the grounds that it is a civil and religious liberty in its own right.[100] But the claim I am examining here is stronger: publishing the truth is supposed to secure *other* liberties. In Greeley's words, liberty of the press is supposed to be the palladium of *all* liberties. For this position to be coherent, it must include some account of how publishing the truth will lead to political action in defense of other liberties.

We can fill out this picture to some extent by referring to a standard Enlightenment argument about the relationship between deference and political subordination. As discussed in Chapter 3, Adam Smith argued that deference prevented the masses from challenging their rulers, even when it was in their best interest to do so. This argument implies that barriers to rational calculation (deference, ignorance, and so forth) are the only things preventing the people from taking action to correct injustices. Of course, this may be the case in some specific historical circumstances. But even if deference, ignorance, and superstition are pervasive obstacles to political action, the proposition that publishing the truth will, as a general rule, undermine tyranny begs two critical questions. First, why should truth automatically prevail over the mistaken opinions that have been propagated by the authorities? Second, why should independent, rational thought necessarily lead to (successful) political action? In many cases, after all, one might rationally calculate that political action would be fruitless.

Take the first question: why should truth prevail over mistaken opinions? I touched on this problem earlier when I considered why, if the truth is obvious, it has only recently been discovered. Frances Wright argued that the truth had been hidden by those in power—most prominently the clergy, whose influence depended on persuading people to believe in lies and superstition, but also the political rulers (who presumably benefited from the deference and passivity of an ignorant public). This was a popular explanation, especially among working-class radicals. As one mechanic congratulated, "It was not till this country was established, that an advocate could be found bold enough to attack the strong holds of priestly and monkish power. Before that time, religious usurpation was merely whispered, but thenceforth it was openly and publicly denounced; and political freedom was followed in many cases with total indifference to the vain ceremonies and dogmas of its ambitious supporters. . . . Ever since their enemies have increased, and they have never been able to silence the powerful voice of science and philosophy."[101] This sounds very much like Wright—but Wright, unlike this optimistic mechanic, did not believe that religious usurpation *was* being openly and publicly denounced in the United States. On the contrary, she considered Americans to be far too subservient to their clergy.[102] How, then, did she explain the failure of truth to prevail in a country where the state did not actively prohibit its dissemination?

For Wright, the major obstacles to the triumph of truth, besides its actual suppression by governmental authority, were passion and interest. The negative effects of passion on the search for truth have already been considered. Passion can affect judgment; thus, as Wright put it, as long as we are "irrational, perverse, ill-natured, violent, prone to misinterpret, to offend in our manner, to irritate in our language, to wound and to be wounded," we are "ill prepared to elicit truth by the shock of opinions in the subtle field of argument."[103] These problems can be overcome if we strive to be dispassionate, but interest posed another set of difficulties. According to Wright, the desire for power and wealth was inimical to truth and free inquiry, since, in order to gain either, one must "assume the semblance of such opinions . . . as rule the ascendant." Our teachers, she argued, "are *compelled* to administer to our prejudices, and to perpetuate our ignorance. They dare not speak that which, by endangering their popularity, would endanger their fortunes. They have to discover . . . not what will search into the hearts and minds of their hearers, but what will open their purse strings."[104] Either the church itself or those upon whom the church was financially dependent controlled the distribution of wealth and power and could therefore provide an incentive *not* to seek and disseminate those truths that would undermine their authority. Given the present distribution of wealth and power in society, then, one would have to be disinterested in order to pursue the truth (or one's interest in the truth would have to outweigh one's interest in not offending the powerful, a possibility that Wright did not explicitly consider).

But the problem with interest is not just that it might distract people from the search for the truth. Material interest, according to standard eighteenth- and nineteenth-century moral philosophy, impairs one's ability to recognize the truth. In Locke's melancholy judgment, "Let ever so much probability hang on one side of a covetous man's reasoning, and money on the other; it is easy to see what will outweigh."[105] Interest, like passion, introduces bias into the judgment that interferes with the triumph of truth. Therefore, although interest might in some cases provide a sufficient incentive to search for the truth, such a strong interest might equally lead one astray. In short, to ensure that the truth will prevail, one first has to ensure that interest will not stand in its way.

This sounds like an argument for a disinterested politics; truth is obvious only to dispassionate *and* disinterested actors, so there is no reason to believe that truth will prevail if political actors are motivated by interest. But what else could motivate them? As Wright pointed out, "Zeal may impart energy to our first movements, but will not generate and nourish those steady motives which, by sustaining equal and healthy exertions, can alone ensure success."[106] What steady motives was she referring to, if not interest? What would prompt a good Enlightenment rationalist to put down the newspaper and go out and fight injustice, not just once in a while, but regularly?

Apparently, some hoped that action would follow automatically from belief, just as belief was supposed to follow automatically (barring the effects of passion or interest) from exposure to the truth. For example, moral reform advocate William Whipper claimed that reform could be accomplished without engaging in electoral politics: "It is our duty to inform and enlighten public opinion on this subject. Let us aim at a correct public opinion, and cease to regard who frames the laws; for it is on this basis that all laws are founded."[107] This argument transforms the conviction that laws should be based on public opinion into a reason not to engage in electoral politics. If laws simply reflect public opinion, then one need only expose the truth and let it shape public opinion; the laws will follow automatically.

Whipper's disavowal of the need for electoral politics was extreme, though not unusual for those involved in the moral reform movement. Others acknowledged that something more than public debate was needed to accomplish political change. The workingmen's movement, for example, focused on the need to elect representatives from the working class to pursue their interests in the legislatures. William Heighton insisted that "[w]e shall never reap any benefit from [the government] until we have men of our own nominating, men whose interests are in unison with ours."[108] So was it interest that was supposed to motivate these workers to go to the polls? Perhaps; the literature of the workingmen's movement contained positive as well as negative references to interest. For example, workers' advocates argued that the end of politics was to "promote the just interests . . . of each individual," and that interest was the most reliable influence in politics: "Was ever a class of men heard of, who acted in direct opposition to what they conceived to be their interest?"[109] But usually such positive references to interest implied not a narrow and short-sighted individual interest but something like class interest, or even "the real prosperity and welfare of *all classes.*"[110] So we are left with essentially the same question: what would motivate a good Enlightenment rationalist to fight for the real interests of all classes?

It may be useful at this point to look more closely at the concept of "interest" and its relationship to principle. The concept of interest, as Albert Hirschman has explained, originally entered into political theory in the late sixteenth century, as a counterbalance to the passions that were thought to drive destructive state policies. Increasingly applied to groups and individuals, the term came to denote a kind of rationalized passion, a desire that is the fruit of careful reflection and consideration. Thus a variety of Enlightenment theorists seized on interest as a safer and more reliable guide to action than the wayward passions.[111] Nevertheless, the core of interest is essentially passion, or desire, which is why it can motivate action (as reason alone presumably cannot) and why it can bias the judgment as passion does. Moreover, since interest involves reflection and calculation, people may be mistaken about their interests, as they seldom are about their feelings (a debatable proposition certainly, but a necessary assumption for this argument).

If individual interest is a rationalized, long-term sort of passion, then public interest may be conceived as even more rationalized and long term—the concrete benefit of the whole society, which may be inconsistent with an individual's short-term interest (hence the difficulty of collective action). Of course, as interest becomes more rationalized in this way, it moves further away from passion, the basic spring of human action. Acting out of a concern for the public interest, then, begins to look like acting on reason alone, or acting on principle, on a conviction about what is right. The question here is which of these possibilities—individual interest, the public interest, or principle—ought to be or can be relied on to govern political action?

William Elder's discussion of this question, in reference to the advisability of forming an abolition party, is instructive. The chief problem with principle, he noted, is that "the multitude of working men . . . are too much occupied with their own social and pecuniary privations. . . . They are not so much at ease in their own condition as to feel the impulses of a disinterested philanthropy."[112] He did not mean to suggest that principle cannot guide mass politics; on the contrary, even the impecunious worker will act on general principles when they relate to his own material conditions: "[I]t is the great problem of labor, its relations to capital, or the *system of property*, that occupies these people. Bring them a system of rights and remedies in this interest and they will listen." But when political philosophy ventures too far from the public's immediate interests, "they are not concerned." The matter of slavery, for example, excites little interest among white workers because it "touches the free laborer nowhere near enough to be felt vehemently." While the public may occasionally act out of disinterested philanthropy—"[a] great idea may, indeed, monopolize the attention of a community for a time"—it is not reliable; "we must not expect conformity to good conscience and the Divine will in the administration of affairs."[113]

For Elder, then, interest is a more reliable motive than principle; unfortunately, interest is unlikely to produce action on behalf of despised minorities such as the slaves. But even if we could achieve a politics of principle, we might not want to. Elder worried that too great a devotion to principle made one less fit for republican politics. "The anti-slavery man who is most capable of sacrifice," for example, "is also the least disposed to compromise." A principled man "is intent on saving his own soul and maintaining his consistency of principle, whatever becomes of the enterprise." In other words, although he may be acting rationally in the sense that he is following abstract principles of justice, he may not be exhibiting instrumental rationality, a prudent concern with choosing the proper means to effect his goal. And instrumental rationality, "the adjustment, every moment demanded, of principles to affairs, in order to effect the greatest possible good in the circumstances," is what politics requires. Elder's primary concern was that principled actors may be less effective: "[A] man may justify himself by doing no wrong, though at the expense of doing nothing useful for the excellent end in view."[114] But one might equally fear that the only people who consistently act out of principle are deranged fanatics, a charge leveled with depressing consistency at the abolitionists. Antebellum politics provided ample evidence, in such figures as William Lloyd Garrison and John Brown, that passion and principle do not necessarily conflict with each other; on the contrary, principles might inspire passion, and a potentially destructive passion at that.

In sum, we have a complicated set of problems related to motivation. On the one hand, if we rely exclusively on appeals to interest to motivate political action, politics may be overridden by the kind of narrow, selfish interests that bias the judgment and lead to conflict. Appeals to the public interest or principle, on the other hand, are too abstract to motivate a majority of the citizens consistently. And those who *are* motivated by such appeals may be unwilling to compromise their integrity by getting involved in the give-and-take of politics; or even worse, they may be crazy zealots unwilling to observe the basic rules that contain political conflict. The prospects for the triumph of truth look fairly bleak.

The neoclassical model avoided these difficulties because it accepted conflict as endemic to politics and discarded truth as a goal of public debate; the problems of conviction and motivation arose under the Enlightenment model only because it maintained an ideal of conflict-free, wholly rational debate that would tend ineluctably toward the truth. But its very failure to give a satisfactory answer to these problems was also, in a sense, its chief virtue. By glossing over the problems of conviction and motivation, the Enlightenment model was able to preserve the rational independence of the audience. Under this model, the only agent is truth: it is truth that exercises its irresistible power over the mind of the audience, that convinces and motivates—not, as in the neoclassical model, the eloquence of the orator. This formula corrects the problematic relationship between the speaker and the audience under the neoclassical model, in which the speaker was considered to dominate the will of the audience and thereby impair its rational independence. It allowed John Ferral, for example, to attribute the general strike to the effect of the Boston circular—the argument itself—and not its author, Seth Luther, thus protecting Luther from the charge of demagoguery. This was the strength of the Enlightenment model: the audience does not submit its will to another person, but to truth and reason—which is, of course, the very definition of rational independence.

Nevertheless, the pervasive influence of this model of public debate is somewhat puzzling. Although it preserved the public's rational independence, it did so in a singularly unconvincing manner. After all, truth does not auto-

matically vanquish error—at least not without assistance from "artful persuasions"—and even if it did, laws do not automatically follow from a change
in public opinion. So why were Horace Greeley, Nicholas Biddle, Frances
Wright, and William Heighton (to name only a few) so insistent that the
right would prevail, given free and open discussion? Such language can be
attributed in part to simple bravado; expressing an inordinate confidence in
one's own cause can help to rally supporters. But there are less Machiavellian
explanations for this vocal faith in the power of truth. This rhetoric had deep
roots in antebellum political culture, harmonizing with two important political languages: Christian millennialism and the eighteenth-century revolutionary tradition.

Christians shared the Enlightenment faith in the irresistible power of
truth, but they had a different truth in mind. Quaker preacher Lucretia Mott
sounded like an Enlightenment rationalist when she argued that the "enquir-
ing state of the public mind in England" would soon lead to the abolition of
capital punishment. But Mott rested her faith in the inevitable triumph of
truth on the work of the Holy Spirit: "As enquiry proceeds, men will discover
the principle of forgiveness, and will feel the power of the spirit of love."[115]
This tendency to assimilate Enlightenment truth (facts, figures, and general
scientific principles) and Christian truth (God's revealed will) permeated the
political discourse of the moral reformers. Thus, when abolitionist Angelina
Grimké insisted that "if the organ of vision is only clear, the whole body . . .
will soon be thrown into powerful action," she was not only expressing a
naive confidence in the agency of Enlightenment truth; she was expressing
faith in the agency of God, working through men to accomplish "the great
and glorious work of reforming the world."[116] Because Christian and Enlightenment concepts of truth were fused in the rhetoric of moral reform, the
Christian faith in the coming of the millennium (which was thought by
many evangelical Christians to be imminent) gave some support to the Enlightenment model's assumption of the irresistibility of truth.

This trope also echoed eighteenth-century revolutionary rhetoric, which
remained popular among working-class radicals. As discussed in Chapter 1,
the Whig tradition took the spontaneity of mass political action as evidence
that the people's cause was legitimate (since only a real, concrete grievance
could arouse the usually lethargic public). This element of the revolutionary tradition had remarkable longevity in American political discourse, particularly in northern cities where the workingmen's movement kept the tradition alive. Antebellum actors regularly referred to the spontaneity of mass
movements (such as rallies, strikes, or electoral successes) to demonstrate the
legitimacy of their cause. "A rising of the democracy *en masse*," claimed one
editor, "is an indication of popular feeling too significant to be mistaken."

Such general uprisings were reliable because they were unlikely to be the result of conspiratorial machinations—or else the conspiracy must be "coextensive with the State," as one editor felicitously put it. The people can be counted on to know their best interests without being told by politicians; they manifest "a perfect knowledge . . . of the character, deeds, and intentions of their opponents. . . . There is an intelligence in democracy which cannot be denied."[117] This language actually goes beyond the Enlightenment distrust of persuasive speech, making public deliberation itself seem suspect—as though deliberation should not only take place in private but shouldn't even be influenced by public argument. This isn't entirely consistent with the Enlightenment conviction that the free play of reasoned argument is critical to an informed judgment, nor with Americans' long-standing fear of politics conducted in private (it carries connotations of conspiracy). Nevertheless, the language of spontaneity resonated with the Enlightenment conviction of the irresistibility of truth. For example, John Ferral drew on both traditions in describing the effect of the Boston circular. The circular, he claimed, had simply put the truth before the people; the general strike was a spontaneous expression of "that sympathy of feeling, which pervades all intelligent working men." No exhortations or organizational efforts were needed; once the workers had learned the truth, "one motive seemed to pervade the mass," producing a "harmonious and almost simultaneous action of the great body of the useful classes in this great and glorious cause."[118] The automatic impact of truth helped to account for the spontaneity of mass political action.

Conversely, the Whig tradition supplied one of the missing elements in the Enlightenment model, in the conviction that the public will be motivated to take political action when their basic rights are violated. If the people are generally jealous of their rights and can be counted on to know what they are (both problematic assumptions—recall the hapless Barbadians), then revealing the truth about government abuses may be enough to motivate them to act. Happily, rights, in the Whig tradition, combine interest and principle in just the right way: people are presumed to have a concrete interest in the protection of their rights and to feel it when those rights are violated (so errors in judgment are unlikely). But rights are also the particular expression of general political principles. Therefore, acting in defense of rights can further both individual interest and general principle. Unfortunately, this solution to the problem of motivation comes at the expense of limiting the scope of popular political action to redressing serious invasions of basic rights. Eighteenth-century Whigs, of course, never suggested that popular participation should go beyond this watchdog role; as Madison put it, the people's "eyes must be ever ready to mark, their voice to pronounce, and their arm to repel or repair aggressions on the authority of their constitutions," and that should be sufficient.[119] Antebellum Democrats, in contrast, expected the people to *govern,* and the Whig tradition (which typically characterizes the public as apathetic about government except when their liberties are at stake) provides little help in explaining how they would be motivated to do so. But at least to the extent that popular politics could be conceptualized as resistance to serious but secret government oppression, the eighteenth-century revolutionary tradition provided some crucial support to the Enlightenment faith in the power of truth.

At least some antebellum actors, then, may have had reason to insist on the automatic power of truth. But the lack of attention in the Enlightenment model to the actual mechanisms needed to persuade or motivate the public demands further explanation. I suggest that these problems were neglected because, during this period, the dominant concern among the political elite, especially in politically turbulent cities such as Philadelphia, was not motivating political action but constraining it. Given the general anxiety about riotousness, any action taken to arouse the masses was vulnerable to the charge that it promoted licentiousness. No one complained that the public was apathetic; on the contrary, the typical complaint about mass politics was that the public was too involved. The populace is "already too excitable, and too prone to violence," complained the *Pennsylvanian.* Both the *Philadelphia Evening Bulletin* and the *Public Ledger* similarly criticized political campaigning on the grounds that it excited the people and led to riotousness.[120] But this conservative temper also infected the discourse of the activists who wanted to promote popular excitement, perhaps because expressing confidence in the irresistible power of truth constituted an implicit disavowal not only of the "artful persuasions" of rhetoric but also of violence and mob action. If one believes that the truth will prevail automatically, one needn't try to arouse the masses by appealing to their passions. For example, nativist John Hancock Lee used this language to disassociate his party from the riots it was widely accused of provoking. In contrast to the typical characterization of members of the Native American Party as rabble-rousing demagogues, he insisted, "Never did a movement, commenced with so little noise, parade and show, commend itself so forcibly to the understandings and better feelings of the people." The movement, then, was not engineered; it "commended itself." Party leaders did not need to resort to potentially disorderly "parade and show," because they had truth (both Enlightenment and Christian) on their side: "As though the hand of Providence were in the work directing and controlling it, the measures of the new party met with the general approbation of all who were not governed by opposing political party principles, or blinded by the misrepresentations of those whose interests depended upon arresting the progress of the principles of the new associations."[121] Lee thus drew on the doctrine of the irresistibility of truth to describe the movement as a spontaneous reaction by reasonable citizens to self-evidently true principles, thereby countering claims of demagoguery and riotousness. In this way, expressing belief in the irresistible power of truth could legitimate one as a political actor; it identified the speaker with the politics of rationality and order, rather than passion and violence.

Of course, one might also take this language not simply as declaring faith in the truth but as expressing an ideal that the political community should aspire to. After all, rational, dispassionate debate *would* be sufficient for the triumph of truth if the public were rational, dispassionate, and already committed to political action in the service of the public good.[122] In other words, this model of debate assumes—or, more properly, promotes—a particular conception of the political community: It should be composed of intellectually independent rationalists who are impervious to emotional or ethical appeals, but who can be moved to action on a regular basis by appeals to reason. They should be open to persuasion only by objective, factual information and concerned only with the general welfare rather than particular interests. There would be no leaders or followers in this community; equality would be ensured because rational independence would be preserved. It would be, in short, a community of reasonable people, reasoning together.

To the extent that the Enlightenment model served as an ideal to be aspired to, it expressed perfectly the values that antebellum Americans apparently wanted their politics to embody: rationality, order, and equality. Unfortunately, this ideal left little room for the actual mechanisms by which the people were being mobilized to participate in political debate, a point illustrated vividly by Enlightenment criticisms of the party press. The existence of parties, and in particular their close association with the press, was a major problem for advocates of the Enlightenment model. The difficulty was not that the party press imperfectly realized the Enlightenment ideal but that, when evaluated in Enlightenment terms, institutionalizing public debate in the party press looked like a mistake altogether. Moreover, this incompatibility between the Enlightenment model and the party press points toward a deeper tension between the Enlightenment model of political debate and partisan mass politics in general. The Enlightenment model not only obscured the problems of persuasion and motivation; it posed a significant barrier to legitimating the actual mechanisms of popular politics.

The Problem of Parties

The party press was, and was understood to be, the primary vehicle for political debate. But the party press was, of course, partisan, and therein lay the trouble. The problems created by this manner of institutionalizing political debate are neatly illustrated in Nicholas Biddle's unhappy experience with the press during the Bank War. In 1830, Biddle, in his capacity as president of the second Bank of the United States, was just beginning his long struggle to persuade Congress to renew the bank's charter. President Jackson's annual message to Congress had signaled the party's official position against renewal, a position that was soon being argued in the Democratic papers—most prominently, New York's *Courier and Enquirer*. One of Jackson's chief objections to the bank was that it had impaired the soundness of the currency, a claim that convinced Biddle that opposition to the bank was based mainly on ignorance. To correct public—and presidential—opinion, Biddle prepared a report on the soundness of American currency. He submitted this document to the Senate Finance Committee's Senator Smith, and it became the committee's offical report. He then sent copies of this report and the House's report (which also defended the soundness of the currency) to the party papers, paying some editors to publish them, and he published them himself as pamphlets—at the bank's expense.

The practice of paying editors to publish material was common, but Biddle nevertheless considered it necessary to defend himself. He explained, "The whole influence of [Jackson's] government and of the presses subservient to his government, is employed in endeavoring to break down the Bank. In this situation, the Bank can only find safety in such explanations of its proceedings as will satisfy the country that it has been unjustly assailed and that its operations are highly beneficial. But how is it to make these explanations except through the press, the only channel of communication with the people? And if it employs that channel, why should it ask of printers to insert its explanations gratuitously?"[123] By anthropomorphizing the bank, Biddle was able to apply the language of Enlightenment rationalism to the situation, framing it as a conflict between the government, which was supposedly spreading lies to further its oppressive ends, and the citizen (the bank), which was simply trying to defend itself (himself?) by countering the government's lies with the truth.

But Biddle had more difficulty justifying his next step. He decided that he needed to secure the continuing support of the Democratic press. Fortuitously, one of the owners of the *Courier and Enquirer* was planning to sell his interest, and Mordecai Noah, an editor on the paper, was interested in buying it. All he needed was a loan of $15,000. Biddle was informed of this situation by Silas Burrows, a rather shady and, as it turned out, untrustworthy character that Biddle relied on for information about New York politics. Burrows told Biddle that Noah's opposition to the bank would dissolve if he could secure a loan from the bank. Biddle accordingly arranged the loan, without informing the bank's directors. After Noah bought a share of the paper, its position on the bank *did* change—but not, apparently, as a result of the loan, since Burrows later claimed that he never told Noah where the loan had come from. The change in editorial opinion more likely reflected a change in the position of the New York Democratic Party, whose leaders had concluded that Jackson's attacks on the bank were hurting his reelection chances. In fact, the whole premise of Biddle's plan was questionable—the newspaper could not easily take a position that was at odds with the local Democratic Party, since it was the party's organ. It depended on the party's political advertising and patronage, and the political editor was appointed by the party's General Committee.[124]

This was not the only loan the bank made to newspapers, though it was apparently the only one made with the intent of influencing editorial policy. But the fact that the bank made loans to newspapers at all became a major issue during the 1832 congressional investigation into the bank's practices. The details of this particular loan were not discovered during the investigation, but the possibility that they might be prompted Biddle to confess his machinations to the bank's directors. Biddle survived the controversy, but director Thomas Cadwalader was so shocked by the affair that he considered resigning.[125] Whereas the practice of paying editors to print the congressional reports was relatively easy for Biddle to justify in terms of the Enlightenment model, he had no defense for the practice of paying editors to change their own opinions. His official position reflects the Enlightenment ideas informing his understanding of acceptable political practice: "The Bank is glad to have friends from conviction, but seeks to make none from interest."[126] To an Enlightenment rationalist, paying an editor to espouse one's own views looks too much like the practices used by oppressors to perpetuate their lies; the truth, after all, is not supposed to need such help.

Biddle's embarrassments illustrate the unhappy reality facing a dedicated Enlightenment rationalist in the antebellum era: interest, in the form of money and power, was the engine driving political debate. The party press was not, or not only, an open forum for political discussion; it was part of a larger system for distributing political power. After all, party newspapers were established for the express purpose of advancing political doctrines or electing persons to office. They were therefore intimately involved in webs of financial and political dependence. To antebellum critics of the press, these dependencies created two obstacles to free inquiry: corruption and partisanship.

Corruption

In theory, the press was supposed to remain independent of the government so that it could criticize the exercise of government power. If the press were dependent on the government, that interest might impair its ability and willingness to report the full truth. In fact, however, the party presses *were* dependent on the government, particularly when their respective parties were in power. Party papers were financed by parties both in the form of initial capital and in the promise of government printing jobs, which the party could secure if and when it captured the legislature. These printing jobs were a standard form of patronage, and defection from the administration's positions was considered a reason to refuse such patronage (whether it was a legitimate reason is less clear, as we shall see). Party newspapers depended heavily on such subsidies.[127]

Although patronage was standard practice, it was not taken for granted. One bemused editor noted the uproar in New York when the *Courier and Enquirer* attempted to secure, by legislative enactment, the exclusive right to publish the government's official list of insolvents. "[W]hat is the difference," he wondered, "between an enactment to give a certain partizan paper all the profits of public printing, and the *custom* of doing the same? We never think of complaining that the Jackson papers of Philadelphia, obtain all the public patronage in that way."[128] But people did complain; the press's dependence on patronage was a favorite theme of newspaper editors. The editor of the *National Gazette* pointed out the basic contradiction between the custom of patronage and the role of the press: "[T]here can be no real independence of the press where patronage is . . . indiscriminately bestowed, or given, preferably, to mere party-prejudices and designs. The situation of the conductor is too precarious to admit of an unreserved discussion of all questions of national or municipal concern—of the indication of all abuses, and full resistance to all irregular or inordinate schemes or wishes. Several of the most important topics are *tabood* [*sic*]."[129] This editor, at least, did not consider patronage to be legitimate. On being accused of being one of the host of newspapers "rewarded" by Jackson, he indignantly insisted that he had "neither sought nor received any benefit from the President;—no attempts have been made upon the independence of this gazette."[130]

Clearly, a newspaper could not plausibly maintain its independence from the government if it was supported by the party in power. But the liberty of the press was considered to be impaired not only by a newspaper's relationship with the government but also by its relationship with political parties. One editor declared that "[n]o journals are less entitled to be called free, than those which acknowledge the epithets *Administration* or *Opposition*." This position reveals the conflict between the antebellum American and the Habermasian interpretations of the relationship between the press and the state. As Habermas explains it, the press is free if it is in a position to criticize the exercise of government power. In his view, the fact that the opposition's desire to secure power constitutes its primary motive to engage in this exercise is not a problem.[131] But for observers of antebellum politics, this dynamic *was* a problem. According to them, opposition papers were also corrupt, because "if they do not exist through funds contributed to maintain them in a prescribed or stipulated course of doctrine and action, they studiously minister to the aims of particular men or associations, they push aside truth and right; as they eagerly contend for party objects."[132]

The problem with the party press was that it was not disinterested. It had a financial interest through which it was linked to the interests of power-seeking politicians. This knot of interests conflicted with its mission of revealing the truth. As Frances Wright argued, those seeking power have as much incentive to obscure the truth as those who currently hold power. According to the *National Gazette,* "The devoted advocate, or fixed enemy, of the administration . . . is really shackled and lamentably warped. . . . When either of them . . . undertakes to convey sentiments and conclusions of his own, it must ever be on one side—with a special oblique directon."[133] *Niles' Register* put the matter even more plainly: "It is against *standing orders* to acknowledge truth made manifest,—a falsehood or calumny, once fairly afloat, is rather bolstered by new emissions than corrected, that the people may be undeceived and rightly understand the character of public men and public measures."[134] Both opposition and administration papers, then, were perverting the quest for truth. Biddle, according to this reasoning, was just as culpable as Jackson in linking the newspapers' financial interests to his political agenda; even his practice of paying editors to print the House and Senate reports was questionable. Interest inevitably impairs the search for truth. Any connection between truth seeking and power seeking was, for antebellum rationalists, a contradiction.

Partisanship

Unfortunately, it was not simply newspapers' financial dependence on parties that impaired their ability to seek the truth. Partisanship itself was often considered to be incompatible with the rational independence that was essential to truth seeking. Biddle, for example, contrasted the "intemperance of party" with "a manly independence founded on honor and maintained with firmness without descending to adopt the prejudices or to be guided by the passions of others." Similarly, Governor Johnston distanced himself from partisan appeals in a campaign speech by insisting that he would "not ask men to desert a party to which their prejudices confined them"; instead, he would "address himself to their reason."[135] Partisanship implied prejudice and passion, rather than a manly and honorable rational independence. According to one editor, "Strong party feeling, vehement and interested zeal, are apt to weaken the force of conscience; to counteract the sense of honor; or, at least to pervert the judgment." Another argued that "adherence to a party name" created an "imaginary interest" that interfered with independent judgment; "break the association in your minds between correctness and that name, and you will . . . readily perceive truth."[136] In fact, passion and prejudice had a supportable claim to be not only attendant on but the very foundation of party politics. The rhetoric surrounding elections was ladened with references to passion, zeal, and spirit. Elections were likened to battles: "All parties are buckling their armor, drumming up recruits, and striving to arouse the enthusiasm of rank and file." Rather than expressions of rational opinion, they were viewed as the "practical test of [a man's] devotion" to the country or the party. An appeal to party was generally understood to be an appeal to passion and prejudice.[137]

This association of partisanship with passion and prejudice was not always pejorative, however. The occasionally positive view of passion with respect to parties reveals the origins of antebellum conceptions of party in the eighteenth-century Whig revolutionary tradition, in which passion was valued to the extent it was directed at protecting liberty.[138] Gerald Leonard's study of antebellum partisanship offers a cogent explanation of its eighteenth-century roots. Leonard points out that a discourse of party—that is, a discourse that went beyond simple condemnations of parties—emerged in the eighteenth century, and it bore little resemblance to the modern conception of parties as vehicles for mobilizing public opinion and organizing political debate. The eighteenth-century discourse of party was constitutional; it grew out of England's seventeenth-century struggles to establish a durable constitutional order and entered American political discourse as part of the Whig opposition tradition. This Anglo-American discourse of party began with the concept of a balanced constitution, in which the three estates, or "parties"—the monarchy, the nobility, and the democracy—would balance one another's striving for power and thus preserve liberty. When antebellum Americans used the word "party," they generally meant to designate these constitutional orders. The different parties, under this view, represented different constitutional orientations, and partisanship meant not commitment to any particular set of policies or persons but commitment to a constitutional order. Thus the early-nineteenth-century Federalist and Democratic Parties were popularly considered to be the parties of aristocracy and democracy, respectively, defined less by their policies than by the constitutional classes they represented.

By the age of Jackson, the democratic orientation was the only one that could claim legitimacy, but the Democratic Party understood in this constitutional sense was strongly legitimated. Partisanship, then, was not necessarily a bad word. If one could plausibly characterize one's party as the true defender of the democratic constitution, passionate commitment to it was perfectly legitimate, even desirable. Defenders of partisanship thus argued that "if you are of no party, you are a political drone, destitute of all patriotic zeal, and perfectly willing that your country should be improving or degenerating, without lifting your finger to aid what you might believe to be the cause of truth, liberty and justice."[139] In contrast, if one's party represented an aristocratic or, even worse, monarchical orientation, it was wholly illegitimate, a mere faction that threatened the unity essential to a republican constitution.[140]

This background explains why antebellum politicians, even in the face of strong norms against party-as-faction, still claimed enduring allegiance to their own parties. Winfield Scott, for example, was drawing on the constitutional sense of party when he declared, "Brought up in the principles of the revolution—of Jefferson, Madison, etc.—under whom in youth I commenced my life, I have always been called—I have ever professed myself, simply a Republican or Whig, which with me was the same thing."[141] This commitment to the constitutional party of republicanism did not conflict with the ideal of a politics of rational public debate; as discussed earlier, a common commitment to republicanism was a prerequisite for such debate. In fact, under the Enlightenment model, a consistent partisanship could indicate that one's party was indeed the true defender of the nation's basic principles—such heroic consistency could be explained by the obvious and irresistible power of truth on one's opinions. For example, the editor of *Niles' Register* boasted of "the steadiness of our own course" that caused others to be "jostled by running a-foul of us." He insisted that "[o]n no matter of policy or principle, has the character of the REGISTER been changed, from its beginning—but thousands who cheered us in our course years ago, have abandoned their opinions,—and tens of thousands that were indifferent have become enlightened."[142] He thus offered his consistency as evidence of a long-standing conviction based on an enlightened perspective.

But if Niles could celebrate his consistency in matters of policy as well as principle, Enlightenment rationalism also provided ample grounds for attacking such consistency. Passionate devotion to the constitutional principle of republican government is one thing; passionate devotion to particular policy measures is, arguably, another. But the line between principle and policy was vague, and parties were often perceived as requiring just such devotion to particular policies.[143] The most ardent defenders of party insisted that "every man should sacrifice his own private opinions and feelings to the good of his party—and the man who will not do it is unworthy to be supported by a party, for any post of honor or profit."[144] Some parties even asked their members to sign loyalty oaths, such as this Native American oath: "We, the undersigned, Native American Citizens of the City and County of Philadelphia, do hereby pledge ourselve to cast suffrages for no other candidate for office, who is not an advocate of the principles promulgated by the National Native American Convention . . . and who does not uphold these principles as the only true basis of political organization."[145] Binding oneself to a party platform could be characterized as a rigid refusal to consider and reflect on opposing viewpoints—a major epistemic error under the Enlightenment model of public debate. A sign of true intellectual independence, some suggested, was a heroic *lack* of consistency, representing one's refusal to be bound by party doctrine. In language that hints at the emerging understanding of party as a vehicle for promoting particular policies, one editor commented, "In times of high excitement, it is somewhat difficult for a man of an independent mind to conduct himself conscientiously, without losing the favor of all parties, and becoming the object of almost universal coldness and distrust. Such a man will see in every party, some things which he cannot approve; and if he is in the habit of expressing his mind freely on all occasions, he may excite the bitterest dislike to himself in the very party, for which he has, on the whole, the highest esteem."[146] Similarly, the *Philadelphia Evening Bulletin* speculated on Zachary Taylor's political affiliation, concluding that Taylor's sterling character indicated that he was neither a Whig nor a Democrat, but "that he has frequently voted for both parties, now for the Whigs; now for the Democrats, as he considered either right. An honest patriot finds it difficult always to go with the party to which he nominally belongs. To be a partisan, in the usual sense of that term, requires more pliability of conscience than high-minded citizens usually possess."[147] For this editor, inconsistency in one's partisan affiliation indicated a consistent adherence to one's conscience. (As it turned out, however, the editor guessed wrong—Taylor opted for partisan consistency, declaring that he was and always had been "a Whig in principle.")[148]

In sum, partisanship was generally interpreted as a wholehearted commitment to a set of political principles and—more problematically—the policies that flowed from those principles. Such a commitment could be characterized as a rational conviction resulting from critical reflection, or as an obstinate prejudice barring critical reflection. If it was the latter, it looked very much like intellectual deference: passively submitting to "the dictation of others" rather than thinking for oneself.[149] Partisanship, then, was a slippery matter that had to be negotiated very carefully. Consider the *Democratic Review*'s biographical sketch of Charles Ingersoll. The *Review* acknowledged that Ingersoll had been a federalist, when James Madison "and other apostles of the democratic party were called federalists." But "[i]n the mutations of parties and of men, Mr. Ingersoll, who has always . . . been characterised by the utmost independence of opinion, has no doubt occasionally opposed those with whom he has generally coincided." In other words, he has always been a democrat but has sometimes disagreed with whichever party represented true democratic principles. Nevertheless, his lack of partisan consistency is to be interpreted as consistency of opinion. Still, this consistency should not be read as intellectual rigidity: "[H]e is yet, no doubt, willing to acknowledge that with the progressive development of political experience, his mind has gradually opened to convictions of democratic excellence." And yet "he has always been among the hardiest pioneers of the loftiest American patriotism, lived in the full faith of the real presence of popular sovereignty and radical politics." His democratic sentiments, then, are both an "ingrain attachment" and the result of rational, open-minded reflection.[150] The reader may judge whether this attempt to reconcile principled consistency with open-mindedness is persuasive. At any rate, it illustrates the conflict between the antebellum conception of partisanship and the principles of Enlightenment rationalism.

Editors of party newspapers were especially likely to get caught in this conflict. They did not just *appear* to be submitting to the dictation of others but explicitly *promised* to submit to their patrons' dictation. As one editor put it, "when subscribers are received on the condition, express or implied, that the paper is to espouse a certain cause, to uphold certain doctrines, or to advance the political interests of certain men, the publisher binds himself to a contract. . . . He indentures himself to, perhaps, several hundreds or thousands of task-masters, all severe in their exactions and disposed to visit with stern rebukes every deviation from what each considers the proper course."[151] The language of slavery is telling. Not only did editors surrender their rational independence by virtue of their partisanship, but they often surrendered it to power-seeking politicians—and they did it for money. It was little wonder, then, that Nicholas Biddle thought that the editor of the *Courier and Enquirer* would be receptive to bribery; one might plausibly conclude, from the complaints voiced in the press itself, that the profession was dominated by political prostitutes.

This is, of course, the least charitable interpretation of the party press. One could also characterize a newspaper's partisanship as the result of the inevitable operation of truth on the editor's convictions. It might then plausibly earn the sort of praise Charles Leland bestowed on Greeley's *Tribune,* as serving the cause of human freedom. Similarly, a newspaper's financial dependence on a party or its subscribers might be dismissed as harmless when the editor and the paper's patrons already share common political convictions based on their independent rational inquiry and reflection. But the relentless criticism of the press (most vociferously by the press itself) indicates how vulnerable it was to the charges of corruption and intellectual servility. As long as political debate was embedded in the interest-driven system of partisan politics, it was inevitably in tension with the ideal proposed by the Enlightenment model.

Antebellum editors did find a solution to this problem, however. They knew what the goal was; as one editor explained, "[W]hat we term freedom of the press, is, a dignified and honourable impartiality in every emanation from it, whether concerning the government, or parties, or individuals, by its editor; whether approbation or offence follows, having a due regard to the interest of the country, to the feelings of individuals, to chasteness of language, and to *truth*."[152] In order to realize this ideal of objectivity, publishers simply had to free their newpapers from dependence on party and government. The penny press pioneered this type of independent journalism. It not only made use of innovations in printing that made mass production cheaper and easier but also utilized new types of financing mechanisms—advertising and large volume circulation. Whereas newspaper advertising had previously been dominated by shipping news, public sales, and legal notices, the penny newspapers opened their pages to any sort of advertisement, from want ads to patent medicines to abortionists. Advertising in penny papers was made particularly attractive by their large circulations; Philadelphia's *Public Ledger,* for example, reached a circulation of 20,000 within eighteen months, when other papers in the city had circulations of about 2,000. These large volumes were accomplished by the innovative practice of selling papers on the street instead of by subscription. This practice also had the felicitous effect of moving sales to a cash, rather than credit, basis. Such innovations gave the penny presses financial independence, thus allowing them to focus on their mission of simply and objectively revealing the facts about political matters. As Michael Schudson aptly put it, "[T]he world of parties became just a part of a larger universe of news."[153]

This transformation in journalism, in which newspapers freed themselves of government and party patronage in favor of advertising and sales, is the critical moment in Habermas's story of the decline of rational-critical debate in the press—it is the point at which the press "became enmeshed in a web of interests," becoming the tool of capitalists at the expense of its political function.[154] But, as should be clear by now, antebellum editors and publishers interpreted the situation differently. They engineered this transformation in order to *extricate* newspapers from the web of financial and political interests that, in their view, interfered with their objective pursuit of the truth. As Horace Greeley explained, his penny paper was to be "a journal removed alike from servile partisanship on the one hand and from gagged, mincing neutrality on the other."[155] But it is not coincidental that the penny press, once it was freed from dependence on parties, moved away from politics altogether, focusing on reporting crime and other "sensational" subjects instead of political argument and editorials. Habermas implies that this move was driven by the profit motive, but Schudson correctly points out that this explanation is too simplistic. Unlike colonial printers, who explicitly cited profitability as their main reason for avoiding politics, antebellum newspaper publishers argued that they had a political duty to make newspapers more profitable; in this way, they could achieve financial independence and better fulfill their truth-seeking mission.[156] However, Habermas is probably right in pointing to this desire for profitability as driving newspapers away from their focus on political argument and mobilization; politics, apparently, didn't sell.[157]

Thus, although the penny press might have enhanced the legitimacy of American journalism by freeing itself from the state and parties, it did not provide a solution to the question at hand: how might the people legitimately be mobilized into politics? Parties remained the primary institutional answer to that question, and in practice, parties and partisanship thrived during the antebellum era. But their legitimacy continued to be undermined by the Enlightenment ideal of public rationality. To the extent parties relied on interest and passion to persuade and motivate, they were vulnerable to the complaint that they diminished the rational independence of the public and the quality of public debate.

In sum, the Enlightenment model imposed severe constraints on legitimate political debate, particularly when contrasted with the neoclassical model. Ironically, despite its elitism, the neoclassical tradition actually accommodated popular politics better than did the purportedly egalitarian tradition of Enlightenment rationalism. Under the neoclassical model, political speech was aimed at persuading people to take action, not at preserving their rational independence. This model was able to endorse a rich variety of rhetorical techniques designed to arouse the public, shape their desires, and inform their judgment. To be sure, it also endorsed conflict and inequality. But the Enlightenment model, with its hostility to passion, prejudice, and interest, had difficulty endorsing any popular politics at all.

Conclusion

I argued in Part I that rational public debate was originally promoted as a solution to the problem of riotousness—a way for the citizens to actively participate in politics without threatening social order and undermining the legitimacy of the regime. But it was far from self-evident whether and how a popular politics of public debate could achieve this goal. On the one hand, the neoclassical model was consistent with the ideal of a popular politics of public debate, but it described political debate as driven by individual glory seeking, producing disorder, inequality, and conflict. On the other hand, the Enlightenment model described political debate as a rational, dispassionate pursuit of the truth, thus highlighting the ways in which passion and interest might interfere with public rationality and order. But it offered no coherent account of a politics free of passion and interest, relying instead on the wholly implausible power of truth to persuade and motivate political action. Thus the Enlightenment model works only if we borrow from the Whig tradition and limit popular politics to redressing serious governmental abuses, or else make some heroic assumptions about the public's zealous (but not too zealous) commitment to the public good. And even if the Enlightenment model did make sense on a conceptual level, its practical effect was to undermine the legitimacy of the very institutions that were mobilizing the mass public to participate in political debate: parties and the party press. In sum, the Enlightenment model, as it took shape in antebellum public discourse, offered an impoverished vision of popular politics—a vision that exalted rationality at the expense of passion, interest, and eloquence.

At this point, the idea of shaping popular politics around the value of rational public debate should look less obvious and unproblematic. Worries about the rationality of popular politics only became more intense as public debate replaced mob action as the dominant mode of participation; if violence could be excluded from politics, passion and interest apparently could not. But for some critics of rational debate, its problems lay in another direction altogether. A group of abolitionists, disillusioned by their experiences with public argument, went beyond complaining about its lack of rationality and began to question the premises, both moral and epistemological, underpinning the Enlightenment ideal. Against this ideal, they offered an alternative practice of narrative testimony, or public storytelling, that embodied a radically different conception of democratic politics.

PART THREE
NARRATIVE TESTIMONY

5

STORYTELLING

In 1840, the *Pennsylvania Freeman* excerpted a report written by Horace Mann on the dangers of reading fiction. Fiction, he warned, has a "weakening and dispersive influence" on morals. It portrays trials and temptations that "are rarely such as any human being will fall into" and virtues that "few will ever have an opportunity to achieve." It arouses sympathy and aversion, but the reader, he feared, would be unable to relate such sympathy and aversion to real life. Worse, "[i]n the mean time, the understanding sleeps; the intellect is laid aside. Those faculties have nothing to do, by which we comprehend our position in life, and our relations to society,—by which we discover what our duty is, and the wisest way to perform it. The mind surrenders itself to the interest and excitement of the story, while the powers by which we discern tendencies and balance probabilities, are discarded."[1] Fiction, then, impairs the rational faculties without educating the moral ones.

Ironically, the *Pennsylvania Freeman* printed this critique of fiction next to a partially fictionalized story entitled *Pinda: A True Tale*, by Maria West Chapman. Pinda gained notoriety in abolitionist (and antiabolitionist) circles as a slave who refused to escape from her master when he brought her to Massachusetts. Defenders of slavery portrayed her as a "contented slave." But Chapman told a different story. In her version, Pinda had refused to escape because she thought that her master might take revenge by punishing her husband, also a slave. On returning to the South, however, Pinda and her husband agreed that she should escape if her master took her north again. He did, and Pinda took advantage of the opportunity to claim her freedom— even while her master was holding forth on the virtues of slavery to a company of abolitionists.[2]

Chapman's story wasn't supposed to be purely fictional, and we have no reason to believe that she made up the basic story line. But it wasn't clearly nonfiction either. She told the tale in the same style as similar romantic (and fictional) stories about escaped slaves, leaving out the usual assurances that the story was factual and failing to inform the reader how she learned such details as the characters' emotional states and the content of supposedly private conversations. Moreover, she drew on the standard conventions of sentimental novels in describing the settings and the psychological traumas of the characters. Even the dialogue was stylized and romantic: " 'Dear wife,' said

Abraham to Pinda, as they stood by the door of his little hut, in the yellow
moonlight of a Savannah evening,—'you must never lose another chance for
freedom out of regard to me.' "[3] The romance of the story challenged the
boundary between fact and fiction. And Chapman wasn't alone. Other abolition advocates (most notably Harriet Beecher Stowe) crossed the line, offering frankly fictional and romantic stories as politically relevant literature.
How do we explain this use of romantic storytelling by a group of people
who were vocally and insistently dedicated to a politics of reason? If romance
was supposed to weaken the rational faculties and impair the judgment, why
were abolitionists so willing to exploit the genre?

This chapter and the next examine the three major lines of argument justifying the use of slave narratives in political debate. In this chapter I consider the claim that slave narratives are analogous to judicial testimony, designed simply to establish the facts—thus making a place for testimony
within the Enlightenment model of political argument outlined in Chapter
4. But critics were quick to point out the problem with this analogy: Romances, unlike judicial testimony, don't carry any guarantee that the information they convey is true. Storytellers take dramatic license; their tales can
hardly serve as reliable sources of information about complex social issues.
The next chapter, then, turns to the claim that slave narratives could generate
sympathy for the slave. According to the abolitionists, sympathy had political value in that it could motivate political action—a fairly straightforward
claim, but one that left the narratives open to the charge that they only arouse
the passions without informing the judgment. The third justification for slave
narratives, however, offered an answer to such concerns: the abolitionists presented slave narratives not only as judicial testimony but also as religious
testimony—a form of discourse designed to influence and reform moral sentiments, and therefore an important prerequisite to reasoned public debate.
This argument, I suggest, represents a significant departure from the framework of Enlightenment rationalism; drawing on a Protestant language of
moral corruption and reform, the abolitionists developed a way of talking
about political action that de-emphasized reasoned argument and opened the
door to romance and eloquence. The result was a rhetoric that affirmed the
Enlightenment project of rationalizing politics even while it undermined
the central supports of that project: faith in the accessibility of truth and in
the rationality of the public.

The Enlightenment of Frederick Douglass

The slave narratives are themselves a paradoxical conjunction of reason and
romance: they are romances about the enlightening power of reason. They

thus have a moral and political purpose that relates them to the politics of reason, even while taking a form that seems to distance them from such rationalist ideals. Understanding this paradox is critical to understanding the challenge posed by the slave narrators to the conventions of political action—a point best illustrated in the narratives of Frederick Douglass.

In 1845, Frederick Douglass finally gave in to the entreaties of his public and published his *Narrative,* an account of his life as a slave. Douglass had already been lecturing throughout the North for four years, impressing audiences in Ohio, New England, New York, and Pennsylvania with his commanding presence, his oratorical prowess (unusual for a fugitive slave), and his dramatic stories. Although his early speeches apparently avoided the subject, by 1845, his life story and personal experiences as a slave had become his most popular topic. Responding to both public demand for his biography and the proliferating questions about its authenticity, he followed the example of other escaped slaves and published what was to become the most famous and widely read fugitive slave narrative. The first edition of 5,000 copies sold out in a matter of months.[4]

The demand for Douglass's *Narrative* was impressive, but not surprising. By the time it was published, fugitive slave narratives were an immensely popular genre in the North. They had their roots in the more explicitly religious conversion narratives that were popular in the eighteenth century, but their success in the antebellum era is probably due to the fact that they incorporated elements of traditional adventure stories, captivity narratives, African oral literature, and conventional sentimental romance novels.[5] They were a unique addition to American letters; many ran through a number of editions, and the most popular sold as many as 6,000 copies in three years (well under the 70,000 copies of *Fern Leaves from Fanny's Portfolio* sold in one year by sentimental writer Fanny Fern, but considerably more than the 300 copies Henry David Thoreau and Nathaniel Hawthorne could expect to sell in a good year).[6] Fictional accounts of fugitive slaves were equally popular; *Uncle Tom's Cabin* was only one of several novels modeled on factual narratives.

But the emergence of slave narratives as a major genre in American letters was also due to the fact that, beginning in the 1830s, abolitionists began promoting this literature as a way to spread antislavery sentiment. Until this time, most slave narratives had been published as religious tracts and focused on the slave's religious conversion. William Lloyd Garrison, however, saw a different potential in the narratives; when 50,000 copies of the narrative of Nat Turner were sold in Baltimore in 1831, Garrison's *Liberator* expressed the hope that the story would produce some sympathy for the condemned man.[7] Soon the antislavery press, concentrated in New York, Boston, and Philadelphia, was seeking out and printing slave narratives. The first book-length narrative (of Charles Ball) was published in 1837. The next step was the lecture circuit. Frederick Douglass and Lewis Clarke were the first stars of the antislavery circuit, but after 1840, every major slave narrator also performed on stage. By that time, the narratives had developed a more pronounced ideological edge; narratives like Douglass's were not simply adventure stories but incisive critiques of southern slavery and sometimes even northern racism. But despite their transparently propagandistic tone, the stories were so popular that the sensational press and independent printers began to publish them as well.[8] Thus slave narratives were an integral part of the political culture in the North, particularly in centers of abolitionist activity such as Philadelphia, New York, and Boston.

The importance of slave narratives to the development of American literature is well recognized. The major studies focus on these texts primarily as literary acts and argue that their central theme is the problem of identity. William Andrews, for example, interprets the slave narrative as an attempt to explain and justify the self, an act of self-liberation through writing. Frances Smith Foster also emphasizes the search for identity as the slave narrator's central rhetorical problem, and Charles T. Davis and Henry Louis Gates characterize the narrative as an "attempt to write oneself into being."[9] Although generally sensitive to the political dimension of the narratives, these analyses focus on the attempt to find an authentic literary voice—a legitimate concern, but one that is fairly remote from my central question: how such stories fit into the conventional practices of antebellum politics. I want to understand the narratives as political, rather than simply literary, acts. Thus, while I agree that "coming into being" is a central theme in the stories, I give that interpretation a less literary meaning: the narrators did become authors, but their stories were first and foremost about becoming political actors— freemen and citizens. Of course, achieving an authentic public voice *is* an act of political significance, but to focus on this dimension of the narratives is to neglect the larger picture, the transformation from slave to citizen. Moreover, focusing on authenticity and self-creation does not help us understand the political significance of the closely related fictional narratives (typically written by white abolitionists). In fact, it tends to re-create the debates over authenticity that have always plagued these narratives, without shedding much light on what is at stake in that debate.[10] My analysis, then, departs from the standard readings of the narratives by concentrating on the problem of becoming a political actor, rather than on the problem of becoming an authentic author.

From this perspective, fugitive slave narratives are stories about the birth of political consciousness, the transformation of the subject into a political agent. They are essentially narratives of political enlightenment. As such, they start from the premises and commitments of Enlightenment rationalism outlined in the last chapter, and revolve around the problems of epistemology and agency endemic to this approach to political action: how do we know political truths, and how and why are we moved to act on them? In the narratives of escaped slaves, these questions were framed in a way that resonated forcefully with American political traditions; specifically, how do we recognize that we are oppressed, and what will motivate us to resist? The answers were not uniform, but they shared a basic structure, best exemplified by the two early narratives of Frederick Douglass: the *Narrative* and the 1855 *My Bondage and My Freedom*. Douglass's approach to these questions, I argue, adds important dimensions to the rationalist framework by clarifying the place of character and intuition in Enlightenment thought, thus paving the way for the abolitionists' departure from Enlightenment rationalism altogether.

The Liberation of Frederick Douglass

Douglass's *Narrative* is a romance of enlightenment, following Douglass from the time he was a child, "occasionally oppressed by what he could not well account for" and "peering and poking about among the layers of right and wrong," through his "notable" discovery that "liberty and right, for all men, were anterior to slavery and wrong."[11] This journey from ignorance to understanding structures the entire story, beginning with the conventional starting point for slave narratives: how Douglass discovered that he was a slave.

Like most other narrators, Douglass emphasizes that he spent his childhood in happy ignorance of his status. "It was a long time," he tells us, "before I knew myself to be *a slave.*" Only gradually did he learn that he and his family belonged to "Old Master." The fact was a "distressing revelation" to him, though he admits that he didn't fully understand what it meant.[12] Over time, his experiences on the plantation brought home to him the meaning of slavery—experiences he shares with the reader in unsparing detail: his unhappiness that (unlike white children) he didn't know his birth date, his sudden removal from his grandmother's house to his master's, and such dismal incidents of plantation life as whippings and the haunting sound of slave songs (to which he traces his "first glimmering conception of the dehumanizing character of slavery").[13]

By dwelling on this first stage of his enlightenment, Douglass makes the point that there was nothing self-evident about the "truth" that he was a slave. Beyond that, this opening discussion makes a connection, common in Enlightenment rhetoric, between slavery and ignorance; for Douglass, to be a slave is, in important respects, to be deprived of essential knowledge about one's condition and history. At the same time, Douglass establishes himself as a good rationalist, operating in a fashion that Frances Wright would approve of: observing the facts of his condition, examining, comparing, and drawing conclusions. But his story takes a different turn when he is sent to Baltimore to live with a relation of his master's. Douglass overhears his new master instructing his mistress not to teach him [Douglass] how to read: " 'Learning to read would spoil the best nigger in the world. Now,' said he, 'if you teach that nigger (speaking of myself) how to read, there would be no keeping him. It would forever unfit him to be a slave.' " Douglass "instinctively assented to the proposition," calling it a "new and special revelation." It explained to him (he said) both the nature of the white man's power over the slave and the "pathway from slavery to freedom."[14]

Douglass's connection between reading and freedom also rehearses a familiar Enlightenment trope—that reading, by facilitating reasoned inquiry, has a special connection to truth. But what should we make of his reference to "instinct"? It's not an abberation; the language of instinct or intuition becomes more pronounced as we move to the next stage of Douglass's enlightenment—his conviction that slavery is not only undesirable but also unjust. In fact, to call this "the next stage" is misleading. In contrast to his protracted study of the nature of slavery, his enlightenment about the morality of slavery was easy and automatic: he claims that he knew slavery was wrong ever since he began to think about it. "I was just as well aware of the unjust, unnatural and murderous character of slavery, when nine years old, as I am now."[15] Thus, although he had to learn the facts of his condition, he did not have to learn how to make moral judgments about it. His knowledge of right and wrong, particularly on the question of slavery, was innate. To underscore the obviousness of this proposition, he points out that even the white boys of Baltimore that he played with thought that Douglass had a right to freedom. Their condemnation of slavery, he concludes, "springs from nature, unseared and unperverted"—as did his own.[16]

Moral reasoning, in contrast to moral instinct, played a limited role in Douglass's enlightenment, serving mainly to provide him with the tools to defend his instinctive rejection of slavery. He wasn't even exposed to moral arguments against slavery until he learned to read and started reading the *Columbian Orator,* a collection of pieces used by schoolchildren to practice public speaking. He read Richard Sheridan on Catholic emancipation and speeches by Lord Chatham, William Pitt, and Charles Fox; he was particularly impressed, he tells us, by a dialogue between a slave and his master in which the slave convinces his master to free him.[17] These texts, he says, "gave tongue to interesting thoughts of my own soul, which had frequently flashed through my mind, and died away for want of utterance." Reading them "enabled me to utter my thoughts, and to meet the arguments brought forward to sustain slavery."[18] The arguments against slavery did not so much convince him that slavery was wrong, then, but merely allowed him to articulate his own feelings on the subject.

Douglass's reliance on innate feelings and instincts to explain this process of conviction may seem rather vague, but it would have been familiar language to his audience, and not inconsistent with the teachings of the Enlightenment. Rousseau and Voltaire, after all, were among the eighteenth-century Enlightenment philosophers who contributed the emergence of feeling as an alternative to rationalization of moral judgment.[19] (The Enlightenment, remember, was a complex phenomenon that defies simple generalizations. It was about reason and feeling, instinct and argument.) More specifically, the language of feeling and intuition echoes a common theme of the Scottish Enlightenment, the idea that moral judgments derive from an innate "moral sense." The concept was a major topic of debate among such philosophers as the Earl of Shaftesbury, Frances Hutcheson, Thomas Reid, and Adam Smith; their ideas were transmitted to America during the second half of the eighteenth century via such figures as John Witherspoon (president of Princeton College from 1766 to 1794), David Tappan (professor of divinity at Harvard from 1792 to 1803), and Timothy Dwight (president of Yale from 1795 to 1817). As historian Herbert Hovenkamp points out, for the first half of the nineteenth century in America, "the men who taught the most popular courses in moral and analytic philosophy, who questioned and licensed ministerial candidates, who produced the scientific thinkers and wrote the college textbooks, were disciples of the Scottish Enlightenment."[20]

By virtue of these influences, Americans were familiar with the claim that moral judgments were rooted in feeling, in particular those feelings of approval or disapproval that spring up naturally when a person observes a virtuous or vicious act. This moral sense, often analogized to the aesthetic sense (the capacity to be pleased by art or music), was supposed to be grounded in human nature—in the words of Shaftesbury, "a first Principle in our Constitution and Make" that could be displaced only by "contrary Habit and Custom." Like Douglass, partisans of the concept tended to discount the role of reasoning in moral judgment. "[M]ust a Man have the Reflection of Cumberland, or Pufendorf, to admire Generosity, Faith, Humanity, Gratitude?" asked Hutcheson, "Or reason so nicely to apprehend the Evil in Cruelty, Treachery, Ingratitude?" Untutored instinct was supposed to be a superior guide to conduct than the disputations of the learned; the authority of the moral sense rested on its naturalness. As Shaftesbury insisted, nature does not teach vice: "The Wrong Sense or False Imagination of Right and Wrong . . . can proceed only from the Force of Custom and Education in opposition to Nature."[21]

Such language should not be taken to suggest that education and reason could play no legitimate role in forming moral judgment. Thomas Reid, for example, posited an intuitive moral sense only to uncover a host of sources of error, including too great a willingness to rely on authority and a tendency to assume that things are simpler than they are. Prejudice and passion, of course, might also bias the judgment. Thus, while moral judgments initially spring from nature, they need careful cultivation of character and reason to develop properly.[22] Nevertheless, this understanding of moral judgment gives an at least plausible explanation of why intuition should be trusted over received views. And clearly this school lent some badly needed support to the popular version of Enlightenment rationalism by suggesting that even moral truths are (in principle) discoverable by any rational person.[23]

Douglass's story illustrates how the language of moral sense could be combined with the Enlightenment model of political argument so that moral instincts—rather than arguments—do the work of persuasion and conviction. My point here is not to suggest that Douglass studied Reid or Shaftesbury; the language and assumptions of moral intuitionism were pervasive in antebellum America. My interest is in how moral intuitionism solves certain problems created by Douglass's commitment to Enlightenment rationalism. Its political advantages are obvious. First, it can be part of a strategy of inclusion and exclusion—a way for Douglass to establish himself as a member of the same moral community as his audience (since they all share the same moral intuitions) and, perhaps more importantly, to exclude from his conception of the community anyone who doesn't share his intuitions. This is undoubtedly a critical part of Douglass's rhetorical strategy, since the problem of inclusion was at the heart of racial politics. But moral intuitionism had other advantages as well. For example, because Douglass's convictions were based on intuition, no one had to tell him that slavery was wrong. Thus there was no danger that he was simply misled by (for example) meddling abolitionists. This is important not only because it allowed Douglass to assert his own rational independence but also because it allowed him to downplay the influence of abolitionist literature on his enlightenment. Although he learned about abolitionism while in Baltimore, it wasn't the abolitionists' arguments that impressed him. "I must say, that, ignorant as I then was of the philosophy of that movement, I believed in it from the first." He believed in it because the abolitionists hated slavery and "alarmed the consciences of slaveholders."[24] In other words, he recognized them as allies, but his hatred of slavery had nothing to do with their influence. Douglass's intuitionism thus protected abolitionists from the charge that they were responsible for the discontent of slaves, while contributing to the impression that his moral sentiments were gifts of nature and therefore both reliable and inarguable.[25]

Moral intuitionism seems to fit easily into the Enlightenment framework of political argument that Douglass was working with, which (as discussed in Chapter 4) assumes a fairly high level of consensus on basic values—thus downplaying the need for political debate about values. But if intuitionism explained how one might make reliable moral judgments without hearing arguments, it did not rule out the possibility of debate on values altogether, even among those whose moral sentiments have been properly educated and refined. Reid, for example, postulated basic principles that were much more abstract than Douglass's proposition that slavery is wrong: that some human actions merit praise and some blame, that involuntary actions do not deserve praise or blame, and that we ought to try to be informed of our duties and to perform them, to name a few. He thus left ample room for moral ambiguity, acknowledging that most human actions are open to varying interpretations. Moreover, he admitted that reasonable people may differ even about basic moral principles, and that when such differences arise they should be met with arguments.[26] In other words, Reid recognized a legitimate kind of moral discourse that does not proceed from first principles but attempts to establish them.

Douglass seems to leave less room for legitimate disagreement than Reid, but he does implicitly acknowledge that the reader might question Douglass's moral intuitions. After all, both Douglass and his audience knew that some slaves and most slaveholders claimed to have precisely the opposite intuition, that slavery was morally justified. Douglass attacked this problem on two fronts. First, he defended the naturalness of his own intuitions; slavery, he insists in his opening chapter, never seemed natural to him, even when he was a child. (Moral intuitionism provides grounds for giving special weight to the intuitions of children, since their intuitions have not yet been deformed. However, one might complain that their intuitions are unreliable because they have not yet been sharpened and refined. Douglass does not consider that possibility.) Similarly, Douglass undermines the authority of his fellow slaves' opinions by explaining how their intuitions get perverted by their circumstances and treatment. Slaveholders, he argued, warp slaves' moral instincts by brutalizing and degrading them. This, for example, is Douglass's complaint about the custom of giving slaves holidays, encouraging them to "[plunge] . . . into the lowest depths of dissipation."[27] Only a slave who can resist this degradation will have within him (and the gendered term may be necessary here) the resources for recognizing the truth in his innate feeling of manhood.

An obvious objection to this reasoning is that Douglass was himself a slave. How did *he* escape its alleged brutalizing effects? Before we accept Douglass's thesis that slavery impairs the moral sense, we would want to know more about what set him apart from the others. I return to this problem later. Here I want to consider a second objection. His explanation works only if one accepts the premise that slaves are equal to other men; if slaves are naturally inferior, then their treatment isn't degrading but appropriate to their capacities and conducive to their moral development. A defender of slavery would argue that it is Douglass's moral faculties that are deranged. And how are we to decide who's right? This is perhaps the most striking feature of Douglass's reliance on moral intuitionism. It deflects argument from the moral issue itself to the question of whose intuitions to trust, and why. It therefore raises issues of character and ethos that are potentially at odds with the Enlightenment commitment to impersonality in political debate.

But Douglass does not rely solely on the authority of his own intuitions. He also produces an argument to support his claim that slavery is wrong. It is an ad hominen argument, but given the importance of character in arguments from moral intuition, we shouldn't be surprised to find Douglass raising doubts about the sincerity of his opponents. And in fact, his argument is of a kind that even Reid considered persuasive: that slaveholders are inconsistent, treating slaves as property while claiming that they are men.[28] To appreciate the argument, we have to begin with the conventional justifications of slavery, which Douglass does not bother to rehearse. The dialogue between master and slave in the *Columbian Orator* states the case concisely: The master claims that it is "the order of Providence that one man should be subservient to another." Moreover, the slave owes obedience to the master for the benefits the master has conferred on the slave, which include providing for the slave in his old age.[29] More extended defenses of slavery based black slavery on the claim that blacks were an inferior race who were better off as servants, and that the practice had biblical sanction in Noah's curse on Canaan (claimed by the defenders of slavery to be the progenitor of the black race), which condemned him to slavery.[30] All these defenses maintained the basic humanity of slaves but posited that the relationship between master and slave was legitimate because it was analogous to that between a father and child.

Douglass found these arguments unpersuasive, insisting that "to make a contented slave, it is necessary to make a thoughtless one. . . . He must be able to detect no inconsistencies in slavery; he must be made to feel that slavery is right; and he can be brought to that only when he ceases to be a man."[31] In other words, only an unthinking brute would fail to recognize the irrationality of slavery. But where in particular does the defense fail? Two contradictions stand out. The first was brought home to Douglass by the process of valuation. A valuation occurs when a slave owner dies and his or her estate is divided. Douglass experienced this process firsthand, and it gave him "a new conception of [his] degraded condition." The slaves were "ranked with horses, sheep, and swine. There were horses and men, cattle and women, pigs and children, all holding the same rank in the scale of being."[32] Douglass echoes other fugitive slaves in identifying valuations, along with auctions and the internal slave trade, as activities that unmask the lies of the slaveholders. The buying and selling of slaves reveals the fundamental fact that slaves are property, that economics and not paternal affection governs their treatment.[33]

The second contradiction lay in the master's claim to ownership of the slave's labor, represented by his alleged right to all the slave's earnings. Douglass argued that his master was unable to maintain this fiction. He allowed Douglass to hire out his own time, working as a caulker; his mistake was that he let Douglass keep one cent on every dollar he earned. Douglass identified this as "a sort of admission of my right to the whole," and evidence that his master didn't really believe that he had a right to Douglass's labor.[34]

It is important to understand the role that these inconsistencies played—or didn't play—in Douglass's enlightenment. It is not that they caused Douglass a kind of cognitive dissonance, leading him to question, and finally reject, the justification of slavery. He *always* (or at least since he began to think about it) knew that slavery was wrong. The inconsistencies in slaveholder ideology are offered simply to demonstrate to the reader the reliability of Douglass's moral intuitions, in contrast to those of his (at least irrational, if not hypocritical) opponents. Douglass's own enlightenment did not depend on recognizing these inconsistencies; it followed automatically from his innate, untutored feelings.

If innate feelings were central to Douglass's realization that slavery was wrong, they were equally critical to his decision to escape—the third stage of his enlightenment. This stage implicates the problem of motivation, which turns out to be a particularly difficult one for fugitive slaves. The problem lies in explaining why, if slavery was as bad as Douglass claimed, more slaves didn't escape. His own resolution to escape—or perhaps I should say his determined desire to be free—formed after he learned to read in Baltimore, which (as his master promised) made him discontented with being a slave. Shortly thereafter, a pair of Irish dockworkers suggested that he should escape to the North, and Douglass decided to do so.[35] But knowing where to escape to is one thing; mustering the resolve to do it is another. Douglass doesn't actually attempt an escape until he is sent back to his old master on the plantation, who hires him out to a man who is notorious for "breaking" slaves. This is a turning point in Douglass's life. The harsh treatment he received from this Mr. Covey nearly destroyed him, he tells us, breaking him "in body, soul, and spirit." He was "transformed into a brute." But not entirely; watching the ships sailing in Chesapeake Bay, he still considered plans for escaping, albeit with a marked lack of resolution: "O, why was I born a man, of whom to make a brute! The glad ship is gone; she hides in the dim distance. I am left in the hottest hell of unending slavery. . . . I will run away. I will not stand it. Get caught, or get clear, I'll try it. . . . I have only one life to lose. . . . Let but the first opportunity offer, and come what will, I am off. Meanwhile, I will try to bear up under the yoke. I am not the only slave in the world. Why should I fret? I can bear as much as any of them. Besides, I am but a boy, and all boys are bound to some one."[36]

His determination to escape revived after an incident that, in his words, transformed him back into a man. Douglass was finally driven by Covey's meanness to return to his master to complain. His master, however, sent him back to Covey, at which point Covey attempted to punish Douglass by whipping him. Douglass, however, suddenly decided to fight back. "[F]rom whence came the spirit I don't know," he tells us (unhelpfully), but after scuffling for nearly two hours, he drove off Covey's attack and avoided the whipping. This resistance, he maintains, "rekindled the few expiring embers of freedom, and revived within me a sense of my own manhood." Importantly, he adds that "[t]he gratification afforded by the triumph was a full compensation for whatever else might follow, even death itself." In short, he concluded that the satisfaction of resisting oppression outweighed the costs, and this was enough to solidify his resolve to escape. "My long-crushed spirit rose, cowardice departed, bold defiance took its place; and I now resolved that, however long I might remain a slave in form, the day had passed forever when I could be a slave in fact."[37] This event explains not only how he resolved to escape but more generally how he resisted the brutalizing effect of slavery and its paralyzing impact on the moral sense. He *was* degraded by captivity like other slaves but was regenerated by this exceptional act of resistance—the product not of habit, reason, or training but of an innate, indomitable will.

Douglass did not hesitate to underscore the gendered element of this regeneration through violence.[38] The influence of the eighteenth-century Whig tradition may be at work here; for Douglass, the status of freeman is intimately bound with masculinity and the masculine virtues, among which physical courage is primary. "A man, without force, is without the essential dignity of humanity. Human nature is so constituted, that it cannot *honor* a helpless man, although it can *pity* him; and even this it cannot do long, if the signs of power do not arise."[39] Of course, such resources would not be available to a woman who did not want to challenge the conventions of femininity, which complicates the problem of motivation for female narrators. In *Incidents in the Life of a Slave Girl,* for example, Harriet Jacobs attributes her resistance to slavery to the very feminine virtue of domesticity: she wanted a home like her free grandmother had had, a desire that slavery consistently frustrated. Ellen Craft relied on her husband's courage and her faith to carry her over the threshold to freedom, thus managing to make her act of resistance look like as an expression of feminine dependency and Christian humility.[40] In contrast, Sojourner Truth (no respecter of the conventions of femininity) glossed over the problem. Although she echoed Douglass's conclusion that slavery leaves the slave dispirited and unable to resist, she offered no explanation as to how she escaped this fate. At the key point in the narrative, her master reneges on his promise to free her, so she simply decides to leave—and does.[41]

Douglass's escape wasn't so easy. Inspired by his successful resistance of Covey, he persuaded some of his friends to join him in an attempt. Again, he dwells in detail on the difficulty of the decision. "Whenever we suggested any plan, there was shrinking—the odds were fearful. Our path was beset with the greatest obstacles. . . . At every gate through which we were to pass, we saw a watchman—at every ferry a guard—on every bridge a sentinel— and in every wood a patrol. . . . Here were the difficulties, real or imagined." They faced a "doubtful liberty" if they succeeded, and "almost certain death" if they failed.[42] These endless deliberations do more than heighten the drama of the story; they also underscore the point that merely knowing the truth is not sufficient to prompt action against injustice. To act in the face of all their uncertainties required more than ordinary fortitude; it required a heroic spirit.

Unfortunately, not all his friends shared that spirit; one of them betrayed the conspirators, and the plan failed. It was four years before Douglass attempted another escape, prompted this time by his master's decision to let him hire his time. As discussed earlier, this arrangement again brought home to Douglass the injustice of slavery; once he was arranging contracts and managing his own time, he became frustrated with his master's attempts to control him. Apparently this time the decision to escape was easier. He knew that slavery was undesirable and unjust and that the rewards of resistance, even if it failed, would outweigh the costs. His enlightenment was complete. His first innate feelings of manhood, refined by reflection and exposure to rational arguments, provided the impetus for him to resist oppression—an impulse that was so satisfying that it became a habit of character that finally led him to take positive action and escape.

Most of the elements of Douglass's story are familiar to us by now. He draws on Enlightenment rationalism in portraying truth as easily recognizable and on the Whig tradition of resistance (complete with its gendered concept of civic virtue and its sanction of violence) in explaining how he was finally motivated to take action. But what should we make of this new element, his "moral sense"? Reliance on such moral intuitions wasn't unique to Douglass. Most slave narrators gave their innate moral sense a central role in their enlightenment. For example, Mattie Griffiths's fictional slave, like Douglass, attributed her conviction that slavery was wrong to some "glimmering ideas of justice," which were later developed and refined through exposure to abolitionism. James Pennington also drew on moral intuitionism when he asserted that he rejected colonization in favor of abolitionism "without bias or advice from any mortal," as did Josiah Henson in finding in his (as yet unconverted) moral nature the "righteousness of indignation against the cruel and oppressive."[43] I do not mean to suggest that narrators never tried to rationalize their rejection of slavery; the point is that such rationalizations typically played a relatively small role in their enlightenment, compared with their moral intuitions.

I have already considered the strategic reasons for emphasizing intuition over argument, but what does moral intuitionism add to our understanding of political conviction and motivation? Apparently, very little. Despite their philosophical pedigree, Douglass's innate feelings are ultimately no more satisfying as an explanation of his own convictions than is the "irresistible power of truth." How does he know—or better, how does the audience know—that these feelings are universal and reliable? After all, Douglass admits that the treatment slaves receive can alter their moral intuitions, making them feel less than human, or at least an inferior kind of human. For example, he explains the general docility of slaves by the fact that they are "[t]rained from the cradle up, to think and feel that their masters are superior, and invested with a sort of sacredness," so that "there are few who can outgrow or rise above the control which that sentiment exercises." Douglass was one of the few who "got free from it."[44] But, as already mentioned, it could be that such an upbringing is appropriate to this race, and that it is Douglass's moral faculty that is defective. And, pace Reid, pointing to the inconsistencies between the slaveholders' ideology and their practice proves little; the "free" labor system of the North was also rife with inconsistencies (as slaveholders often pointed out).

Nor do Douglass's innate feelings help us make sense of the problem of motivation. Acting, Douglass reminds us, involves all sorts of risks; it requires courage that the oppressed are unlikely to have, and desire that those who are born free are unlikely to feel. How, then, can the oppressed and apathetic be motivated? Must we rely on the apparently rare and inexplicable "spirit" that finally moved Douglass to resist? If so, what are the implications for democratic politics generally? Douglass comes across in this narrative as a unique case, unusually spirited and exceptionally lucky (a fact he admits himself, attributing his success to "a special interposition of divine Providence").[45] If his story is exceptional, then perhaps all we can learn from it is that only extraordinary people like Douglass can be counted on to perceive and act on the truth—which hardly bodes well for the progress of truth and reason, particularly in a democracy that lodges political power in the vast, unexceptional majority.

To make sense of his account of political enlightenment, we need a more illuminating account of how moral judgment is formed and how it can be perverted—or at least how we decide whose intuitions are reliable—and some explanation of how the general public (even those who lack Douglass's spirit) can be moved to act. In short, Douglass's references to his moral sense raise more questions about political enlightenment than they answer. So what is their role in political argument? More specifically, how exactly was Douglass's account of his political enlightenment supposed to enlighten the public about slavery—to fill its readers (as Garrison put it) with "an unutterable abhorrence of slavery" and animate them "with a determination to seek the immediate overthrow of that execrable system"?[46] Clearly, the persuasive force of the story did not lie in its inescapable logic; Douglass's reliance on the ill-defined concept of "moral sense" and the dubious authority of his own moral intuitions left his opponents plenty of room to dispute his conclusions. Was he just a bad rationalist, then, and Garrison too optimistic? Or was he up to something other than reasoning with the reader?

The Turn to Narrative

The remainder of the story, which turns from Douglass's own enlightenment to his attempts to enlighten others, suggests the latter. After his escape, we find Douglass in New Bedford, where he completes the process of becoming a freeman: he marries, chooses a name, begins to work for himself, and starts reading the *Liberator*. His accession to the status of political actor is complete when he attends an antislavery convention in Nantucket in 1841. There, he says, "I felt strongly moved to speak. . . . The truth was, I felt myself slave, and the idea of speaking to white people weighed me down." But (as Garrison told the story in his introduction to the *Narrative*), he "proceeded to narrate some of the facts in his own history as a slave, and in the course of his speech gave utterance to many noble thoughts and thrilling reflections."[47]

We should not be surprised that Douglass chose this act of public speaking to culminate the story of his transformation into a political actor, given the importance of oratory in antebellum political culture. But we should wonder why his oration took the form not of an argument but of a story: the facts of his life as a slave. After all, narrative played no part in awakening his political consciousness; it was not through hearing or telling stories that he learned to recognize injustice or was moved to take action. Like a good Enlightenment rationalist, he was influenced by his innate sense of right and wrong, by his own experiences and perceptions, and (to some extent) by the abstract arguments contained in the *Columbian Orator*. (Not a single excerpt in the book is a story; they are either arguments or expressions of sentiment.) Why, then, would Douglass choose to take his first step into abolitionist politics not by arguing his position but by telling a story?

The question is particularly puzzling because of the status of storytelling, particularly romantic stories, during this era. Horace Mann's warning about the dangers of fiction expressed the standard complaints about novel reading, complaints that dovetail easily with the assumptions and convictions of Enlightenment rationalism.[48] According to the critics of fiction, one cannot learn the truth from novels because the stories they tell aren't true. Novel writers, of course, objected that their stories, though factually false, taught moral truths; they informed the reader's judgment by pointing out the rewards of virtue and the costs of vice and provided models of moral excellence that the similarly situated reader could imitate. But critics worried that the world of romance was too far removed from everyday reality to provide good moral guidance; moreover, they charged that many novelists didn't even try to provide such guidance but created instead a fictional world in which vice is rewarded, villains are heroes, and virtues are vilified. A novel reader who took this world as an accurate picture of reality would lose the ability to recognize moral truths, to identify the truly virtuous and the truly evil. Behind such complaints may lurk the worry that novel writers, as a class, are not the sort of people we would want in charge of moral education; it is probably not coincidental that novel writing was generally considered a feminine occupation. But regardless of the reliability of the author's moral compass, novels posed another moral danger: Critics argued that novels appeal to the passions rather than, and at the expense of, the intellect. A novel reader, they worried, may come to view "sober thoughts" as "unwelcome intruders, which come to break the delusions, and to repress an insane exhileration [*sic*] of the feelings."[49] Thus, reading novels "saps the foundations of virtue and loosens the moral principles generally. The victim never goes so far as to break the laws, but is always lax in his or her notions of what is proper and right."[50]

To appreciate these complaints, we should keep in mind that the critics of novels probably did not object to all kinds of fantasies and fictions. For example, we do not find many critics worrying (à la Cervantes) that novels were filling the minds of young men with fantasies about war and heroism. (After all, the country's military power depended on a ready stock of romantic, foolhardy young men willing to risk their lives for noble ideals.) The fantasies that critics were worried about had to do with sex—with the stupid choices that young men and especially young women (novel reading was also widely considered a feminine occupation) make when under the influence of romantic novels. Love was the central theme in most novels, the "*principium et fons* of every movement*,*" and the conflict between desire and sexual mores was usually the central problem.[51] Significantly, many of the early critiques of novel reading in the United States referred to the sad case of Elizabeth Whitman, a beautiful young Connecticut woman who was, unfortunately, a novel reader. According to contemporary accounts, her reading habits impaired her judgment, leading her to reject a number of respectable suitors and become romantically involved with an unreliable scoundrel, who subsequently left her alone and pregnant. Her child was stillborn, and she died shortly after it was born. A number of newspapers reported the story, finding it an excellent example of the perils of novel reading.[52] Behind the complaints about novels lay fears about the real dangers facing young women like Whitman whose romantic fantasies led them to violate sexual mores.

Were slave narratives, like romantic novels, vulnerable to the charge that they propagated dangerous fictions? The narrators typically tried to defend themselves from such charges by insisting that their stories were not fiction at all, but strictly factual. The transcriber of Charles Ball's narrative, for example, insisted that he had simply recorded the facts and tried to "render the narrative as simple, and the style of the story as plain, as the laws of the language would permit." His aim was not to create entertaining fantasies but "[t]o introduce the reader, as it were, to a view of the cotton field, and exhibit, not to his imagination, but to his very eyes, the mode of life to which the slaves on the southern plantations must conform."[53] Ball himself echoes this denigration of imagination: "[A] man's knowledge is to be valued, not by that which he has imagined, but by that which experience has taught him." Thus he is "content to give facts as [he] saw them."[54] But, as Maria West Chapman's story about Pinda suggests, in storytelling, the line between truth and fiction is ambiguous. Frankly fictional novels about slavery also claimed to be factual. Harriet Beecher Stowe, for example, insisted that *Uncle Tom's Cabin* was a "work of fact" rather than fiction and that she "aimed, as far as possible, to say what is true, and only that."[55] In fact, novelists of all genres often advertised their work as founded on fact; some even included letters testifying to the truth of the story.[56] But the claim of being "founded on fact" actually tells us little about how much artistic license went into depicting the situations, characters, and dialogue. Stowe, for example, described her "factual" work as a "mosaic," a collection of events and characters drawn from real life and pasted together into a story—which seems a very short distance from fiction.

Even true slave narratives relied heavily on novelistic conventions that sometimes undermined their claim to authenticity. The memoirs of Lunsford Lane, for example, were advertised as plain facts, simply "a transcript" of social history, presented in a "plain style."[57] But it begins on an unmistakably romantic (if syntactically fractured) note: "Upon a pleasant afternoon in October, a slave, completing the day's labor some hours sooner than usual, his bosom swelling with emotions peculiar to a man about enjoying his first moment of freedom, when from being a chattel, he is about to experience the liberty wherewith God and Nature hath made him free!"[58] The story continues in this vein, replete with the usual novelistic conventions such as long and detailed embedded narratives and eloquent soliloquies (at one point the hero tells his wife that he is "borne up as if on eagles' wings").[59] And what should we make of the passage in Charles Ball's narrative recounting the speech he addressed to his dog before leaving it behind on the plantation? "Poor Trueman, faithful Trueman," he recited, "fare thee well. Thou hast been an honest dog, and sure friend to thy master in all his shades of fortune. When my basket was well filled, how cheerfully we have partaken together of its contents. I did not then upbraid thee, that thou atest in idleness the proceeds of my labour, for I knew that thy heart was devoted to thy protector. In the day of my adversity, when all the world had forsaken me, when my master was dead, and I had no friend to protect me, still, poor Trueman, thou wert the same."[60] And so it goes on, for two long paragraphs. Was this an accurate depiction of historical events, or (possibly tongue-in-cheek) romance?

To further confuse the issue, reactions to the slave narratives often put them in the category of romance, even while acknowledging their authenticity. Their heroes, claimed one review, made "the ordinary characters of romance . . . dull and tame." Some saw in them evidence that "the elements of poetry and romance" had not faded from the "tame and monotonous social life of modern times," and Angelina Grimké described them as tales of "romantic horror."[61] Thus slave narratives, even those grounded in facts, were open to the criticism that they appealed to the passions and impaired the reader's ability to distinguish truth from fantasy.

The charge could be devastating. If abolitionists relied on novelistic romances to make their case against slavery, their opponents could claim that their case was based on fantasies and delusions. And that is exactly what defenders of slavery did claim. If one is to understand southern society, warned one critic, "the vision should not be strained through the magnifying lenses of idle rumor and imaginative story."[62] Mary Eastman castigated Harriet Beecher Stowe for her descriptions of the squalid conditions of slave life: "Who . . . could read without an indignant thought" such descriptions? But they're not true, said Eastman. Nor are Stowe's characters accurate—the too-saintly Tom, the too-vicious slave driver Legree. And needless to say, the horrors and cruelties Stowe describes are "delusions."[63] The abolitionists, complained Eastman, had brought a dangerous element of fantasy and romance into politics: "It will do well enough, in a book of romance, to describe infants torn from the arms of their shrieking mothers, and sold for five and ten dollars. It tells well, for the mass of readers are fond of such horrors; but it is not true. . . . How did the snows of New England ever give birth to such brilliant imaginations!"[64] The dangers of such imaginations are even more serious than the dangers of romance novels; they might lead to emancipation and to "[s]cenes of blood and horror—the desolation of our fair Southern States—the final destruction of the negroes in them."[65] Slavery, like sex, was a matter in which fictions and fantasies could be particularly dangerous.

Of course, another complaint about storytelling is that it simply isn't as impressive an exercise of reason as abstract argument. This, at any rate, seemed to be Douglass's view of the matter. Wanting a chance to exercise his mental powers, he initially resisted the efforts of abolitionists to confine him to autobiographical stories in his speeches: "I was growing, and needed room."[66] His early speeches dwelled less on his personal life than on more general arguments against slavery. However, even Douglass gave in to the pressure to expand on his life story, partly because people began to question its authenticity, but also no doubt because this is what people wanted to hear. "Almost everywhere I go," he complained, "I am strangely pressed to tell the story of my life; and if I responded to all the demands made upon me on this behalf, I would have time for little else."[67]

Given the general denigration of romantic storytelling, why did Douglass and other abolitionists keep feeding the northern appetite for fugitive slave narratives? Why venture into the disreputable world of romance at all? To be sure, romantic stories were popular and a good way to secure an audience for abolitionist arguments—the means by which "[c]uriosity, discussion, investigation are stimulated, and public attention forcibly drawn to the subject."[68] But most abolitionists accorded the narratives a more central role in antislavery politics. The stories, they insisted, did not simply embellish a politics based primarily on rational arguments; rather, they were necessary because rational arguments were not enough to convince and motivate northern audiences to oppose slavery. Specifically, slave narratives were supposed to serve three purposes: they established a common body of facts from which to argue, they moved the general public to take action on behalf of an oppressed minority, and they accomplished the moral reform of the public that was needed before rational appeals could work. Examining these arguments in detail should give us some insight into what Douglass was up to in his narrative, why moral intuitions—rather than reasoned arguments—were so central to his story about political enlightenment, and what claims and commitments are behind the practice of political storytelling.

The Truth about Slavery

"Slavery has never been represented; Slavery never can be represented."[69] So asserted William Wells Brown, a popular fugitive slave speaker, in a lecture delivered in Boston in 1847. It is a strange statement, coming from someone whose vocation was representing slavery to northern audiences. It seems to make an epistemological point similar to that made by Frances Wright: that words cannot transmit knowledge as direct experience can. But Brown was making exactly the opposite claim: words *can* transmit direct sensory knowledge, and that was why he was unable to talk about all the evils of slavery. The truth, he claimed, was so shocking that the conventions of public discourse did not allow him to reveal it. "Your fastidiousness would not allow me to [represent the real condition of the slave.] Were I about to tell you the evils of Slavery, to represent to you the Slave in his lowest degradation, I should wish to take you, one at a time, and whisper it to you."[70] Brown's statement is not an attack on testimonial evidence but a tribute to its power to represent the truth about slavery.

His colleagues in the abolition movement agreed that one of their primary tasks must be the accurate representation of slavery, and this was one of the initial justifications for the publication of slave narratives. In 1839, for example, Theodore Weld published *American Slavery as It Is,* a collection of slave narratives and other material (taken mostly from southern newspapers) purporting to show the actual condition of slaves. He presented the pamphlet as a brief against slavery, subtitling it "Testimony of a Thousand Witnesses" and asking the reader to act as a "juror to try a plain case and bring in an honest verdict." The issue, he insisted, was one of fact: "What is the actual condition of the slaves in the United States?" This was not a matter of "sympathy or poetry," or even argument. Once the facts were established, the verdict was assured: "The case of Human Rights against Slavery has been adjudicated in the court of conscience times innumerable. The same verdict has always been rendered—'Guilty'; the same sentence has always been pronounced, 'Let it be accursed.' His heart is false to human nature, who will not say 'Amen.' There is not a man on earth who does not believe that slavery is a curse."[71]

All the abolitionists needed to do, then, was to present the facts about slavery through testimony.

Slave narrators frequently drew on this judicial analogy to explain their purposes. Moses Roper laid his narrative before the reader as "an impartial statement of facts"; Lunsford Lane's narrative was written to show "what it is to be a *slave*"; and Harriet Jacobs wrote her narrative to "add [her] testimony to that of abler pens to convince the people of the Free States what Slavery really is."[72] Charles Ball's narrative similarly began by explaining that "[t]he system of slavery, as practised in the United States, has been, and is now, but little understood by the people who live north of the Potomac and the Ohio." Thus he "endeavoured, faithfully and truly, to present to the reader, some of the most material accidents that occurred to [him], in a period of thirty years of slavery in the free Republic of the United States; as well as many circumstances, which [he] observed in the condition and conduct of other persons during that period."[73] This, then, was one justification for storytelling: it was a way to establish the facts about slavery.

Under this interpretation, narratives seem to fit easily into the Enlightenment model of political argument. After all, we can't have intelligent debate about an institution if we don't know what it is. But the claim that northerners didn't know about slavery complicated the Enlightenment model by distinguishing between two kinds of facts that may be relevant to political debate: those that are generally accessible to anyone, and those that aren't. Rationalists such as Matthew Carey and Frances Wright began from the premise that truth is easily accessible to anyone who cared to find it out.[74] Abolitionists found slavery a striking exception to that premise, identifying two major obstacles to discovering the facts about slavery. The first was that the United States was a big country. Slavery was confined to the South, and few northerners spent much time there. According to Ball, "A person who has not been in the slave-holding states, can never fully understand the bonds that hold society together there"; moreover, "the reader who has never resided south of the Potomac, will never be able to perceive things precisely as they present themselves to my vision."[75]

But even northerners who did travel in the South might not get an accurate picture of slavery. After all, they could see only what was presented to them, and southern slaveholders did not advertise the darker aspects of slavery. The slaveholder entertaining a northern visitor, argued Jacobs, "makes himself as agreeable as possible; talks on theology, and other kindred topics. . . . After dinner [the visitor] walks round the premises, and sees the beautiful groves and flowering vines, and the comfortable huts of favored household slaves. The southerner invites him to talk with these slaves. He asks them if they want to be free, and they say, 'O, no, massa.' This is sufficient to satisfy him. . . . What does *he* know of the half-starved wretches toiling from dawn till dark on the plantations?"[76] As Weld pointed out, "What insight do casual visitors get into the tempers and daily practices of those whom they visit, or of the treatment that their slaves receive at their hands. . . . What opportunity has a stranger, and a temporary guest, to learn the every-day habits and caprices of his host?"[77]

Although the difficulty of finding out the basic facts of social relations may seem peculiar to slavery, one sympathetic reviewer of *Uncle Tom's Cabin* considered it a more general problem: "[The novel] has astonished many also in the South, who, judging of the state of society only from what passes before their eyes, are ignorant of the existence of what they do not see, or indeed of the true meaning and nature of what they do see, until their attention is forcibly called to it. *Nothing is more common than such ignorance of what is passing around us.* How few know or think of the scenes of misery and destitution in our cities; yet they exist within a few squares of the comfortable and luxurious homes of wealth."[78] Against the assumption of a common, stable body of knowledge proposed by the Enlightenment model of political debate, this author points to the differing levels of knowledge—and certainty—that political actors bring to debate. It is this uneven distribution of information that gives testimony a central place in politics. And testimony, in turn, introduces a host of epistemological problems, revolving around two questions: Is the testimony generalizable, or is it just a partial, one-sided view of the subject? And, equally worrisome, is the witness telling the truth?

Generalization

Among the testimonials collected by Theodore Weld in *American Slavery as It Is* is a letter from William Leftwich detailing the condition of slaves on his uncle's estate. After describing his own unhappy experiences working for his uncle, he offers to "relate a few facts, showing the condition of the slaves *generally.*" He proceeds to describe three incidents in which his uncle whipped a slave. One earned the punishment by trying to escape, another was suspected of stealing, and the third's offense was unspecified; all were brutally beaten. The writer adds that he "could spend months in detailing the sufferings, degradation and cruelty inflicted upon slaves," but of course he does not do so. So we are left with three whippings by which to judge the condition of the slaves *generally.*[79] Defenders of slavery seized on the inadequacy of such evidence. "Can we judge of society by a few isolated incidents?" asked an indignant Mary Eastman.[80] A favorite strategy of antiabolitionists was to relate examples of cruelty exercised by northern employers toward their workers and to ask, "should we from this instance undertake to judge of the usual conduct of those having *white servants* . . . under their care in [the North]? . . . Surely no reasonable being would do any such thing; and yet it would be just as rational and proper, to make up a general opinion from this solitary case, as it would be to judge of the usual treatment of slaves at the South, from some instances of abuse, which an abolition writer might collect, or which, in the exercise of his ingenuity, he might invent."[81]

The attack was a potentially effective critique, since it made the abolitionists look like hypocrites as well as challenging their picture of slavery. And slave narratives were particularly vulnerable to this kind of complaint, since fugitive slaves could testify only to their own limited experience. Josiah Henson's narrative illustrates the problem. After describing the brutal treatment he received from his master, Riley, Henson tries to make a general point about the nature of slavery. First, he acknowledges that Riley's character was "by no means an uncommon one in any part of the world." The problem with slavery, he suggests, is "that a domestic institution should anywhere put it in the power of such a one to tyrannize over his fellow beings."[82] This is a good point, perhaps, but it is vulnerable to the argument that there are any number of commonly accepted relationships that allow for such abuse: between employer and employee, husband and wife, father and child, and so on. His second attempt to generalize is no more successful: "The natural tendency of slavery is to convert the master into a tyrant, and the slave into the cringing, treacherous, false, and thieving victim of tyranny. Riley and his slaves were no exception to the general rule, but might be cited as apt illustrations of the nature of the relation."[83] But Henson has already acknowledged that such characters are not uncommon in places that don't have slavery, and one isolated case hardly proves a general rule—perhaps he was brutal for some other reason. Slave narratives simply collected numerous unsystematic observations. How can one make general claims about the nature of slavery from this evidence?

Abolitionists were sensitive to the problem. Weld, for example, hoped to silence his opponents through the "accumulation of proof" by collecting "affirmations and affidavits, by written testimony and statements of a cloud of witnesses . . . and all these impregnably fortified by proofs innumerable."[84] His idea was to gather so many statements about the cruelty of slavery that they could not be dismissed as a few isolated incidents. But abolitionists frequently expressed frustration that their massive data failed to make an impact. As Jacobs complained, "Surely, if you credited one half the truths that are told you concerning the helpless millions suffering in this cruel bondage, you at the north would not help to tighten the yoke."[85] Unfortunately, there was no consensus on how many specific incidents of abuse would be enough to demonstrate the general character of the system.

But the abolitionists had other strategies for drawing general conclusions from specific cases. A common one was to describe the best cases, the conditions of the most favored slaves and the practices in the border states (which were considered to be less brutal than those of the Deep South). Angelina Grimké, for example, claimed that she knew "almost nothing of slavery on *plantations*" and offered to describe only "the treatment of '*house-servants*,' and chiefly those belonging to the first families in the city of Charleston."[86] Similarly, Lunsford Lane's narrative, according to his amanuensis, contained "the particulars of a life replete with incident, not of what slavery is under its most revolting features, but of what it is to be a slave, with a sensitive nature, under the most favorable circumstances."[87] (Lane lived most of his life in Raleigh, North Carolina, in the service of a wealthy family.) Henry "Box" Brown took the same approach: "It is not my purpose to descend deeply into the dark and noisome caverns of the hell of slavery; . . . Slavery . . . has two diverse sides to it; the one, on which is fearfully written in letters of blood, the character of the mass who carry on that dreadful system of unhallowed bondage; the other, touched with the pencil of a gentler delineator, and telling the looker on, a tale of comparative freedom, from the terrible deprivations so vividly portrayed on its opposite side."[88] Brown promised to present the "beautiful" side of slavery; he was not whipped or starved, but still suffered "those lashings of the heart, which the best of slaveholders inflict upon their happy and 'well off' slaves."[89]

Why ask the public to judge a system by its *best* case? This strategy had a number of advantages. In the first place, it allowed the abolitionists to reinforce the point that even many southerners had a limited knowledge of slavery and to invite the audience to imagine even worse cruelties—thus enlisting their most perverse fantasies in the cause of condemning slavery: "Let us hear . . . what [slavery] is at its best estate," suggested Wendell Philips, "and then imagination may task her powers to add dark lines to the picture, as she travels southward to that . . . Valley of the Shadow of Death, where the Mississippi seeps along."[90] The strategy also solved a dilemma for slave narrators—namely, whether to present themselves as typical slaves or exceptional ones. If they were typical, the reader could generalize more easily from their experiences, but it would be hard to explain why *this* slave was able to resist the allegedly degrading effects of slavery and escape. We have already encountered this problem in Douglass's *Narrative*. Was Douglass an exceptional character, a rare example of a black man for whom slavery was unsuitable, or were his experiences and feelings typical? If slavery generally turns the slave into a "cringing, treacherous, false, and thieving victim of tyranny," how did Josiah Henson and other narrators escape this fate? And why do we find, against the constant complaint that slavery necessarily degrades the slave, statements like that of Henry Brown, who insisted in his narrative that "all slaves harbor the hope of future freedom," and William Wells Brown, who asserted that "none but a slave" could truly value liberty?[91] This tension between the fugitive's status as a hero and his or her status as representative infects most of the narratives.[92] But claiming that the narrative describes the best case helps to resolve this tension: one explanation for these slaves' ability to escape the worst effects of slavery is that their circumstances were more favorable than those of most slaves. Douglass spent most of his young life as a house servant in Maryland; Henry Brown, also a house servant, was spared the worst physical cruelties; Charles Ball and Lunsford Lane were from Maryland rather than the Deep South; and William Wells Brown spent most of his servitude in St. Louis, where he even worked for Elijah Lovejoy for a time. Their relatively favorable conditions could account for their exceptionally strong characters, without undermining the claim that slavery as a rule turns men into beasts. As Jacobs explained it, "[H]ow can the slaves resolve to become men? There are some who strive to protect wives and daughters from the insults of their masters; but those who have such sentiments have had advantages above the general mass of slaves. They have been partially civilized and Christianized by favorable circumstances."[93]

So the slave narrators may not have been typical in all respects, but one could nevertheless draw general conclusions from such "best cases." Best cases were offered on the implicit assumption that one can deduce the permanent, inescapable defects of a system of social organization by focusing on how it works under the most favorable circumstances. According to the abolitionists, the permanent, inescapable feature of slavery was the chattel principle, a general principle that necessarily distorted the relationships and characters of the people caught up in the system. As Weld explained, "[H]e who holds human beings as his bona fide property, regards them as property, and not as persons; this is his permanent state of mind towards them. He does not contemplate slaves as human beings, consequently does not treat them as such."[94] If this hypothesis is true, then the negative effects of slavery should show up under even the best circumstances. In fact, one can observe the effects of slavery *best* by examining how it operates in the most civil and respectable homes, since once one has accounted for all the other reasons that a person might be exceptionally cruel—poor upbringing, lack of Christian values, economic necessity, and so forth—only the relation of slavery remains as a plausible explanation.

An obvious response to such reasoning would be to identify other reasons why respectable families might engage in brutality, but that could lead to a general attack on the family as an institution—hardly a viable strategy in the age of "the cult of domesticity." Defenders of slavery avoided that line of argument. Instead, they added to their arsenal another, more direct attack on narrative testimony: they challenged its truthfulness.

Veracity

The veracity of the narratives was questioned from the start. Charles Ball's 1836 narrative, the first of the classic antislavery narratives, was initially denounced as fictional; abolitionists insisted that it was true. Shortly thereafter, the popular narrative of Archy Moore, which was initially considered to be factual, was revealed to be the product of (white) novelist Richard Hildreth. A year later, the narrative of James Williams was declared false by the American Anti-Slavery Society, which had taken upon itself the duty of investigating the truthfulness of the narratives. The narrative of Harriet Jacobs met the same fate; it was popularly thought to have been written by Lydia Maria Child. (In 1987, Jean Fagan Yellin used recently discovered letters to establish Harriet Jacobs's authorship of the narrative.)[95]

The credibility of the narratives was further confused by the general mingling of fact and fiction in abolitionist literature. I have already discussed the difficulty of untangling fact from fiction in romance novels; for slave narrators, the problem was exacerbated by the proliferation of fictional versions of slave narratives, such as Mattie Griffiths's *Autobiography of a Female Slave.* There is nothing in Griffiths's story to indicate that it is fiction. In fact, the narrator insists that she is a "veracious historian": "This book is not a wild romance to beguile your tears and cheat your fancy. No; it is the truthful autobiography of one who has suffered long, long, the pains and trials of slavery."[96] Such protestations were common devices in novels, and readers probably understood that they were not to be taken literally when they appeared in a work of fiction. But in the case of slave narratives, that was precisely the point at issue: is it fact or fiction? For example, Lunsford Lane's (factual) narrative includes the following assertion: "The reader may as well be assured here as at any other time, that the narrative here given to the public is a statement of matters of fact, either received from the lips of Mr. Lane himself, or from information possessed by the compiler by a residence in the South, or drawn from well-authenticated documents."[97] Sarah Hale's (fictional) novel about slavery contains a similar statement about the authenticity of some letters the narrator refers to: "To explain how these letters fell into my hands, would be a long and needless story; but the reader may depend on their authenticity. Yet the veracity of a historian obliges me to acknowledge they have undergone some alterations. The orthography needed many corrections, and the punctuation had to be entirely supplied."[98] How is the casual reader to know which of these statements is to be taken literally?

Or perhaps we should ask, in what sense is each narrative "true"? Romance novelists, after all, had a good claim to be telling the truth, even if their stories were wholly the products of their own imaginations. As a reviewer of *Uncle Tom's Cabin* explained, "Eva and Tom are dreams; the one is a saint, the other an angel. But dreams are founded on realities, and 'we are all such stuff as dreams are made of.' These characters are both exaggerated; but to color and idealize is the privilege of romance, provided the picture does not over-step the modesty of nature or contradict nature."[99] An imitator of Stowe's made a similar point: "[W]orks of the present class are charged by some with exaggeration. In one sense they are exaggerations. There are points in which they do not correspond with the reality. It is, however, only in those respects in which all works of fiction resting on a basis of fact transcend the actualities of life. The tame, the common-place, the repetitious are thrown out of view, just as the painter omits many of the trivial objects in his landscape, and yet is true to nature and fact."[100] Thus, even if the story had only a slight con-nection to its factual basis, it might still be true; romance novels claimed to deal in a different kind of truth than the factual, verifiable sort of truth that politics was supposed to be based on. They purported to teach *moral* truths, general principles of right conduct and its consequences that transcended the actor's specific circumstances.[101] But defenders of slavery objected to this "throwing out" of the tame, commonplace, and repetitious. Political argu-ments, they insisted, are not supposed to transcend the "actualities of life." Thus, despite their claim to some essential truthfulness, every slave narrative raised the question, is this truth or fantasy?

The question became a central axis of the abolition debate as it took shape in the 1830s. Defenders of slavery argued that the institution was actually beneficial to slaves, raising them "to a condition of moral, intellectual and civil improvement, and to a state of protection, comfort and happiness never elsewhere, not in any period of the world's history, known to any portion of the negro race."[102] This claim would be hard to maintain if the cruelties and hardships documented by the abolitionists were true. So the pro-slavery case rested in part on the claim that the abolitionists lacked credibility: "[T]here has been, and continues to be, a vast deal of misapprehension on this subject [the effect of slavery on morality], especially amongst those Abolitionists who suppose, *or pretend,* that in slavery of South, there is a continued succession of crimes, as well as of injustice and cruelty."[103] "[A] few flashes of truth," suggested Mary Eastman, "would make [the abolition cause] decidedly more respectable." As it was, abolitionists were guilty of "gross misrepresentations," either deliberately deceptive or culpably negligent in not taking proper means to "find out the delusions under which they labor."[104] Slave stories are mere "literary fancies," another critic charged, citing *Uncle Tom's Cabin* as an example: "The truth is, that all these characters, Tom, Topsy, Cassy, Sambo, Quimby, etc., are not living people; they are only Mrs. Stowe's feelings dressed up—her emotions transfigured on paper. When we go to the South we will not look out for one of them—either in Kentuck or Louisiana. We know they are not there."[105] One southerner argued that one simply could not expect truth from abolitionists; after all, the documentary evidence against slavery comes from "acknowledged abolitionists of the ultra stamp," who may be "mistaken in their calculations, being liable to derangement through their mad fanaticism or subject to blindness to the truth through the bias of selfish prejudice."[106]

If abolitionists' trustworthiness was suspect, that of fugitive slaves was even more so. One commentator noted that slaves, like everyone else, have a one-sided view of slavery. The narratives "give, doubtless, a just idea of what slavery is to the slave. But, on the other hand, . . . we have no doubt that they convey an altogether erroneous idea of the general character of the masters."[107] But the more serious problem is that slaves, and especially fugitive slaves, were stereotyped in the North as in the South as untrustworthy. Before the 1830s, even abolitionists in northern cities such as Philadelphia tended to characterize blacks in general as "degraded and vicious," loose in both morals and conduct.[108] Although this depravity was typically attributed to the heritage of slavery, it was still sufficient to impair slaves' and even free blacks' reputation for truthfulness. As Gerrit Smith put it, "Simple-hearted and truthful, as these fugitives appeared to be, you must recollect that they are slaves—and that the slave, as a general thing, is a liar, as well as a drunkard and a thief."[109] Similarly, Mattie Griffiths's protagonist in *Autobiography of a Female Slave* complained, " '*Honest for a nigger*,' is a phrase much in use in Kentucky. . . . It was so common a charge—that of liar and thief—that despite my practice to the contrary, I almost began to accept the terms as deserved."[110] The stigma was reinforced by the common rule that blacks could not give testimony against whites in court, and even those who criticized the rule acknowledged the general untrustworthiness of such testimony: "Cannot a negro tell what he knows, and describe what he has seen and heard? And is it not sufficient that he is subjected to cross-examination, that court, bar, and jury are composed of the superior race, and that his testimony will be received with caution, *because of his color and condition?*"[111] In short, slaves were simply designated liars; they were people whose presumed character, condition, or capacity warranted an automatic dismissal of their testimony.

Abolitionists, either sharing this prejudice or at least recognizing it, did not rely only on testimony from slaves. Theodore Weld's strategy was to forestall accusations of untrustworthiness by using "the testimony of slaveholders in all parts of the slaves states, by slaveholding members of Congress and of state legislatures, by ambassadors to foreign courts, by judges, by doctors of divinity . . . by planters, overseers and drivers."[112] Much of his pamphlet, *American Slavery as It Is,* consists of extracts from speeches of slaveholders and, especially, from southern newspapers. Notices of escaped slaves like the following were useful for providing evidence of the brutal treatment of slaves: "$100 will be paid to any person who may apprehend and safely confine in any jail in this state, a certain negro man, named ALFRED. And the same reward will be paid, if satisfactory evidence is given of *his having been killed.* He has one or more scars on one of his hands, caused by his having been shot."[113] Other notices listed the burns, scars, and other deformities by which escaped slaves could be identified, which Weld helpfully linked to typical punishments meted out to slaves. A particularly chilling one read: "Ranaway, a negro woman and two children; a few days before she went off, *I burnt her with a hot iron,* on the left side of her face, *I tried to make the letter M.*"[114] Since slaveholders, as Weld explained, had no interest in making slavery look worse than it was, such evidence should be reliable.[115]

But it was also necessarily fragmentary, in contrast to the detailed slave narratives. These the abolitionists took pains to authenticate, investigating their truthfulness and prefacing them with letters from whites of good reputation testifying to the good character of the writer.[116] The problem for the slave narrators was that the people who typically investigated the stories or wrote the letters were themselves abolitionists, or became associated with the cause by their testimony. Did it help the credibility of Douglass's narrative that it was introduced by William Lloyd Garrison and Wendell Philips, whom the pro-slavery contingent had already branded as fanatics? Douglass didn't think so. As he explained to a southern editor who confirmed that Douglass had in fact been a slave: "Our cautious and truth-loving people in New England would never have believed this testimony, in proof of my identity, had it been borne by an abolitionist. . . . Not that they really think an abolitionist capable of bearing false witness intentionally; but such persons are thought fanatical, and to look at everything through a distorted medium."[117] Testimonials, then, had limited value in authenticating the narratives.

But slave narrators had another response to the problem of veracity: they attacked the image of slaves as liars not by denying that slaves often lie but by unpacking what makes slaves lie and under what conditions they will tell the truth. Slaves, narrators insisted, were not naturally disposed to lie. Consider the story of James Pennington. Captured as he was trying to escape, his captors asked him who he belonged to, a question that presented him with a "great moral dilemma": "The facts demanded were in my breast. I knew according to the law of slavery, who I belonged to and where I came from, and I must now do one of three things—I must refuse to speak at all, or I must communicate the fact, or I must tell an untruth. How would an untutored slave . . . be likely to act in such a dilemma?"[118] Of course he lied, telling them that he was free, but not without some moral anguish. He did offer a rationalization, concluding that the facts in this case were his "private property" and that his captors had no right to them—a weak argument, however, because his captors were under a legal obligation to turn in escaped slaves, and his status as a slave was hardly a private matter. A more compelling justification was the fact that, if he told them that he was a slave, "[i]n forty-eight hours, I shall have received perhaps one hundred lashes, and be on my way to the Louisiana cottonfields."[119] How can anyone be expected to tell the truth under such circumstances? Thus, after escaping from these men and being recaptured, he lied again, more creatively: he told his captors that he had been part of a large gang of slaves headed for Georgia, but they had contracted smallpox. As a result, no one wanted to claim them. Fortunately for Pennington, this lie was effective; his captors didn't want to claim him either, and he managed to escape again.

But despite the success of the strategy, Pennington was uncomfortable with lying. "If you ask me if I expected when I left home to gain my liberty by fabrications and untruths? I answer, No! my parents, slaves as they were, had always taught me, when they could, that 'truth may be blamed but cannot be ashamed': so far as their example was concerned, I had no habits of untruth."[120] It was not his character, then, but his extraordinary circumstances that led him to lie. William Wells Brown made the same point by telling how he tricked another black man into taking a whipping meant for himself. His master had sent him to the jail with a note instructing the jailer to administer a whipping to the bearer. Brown told a passing black man that the note instructed him to pick up a trunk at the jail and be paid a dollar for it, and asked him to do the job. His victim went to the jail and received Brown's punishment. According to Brown, "This incident shows how it is that slavery makes its victims lying and mean; for which vices it afterwards reproaches them."[121]

These stories (at least on the surface) refute the conception of slaves as a dangerously alien population lacking normal human virtues. Slaves, they imply, are just like anyone else—if taught to be truthful as children, they will be truthful, or at least as truthful as possible. Whether they make this claim successfully is another matter. Although Pennington seems genuinely contrite over his need to lie, Brown seems to take pleasure in tricking his fellow slave and to have a certain pride in his cleverness. And he wasn't alone; many slave narrators appeared from time to time in the guise of the trickster, a familiar figure in African and Native American folklore—an amoral sprite who takes pleasure in causing trouble and whose pious expressions of remorse are not to be taken seriously.[122] The trickster aspect of Brown's character undermines his claim to truthfulness and normalcy; we aren't sure whether he is really a conscientious truth-teller or merely posing as one. Alternatively, his story could be read as attacking the norm of truthfulness itself, by adopting a mocking tone toward this normally sacrosanct value. Under this reading, Brown is involving the reader in his defiance of conventional morality, saying, in essence, "Whatever your pretensions to honesty and fair dealing, you appreciate the joke as much as I do."

The trickster motif was (appropriately) difficult to control; it might obscure or confuse the moral stance from which the narrator was criticizing slavery. (What are we to make of Brown's complicity in the whipping of another slave?) But the treatment of truthfulness in the narratives was problematic for other reasons. Narrators generally treated truthfulness as a habit, an ingrained disposition to act in a particular way. In discussions of honesty, then, habit joined the triumvirate of reason, passion, and interest as a possible explanation of human behavior. Its virtue for the slave narrators is that it allowed them to distinguish between truly untruthful characters and those who lie only under unusual circumstances. James Pennington, for example, claimed that he was habitually truthful, even though his self-interest led him to lie to his captors. But this kind of explanation led to the following problem: if truthfulness is *always* against one's interest, how would one ever develop the habit of truthfulness? The very condition of being a slave (reminded one abolitionist) is antagonistic to truthfulness: "The negro, like other men, naturally desires to live in the light of truth; but he hides in the shadow of falsehood, more or less deeply, according as his safety or welfare seems to require it. Other things being equal, the freer a people, the more truthful; and only the perfectly free and fearless are perfectly truthful."[123] The argument refers to the familiar conflict between truth and interest, and the usual pessimistic assumption that interest always wins. In this case, the pull of interest defeats truth by a kind of preemptive strike, preventing slaves from ever developing the habit of truthfulness. So why should we believe any of the slave narrators?

But the conflict between truth and interest can work in the abolitionists' favor, too. If interest leads slaves to lie, then how reliable are reports from slaves that they are contented? Frederick Douglass explained that masters would punish slaves for complaining, which naturally had the effect of teaching them to lie about their condition: "They suppress the truth rather than take the consequences of telling it, and in so doing prove themselves a part of the human family."[124] The same reasoning, from Theodore Weld, undermines the credibility of slaveholders who defend the institution: "Now let candor decide between those two classes of slaveholders, which is most entitled to credit; that which testifies in its own favor, just as self-love would dictate, or that which testifies against all selfish motives and in spite of them. . . ."[125] Thus neither slaves nor slaveholders can be trusted when they claim that slavery is beneficial to the slave.

By now it should be apparent that the debate over the veracity of narratives, rather than settling the issue of who could be trusted, simply proliferated reasons not to trust anyone. Abolitionists and their supporters can't be trusted because they are deluded by romantic fantasies or swayed by sentimentalism (or simply motivated by greed).[126] Slaves and slaveholders who defend slavery can't be trusted because their interests impair their credibility; and even impartial observers can't be trusted because they aren't likely to see what's actually going on. So instead of producing a consensus about the facts of slavery, the narratives became mired in epistemological uncertainty, prompting apparently endless and irresolvable disputes over the truth about slavery.

Conclusion

In sum, slave narratives were not particularly effective at establishing the facts about slavery. Despite the best efforts of the abolitionists, they remained vulnerable to the charge that such cases were not typical, or that they simply couldn't be believed. To their critics, they were too romantic, obviously designed to sell and to entertain, and written and published by interested parties whose trustworthiness was already suspect. All they could do was raise questions about the actual conditions of slaves, while making it difficult for anyone to resolve those questions authoritatively. Such an evaluation, of course, ignores the incisive theoretical arguments elaborated in many of the narratives about the nature of the master-slave relationship. But if the value of the narratives actually lay in their theoretical arguments, why not just make arguments and leave off storytelling, which only seemed to undermine the speaker's credibility?

Some abolitionists did, in fact, leave off storytelling, a strategy represented by Hinton Helper. Helper was a free labor abolitionist, part of a movement that began to gain prominence in the 1840s.[127] The free labor camp, including such theorists as Theodore Sedgwick, Henry Carey, and Frederick Law Olmsted, opposed slavery primarily on economic grounds, and their theoretical arguments paved the way for Helper's rejection of narrative testimony in favor of economic data. As he explained in his 1857 treatise *The Impending Crisis of the South,* "Yankee wives have written the most popular anti-slavery literature of the day. Against this I have nothing to say; it is all well enough for women to give the fictions of slavery; men should give the facts."[128] So much for the novelists' insistence that they *were* giving the facts. The relevant facts, for Helper, were not the psychological insights of (female) novelists but hard, manly numbers. He offered an analysis of the impact of slavery on the southern economy based on census data, which lent his work an aura of scientific objectivity that slave narratives couldn't achieve. Instead of examining the complexities of the master-slave relationship, Helper took a survey of "the relative position and importance of the several states of this confederacy"—their populations, exports and imports, and the cash value of their real estate and other property. Using this data, he argued that the problem with slavery was that it was economically inefficient; it had depressed the economy of the South.[129]

Clearly, one of the virtues of such arguments was that they relied on publicly available and widely accepted data, and so were less vulnerable to the problems of credibility that plagued narratives. Or so Helper believed; he offered to rest his case on "incontrovertible facts and statistics" whose magic would, he claimed, "soon terminate the existence of slavery." His numbers, he noted, "have been obtained from official sources, and may, therefore, be relied on as correct." And they were generalizable; a statistical description of a country, he argued, "more perfectly explained its social condition than general statements, however graphic or however accurate."[130]

Helper's critics disagreed, of course. According to Samuel Wolfe, statistics are an "effectual and plausible mode of deceiving and misleading the human understanding" because people are "too apt . . . to take whatever is presented to their understanding in the shape of figures, as so;—believing it to be a work of too much labor for figures to lie."[131] In other words, statistics are more misleading than slave narratives because the very genre of romance raises the issue of credibility in a way that the genre of scientific discourse does not. However, Wolfe's quarrel with Helper centered less on whether his numbers were accurate than on how to measure economic productivity; Wolfe argued that export revenue alone should be the proper measure.[132] Debate over how to interpret the numbers continued (and continues to this day), but at least it was informed by a higher degree of consensus on what the basic facts were.

One might have expected economic arguments to supplant the slave narratives, being generally more credible and "manly." But in fact, abolitionists kept writing and selling narratives throughout the 1850s, without making

any attempt to disassociate the factual narratives from fictional romance novels. The frankly fictional *Uncle Tom's Cabin,* after all, was widely hailed as the
most effective piece of abolitionist literature ever written.[133] It was followed
by a host of imitators—including pro-slavery versions of the genre, such as
Mary Eastman's *Aunt Phillis's Cabin* and W. L. G. Smith's *Life at the South:
or "Uncle Tom's Cabin" as It Is.*[134] By the late 1850s, the general public no
longer seemed to care whether narratives were fact or fiction; as Mary Starling
put it, "In an atmosphere saturated with slave stories, fact and fancy came
together to form one thing: books on slavery."[135] The narratives remained
central to the abolition movement—but for reasons other than their ability
to establish the facts about slavery. The following chapter explores these
reasons.

6

SYMPATHY

The previous chapter considered the claims of slave narratives to be (despite appearances) legitimate entries in the politics of reason—not sentimental flights of fancy, but a useful corrective for our limited information and partial, distorted perspectives. But more prominent in abolitionist rhetoric was the claim that the political value of slave narratives lay not in their stock of information about slavery but in their ability to generate sympathy for slaves. Thus while Theodore Weld began *American Slavery as It Is* by promising to prove the facts of slavery, his English colleague Wilson Armistead began one of the most widely distributed antislavery pamphlets by promising to "increase a feeling of sympathy for that portion of suffering humanity whose own voice has but little chance of being heard." The pamphlet was aimed at keeping the public mind "alive to the great subject of the negro's wrongs, till such time as they are effectually redressed." Similarly, Harriet Jacobs declared that although she did not hope to receive sympathy for her own sufferings, she did want "to arouse the women of the North to a realizing sense of the condition of two million women at the South." James Pennington hoped to "elicit your sympathy in behalf of the fugitive slave, by shewing some of the untold dangers and hardships through which he has to pass to gain liberty." And white narrators also offered testimony "to awaken more feeling at the North in behalf of the slave."[1]

I suppose this sounds, to us, like a patently obvious strategy. But for the abolitionists (and perhaps for us, too), the politics of sympathy was treacherous territory both conceptually and politically. Conceptually, for example, are "sympathy," "a realizing sense" of the slaves' conditions, "feeling in behalf of the slave" all talking about the same thing? What exactly is sympathy, anyway—a feeling, a faculty, a psychological process? And politically, how does the politics of sympathy stack up against the politics of reason? Why didn't these calls for (maudlin, romantic, feminine) sympathy undermine the legitimacy of the whole effort? In short, how exactly was sympathy supposed to advance the cause of abolitionism?

Here I want to unpack the concept of sympathy and its possible political uses by exploring the two remaining justifications for storytelling: first, that sympathy could motivate action in behalf of slaves, and second, that sympathy could purify and reform the public's moral nature. Sympathy and storytelling (I argue) were linked in important ways; thus no simple rationalist justification for political storytelling can account for its role in abolitionist politics. On the contrary, for the abolitionists, the chief virtue of sympathy was that it gave them a way out of the framework of Enlightenment rationalism, allowing them to offer a description of democratic politics that accorded a legitimate place to passion, eloquence—even, perhaps, violence.

Who Cares about Slaves?

"Northerners," asserted Harriet Jacobs, "know nothing at all about Slavery. They think it is perpetual bondage only. They have no conception of the depth of *degradation* involved in that word, SLAVERY; if they had, they would never cease their efforts until so horrible a system was overthrown." Such expressions of faith in the power of truth to motivate action are already familiar to us from Chapter 4; Henry Box Brown echoed Frances Wright and William Heighton when he asked, "O, who can hear of these cruel deprivations, and not be aroused to action in the slave's behalf?"[2] But in fact there were far too many people who could hear of such cruel deprivations without raising a finger in the slave's behalf. As William Elder pointed out, a sense of civic duty was not sufficient to motivate large numbers of citizens to defend the slave. "[T]he multitude of working men," he argued, are "much too occupied with the general interests of productive industry, and the more equal distribution of wealth in their own world, to give an effective sympathy to the slave of the South."[3] People may act consistently on general principles, he suggested, but only when their concrete interests are at stake. Thus Elder and others in the free labor movement looked for ways to tie abolition to the interests of northern workers. Theodore Sedgwick, for example, argued that slavery and free labor cannot coexist; if tolerated, the slave system would eventually destroy the country's republican institutions. Increasingly this camp of slavery opponents raised the specter of "slave power," a southern conspiracy to seize political power and destroy the liberties of northern citizens in order to protect their cherished system.[4] Presumably, the threat to their political liberties would motivate northern workers to oppose slavery.

But the slave narrators suggested that there was something besides abstract principle and concrete interest that could motivate political action: sympathy. Even if their interests weren't at stake, northern workers could give an "effective sympathy" to slaves—meaning not just compassion but also active involvement in the cause of abolition. Wilson Armistead's claim that arousing sympathy for slaves could keep the public mind "alive to the great subject of the negro's wrongs, till such time as they are effectually redressed," makes this connection between sympathy and action explicit, as does Josiah Henson's declaration that he wanted to inspire "a deeper interest" in his race ("interest" here meaning concern), which he hoped would "lead to corresponding activity in their behalf."[5] Thus we might read Harriet Jacobs's and Henry Brown's faith in the narratives' motivational potential as referring not to the irresistible power of truth but to the irresistible power of sympathy.

This sounds promising; maybe sympathy can lead us out of the impasse between reason and action explored in Chapter 4 (that is, the conclusion that the only legitimate basis for political action is reason, which has no power to motivate political action). But before considering whether and how sympathy can serve as a basis for political action, we need to be clear about what abolitionists meant by this notoriously slippery term. We've already encountered sympathy in Chapter 3, in explanations of the skillful orator's ability to influence the audience, the lower classes' tendency to defer to the aristocracy, and the strange powers of mesmerism. These examples only begin to illustrate the central place sympathy held in antebellum moral philosophy. The term was ubiquitous—and not just in the respectable pages of philosophical treatises. One of the first American novels, by William Hill Brown, is entitled *The Power of Sympathy.* It recounts the tragic story of a pair of lovers who discover that they are brother and sister. They blame familial sympathy for their fatal attraction; despite the fact that they were separated at birth, they were "ALLIED by birth, and in mind, and similar in age—and in thought still more intimately connected" by "the sympathy which bound [their] souls together."[6] (Not coincidentally, Brown establishes the young heroine as acutely and dangerously susceptible to sympathy by showing her ardent compassion for slaves.)

Brown's sympathy is a spiritual link, although apparently enhanced in some obscure way by biological connection. For followers of Franz Mesmer, in contrast, sympathy could be conceived as the natural product of a physical, if etheric, substance, the invisible, fluidlike medium that binds all human beings and, mysteriously, allows the mesmerist to establish dominance over the will of his subject. This notion of sympathy, strange as it sounds, was also widely circulated, popularized by mesmerists' lectures and stage performances (and its creepier implications explored by writers such as Edgar Allen Poe).[7] But more common, probably, was Adam Smith's conception of sympathy as a "kind of pity or compassion" produced when, "[b]y the imagination we place ourselves in [another's] situation, we conceive ourselves enduring all the same torments, we enter as it were into his body, and become in some measure the same person with him." So "[h]is agonies, when they are thus brought home to ourselves . . . begin at last to affect us." In other words, we can, by a process of imaginative identification with another person, experience his or her feeling of pain (or joy); this somewhat weaker but analogous emotion is sympathy. (Thus Smith defines it as "our fellow-feeling with any passion.")[8]

Smith's account, however, conflates two distinct dimensions of sympathy: the process by which we come to experience another person's feeling, and the feeling (often, but not always, compassion) that results from that process. In many contexts, the distinction is unimportant; sympathy can stand for the whole psychological progression from imaginative identification to compassion. Thus sympathy was often used simply as a synonym for compassion or pity. The author of the popular novel *Charlotte Temple,* for example, tells us that "the tear of compassion" falls for its sad heroine, and "the soul melts with sympathy." The heroine of another romance novel cares for her ailing suitor with the "sympathizing tenderness of a sister" (and later becomes the object of her friends' "sympathizing pity"). Similarly, when Fanny Fern's Ruth Hall craves sympathy for her sufferings, she is asking only for compassion and gentler treatment from her relations, not spiritual bonding.[9] And Nathaniel Hawthorne plays on this sense of sympathy in *The Blithedale Romance,* albeit distinguishing "common pity" from the narrator's true sympathy for the lovelorn heroine: "[A]s Zenobia leaned her forehead against the rock, shaken with that tearless agony, it seemed to me that the self-same pang, with hardly mitigated torment, leaped thrilling from her heart-strings to my own."[10] Abolitionists, too, used "sympathy" to express compassion; Angelina Grimké offered "sentiments of sympathy" to William Lloyd Garrison as he battled proslavery mobs in the summer of 1835, while her sister Sarah insisted that slaves had as great a claim as seamen to "the sympathy and benevolent effort" of southern evangelists. While dwelling on the suffering of seamen, she asked, "was there no cord of sympathy in thy heart to vibrate to the groans of the slave?"[11] Thus Pennington's proposal to "elicit your sympathy in behalf of the fugitive slave," like Weld's desire to "awaken more feeling at the North in behalf of the slave," can be read simply as an intention to generate compassion for slaves.

In some contexts, however, "sympathy" could lose its association with compassion and refer solely to the process of imaginative identification—which, importantly, needn't be confined to another person's feelings. Sympathy could give one access to another person's thoughts and perspective, as well as his or her feelings. (This meaning, no doubt, was supported and given content by the development of mesmerism and the popular interest in spiritualism, but also by its use in neoclassical rhetoric; a good orator could make the audience not just feel but also think and see the world as he did.) Under this reading, sympathy might have a cognitive dimension; adopting another person's perspective could, for example, cure the ignorance of "what is passing around us" that results from our partial, one-sided view of the world.[12] Also, clearly, it needn't have any special connection with compassion. Seeing the world from another person's point of view *might* facilitate compassion for that person, but it might just as easily foster fear, wonder, revulsion, anger, or contempt. (Imagine looking at the world from the point of view of a racist or a psychotic killer.) Certainly Hawthorne's and Poe's portrayals of mesmerism were innocent of any suggestion that the mesmerist's power might make him, or his subjects, more compassionate.[13]

In short, references to sympathy usually brought into play the idea of imaginative identification and typically (but not always) the implication of compassion stemming from such identification as well. This association with compassion helps to account for the abolitionists' positive view of sympathy, as I discuss later. But even without any special link to compassion, sympathetic identification could be a positive force in politics. While critics of mesmerism were worrying that sympathy could compromise individual identity, abolitionists saw in the phenomenon the means to bridge differences and create unity: because sympathy allows one person to share in the experiences of another, it has the power to extend the feeling of the slave's suffering among the general public, and thus prompt general resistance to slavery. (Remember that the feeling of injustice is, in the still-influential Whig tradition of resistance, the usual impetus to political action.)[14] Importantly, this argument doesn't rest on the claim that sympathetic identification with slaves will necessarily result in warm, benevolent feelings toward them; it might, on the contrary, simply annoy people and induce them to avoid being reminded of the slaves' suffering. But if they *can't* avoid exposure to the slaves' suffering, if abolitionist literature has saturated the community, they might be motivated to relieve the suffering the abolitionists keep reminding them about— for their own sake, if not from any desire to help slaves. Thus sympathy could make particular interests general. In principle, the suffering of a single slave, if communicated properly and thoroughly, could be enough to motivate the entire country to take action. Sympathy, then, made it possible to create a nationwide political movement aimed at protecting the interests of minorities.

Nevertheless, playing on the audience's sympathy looks like a suspect tactic from the standpoint of a committed rationalist. As mentioned earlier, sympathetic identification could have a cognitive dimension; thus, identifying with slaves *might* produce a better understanding of the institution and its effects. This case for sympathy is simply a restatement of the argument laid out in Chapter 5, that slave narratives could inform the public what slavery was really like. But the abolitionists' calls for sympathy appeared to be aimed at generating compassion for slaves, anger at slaveholders, or discomfort at the thought of suffering, rather than (or at least in addition to) fostering rational comprehension of the slave system. After all, if it didn't arouse the passions, sympathy would have little motivational value.

Unfortunately, these were precisely the kinds of appeals to the passions

that opened the abolitionists up to the charge that they were simply demagogues, and that their appeals rested on "sickly" and "mawkish" sentimental-
ity.[15] This sentimentalism, according to the pro-slavery camp, would lead to
a dangerously quixotic kind of politics, full of "enthusiams, ebullitions, animosities" (and "we think there may be better ways of coming at ends considered
good, than by running full tilt against the opposition, like Don Quixote").[16]
Sympathy without a good dose of hardheaded rationalism, then, was hardly
a better basis for politics than interest. And abolitionists, for their part, also
had concerns about a politics based on sympathy. Sympathy worked on the
passions, and the passions are notoriously unstable. Why do some abolitionists "grow cold in their work," asked one antislavery advocate, while others
"pursue the even tenor of [their] way? The difficulty we apprehend lies in the
different ways or doors through which these two persons entered into this
work. One entered through the door of feeling—the other of reason. One
entered by the way of impulse—the other by the way of judgment. . . . And
as they entered, so they continue." So the "lukewarm abolitionist" is guided
by feeling, instinct, and impulse, and "they come and go according to cir-
cumstance."[17]

But this doesn't mean that sympathy couldn't find a secure place in abolition politics. The abolitionists had a more subtle argument to make about
politics and sympathy. It's not just that appeals to passion can motivate political action, but fostering sympathy may be necessary to inform (or reform)
defective moral judgment, thus removing a major barrier to rational argument. This connection between sympathy and judgment is the focus of the
next section.

Romance and Reform

By 1845, after fifteen years of abolitionist agitation, slavery was just as firmly
entrenched as it had been in 1830. William Lloyd Garrison was baffled. Why,
he wondered, were so many people "stubbornly incredulous" about the evils
of slavery? "They do not deny that the slaves are held as property; but that
terrible fact seems to convey to their minds no idea of injustice, exposure to
outrage, or savage barbarity."[18] Why did the abundant evidence of its cruelty
and injustice fail to produce the immediate overthrow of the institution?
More generally, what accounts for the failure of reasoned argument to undermine a practice that (in Garrison's opinion) had no rational justification?

The question plagued abolitionists. As the South produced ever more vocal and vigilant defenders of slavery, the abolitionists' initial confidence that
simply exposing the system would destroy it began to flag. Horace Greeley

complained, "Is it in vain that we pile fact upon fact, proof on proof, showing that slavery is a blight and a curse to the States which cherish it? These facts are multitudinous as the leaves of the forest; conclusive as the demonstrations of geometry. Nobody attempts to refute them, but the champions of slavery extension seem determined to persist in ignoring them."[19] In *Autobiography of a Female Slave,* one of Mattie Griffiths's characters despairs that "I never heard a pro-slavery man who could, upon any reasonable ground, defend his position. The slavery argument is not only a wicked, but an absurd one." Nonetheless, her pro-slavery characters continue to defend the institution— even when soundly outreasoned by eloquent abolitionists. Thus the impatience with argument that Douglass expressed in his 1852 Fourth of July speech echoed a prominent theme in abolitionist literature: "Would you have me argue that man is entitled to liberty? that he is the rightful owner of his own body? You have already declared it. Must I argue the wrongfulness of slavery?"[20] There is a charge of hypocrisy implicit in such complaints, but also a frustration with reasoned argument, even a sense of bewilderment. If all is plain, if the wrongfulness of slavery is inarguable, why does it persist? And if argument cannot defeat slavery, what can?

Moral Blindness

In the face of the apparent impotence of their arguments, abolitionists began to replace their testimonials to the power of truth with explanations for its failure. The problem, as Garrison saw it, was not simply apathy. Rather, the public, perversely, resisted the truth: "In some few instances [the skeptics'] incredulity arises from a want of reflection; but, generally, it indicates a hatred of the light, a desire to shield slavery from the assaults of its foes, a contempt of the colored race, whether bond or free."[21] The last two faults listed here—a desire to shield slavery from attacks and contempt of the colored race—can be read as references to the usual barriers to rationality: interest, passion, and prejudice. But what do we make of this "hatred of the light"? Is it just a distinctive symptom of the influence of interest, passion, or prejudice on reason? Or is Garrison making a different claim, not that reason has been defeated by countervailing psychological influences, but that some precondition for correct moral reasoning is absent in the character of those who defend slavery?

Other abolitionists seemed to detect in slaveholders a moral defect that went beyond the distorting effects of interest and passion: a kind of blindness that affected not the rational faculty but the moral sense. We've already encountered this concept of the moral sense in Douglass's *Narrative,* where it designated a pre- or nonrational capacity to intuit moral truths without the benefit of instruction or argument. Here it reappears, corrupted by slavery, to serve as an explanation for slaveholders' poor moral judgment. Charles Ball's editor, for example, attributed the cruelty of slaveholders to slavery's paralyzing effect on the master's "moral sense," and Harriet Jacobs claimed for slavery the power to "deaden the moral sense" to the point that adultery and other immoralities were taken for granted in the South—not just by slaves but also by their mistresses. Indeed, Angelina Grimké worried as much about slavery's tendency to bring "fearful ruin upon the hearts of *slaveholders*" as she did about its cruelty toward the slaves.[22] A southern abolitionist documented the effect of slavery on his own moral transformation: "When I was quite a child, I recollect it grieved me very much to see [a slave] *tied up* to be whipped, and I used to intercede with tears in their behalf. . . . Yet, such is the hardening nature of such scenes, that from this kind of commisseration [*sic*] for the suffering slave, I became so blunted that I could not only witness their stripes with composure, but myself inflict them, and that without remorse."[23] As Lunsford Lane's biographer explained, "[S]lavery is demoralizing in its influence upon every class over which it holds sway. Let the mind once embrace the heresy that the negro is a chattel, . . . and you may readily account for the whole black catalogue of the wrongs that have been inflicted upon the unoffending race."[24]

We might dismiss these charges of moral incompetence as an attempt to demonize the opposition, a suspect tactic typically condemned as degrading the civility of political argument and posing a serious barrier to rational deliberation. More charitably, they constituted a paratheory—an explanation of why their opponents wouldn't be persuaded by the abolition position. But beyond that, the charge that slavery corrupts the moral sense was the theoretical starting point for the abolitionists' third justification of storytelling, their final argument in behalf of sympathy.

But to understand that argument, we need a better grasp of what this charge of moral blindness means. Exactly what kind of moral fault are these complaints attributing to the slaveholders? Garrison's distinction between "want of reflection" and "hatred of the light" suggests that the problem is not just a failure to reason correctly about moral questions. The defect has something to do with feelings, with the heart. But neither is the complaint simply that slaveholders often have the wrong emotional response to the cruelties of slavery—not that this wasn't a common charge. Abolitionist literature frequently held up for public censure the wholly inappropriate reactions of slaveholders to the suffering of slaves. Mattie Griffiths, for example, describes a white woman "of conceded refinement" playing with her baby while "her husband was in the kitchen, with a whip in his hand, severely lashing a negro woman, whom he had sold to a trader—lashing her because she refused to go cheerfully and leave her infant behind." The mistress reacts to the slave's entreaties with "a derisive sneer": "Go away, you impudent wretch, you don't deserve to have your child. It will be better off away from you!" Griffiths notes that the white woman "was known to weep violently" for an Irish woman who couldn't afford to bring her children to America. Similarly, in *Uncle Tom's Cabin*, Harriet Beecher Stowe portrays a grief-stricken slave sobbing on being parted from her husband, while a white woman calmly comments, "We can't reason from our feelings to those of this class of persons"; the other onlookers to this scene respond by turning away or thinking about something else—"and all went on merrily, as before."[25]

But the claim that defenders of slavery have an impaired moral sense goes beyond the complaint that their lack of anger at injustice or compassion for its victims is morally repugnant. It seems to assert, in addition, that their failure to feel the appropriate emotions when faced with injustice prevents them from *recognizing* it as injustice. The failure of compassion, under this view, is intimately (but somewhat obscurely) related to the failure of correct moral judgment. As Theodore Weld explained it, the belief that slaves are chattel prevents the master from "contemplat[ing] slaves as human beings." The slave owner therefore watches "with entire indifference" while slaves suffer cruelties that would, if inflicted on whites, "fill him with horror and indignation." As a result, he "regards as good treatment of slaves, which would seem to him insufferable abuse if practiced on others." Lunsford Lane's biographer makes a similar point: slave owners are able to view their treatment of slaves as proper only because they believe that "[n]iggers have no feelings; it don't hurt 'em to have their domestic life made the plaything of white men's cupidity and lust." Angelina Grimké stated the problem succinctly: "*One who is a slaveholder at heart never recognizes a human being in a slave.*"[26]

These complaints bring us back to the conceptual terrain mapped out earlier in the discussion of sympathy, where imaginative identification figures prominently in the successes or failures of compassion. What the abolitionists were describing was a situation in which slaveholders saw a slave being whipped, beaten, or otherwise abused and *failed to sympathize with the slave*—that is, they neither identified with nor felt compassion for the slave. That much is clear, but the connection between this lack of sympathy and the slaveholders' poor moral judgment is more obscure. Allegedly, the failure of sympathy blinds the slaveholder to the slave's humanity, so that he or she fails to take the slave's feelings and welfare into account in judging the morality of slavery. The claim, then, is that the slaveholders' moral evaluation of their practices is distorted by their inability to sympathize with the slave. But at the same time, their failure to sympathize seems to be the result of a cognitive error (the belief that slaves are chattel, or that they have no feelings that count) that in itself might be considered a failure of correct moral reasoning. It's not clear which comes first, incorrect reasoning or the inability to sympathize.

One way to untangle this argument is to posit sympathy (in its dual aspect as identification with and compassion for a sufferer) as an important adjunct to reason in making moral judgments; certainly such a claim would go a long way toward giving it a legitimate place in a politics of reason. But there are a number of ways that this could work. Were the abolitionists, for example, claiming that sympathy is a more reliable guide to moral judgment than reason? Is the claim that (as one slavery opponent in *Uncle Tom's Cabin* insists) "[y]our heart is better than your head in this case"?[27] But why would it be? After all, one can easily imagine situations in which sympathizing with a sufferer would lead to an incorrect moral judgment. This was, in fact, the argument of the defenders of slavery, who claimed that people like Frederick Douglass were just oversensitive, so their suffering shouldn't be taken into consideration in evaluating the institution. But even if we dismiss this charge as patently obtuse and self-serving, we still might not conclude that the failure of sympathy accounts for the slaveholders' poor moral judgment. Consider again the abolitionists' argument: the failure to sympathize (whether the cause or the result of the belief that slaves aren't fully human) leads to another cognitive error that impairs moral judgment—specifically, the slaveholder continues to approve of slavery because *he doesn't know that it causes (morally relevant) harm.* Sympathizing with the slave corrects this cognitive error (along with the also blameworthy insensitivity to the slaves' suffering, and perhaps the belief that slaves are inferior). At the very least, then, sympathy may be a good way to gain access to information that is critical to making a correct judgment—namely, whether a practice is causing harm. But can we make a stronger claim: that the *only* way to know that a practice is causing harm is to feel sympathy for the victim? If this is true, then sympathy is not only helpful but also essential to correct moral judgment, and its failure is therefore an adequate explanation for slaveholders' obstinate defense of the peculiar institution.

Whether this stronger position makes sense depends in part on what constitutes adequate knowledge of another person's subjective experiences. Do we have to actually experience a person's suffering through sympathetic identification to "know" that he or she is suffering? Or is abstract, cognitive knowledge enough? (And is such abstract knowledge of an emotional phenomenon possible?) What if we are told by someone we trust that the person is suffering, so that we don't have to sympathize with the victim ourselves? For example, imagine a sophisticated computer program designed to decide moral issues by applying a set of moral rules to a given fact situation. If we gave the computer the information that a given practice would cause X units of pain (information gathered from the victims or from others who are capable of sympathizing with the victims) and let it run the relevant calculations, would it reach the same conclusion as a sympathetic person applying the same rules? Or would the computer lack some critical information, some knowledge that can be gained only by experiencing (directly or through sympathetic identification) the harm complained of?[28]

Such questions could arise even if one believes that moral opinions originated in sympathy rather than reason. One might argue (as Adam Smith does) that moral judgments grew out of feelings of sympathy but have since been elaborated into general rules that can be applied by people who do not feel any sympathy at all.[29] Under this view, a computer (or a rational but insensitive slaveholder) might not be able to generate a moral system but could still operate within one. However, it might not be able to revise its moral rules when faced with new situations—an important point if one believes, as many abolitionists did, that the current system of morality is defective and in need of reform. I examine how abolitionists enlisted sympathy in this project of moral reform later; here it is enough to note that the role of sympathy in politics may depend on one's commitment to moral progress.

But there are other ways to make the case that sympathy is essential to moral judgment. One could, for example, draw on traditional Christian morality and the association of sympathy with compassion, and argue that exercising moral judgment without sympathy (for the victim or even the perpetrator of injustice) is itself a morally suspect activity. After all, the New Testament repeatedly enjoins passing judgment, characterizing it as a usurpation of God's prerogative and the failure of charity (which is, in contrast, explicitly commanded). If moral judgment springs directly from feelings of compassion—from charity—then it has a better claim to moral respectability than a judgment that is merely a rational calculus.[30] Alternatively, one could argue that moral judgment can't be reduced to a set of rules, that morality can't be fully rationalized. Under this view, right action would require guidance from some nonrational (spiritual or emotional) faculty. This position would find very little support within the tradition of British moral philosophy inherited by antebellum Americans, the bulk of which clung tenaciously to the principle that reason is a perfectly adequate guide to right action.[31] It could, however, find some support in traditional Calvinism, which starts from the proposition that man's nature—reason, passions, and will—is hopelessly corrupt; one could conclude that reason alone cannot provide adequate guidance to correct moral action. Calvinists, we should note, did not always draw this conclusion, and in any case, this line of reasoning begins to diverge from the picture of sympathy as an adjunct to an otherwise reliable reason.

It may be that neither reason nor sympathy is reliable in the unregenerate, and something else is needed for right judgment—a possibility I explore later.

But one needn't turn to Christian ethics to make sense of the role of sympathy in moral judgment. It was a common theme in British moral philosophy that reason cannot supply the ultimate ends that must inform moral judgment. As Frances Hutcheson argued, moral judgment must be motivated by a desire for the good: "[T]he use of our Reason is . . . requisite, to find the proper Means of promoting publick Good," but "it must be an Instinct, or a Determination previous to Reason, which makes us pursue . . . publick Good, as our end."[32] The point here is that reason can't cause us to value anything; it can only tell us how to pursue what we value. Hutcheson thought that it was the moral sense that caused us to value the good of others, but (as Adam Smith would point out) sympathy is an equally plausible explanation for our altruistic impulses. Of course, this reasoning is vulnerable to some familiar objections. Sympathy might cause us to value the good of others, but what tells us that it is right to do so? Similarly, why should we accept such a narrow definition of reason? Isn't choosing among competing ends also an exercise of reason?

In sum, we can posit a number of possible roles for sympathy in moral judgment: it might be a means of obtaining important information, it might affect the quality of the act of judging, or it might serve to orient one's rational faculties toward the right values. But none of these claims, I suggest, is what the abolitionists were getting at in their discussions of the interplay between insensitivity and faulty reasoning among slaveholders. Their point, I think, was not that sympathy is an important adjunct to reason in individual case-by-case judgments (although it may be) but that slavery infects one's *entire moral nature* in such a way that none of one's faculties can work properly. This is why it's difficult to disentangle the slaveholder's bad reasoning from his or her lack of sympathy and compassion; they are all the result of the same deep moral corruption. The charge of moral blindness, in short, was a claim that for those influenced by the slave system, neither reason nor feelings nor both together are reliable guides to right action. Thus the slaveholders' lack of sympathy as well as their unreliable moral reasoning were *symptoms* rather than causes of moral corruption.

What does this moral corruption mean for politics, then? Here I want to look more closely at how moral blindness infects reason, passions, and the will and how it affects public rationality and judgment generally. The best way into these problems is through Harriet Beecher Stowe, whose dissection of the problem of moral blindness in *Uncle Tom's Cabin* is particularly helpful in clarifying its implications for a politics of reason. This excursion will also help us answer some related questions: How is moral blindness distributed

through the populace? Is it specific to the South, or can it account for northern indifference to the cruelties of slavery? How does it play into political
decisions, such as the decision to support or oppose slavery? In short, what
does a public infected by moral blindness look like, and how does it make
use of and respond to reasoned argument?

The Moral Geography of Slavery

The world of *Uncle Tom's Cabin* poses a stark contrast to the vision of a
uniformly rational public idealized by the proponents of rational public debate. Instead of a community of reasonable, reasoning people, Stowe reveals
a complex moral geography—a public whose moral character varies as much
as the country's physical geography. And one of her principal topics is the
way in which reason operates, or fails to operate, on this moral terrain.

She begins her story with a short character sketch of two common types
of slaveholders, Haley and Mr. Shelby. Haley is a slave dealer, a trade built
on a kind of moral blindness that manifests itself as unmitigated self-interest.
He is, in Shelby's words, "not a cruel man, exactly, but a man of leather,—a
man alive to nothing but trade and profit. . . . He'd sell his own mother at a
good percentage,—not wishing the old woman any harm, either."[33] Haley is
rational enough, but he relies on a calculating kind of reason whose ultimate
end is his own narrowly defined interests. Thus he treats his slaves as a good
farmer treats livestock—as gently as necessary to preserve their value, but
always with an eye to the bottom line. Naturally, such rationality does not
prevent him from being cruel on occasion, when circumstances warrant it.
Nor does it lead to (what Stowe would consider) good moral judgments with
respect to slavery. Although Haley understands that dealing in slaves puts his
soul in danger, he concludes that it is in his interest to continue in this trade
for the time being. According to his calculations, he can delay his own moral
reform without losing his chance for salvation, as long as he is willing to bear
the risk that he will die before he gets around to repenting.[34]

Shelby, in contrast, is the good master, a "fair average kind of man, good-
natured and kindly."[35] He shares the abolitionists' repugnance at the cruelty
of slavery and does his best to treat his slaves well. Neither morally insensitive
nor driven solely by interest, Shelby seems to be the kind of person who
would make good decisions with respect to his slaves; he is, in essence, the
reasonable man that was supposed to inhabit the democratic public. Unfortunately, Shelby is a bad businessman; a streak of bad luck puts him in financial difficulties and he is forced to sell his favorite slave, Uncle Tom, to Haley.
Stowe presents this as a reasonable decision, however, and not just in Haley's
narrowly self-interested sense. Shelby is caught not between moral principle

and interest but between two competing moral duties: his duty to take care of his family and his duty to his slaves. So much for the harmony of interests that slave owners boasted of. As Stowe describes Shelby's situation, it isn't a fluke but a predictable outcome of the slave system: There will always be some incompetent economic actors, and their failures will inevitably impose costs on their dependents. The injudicious slaveholder will then have to decide who will bear those costs—his slaves or his (legitimate) children. The slave system, then, tends to lead good people into moral dilemmas like these, where no course of action is blameless. (Of course, slavery is hardly unique in this respect; Stowe was undoubtedly aware that the northern free labor system could create similar dilemmas. But Stowe, I suggest, would take that as evidence of the imperfection of the northern system, not as a defense of slavery. In any case, her point here seems to be that the exigencies of the slave system mean that consistently correct moral action takes more than the average level of reasonableness.)

Senator Bird is Shelby's northern counterpart, an opponent of slavery who nevertheless gives tacit consent to it by supporting the Fugitive Slave Law (a harsh measure aimed at making it easier for slaveholders to capture escaped slaves). Although Bird plays a small part in the story, his character is central to Stowe's analysis of the impact of slavery on public rationality. His approval of the Fugitive Slave Law provides evidence that the moral corruption that infects the South has spread to the North. Like Shelby, Bird has a "particularly humane and accessible nature" and is appalled at the cruelties of slavery. But, also like Shelby, he tries to let reason and principle rather than sentiment guide his judgment, and his reasonings lead him to conclude that passage of the Fugitive Slave Law is critical to the survival of the Union. To his wife's objections to the act he responds, "Your feelings are all quite right, . . . but then, dear, we mustn't suffer our feelings to run away with our judgment; you must consider it's not a matter of private feeling,—there are great public interests involved" (it is Bird's wife, incidentally, who insists that "your heart is better than your head in this case").[36] Thus the senator is caught in the same kind of moral dilemma that leads Shelby to sell Uncle Tom: oppose slavery or maintain the Union? Moreover, his decision to support the law, rather than resolving the dilemma, just leads him into new difficulties. When a fugitive slave arrives at his door and asks for help, he finds himself caught again between competing moral obligations. Ultimately, he is unable to live by his own principles; he sacrifices consistency, breaking the law he helped to enact by giving assistance to the escaped slave. The point here (or one of them, at least) is that northerners are not free from the moral effects of slavery. The very existence of slavery anywhere in the Union affects public rationality throughout the Union, which makes the value of rational public debate on the topic questionable. The senator's wife may be speaking for Stowe when she complains, "I hate reasoning, John,—especially reasoning on such subjects. There's a way you political folks have of coming round and round a plain right thing; and you don't believe it yourself when it comes to practice."[37] Given the general distorting effects of slavery on reason, Mrs. Bird's sympathy for fugitive slaves seems to be a better guide to moral judgment than abstract rationality.

But sympathy alone does not necessarily lead to good judgment, either. Thus Stowe also criticizes Augustine St. Clare, a southern slaveholder who heartily despises slavery but fails to do anything about it. In St. Clare we see the inefficacy of abolitionism based solely on compassion. His heart is in the right place; he feels so sorry for his slaves that he even refuses to punish them for misbehavior. Unfortunately, his lack of discipline leads to disorder and vice among the slaves, making their condition even worse than it already was. But he also lacks the motivation to take any positive steps to help them. He disavows any personal responsibility for their condition, since "I can't buy every poor wretch I see. I can't turn knight-errant, and undertake to redress every individual case of wrong in such a city as this."[38] This is a weak argument, of course; the fact that he can't redress every wrong doesn't mean that he shouldn't try to redress some of them. St. Clare's real problem is that he's lazy. He once had "vague, indistinct yearnings to be a sort of emancipator," he tells us, but an unhappy romance left him with a "despair of living," and he ended up "a piece of driftwood, . . . floating and eddying about, ever since."[39] Thus he knows what he should do but lacks the will and discipline to act consistently from principle.

St. Clare is paired with his cousin Ophelia, a Yankee spinster who does have will and discipline and frequently shows excellent judgment. But Ophelia is not a particularly admirable figure either; an ardent abolitionist, she detests the slaves themselves (evidence, again, that the moral corruption of slavery has spread to the North). Eventually, her relationship with the slave girl Topsy helps her overcome her antipathy, and her judgment improves as her rigidity is softened by compassion. The contrast between St. Clare and Ophelia might therefore be interpreted as pointing toward a combination of sympathy and "hard," principled rationalism as being necessary for correct moral judgment and action. This would be to make the familiar point that effective philanthropy must be informed by a dual perspective: the philanthropist must be able to see the situation from the point of view of the sufferer as well as from a higher, more enlightened perspective—losing sight of neither the victim's immediate needs nor the need to address the deeper sources of his or her suffering. Alternatively, Stowe might be making a different point, not about the necessity of both reason and sympathy but about

the ineffectiveness of both reason and sympathy without the spiritual und\ -
standing brought by grace. It may be significant that Ophelia and St. Claı
are unable to change each other but just keep debating their differences without coming to a resolution. Their transformations are brought about instead
by the influence of the child Eva and the slave Tom: it is from Eva that
Ophelia learns how to love the slave girl in her care, and it is Tom's steadfast
faith the leads St. Clare to take the Bible more seriously, which in turn convinces him to promise Tom his freedom (a promise that he is, unfortunately,
unable to keep). Moreover, Eva and Tom achieve these victories not by their
reasoning ability but by virtue of their spiritual character and insight. Without this spiritual influence, Ophelia's strong-willed adherence to principle and
duty is no more helpful to the slaves than St. Clare's unfocused compassion
and weak rationalizations.[40]

I consider in the next section the religious context that makes sense of this
interpretation and the relationship between sympathy and grace that Stowe
may be assuming. For now, let us pursue Stowe's suspicion of reason and
principle further by examining the character of St. Clare's brother. This character analysis comes from St. Clare, who may not be a good source of moral
insight, as he is generally out of touch with his own best moral instincts and
sometimes appears as a poseur, spouting flimsy justifications he doesn't really
believe. But his analysis of his brother Alfred is confirmed by Stowe's later
portrayal of the character: Alfred, he tells us, is an aristocrat. "[A]n aristocrat
. . . the world over," according to St. Clare, "has no human sympathies, beyond a certain line in society. In England the line is in one place, in Burmah
in another, and in America in another. . . . What would be hardship and dis-
tress and injustice in his own class is a cool matter of course in another one."
American aristocrats use race to draw the line and refuse to extend their sympathies beyond it. The aristocratic temper, then, is one variety of moral blindness, an important kind of hard-heartedness. What is odd about this analysis,
however, is that Alfred's failure of sympathy is the result not of passion or
interest but principle. St. Clare praises his brother's lack of hypocrisy—he acts
as he believes, on the principle that "there can be no higher civilization without enslavement of the masses."[41] Stowe thus traces moral blindness, in this
case, directly to a plausible rational principle.

Or does she? This portrait of Alfred brings into play the uncertain distinction between principle and prejudice. As discussed in Chapter 4, consistent
adherence to principle (particularly a bad principle) can look very much like
a stubborn refusal to submit one's beliefs to rational scrutiny. It is no coinci-
dence, then, that St. Clare's brother bears a distinct resemblance to his social
antithesis, the slave catcher Tom Loker. Loker democratically extends his lack
of sympathy toward the whole human race; principled in his own way, he

is candidly and unapologetically brutal toward everyone.[42] Although they would despise each other, Alfred and Loker are actually two expressions of the conviction that might makes right. And this principled conviction—or unthinking prejudice?—makes them both impervious to moral arguments against slavery.

We could explore this moral menagerie further, but these examples are sufficient to make the point: in Stowe's America, moral blindness has created an Alice-in-Wonderland kind of world, where reason works in strange and disturbing ways. This alone would draw into question the desirability of a politics of reason, since it suggests that reason won't lead to moral truth. But Stowe's vision raises another equally disturbing point: not only will reason fail to produce truth, it probably won't even produce agreement. Stocked with everything from aristocrats to savages, Stowe's world has a moral complexity that defeats rational consensus—even a morally suspect rational consensus. Moreover, Stowe gives us reason to believe that such complexity is inescapable in a country such as the United States. Sounding occasionally like an early proponent of realism (a literary tradition characterized by a focus on the social and economic sources of individual behavior and character), she suggests that moral disposition is the product of a combination of upbringing, social conditions, and innate character—influences that can vary dramatically in such a large country. Human virtue (St. Clare complains) is "a mere matter . . . of latitude and longitude, and geographical position, acting with natural temperament."[43] Again, we can't assume that St. Clare is speaking for Stowe here, but his position is a plausible explanation for the variety of moral characters we run into in the novel. And if virtue depends on one's circumstances, then a socially diverse country like the United States will inevitably be plagued not just with error but also with dissensus and conflict. St. Clare gives us a glimpse of the full dimensions of such dissensus: His father and his father's brother, he claims, were both aristocrats by disposition, but his father's brother settled in Vermont—"in a town where all are, in fact free and equal"—and thus became a democrat, albeit with a "strong, overbearing, dominant spirit." His father, in contrast, stayed in the South, "where everything acted for [his natural tendency]," and so became a despot.[44] St. Clare himself escaped that fate (we learn elsewhere) only because his mother and her compassionate disposition had a strong influence on him when he was young. In short, the variety of influences that shape moral disposition ensure that even within this small family we will find both aristocrats and democrats, despots and libertines—and little hope of reaching consensus on an issue like slavery.

But what is Stowe's attitude toward this picture of moral determinism? The view that one's political sympathies are more a matter of habit and disposition—of prejudice—than of careful, open-minded reflection was (as discussed in Chapter 4) a prevalent one. For some advocates of partisanship, prejudice was a perfectly satisfactory basis for political action, provided it was the right prejudice (in favor of democracy). But St. Clare's reference to the sources of moral character seems aimed at devaluing his uncle's convictions as "mere" prejudice. Of course, it also relieves St. Clare of responsibility for his own moral disposition, since it is all determined by the accident of birth. And this is where Stowe and St. Clare part company. Stowe does not endorse the view that moral character is fixed once and for all in childhood. Moral growth (and decay) can continue over the course of one's life. Thus St. Clare is influenced (in spite of himself) by his angelic daughter Eva, his cousin Ophelia, and Uncle Tom. One can become better by associating with good people; perhaps more importantly, a morally superior person can improve the character of others.

But not by reasoning with them. For Stowe, moral reform does not depend on the ability to engage in rational argument—which is unsurprising, given her picture of the inefficacy of reason in a society shaped by slavery. Consider young Eva's positive influence on her cousin, Henrique. Henrique, when Eva first meets him, is a young aristocrat, and his relations with his slave, Dodo, are marked by the casual brutality characteristic of that type. When Eva objects to his cruelty, he dismisses her complaint "with unaffected surprise"— he simply can't understand her reasoning. But he likes Eva and wants to win her approval. So he first promises not to beat Dodo in front of her, and then promises to be kind to him, even to love him.[45] His reformation is accomplished by his emotional response to Eva's ethos: Henrique allows Eva to guide his judgment because he is impressed by her character, not by her reasons. The same dynamic is played out between Eva and St. Clare, Eva and the slave girl Topsy, Tom and St. Clare, and a host of other morally asymmetric relationships. The point is, if Henrique becomes an abolitionist, it will probably be due to Eva's influence, just as St. Clare's antislavery sentiment can be traced back to his mother's influence. Stowe thus downplays both the importance of "latitude and longitude" and the value of rational argument in forming political opinions; it is personal relationships, the bonds of ethos and pathos, that ultimately determine the course of moral development.

What, then, does Stowe's moral geography imply for political action? Certainly one of her points is that reasoned argument, without good moral character, just tends to confirm people in their bad habits and faulty convictions. (Stowe's defenders of slavery are skillful reasoners, a talent they employ to defend themselves against their occasional outbursts of sympathy.) But Stowe goes beyond simply pointing out the dangers of misusing reason; she challenges some key background assumptions supporting the case for a politics of rational debate. In particular, against the ideal of a morally uniform, rational public, she offers a vision of the political community that (1) highlights the variety of moral dispositions that might impede the triumph of reason and justice, (2) holds out the possibility of achieving moral consensus by reforming the morally defective, and (3) gives rational argument virtually no role in achieving such reform.

The advocates of a politics of rational argument probably wouldn't dispute Stowe's point that the public as currently constituted is not very rational. They simply drew different conclusions from that observation—not surprisingly, since they were not starting from the same place as Stowe or addressing the same problem. As discussed in Chapters 1 and 2, the arguments in favor of rational debate grew out of a concern that riotousness would undermine the legitimacy of democracy; confining politics to argument was supposed to mitigate the potential for disorder inherent in democratic politics. The need to prevent disorder was then offered as a reason to limit participants to those who are capable of giving and responding to rational arguments. But Stowe is not concerned about the legitimacy of democracy; she takes it for granted as the basic condition of political action. Whatever Stowe's point is, it certainly is not that we should limit decision making to the enlightened few, like Tom and Eva. Nor should we conclude (following a familiar line of argument in the moral reform movement) that Tom's and Eva's purity is possible only because they are outside the corrupting influence of politics—that because we can't prevent the corrupt from entering politics we must abandon politics as an agent of change. Stowe doesn't portray politics as uniquely corrupting; moral corruption in her world is pervasive, infecting every dimension of social life. Nor does she single out politicians for special censure; although she is critical of their flexible principles and self-serving logic, she makes a politician, Senator Bird, one of the most likable and admirable characters in the story.

What Stowe does tell us is that if we engage in political action, the public we have to deal with is a morally defective and irrational one. Thus (contrary to one of the more firmly rooted principles of democratic theory) we cannot assume that every political actor is equally deserving of respect—not, at least, if to respect someone is to treat that person as someone to be reasoned with rather than simply acted upon. Some citizens are brutal and degraded. They simply can't respond to reason, and it would be pointless to address reasoned arguments to them. Nor should we be sanguine about listening to such people; they may have a bad influence on our own moral development. (Uncle Tom faces this problem on LeGree's plantation, where his companions keep presenting him with persuasive arguments to reject virtue in favor of vice.) But that doesn't mean that we are justified in, or even capable of, ignoring such people (not unless we want to live like the high-minded but ineffective St. Clare). Politics may be corrupt, but it is reformable. If we want a politics of reason, then, we have to begin with a politics of reform.

True, for Stowe (as for her sister Catharine Beecher) this interest in moral reform seems to point toward a kind of politics, or prepolitical character development, that would take place mainly in the private sphere, which raises the question of whether we should read Stowe as saying anything about political action at all. But the abolition movement challenged the line between public and private, along with the related distinction between religion and politics. For abolitionists like Stowe, informing and reforming public opinion was a project that reached beyond the public podium and into the drawing room—but that did not mean that it could or should be confined to the drawing room, or that drawing-room conversations should be dubbed "nonpolitical." On the contrary, by publishing *Uncle Tom's Cabin* Stowe brought this project of moral reform into the public sphere. In doing so, she was engaging in a type of public political discourse that departs from the Enlightenment model of rational debate—a type closely modeled on slave narratives.

Narrative and Moral Reform

Stowe's moral geography of slavery helps us make sense of the abolitionists' third defense of slave narratives. The diagnosis of moral blindness, coupled with an understanding of moral development that gave prominence to the possibility of change and growth, is the background for the abolitionists' arguments about how not just to inform public opinion but to reform it—to rectify and purify it, in Angelina Grimké's words.[46] The project called for something other than rational argument. Before reason can work properly, the public must experience some kind of moral transformation; it must be made to *see* the truth. As a reviewer of *Uncle Tom's Cabin* put it, "Those who, having eyes, see not, and ears, hear not, are greatly the majority; and the chief office of the preacher and teacher, the poet and the thinker, is to tell us what we are, and to show us the things that are before and around us."[47] If the chief barrier to abolition is moral blindness, then the abolitionists needed not just teachers and thinkers but also poets and preachers.

The slave narrators, with their engaging style and compelling stories, easily embraced this role. In a well-known passage from the *Chronotype,* a defender of slave narratives recommended them with the claim that "[a]rgument provokes argument, reason is met by sophistry; but narratives of slaves *go right to the hearts of men*."[48] The point here is that slave narratives bypass reason and work directly on the heart—and to appreciate the significance of this statement, it is important to understand that the heart, in nineteenth-century moral discourse, represented the seat of moral and spiritual perception as well as the seat of the passions.[49] The stories, then, were supposed to not only establish the facts of slavery and motivate action but also change the public's moral sentiments. William Craft, for example, hoped that his narrative would "be the means of creating in some minds a deeper abhorrence" of slavery, and William Wells Brown insisted that "[s]laveholding and slaveholders must be rendered disreputable and odious. . . . Honest men must be made to look upon their crimes with the same abhorrence and loathing with which they regard the less guilty robber and assassin. . . . When a just estimate is place upon the crime of slave-holding, the work will have been accomplished." James M'Cune Smith, introducing Frederick Douglass's narrative, similarly argued that slavery would not be abolished until "the people at large . . . feel the conviction, as well as admit the abstract logic, of human equality." And Stowe claimed that the one thing everyone could do to fight slavery was "to see to it *that they feel right.*"[50]

This goal of creating in the audience the proper moral sentiments helps account for the importance of sympathy in abolitionist politics. The point is not that compassion for the suffering slaves would lead directly to correct judgments, but that sympathetic identification with slave narrators would effect a permanent change in people's hearts—that is, in their moral nature. Henry Brown, for example, asked his readers, "as you peruse this heart-rending tale," to "let the tear of sympathy roll freely from your eyes, and let the deep fountains of human feeling, which God has implanted in the breast of every son and daughter of Adam, burst forth from their enclosure, until a stream shall flow therefrom on to the surrounding world, of so invigorating and purifying a nature, as to arouse from the 'death of the sin' of slavery, and cleanse from the pollutions thereof, all with whom you may be connected."[51] The sympathy aroused by the story was supposed to "purify" the moral nature of the reader: Let "truth find an avenue through your sensibilities, by which it can reach the citadel of your soul," commanded Brown. Even a person "blinded to an appreciation of the good, by a mass of selfish sensibilities, may . . . be induced to surrender his will to the influence of truth, by benevolent feelings being cause to spring forth in his heart."[52] In the same vein, Wilson Armistead called on his readers to "follow the dictates of those sympathies which the God of nature hath implanted in our bosoms," and Josiah Henson even referred to "the divinity of a sympathetic heart."[53] Sympathy, here, is doing much more than simply letting the audience understand what it is like to be a slave or making them feel sorry for those who are condemned to slavery. It is somehow serving as a vehicle for a particularly powerful, transformative kind of truth.

Clearly, we have come a long way from the attacks on romantic stories with which I opened Chapter 5. Horace Mann had postulated a negative relationship between sympathy and moral improvement. Far from serving as a vehicle for truth, sympathy with a character in a romance novel was supposed to interfere with the rational faculty and lead the judgment astray. Precisely because they engage our sympathies, novels have a peculiar ability to draw us in, to induce the mind to "surrender itself to the interest and excitement of the story." Especially when reading those written in "an easy, flowing style, which excel in description and the luxuriance of fancy, the imagination is apt to get heated"; judgment suffers as a result of the novel reader's "inflated fancy."[54] According to these complaints, imaginative identification is no path to truth or moral improvement; it merely arouses the passions, transports us to the fantastic realms of romance, and distracts us from the reality of our own situation.

The slave narrators did not exactly dispute this claim—they didn't acknowledge the claim at all. In fact, they didn't seem to be operating within the same universe of discourse as the critics of novels; the tension between reason and passion, which was so central to the case against romance novels, was completely absent in the narrators' unapologetic endorsement of sympathy. Eloquence like Douglass's was praised rather than criticized because it "melted to tears" its hearers; Stowe did not invite or encourage but *commanded* her readers to "See, then, to your sympathies in this matter!"[55] In fact, the confidence with which abolitionists invoked the power of sympathy suggests that they didn't think that the attacks on novels and romance applied to stories about slaves—that sympathy was supposed to operate in a different way in the context of slave stories than it was assumed to in the context of conventional romance novels (which might explain why the editors of the *Pennsylvania Freeman* printed the story of Pinda next to Horace Mann's essay on the dangers of fiction).

This suspicion that abolitionists considered slave narratives to be qualitatively different from romance novels is further supported by the fact that narrators usually did not adopt the usual defense of novel writers: that they provided models of moral excellence and encouraged readers to imitate them by pointing out the rewards of virtue and the penalties of vice. Although they sometimes offered themselves as models for other escaped slaves to imitate, narrators did not suggest that they could serve as moral exemplars for white readers—at least not in any obvious, straightforward sense.[56] The white audience member, after all, was unlikely to find himself or herself in situations even close to the adventures of the fugitive slave. The relationship between sympathy and moral improvement that Brown was pointing toward was something more than that implied by the notion of imitating good people.

Sympathy with the slave was supposed to purify, to cleanse the soul. Where did this idea come from, and how does it work?

It certainly wasn't new. Indeed, even early romance novels (that is, those published in the late eighteenth century) occasionally used such language, although they were more likely to celebrate sympathy for its own sake (a refined sensibility was supposed to add pleasure to a refined and gracious life).[57] But it wasn't this secular literary tradition that provided the crucial support for claims about the transformative power of sympathy. That support, I argue, derived instead from the tradition of Christian spiritual auto-biography.

But this shift to religious discourse might seem precipitate. Why look to religion when we have a perfectly good philosophical movement that might explain this positive view of sympathy? After all, the antebellum era was the age of Romanticism: a broad, rather vaguely defined, but unmistakable intel-lectual trend characterized by an emphasis on subjective experience and the authority of the passions. This philosophical context undoubtedly supported abolitionists' reliance on sympathy as an agent of moral transformation. But obviously we can't cite Romanticism as the source of the abolitionists' per-spective on sympathy, since the claims for sympathy made by abolitionists helped to constitute the movement we call "Romanticism." We can, however, find a plausible source for these claims in the Christian tradition, in particu-lar, the tradition of Christian testimony or spiritual autobiography. Un-like romance novels, by the nineteenth century, spiritual autobiography had a well-recognized claim to being a positive moral influence. Moreover, this claim was based largely on its power to produce sympathy. The model of moral improvement through sympathy that slave narrators relied on more likely derived from this tradition of religious discourse than from, for example, German romantic philosophy. Slave narratives, I argue, were a political ana-logue to conversion narratives and similar forms of spiritual autobiography and were supposed to work on moral sentiments in the same way.

But I want to approach this analogy carefully. Working out the relation-ship between antebellum political and religious practices is trickier than historians usually recognize. Jean Baker, for example, notes the similari-ties between antebellum elections and certain religious rituals and concludes that the political activity derived much of its meaning from religion. Ronald Formisano makes the same claim with respect to Whig campaign rallies, which he interprets as "rally, picnic, and revival all rolled into one."[58] The idea seems to be that participants in (or observers of) a given political practice would notice its resemblance to a religious ritual and therefore interpret it in similar terms. But it is just as likely that the similarity in symbolic form would lead the participants to note the differences between the two kinds of activity. This seems to be what a Democratic observer was up to when he criticized a Whig rally for its "mock religious ceremony" and "blasphemous imitation of the Holy Supper." The criticism assumes that the reader will see the inappropriateness of using religious symbolism in the political sphere. Nor can we conclude, as Baker does, that the interpretation of American democracy as a direct expression of God's will (a long-standing trope in American political discourse) lends religious significance to politics. On the contrary, such claims were often aimed at devaluing politics as having relatively little importance to the life of the nation, compared with religion.[59]

In contrast, sometimes a political activity becomes so imbued with religious meaning that its political significance virtually disappears. Such is the case when a political cause takes on the aspect of a religious crusade, as the moral reform movement (abolitionism included) often did. Thus James Forten admonished the Philadelphia Female Anti-Slavery Society that "yours is the cause of Christianity," and Angelina Grimké described her commitment to abolition as a religious conversion and the antislavery movement as evidence of the approaching millennium.[60] If the participants represent their activities in this light, we might as well interpret those activities not as analogous to religious practices but as religious practices with some political effects. Again, such an interpretation wouldn't necessarily undermine the distinction between politics and religion—it would just bypass that distinction. Observers might see fighting slavery, for example, as an essentially political activity that has strangely and inappropriately taken on the appearance of a crusade, but participants would interpret their actions as religious reform *simpliciter,* quite distinct from politics—in Grimké's words, as "a matter of morals and religion, not of expediency or politics."[61] Neither group would deny that political activity is not properly interpreted as analogous to religious activity.

In the case of slave narratives, however, the analogy works. On the one hand, the narratives were recognizably patterned after the religious practice of giving testimony; they developed out of the genre of spiritual autobiography and were often structured like conversion narratives. Like spiritual autobiographies, they typically depicted the life of the slaves as "secular figurations of scriptural *mythoi*" (as one commentator put it) and compared the journey from slavery to freedom with the journey from sinfulness to grace. James Pennington, for example, tells the reader that, upon winning freedom, he realized that as a "lost sinner" he must "make another escape from another tyrant." William Craft, on reaching Philadelphia after a harrowing escape, compared himself with Bunyan's Christian "when he first caught sight of the cross." Lunsford Lane, on winning his freedom, insisted that "[n]one but him who has passed from spiritual death to life, and has received witness within his soul of God's forgiveness, can possibly have such feeling as mine."[62] On the other hand, the narratives did not simply conflate religion and politics. The narrators consistently treated religious conversion as distinct from political enlightenment and from the transition from slavery to freedom. In fact, as Frances Smith Foster notes, most of the narratives published after 1836 downplayed the religious themes that animated the early slave narratives. Pennington's treatment of his conversion is typical—it occurs after he escapes and appears in the narrative as a digression rather than as an integral part of his life story. (Frederick Douglass, it should be noted, doesn't even mention his conversion in his first two autobiographies.)[63]

This is not to suggest that liberty and grace were, for the slave narrators, unrelated. Besides being analogous, they could be causally connected. Pennington, for example, complained that without liberty, slaves would (by necessity) be kept illiterate and would therefore be denied access to the Bible, the chief means of receiving grace. Christians who defended slavery might respond that literacy wasn't a requirement for salvation, since they could expose slaves to the Gospel through oral instruction, but in doing so they invited an invidious comparison between themselves and the hated Papists. Other narrators reversed the causal relationship, suggesting that, given the brutalizing and degrading impact of slavery, only those who received saving grace would have the understanding and will to pursue political liberty. Charles Ball, for example, attributes slaveholders' reluctance to expose slaves to Christianity to the fear that they would "imbibe with the morality [preachers] teach, the notions of equality and liberty, contained in the gospel." Indeed, some narrators did trace their first notions of self-worth and dignity to such religious instruction.[64] In short, the narratives used grace and liberty as distinct concepts but possibly interrelated processes.

To the extent that the transition from slavery to freedom is similar to the transition from sinfulness to grace, telling the story of one's escape from slavery can be interpreted as analogous to telling the story of one's conversion. This analogy, I suggest, holds the key to the relationship between sympathy and moral reform that defenders of slave narrators were proposing. To unravel this relationship, though, we have to begin with the role of preaching and prophesying in American Protestantism—in particular, in late-seventeenth- and eighteenth-century Calvinism, which is when spiritual autobiography first came into vogue.

Admittedly, Calvinism seems to be an unpromising place to look for affirmation of the power of sympathy. Calvinists begin with the premise that every human being begins life in a fallen state, infected by a moral corruption that affects the reason, the passions, and the will—which seems to rule out both sympathy and reason as reliable guides to moral judgment. In fact, how-ever, most eighteenth-century Calvinists echoed the secular philosophers in defending natural reason as adequate to teach basic morality—at least the level of morality needed to maintain harmonious social life. Reason is lim-ited, of course. It can't bring the sinner to grace, but it can convict him of his own sinfulness; it can lead him to both the discovery of natural morality and the realization that he can never adequately fulfill those obligations because of his own corrupted will (hence the need for grace).[65] Under this reasoning, natural reason should be sufficient to convince slaveholders that slavery is wrong (unless southerners were unusually corrupted because of their upbringing). But natural reason alone might not be enough to eliminate slavery; that was a matter of will, which is radically unreliable among the unregenerate (hence the need for laws and punishment).

Eighteenth-century Calvinists, then, typically endorsed natural, unregen-erate reason as a guide to right action. But this faith in reason began to erode in the early nineteenth century. The reasons for the change are, undoubtedly, complex, but certainly one was the increased intensity of political conflicts between Christian reformers and defenders of a more secular vision of liber-alism in the early 1800s. John G. West, for example, highlights the contro-versy over whether the post office should deliver the mail on Sundays; advo-cates of a strict separation of church and state opposed the proposal to restrict delivery on the Sabbath. They lost, of course, but this and similar debates led many evangelical Christians to question whether natural reason without bib-lical revelation could provide an adequate basis for public judgment.[66] At the same time, Calvinists' traditional distrust of sympathy was coming under attack. Eighteenth-century Calvinists had generally joined with the secular philosophers in preaching the necessity of subordinating the passions to rea-son and in condemning romance and imagination.[67] In the nineteenth cen-tury, however, some theologians began to back away from this position; as Ann Douglas explains, the very people who led the abolition movement (such as Harriet Beecher Stowe) were also advocating a softer, more liberal theology that emphasized God's love for creation over his wrath at our sinfulness and stressed the role of sensibility and sentiment in the conversion experience.[68]

But how should we understand this new, more positive view of sympathy? After all, the passions, like reason, were corrupted by the Fall; if reason was not necessarily superior to the passions in making moral judgments, neither were the passions supposed to be superior to reason. Nor, I think, would most abolitionists dispute that point. Their endorsement of sympathy was rooted not in Calvinist teachings concerning moral judgment but in its teachings and practices related to the process of moral regeneration.

On one point there is no room for debate: Only God, in the form of the

Holy Spirit, is capable of reforming one's moral nature and correcting one's will. But God works through nature, which means that the Holy Spirit must enter the soul through some kind of sensual perception—usually (though not always) by hearing or reading the word of God. As evangelist Charles Finney put it in his 1835 treatise on revivalism, God brings the sinner "where truth reaches his ears or his eyes." Moreover, because it must reform the reason, the passions, and the will, the word of God must reach all the faculties, not just the rational ones. True conversion is not just "a change of opinion" but "a change of the feeling of [the] heart"—in other words, it changes the sinner's whole moral nature, not just his mind. In Perry Miller's memorable words, original sin is "a dislocation of the faculties," and conversion is, in effect, "a realignment of twisted pulleys and tangled ropes, permitting the blocks once again to turn freely and the tackle to run smoothly."[69]

Preaching is the primary means by which God reaches the faculties, since an eloquent preacher can reach the reason, the passions, and the will of the audience simultaneously. And this is where sympathy, especially in the sense of imaginative identification, comes into play. Sympathy (according to the tenets of neoclassical rhetoric) is an important means by which a speaker influences an audience. By establishing a sympathetic bond with the audience, the speaker induces audience members to enter into his subjective experiences, to share his feelings, thoughts, and perspective. It is this ability to make the audience identify with him that makes an eloquent speaker so persuasive.[70]

Of course, this sympathetic identification is precisely the process that Horace Mann thought corrupted the morals of novel readers. But in the religious context, the sympathetic bond between the preacher and the audience has a different significance for moral development: in enhancing the preacher's influence over the audience—by inducing listeners to adopt his (or her) moral perspective—sympathy serves as a kind of conduit for the Holy Spirit. Simply put, because sympathy is what allows the preacher to convey God's truth to the hearer, it is a means of receiving saving grace. Some divines even sound as though sympathy and grace are synonymous. Edward Park, for example, described effective preaching as having the power to "wake the deepest sympathies of quick-moving, wide-hearted, many-sided men" or to "call forth some emotion" that "[animates] the sensitive nature which is not diseased, deepening its love of knowledge."[71] A sympathetic heart, it seems, is particularly responsive to grace.

This context helps account for the tendency to conflate sympathetic identification with compassion; after all, compassion for others should be the natural outcome of contact with the Holy Spirit. Beyond that, however, the result of grace should be improved moral understanding, a kind of enlight-

enment—but this enlightenment should not be understood in a strictly rationalist sense. Converts spoke of experiencing not merely an improved ability to reason but a new kind of perception, a new way of seeing the truth.
In fact, converts described their experience using the same metaphors of vision and light that permeate abolitionist rhetoric. When Garrison claimed
that Douglass's eloquence "rendered far more clear than ever" his "perception
of the enormous outrage" of slavery, he echoed generations of Christians
describing the effect of saving grace: "For as in natural things, you know, that
by the same light whereby I see the Sun, by the same light I know that I see
him: So there is the very manifestation of God to the Soule, it carries a witness in it self, it is so cleare, that when I have it, though I never had it before,
. . . yet I know as it is Gods sight, so know as I see him."[72] Or, as Charles
Finney described the effect of conversion on sinners, "God clears [the truth]
up before their minds, and pours in a blaze of convincing light upon their
souls, which they cannot withstand, and they yield to it, and obey God, and
are saved."[73] Conversion provides the convert with a new sense, an intuitive
kind of spiritual perception analogous to taste or sight. Moreover, the Holy
Spirit is supposed to work in everyone the same way, leading everyone to the
same perception of truth—or at least a perception of the same truth. In this
way, it eliminates not only moral corruption but also the deep sources of
moral dissensus: the different moral perceptions resulting from different
temperaments and social circumstances. Not that every Christian perceives
the full truth immediately, of course. Most theologians allowed for the possibility that grace would be more effective in some than in others, and that
moral education would still be necessary after conversion; this was, in fact, a
major reason for preaching. But within the community of believers, there are
at least grounds for consensus—grounds that are lacking among the unregen-
erate.[74]

In sum, preaching operates not by directly changing the hearer's mind or
will but by creating a sympathetic bond with the audience through which the
hearer gains access to the Holy Spirit. It is the Holy Spirit, then, that enters
the heart and simultaneously reforms the reason, the passions, and the will.
But this dynamic doesn't end the role of sympathy in religious conversion. It
is also central to the problem of verification, or authenticity: How does the
hearer, or anyone else, know that the Holy Spirit was actually present during
the conversion? How can we be sure that the hearer was not simply led by
the preacher's eloquence to believe that he or she had received grace? It is this
concern that (finally) brings us to the early Puritan conversion narratives.

The conversion narrative actually arose out of a larger category of religious
discourse popular in England, termed "prophesying": an extemporaneous
performance, usually by a layperson, combining biblical exegesis, personal

testimony, and exhortation. Like preaching, the primary goal of prophesying was spiritual education, helping one another "grow in grace." The point
was not conversion of unbelievers, however; it was practiced among and for
the benefit of other believers. Its justification therefore depended on the
proposition that even those who are saved do not have a perfect perception
of God's glory. Prophesying allowed believers to share their individual "heart-
knowledge," that knowledge given to them by the presence of the Holy Spirit
in their hearts, and thus gain a more complete spiritual understanding.[75] In
this context, then, sympathy with the speaker serves as a means for the audience to gain access to and share in the speaker's inner experience of the Holy
Spirit. Prophesying by laymen could renew the work of grace in the audience,
just as preaching did, by creating a sympathetic bond between the speaker
and the audience that could serve as a conduit for the Holy Spirit.

But conversion narratives, which apparently originated in the American
colonies, did more. They were a special form of prophesying: a narrative by
a convert describing how he or she came to be convicted and saved. Such
narratives came into use in America in the early 1600s and were soon required by most Puritan churches of anyone who wished to join. Their primary purpose was to demonstrate to the church, represented either by the
congregation or by an audience of church leaders, that the petitioner had
undergone a genuine conversion. Thus the classic conversion narrative was
related before an audience whose role was to judge the authenticity—the
truth—of the story. The practice generated considerable controversy, most of
which focused on this problem of authenticity. No one can know another's
heart, or so conventional Christian doctrine taught. What, then, made the
audience an adequate judge of the authenticity of the narrative? This is where
sympathy again becomes relevant. According to defenders of the practice, the
audience was qualified to judge the narratives because they had all undergone
the same experience. Through the power of sympathy, church members could
test the convert's experience against their own and thus determine whether it
was a true conversion. This shared experience of grace was the basis of what
Puritans called the "fellowship" or "connaturality" of the Spirit, by which
saints knew one another. Of course, this dynamic works only if the convert
can adequately relate his or her experience; as historian Patricia Caldwell argues, defenders of the practice postulated a close relationship between grace
and the ability to speak and judge. It was not that all believers were articulate;
rather, the Holy Spirit animated the speech of all believers (even the least
eloquent) in a way that other believers could perceive.[76]

The conversion narrative, then, was aimed at verifying the subjective experience of the narrator, but, like other forms of preaching and prophesying,
it was also aimed at helping other members of the congregation "grow in

grace." As one narrator put it, they could be both "instrumental in leaving a lasting impression upon the minds of the impenitent" and "encouraging to the justified soul, and a comfort to the sanctified."[77] It's a neat trick, combining spiritual education and verification, but how does it work? The two goals seem to be inconsistent; how can the audience be a reliable judge of the authenticity of the narrative if it is still morally defective and in need of spiritual education? And if the audience members' experiences of grace are different, how can that experience serve as a common basis for judging the authenticity of the narrative?

One way to resolve this problem is by postulating a hermeneutic process of moral development. The believer begins with a set of moral intuitions that have been at least partially purified through contact with the Holy Spirit. These provide the basis for judging the authenticity of the speaker's narrative, which in turn enhances the intuitions already present.[78] We find suggestions of this dynamic in spiritual narratives such as that of Philadelphia preacher Jarena Lee. Already convicted of her sinfulness, she is exposed to a reading of the Psalms: "[A] ray of renewed conviction darted in to my soul. . . . This description of my condition [contained in the Psalms] struck me to the heart, and made me to feel in some measure, the weight of my sins." The truth of the Psalms thus resonated with the glimmerings of truth already present in her soul. And she experiences the same process from the other direction, when she tries to persuade her congregation of her vocation to preach. While delivering an impromptu exhortation, she explains, "God made manifest his power in a manner sufficient to show the world that I was called to labor according to my ability . . . in the vineyard of the good husbandmen."[79] In other words, her listeners recognized the truth of her spiritual experience (her call to preach) by virtue of their ability to recognize the presence of the Holy Spirit in her testimony.

This hermeneutic process seems implied by the practice of conversion narratives, but it wasn't confined to religious discourse. Consider, for example, University of Vermont professor Calvin Pease's explanation of the persuasive power of scientific discourse. Beginning in a religious mode, he claims that "there is . . . within, the 'true light which lighteth every man that cometh into the world'; and true light, more or less, is shining from without; and hearts are open; and the light shall quicken them; and, though for a time deceived, they shall be at last undeceived." This passage describes the hermeneutic process by which one simultaneously recognizes and is transformed by truth—implicitly, here, the Holy Spirit. Pease then uses the same language to describe this process operating in the domain of science: "[T]o [the scientist's] fiery feelings, fiery words give utterance, communicating life and warmth to kindred heart. And wide and numerous is this family of kindred hearts. Such utterances bring us to know this brotherhood. For by pouring in upon the heart the truth and the light warm-gushing from the heart, the powers and longings of that heart are awakened; the presence of the thing it needs stimulates it to make the appropriation, and to seek, earnestly and humbly, for more."[80] Despite its apparently secular context, such language is clearly rooted in Calvinist theology rather than secular moral philosophy or neoclassical rhetoric; it describes the same dynamic of spiritual recognition and growth that animates spiritual autobiography.

This interpretation of how spiritual autobiography works helps us understand how slave narratives were supposed to reform moral sensibilities by arousing sympathy. The dual function of spiritual autobiography—verifying the speaker's moral intuitions and reforming the listener's moral intuitions—captures precisely the role assumed by slave narratives in abolitionist politics: they were supposed to influence the audience by drawing out and enhancing the audience's own intuitive condemnation of slavery—to fill the reader (as Garrison put it) with an "unutterable abhorrence of slavery."[81] They operated on the moral feelings, rather than just the rational faculties. As we have already seen, for example, the persuasive force of Douglass's critique of slavery depends critically on the authority of his moral intuitions. His intuitions are what make him a hero rather than simply a surly, rebellious fugitive; unless the audience accepts these intuitions as reliable, the story loses its coherence and power. But how is the audience induced to accept his intuitions as reliable? Not through argument; Douglass's refusal to provide extensive arguments about the injustice of slavery is significant, and typical of slave narratives. In fact, when Sojourner Truth wanted to impress on the reader the injustice of being separated from her brother and sister, she did so by *refusing* to argue the point: "I make no comment on facts like these. . . . [Readers] will draw their conclusions from the promptings of humanity and philanthropy:—these, enlightened by reason and revelation, are . . . unerring."[82] I suggest that such references to the author's and the audience's moral intuitions—particularly in a context reminiscent of spiritual autobiography—were designed to set in motion the hermeneutic process. Rather than trying to reason the audience into condemning slavery, the narrator called on audience members to measure their own moral sentiments against the narrator's. If the narrator's feelings about slavery and freedom resonate with their own, they should submit to the narrator's moral influence. In other words, they should let themselves be carried away by the narrator's story. In this sense, the narratives operated in the same way that conversion narratives did—not by offering reasoned arguments, but by creating a sympathetic connection through which the speaker's moral intuitions could both influence the audience and be verified by it.

If we remain within this religious framework and look at the narrative as a kind of sermon, addressed by a Christian convert to an audience of believers, then we have a plausible explanation for Brown's faith in the power of sympathy to reform moral sentiments: the narrator's eloquence establishes a sympathetic bond with the audience through which the Holy Spirit moves, entering the hearers' hearts and reforming them. The presence of the Holy Spirit, verified by means of the hermeneutic process, ensures that the audience's reformed moral judgment will be grounded in truth rather than being merely the product of the speaker's rhetorical manipulation of the passions. But can we take the analogy this far? Can we read the narratives as a kind of sermon? This is, to be sure, a fairly common interpretation; William Andrews, for example, characterizes the narratives as attempts to "convert" the reader, and narrators as "preachers from the anti-slavery pulpit."[83] Certainly the narrators took the authority of Christianity for granted; most of them were Christians and could probably assume that their audience was composed of other Christians or people who accepted the moral authority of Christians. Preaching to them wouldn't have been out of the question. Yet the narrators seemed to be trying to escape from the religious framework of conventional conversion narratives, to secularize them. After all, the stories were not primarily about the truths of the Bible but about the more mundane truths of the legal institution of slavery. And, importantly, the narrators rested their moral authority on their experience of liberty, not their experience of grace.

Of course, this secularization might simply be a rhetorical smoke screen thrown up to obscure the fact that the narrators were actually aiming at conversion; maybe we should read the narratives as preaching masquerading as politics. But what if we give them the secular reading they seem to call for— what if they were supposed to be a kind of secular sermon? This interpretation poses a problem for the model of moral reform they proposed: there is no secular equivalent of God. When we take the narratives out of the religious framework, we can no longer attribute the reforming power of sympathy to the Holy Spirit.

So what do we lose when we lose the Holy Spirit? The eviction of God from abolitionism might be a spiritually dangerous strategy (many abolitionists would have said so), but it needn't be fatal to the narrators' reform efforts. The slave narratives could still work as a secular version of a conversion narrative. Under this reading, fugitive slaves were in the position of a petitioner asking to be accepted into a community—not a church, but a polity. The narrators' repeated references to their and their audience's moral intuitions were central to this goal of inclusion, since, as already pointed out, such references tended to exclude those who didn't share the speaker's moral intuitions. But there is more going on here. The narrators weren't just labeling those who supported slavery as the true outsiders; they were trying to *convert* such moral misfits to the antislavery position—or at least to renew whatever faint, tentative antislavery convictions they still harbored. Under this interpretation, slavery was like original sin; it infected American society with a political corruption that only the experience of liberty could correct. The narrators offered that experience. To be sure, their stories were aimed at demonstrating that they valued liberty as much as their free audiences did, but at the same time, they were trying to enhance their audience's own innate (but corrupted) love of liberty by allowing them to share vicariously the fugitive's subjective experience of freedom.

In short, the slave narrators offered themselves not simply as good citizens but as moral heroes come to purify northern politics. Thus Frederick Douglass described himself as another Patrick Henry, and Wendell Phillips analogized him to the founders, who also published their declaration of independence "with a halter about their necks." Henry Brown likewise compared the slaves' pursuit of freedom to the founders' struggle for independence, addressing his white readers as "ye, who know not the value this 'pearl of great price' [liberty], by having been all your life shut out from its life-giving presence." Fugitive slaves had superior insight into the meaning of liberty, according to one commentator, since they had "a practical knowledge of both sides, of the advantages of freedom." William Wells Brown agreed: "I am satisfied that none but a slave could place such an appreciation upon liberty as I did."[84] The slave narratives asked the audience to view the fugitive as politically "saved," as that person celebrated by rhetoricians: the morally superior speaker to whose influence the public should submit its judgment. To sympathize with the slave did not just mean feeling sorry for him or her, then, but accepting and submitting to the fugitive's moral guidance and influence.

Under this interpretation, we do not need to posit any supernatural source for the reforming power of sympathy. It operates in slave narratives as it does in other rhetorical performances, by making the hearer more vulnerable to the pathetic and (especially) ethical appeals by which the speaker persuades the audience to see the fugitive slave as a morally superior person. This acceptance of the slave's moral authority is part of the moral reform that narratives were aimed at, since it carries with it a judgment that slavery is wrong: you can't see the fugitive slave as an American hero and also see slavery as morally acceptable. But equally important to the project of moral reform is the audience's vicarious experience of the slave's journey from slavery to freedom. This subjective experience of liberty promised to lead the audience to a greater hatred of slavery and a more intense appreciation of the value of freedom.

The problem with this secular reading is this: what ensures that the new moral insight produced by the narrative is grounded in the truth? The hermeneutic process of checking the slave's moral intuitions against one's own guarantees that the sympathy aroused by the story won't be the free-floating, reason-impairing sentimentalism of romance novels; it will be a discriminating sympathy, rooted in the audience's own moral intuitions. But why should we trust the audience's intuitions? Have we returned to Shaftesbury's world, where everyone has a natural moral sense that can provide certain guidance? Or is it the common American heritage, the revolutionary tradition, that ensures that everyone will have, buried somewhere in their American hearts, an intuitive understanding of the true meaning and value of liberty? Neither of these possibilities gives us as much certainty as the Holy Spirit would. Natural moral intuitions and civic traditions, unlike grace, are always subject to corruption. And given the amount of conflict in the North over slavery, one might well conclude that northern society was already too corrupt to perceive the truth, even with the fugitives' help. When we lose the Holy Spirit, then, we lose the connection between sympathy and truth. The slave narrator then begins to look like a demagogue, concerned only with manipulating the public, through pathetic and ethical appeals, toward his or her own conception of right and wrong.

In sum, once it has been removed from the religious context, the claim that sympathy can reform moral judgment still sounds plausible, but the claim that sympathy is a vehicle for truth sounds considerably less so. It may just be a vehicle for demagogic manipulation. In that case, maybe we're better off with a politics of reason, after all—but only if the goal is truth. And it's not clear that truth *was* the goal of abolitionism. On the one hand, the abolitionists' charge of moral blindness and corruption assumes a standard of truth that their opponents' reasonings have fallen short of; the problem they identified was not just disagreement but error. Lurking behind their arguments in defense of romance is the ideal of rational consensus and a politics of reason that might prevail in a world made perfect by the power of sympathy. On the other hand, we can interpret this strand of abolitionism as rejecting a strictly rationalist conception of truth in favor of a more Christian conception, in which truth is inextricably linked to compassion. Under this reading, the abolitionists were insisting on compassion *instead of* scientific, factual truth as the proper basis for public policy. Not that scientific truth was necessarily inconsistent with revealed truth—this was still an unpopular position during the antebellum period, despite the increasing conflict between reason and revelation.[85] But the rationalists' concern with factual truth and scientific reasoning seems to miss the point if, as the abolitionists argued, the fundamental social problem isn't factual error or dissensus but that too many people failed to perceive and appreciate the humanity of the slave. If the abolitionists were after truth, it may have been a moral truth captured better by feelings of compassion than by abstract calculations.

But whatever their stance on truth, the abolitionists' critique of public debate and their endorsement of storytelling—limited though it was to the specific circumstances created by slavery—constituted a significant challenge to the politics of reason. They did not simply suggest that sympathy might serve as a useful adjunct to moral judgment. Such a suggestion might introduce some tensions into the rationalist framework supporting the Enlightenment conception of public debate, but it would hardly undermine that framework. The abolitionists' case for sympathy as an agent of moral reform was more radical—they questioned the political value of reasoned argument altogether. Against the confident assumption that the truth is easily discovered and recognized, they identified endemic sources of misinformation and error, both geographic and psychological. Against the ideal of rational debate, they highlighted the critical role played by pathos and ethos in political discourse, even making a good case for deference to the moral, if not social, elite. In short, against the image of an enlightened public, they described a citizenry still fumbling about in the dark: fully responsible for policy decisions, but plagued by epistemological uncertainty (both moral and empirical) and therefore looking—cautiously but inescapably—to one another for information and guidance. This was a world that needed the leadership and inspiration of moral heroes more than it needed disinterested public debate. It was a world in which a responsible political actor might well put his or her faith not in reason and the irresistible power of truth but in sympathy and the irresistible power of eloquence.

Conclusion

The Enlightenment model of public debate doesn't explain the full dimensions of storytelling as a political act. Narrative testimony wasn't just a device to adduce the facts; the roots of the practice are not only judicial but also religious and romantic. It was supposed to engage the sympathies, both to motivate action on behalf of an obscure and despised minority and to reform the moral sensibilities of a public corrupted by its own unjust institutions. Its justification, then, depended on a picture of politics and political community at odds with the image assumed (or promoted) by the proponents of rational

public debate. Clearly, this picture owes more to Christianity than it does
to secular moral and political philosophy—and it is a compelling one, with
important implications for the norms of political action. It begins with the
bleak assumption that not everyone is morally competent, and rational debate with such people is worse than useless. It does not, however, exclude
these irrational people from the democratic public. The morally corrupt public is instead taken as the relevant audience for political discourse, the aim of
which is to remove the major obstacles to correct moral judgment and create
consensus. And its chief means of doing so is sympathy—that mysterious
power, accessed through the spoken word, by which people of superior moral
vision and character (in the judgment of the public) establish their dominion.
Thus the abolitionists' perspective on the public and its problems lent legitimacy to the arts of rhetoric. By focusing on the ethical bonds between citizens and their need for moral guidance, they made a place in democratic
politics for those persuasive techniques that rely less on rational appeals than
on pathos, ethos, and deference.

Have we returned to the world of neoclassical rhetoric, then—the world
that Charles Brockden Brown depicted in *Wieland* as the realm of passion,
domination, and violence? Surely not; surely the dominion of voice looks less
sinister from a Christian perspective than it does from Brown's. The Christian
emphasis on compassion and humility should (one would hope) mitigate the
potential for violence and disorder that Brown thought inherent in democratic politics. But beyond that, the hermeneutic process of moral development implicit in the practice of testimony makes Brown's dismal scenario less
plausible: it ensures that the speaker's moral influence must be grounded in
something other than his or her own passions and will in order to take effect—it must speak, somehow, to the audience's own moral intuitions. Thus
this tradition, more so than the neoclassical tradition, emphasizes the audience's role in evaluating the speaker's moral influence and deciding whether
to submit to it. In doing so, it points to the community's shared moral convictions as a source of stability in democratic politics, even as it provides for
the creation and enhancement of such convictions.

But is this enough? Are calls for love and peace, and dependence on the
moral judgment of the public, sufficient to ensure that the dominion of voice
won't lead to riot and ruin? Against this hope stands the grim history of
violence leading up to the Civil War: race riots, Bleeding Kansas, Harpers
Ferry. Abolitionists have been blamed for precipitating such conflict by raising the stakes of the antislavery movement to the point where violence looked
justified. This criticism seems to be off the mark; antebellum politics, as
we discovered in Chapter 2, was already saturated with violence when the
abolitionists began agitating for reform. If many of them eventually con-

cluded that some things are worth fighting for, they also tempered the culture of violence by promoting the rather novel idea that many, and perhaps most, affairs of politics are *not* worth fighting for. But we do need to explain how even a thoroughgoing pacifist like Garrison could offer the following comment on John Brown's raid: "The particulars of a misguided, wild, and apparently insane, though disinterested and well-intended effort by insurrection to emancipate the slaves in Virginia, under the leadership of Capt. Brown . . . may be found on our third page. Our views of war and bloodshed, even in the best of causes, are too well known to need repeating here; but let no one who glories in the Revolutionary struggle of 1776 deny the right of the slaves to imitate the example of our fathers."[86] The tone is ambivalent, but not ambivalent enough to mask the implicit endorsement of violent resistance. The abolitionists' celebration of John Brown as a martyr to freedom confirmed the implicit connection in abolition politics between romance and violence—a connection first established, not coincidentally, by the abolitionists' promotion of the narrative of Nat Turner, which was the beginning of the turn to narrative and romance in abolition politics. The problem for peace-loving abolitionists was this: if the charge of moral blindness is correct, then the public needs the moral vision and guidance that only a passionate, charismatic believer like John Brown can provide. They may have deplored his tactics, but they couldn't reject his vision of politics as the domain of violence. Romance requires heroes, and it is violence and conflict, not peace and charity, that give birth to them.

CONCLUSION

I began this study with a quotation from Frederick Douglass's Fourth of July speech explicitly rejecting the politics of reason and the ideal of rational deliberation. It seems fitting to end by considering what Douglass proposed as an alternative. If there was nothing left to argue, what was the point of the speech? What was he planning to say to those people gathered in Rochester, New York, on July 5, 1852?

Clearly, Douglass thought that he had some legitimate options for political action beyond rational argument. He began, for example, with an apology. He asked the audience's indulgence for his "limited powers of speech," his lack of "elaborate preparation," and the "little experience" and "less learning" with which he was able to "throw [his] thoughts hastily and imperfectly together."[1] This must have sounded reassuringly familiar to the audience; introductory apologetics were de rigueur for antebellum public speakers. But Douglass's apologies weren't just the usual formulaic throat clearings. From any other orator they might have come across as false humility or even a sincere lack of confidence; from Douglass, they sound more like his famously acerbic sarcasm. *His* apologies, he reminded them, were supposed to have a more solid foundation in reality than most people's. He was, after all, a slave—an inferior being lacking the intellectual and moral capacity to make the speech he was about to make. His apologies were a challenge, an announcement that he was about to unsettle his audience's comfortable expectations.

Then, suprisingly, he launched into the conventional celebratory story about America's struggle for freedom. Nothing new or strange here, he assured them. He was just repeating what they already knew: how the revolutionaries, "accounted in their day, plotters of mischief, agitators and rebels, dangerous men," presumed to disagree with and rebel against their rulers. Simply put, they resented the tyrannical treatment they were receiving from the British government, and, not content to submit, they decided to separate from the Crown. It was hardly the counsel of prudence, Douglass pointed out: "The timid and the prudent . . . were, of course, shocked and alarmed by it." But "[o]ppression makes a wise man mad." Although the rebels were "quiet men" who "believed in order," they were also brave men—men of spirit—who "preferred revolution to peaceful submission to bondage." And

236

that they succeeded against the "lovers of ease" and "worshippers of property," declared Douglass, was cause for rejoicing. "You may well cherish the memory of such men. They were great in their day and generation. . . . They seized upon eternal principles, and set a glorious example in their defence. Mark them!" What were those eternal principles, and how were they violated? Douglass refused to elaborate: "I need not enter further into the causes which led to this anniversary. Many of you understand them better than I do. You could instruct me in regard to them."[2]

So he began with a story of spirited, passion-driven resistance to authority, an ethical appeal to the moral example of the founders (rebels, plotters, and agitators), and a refusal to reason with the audience about the moral principles they acted upon. Then, turning to the present, Douglass changed tone. This was not going to be another collection of self-congratulatory platitudes, nor a learned disquisition on the meaning of American independence. It was a jeremiad. His subject wasn't liberty, but slavery—American slavery. He came not to praise but to "question and denounce": "I do not hesitate to declare, with all my soul, that the character and conduct of this nation never looked blacker to me than on this 4th of July! . . . America is false to the past, false to the present, and solemnly binds herself to be false to the future."[3] He singled out the internal slave trade, the Fugitive Slave Law, and the church establishment in particular for denouncement. He described for his audience "the bleeding footsteps" and "doleful wail of fettered humanity"; he accused legislators of having perpetrated (in the Fugitive Slave Law) a "glaring violation of justice" with "diabolical intent," and the church of promoting a "religion for oppressors, tyrants, man-stealers, and *thugs*." Moreover, he steadily refused to support these judgments with arguments. Insisting that the audience was already convinced of the moral principles he was defending, he called for "scorching irony" in place of "convincing argument": "For it is not light that is needed, but fire. . . . The feeling of the nation must be quickened; the conscience of the nation must be roused." He wasn't interested in persuading the audience with reasons; he wanted to shame them, to make them feel the outrage *he* felt about the injustice of slavery.[4]

And yet, what was all this impassioned rhetoric in aid of? Nothing less than the march of reason and progress: There was a time (Douglass concluded) when "[l]ong established customs of hurtful character could . . . fence themselves in" and "[k]nowledge was . . . confined and enjoyed by the privileged few," but such is the case no longer. "A change has come over the affairs of mankind. . . . No abuse, no outrage . . . can now hide itself from the all-pervading light. The iron shoe, and crippled foot of China must be seen, in contrast with nature. *Africa must rise and put on her yet unwoven garment.*"[5] So he ended his jeremiad, unexpectedly, on an optimistic note: a prediction of the coming utopia, using an Enlightenment (and millennial) lexicon to spell the doom of slavery.

Where does this collection of storytelling, ethical appeals, pathos, and Enlightenment utopianism fit into American politics—as a blatant violation of the norms of political action, or as a legitimate entry in the lists of political conflict? Those advocating a politics of rational deliberation would have a hard time endorsing Douglass's tactics: his refusal to support his position with reasons or to acknowledge any possibility of legitimate disagreement, his ad hominen attacks on the motives of his opponents, his avowed intention to increase the level of passion animating this debate. If we were as committed to rational deliberation in practice as we are in theory, we wouldn't be able to celebrate this speech as we do—as an expression of resistance, as an attempt to motivate action on behalf of a despised minority, and as a means of gaining moral influence over the public.

The point, of course, is that we *aren't* that committed to a politics of rational deliberation, and for good reason. American political culture supports competing and sometimes conflicting conceptions of democracy, many of which devalue argument in favor of other forms of political action. Rioting, as I argued in Part I, was for a long time after the founding a more obvious vehicle for democratic politics than was debate. And if a legitimate role for mob action isn't a live possibility anymore, a legitimate role for peaceful yet disruptive resistance still is—particularly since concerns about the effect of social disorder on the legitimacy of democracy no longer carry much weight. Think of political activists in the 1960s throwing dollar bills onto the floor of the New York Stock Exchange, trying to levitate the Pentagon, or burning flags, bras, and draft cards. As disruptive and upsetting as these performances may be, we can't quite bring ourselves to suppress them. Perhaps some of this reluctance stems from concerns about censorship; if we interpret such activities in terms of the categories of argument versus violence or disorder, as First Amendment doctrine typically does, then burning a draft card might deserve protection as a kind of second-rate form of political argument.[6] But what, then, is the political opinion behind throwing dollar bills onto the floor of the stock exchange? I suggest that these antics make more sense as part of the tradition of resistance, with its emphasis on public-spiritedness, direct action instead of endless deliberation, and defiance of conventions, norms, and authorities. In other words, we value this kind of political action not because it is another way of making an argument but because it *isn't* just another way of making an argument. It generates heat, not light.

Similarly, argument itself doesn't always look as peaceful and harmless as we would like it to be. This point was the focus of Chapters 3 and 4: the fear that a politics of public debate would erode the rational independence of the audience by subjecting it to skillful rhetorical manipulation, and the related difficulty of explaining how reason and truth, without the assistance of such rhetorical maneuvers, could prevail against interest, passion, and prejudice. These worries underlie much of the distrust of political speech that pervades American political culture—a distrust that ultimately rests on a too-stringent ideal of rational independence, inherited from the tradition of Enlightenment rationalism. If rational independence requires that one's deliberations be perfectly free from the influence of other people's interests and passions, it poses a daunting obstacle to any coherent account of how people may legitimately influence one another through speech. Thus the tradition of Enlightenment rationalism itself contributed to our suspicion of political argument; it replaced the rich tradition of neoclassical rhetoric with implausible and incoherent assertions about the irresistible power of truth, while failing to eradicate our lingering fear of demagogues and "the dominion of voice."

Importantly, though, the triumph of Enlightenment rationalism wasn't complete. The questions it left open, revolving around the problems of conviction and motivation, were the starting point for the abolitionists' attack on the value of political argument—the third of these antideliberative themes in American politics. As I argued in Part III, the abolitionists reformulated the language of Enlightenment rationalism by drawing on Protestant notions of moral corruption and reform, which in turn de-emphasized the role of reason and rational argument in moral judgment. Putting politics in this Christian framework, however, allowed the abolitionists to talk about how people could legitimately influence one another through the eloquence of the spoken or written word. Abolitionism thus simultaneously devalued rational argument and promoted a more positive view of political oratory; the "dominion of voice" sounds less sinister when it's practiced by peace-loving and essentially egalitarian Christians.

Unless, of course, we fear that Christian values are a danger to the republic. In that case, we might worry that the abolitionists rescued the arts of rhetoric by Christianizing politics. Certainly their conflation of religion and politics could have unhappy consequences for tolerance and diversity. Interestingly, though, this isn't the complaint we usually level at the abolitionists; we typically see them implicated not in bigotry but in political violence. The problem, as I have argued, is not that they promoted liberty as a value worth fighting for but that they identified as their country's most pressing need the guidance of moral heroes—and it's hard to endorse the heroic ethic without accepting a vision of politics as the realm of conflict, glory, and violence. An American hero may be a pacifist—Martin Luther King, Jr., may win more respect than John Wayne—but generally even pacifists must become enmeshed in the violence and brutality of American politics, if only as victims, in order to achieve the status of heroes.

The obvious response to this complaint is that the abolitionists didn't promote political violence, they just recognized it. From their perspective, it was precisely because political conflict in the United States was so violent that we needed moral guidance. Thus, rather than dealing with the threat of violence by redefining violence as nonpolitical—the strategy adopted by proponents of the politics of reason—they pointed to the violent character of political conflict to justify their case for constant moral reform and development as an inescapable element of democratic politics. By focusing on the moral character of the public, questioning its ability to see the truth and respond to reason, the abolitionists made one of the strongest cases against the politics of reason, and one that still resonates 150 years later—which is why Douglass's call for less argument and more passion still sounds like a compelling answer to the question of means.

Theory and History Revisited

What, then, does this excursion into antebellum politics contribute to democratic theory? I complained at the outset that contemporary democratic theory is dominated by proponents of rational deliberation, to the point that democracy and reasoned public debate are almost synonymous, or at least necessarily interconnected, to many theorists. I have tried throughout this study to underscore the contingency of that connection, arguing that it was the product of a specific set of problems (such as legitimating democracy) and was deployed for limited, strategic reasons (such as quelling mob action). Democracy can be, and has been, conceived otherwise, as rooted in popular resistance to authority or in practices that forge ethical bonds among citizens. Although coffeehouses may have contributed something important to the idea of democracy, so did tea parties and romance novels.

But beyond pointing out that democracy and reasoned argument don't necessarily imply one another, I wanted to highlight some of the limitations of conceptualizing democracy as an exercise in rational deliberation. One worry is that such conceptions undervalue nondeliberative dimensions of democratic politics. What, for example, is the status of such actions as heckling a speaker or destroying a billboard? Proponents of rational deliberation might observe that these tactics defeat argument by silencing one's opponent or, alternatively, that they promote argument by raising awareness of new issues or undermining the moral authority of the speaker. But their concern with how such acts relate to reasoned argument obscures the other ends served by acts of resistance, such as cultivating a general climate of public-spiritedness or mobilizing supporters. Similarly, tactics such as storytelling (or Douglass's jeremiad) may be aimed not at informing rational judgment but at promoting deference to morally superior people—a goal that looks deeply suspicious from a rationalist perspective. These nondeliberative ends are hard to formulate within the conceptual framework of deliberative democracy.[7]

Another concern is that theories of deliberative democracy may overvalue reasoned argument. This study identifies some of the reasons not to value political argument too highly: a politics of rational debate might become a vehicle for demagogues or a substitute for action; it might delegitimate our more compassionate impulses or reinforce (or at least fail to change) corrupted moral intuitions. And we can expand the list. Jane Mansbridge, who is far from hostile to democratic deliberation, nevertheless worries that deliberation may reinforce the status quo if marginalized groups lack the resources and skills to participate.[8] And even if the means of participation are widely available, the conventions that structure rational deliberation may exclude some voices or claims. For example, before we begin to debate, we have to decide issues of standing—who is allowed to make what kinds of claims. The politics of reason may be of limited value in dealing with such issues, since they are deeply rooted in social conventions that aren't particularly amenable to rationalization. As Angelina Grimké pointed out, the master may simply refuse to take reproof from the nursery maid—unless the nursery maid hits him over the head with a (preferably verbal) sledgehammer.

Proponents of deliberation rightly point out that such complaints constitute an argument for more and better public debate, with perhaps some limited role for unconventional or attention-getting tactics that would otherwise degrade the quality of deliberation.[9] Both sides of the debate endorse the politics of reason to the extent they use the ideal of rational deliberation as a critical standard against which to measure actual practices. Richard Rorty, however, objects to the ideal of reasoned deliberation itself. He argues that the language in which we deliberate may contain built-in biases that limit the kinds of claims people can make. "[M]ost oppressors," he points out, "have had the wit to teach the oppressed a language in which the oppressed will sound crazy—*even to themselves*—if they describe themselves *as* oppressed." The way to escape the language of the oppressors is to shift to a different vocabulary, even to create a new language—a process more poetic than rational, by which new words are created or old words and phrases are given new emotional content.[10]

These are familiar complaints about placing too much value on rational deliberation. My aim was to develop the case against argument in a slightly different direction, first by raising doubts about whether we even know what we mean by "rational deliberation." As I argued in Part I, what counts as reasoned public debate depends on what counts as violence—and that can change. The line between violence and argument is contingent and highly contestable. Similarly, I argued in Chapter 3 that the concept of rational argument depended on a particular (eighteenth-century) picture of human psychology, and on a conception of rational independence that rules out appeals to ethos and pathos. Neither faculty psychology nor the political program supporting the ideal of rational independence—namely, undercutting deference relations—has as much relevance today as it did in the 1830s. So maybe we should reevaluate the restrictions on ethos and pathos, as well as the violence versus argument distinction, that together structure the category of reasoned public debate.

Along the same lines, I want to question whether we know *why* we want a politics of reasoned argument. The rule of reason sounds appealing from the standpoint of equality and liberty: the practice of rational debate requires us to treat one another as equals (under one rather thin conception of equality as meaning "equally rational") and rules out certain tactics commonly considered coercive (although, as I have already pointed out, what counts as coercive is debatable—having one's cherished beliefs subjected to logical scrutiny may feel coercive, too). But perhaps our preference for rational deliberation also reflects a conservative concern with maintaining social order, or a somewhat anachronistic fear that social disorder will undermine the legitimacy of democracy. More cynically, our affirmations of the value of reasoned argument may not reflect any underlying concerns at all but simply the strategic calculation that aligning one's cause with the "irresistible power of truth" will help to legitimate it. Such suspect motives give us a good warrant for adopting a more critical stance toward rational deliberation, which is what I'm after. When subjected to closer scrutiny, the values underlying the ideal may turn out to be less compelling than we thought, or better served by other practices.

Finally, I wanted to foreground some of the more problematic assumptions that have traditionally supported the value of rational deliberation: that truth is accessible to everyone, that we can expect a basic level of rationality from the public (or at least that we can ignore the irrational people), that everyone is equally deserving of respect. Not all contemporary theorists make such assumptions; the point is that we should question those who do. They stack the deck in favor of rational argument. Once we abandon these assumptions, the politics of reason looks less like an obvious goal and more like one option among many for democratic political action.

NOTES

Introduction

1. Frederick Douglass, "What to the Slave Is the Fourth of July?" [1852], in *The Frederick Douglass Papers,* ed. John W. Blassingame, 2 vols. (New Haven, Conn.: Yale Univ. Press, 1982), 2:370.

2. James Fishkin, *Democracy and Deliberation* (New Haven, Conn.: Yale Univ. Press, 1991), 34, 40; David Yankelovich, *Coming to Public Judgment* (Syracuse, N.Y.: Syracuse Univ. Press, 1991), 240; Amy Guttman and Dennis Thompson, *Democracy and Disagreement* (Cambridge, Mass.: Belknap Press, 1996), 1, 52. See also John Dryzek, *Discursive Democracy* (Cambridge: Cambridge Univ. Press, 1990); Benjamin Barber, *Strong Democracy* (Berkeley: Univ. of California Press, 1984), 173 (advocating a conception of democracy centered on "talk" but not exclusively reason giving); Joshua Cohen, "Deliberation and Democratic Legitimacy," in *The Good Polity,* ed. Alan Hamilton and Philip Pettit (Oxford: Basil Blackwell, 1989); Bernard Manin, "On Legitimacy and Political Deliberation," *Political Theory* 15 (Aug. 1987): 338–68. The consensus is not complete, however. See, e.g., Martha Nussbaum, *Poetic Justice* (Boston: Beacon Press, 1995) (on the political uses of novels); Richard Rorty, *Contingency, Irony, and Solidarity* (Cambridge: Cambridge Univ. Press, 1989) (the same); Jane Mansbridge, *Beyond Adversary Democracy* (New York: Basic Books, 1980) (identifying obstacles to democratic deliberation); Lynn Sanders, "Against Deliberation," *Political Theory* 25 (June 1997): 347–76.

3. Guttman and Thompson, *Democracy and Disagreement,* 43–44, 57–58; Barber, *Strong Democracy,* 20–25, 118; Dryzek, *Discursive Democracy,* 13; Cohen, "Deliberation and Democratic Legitimacy," 18–19; Manin, "On Legitimacy and Political Deliberation," 355–57. See Cass Sunstein, "Beyond the Republican Revival," *Yale Law J.* 97 (1988): 1539–90, 1542–47, for a cogent statement of the debate between pluralist and deliberative conceptions of democracy.

4. Jürgen Habermas, *The Structural Transformation of the Public Sphere* (Cambridge: MIT Press, 1993).

5. Don Herzog, *Happy Slaves* (Chicago: Univ. of Chicago Press, 1989),

23. My only quarrel with Herzog's approach is his suggestion that we assume that actors are always trying to make their inherited web of beliefs and practices more coherent. Sometimes actors do strive for greater coherence, but we should recognize that they sometimes choose to live with cognitive dissonance or deliberately foster incoherence to suit their other purposes.

6. Ibid., 29–33.

7. For a good discussion of the differences between northern and southern traditions of mob violence, see David Grimsted, *American Mobbing, 1826–1861: Toward Civil War* (New York: Oxford Univ. Press, 1998).

1. Eighteenth-Century Riots

1. Thomas Jefferson to W. S. Smith, Nov. 13, 1787, in *The Works of Thomas Jefferson,* ed. Paul Ford, 12 vols. (New York and London: G. P. Putnams' Sons, 1904), 5:362.

2. Thomas Cope, *Philadelphia Merchant: The Diary of Thomas Cope, 1800–1851,* ed. Eliza Harrison (South Bend, Ind.: Gateway Editions, 1978), 23, 41.

3. Pauline Maier, *From Resistance to Revolution* (New York: Alfred A. Knopf, 1972), 4. See also Paul Gilje, *The Road to Mobocracy* (Chapel Hill: Univ. of North Carolina Press, 1987); Pauline Maier, "Popular Uprisings and Civil Authority in Eighteenth-Century America," *William & Mary Quart.,* 3d ser., 27 (1970): 3–35; Gordon Wood, "A Note on Mobs in the American Revolution," *William & Mary Quart.* 3d ser., 23 (1963): 635–42; Stanley Elkins and Eric McKitrick, *The Age of Federalism* (Oxford: Oxford Univ. Press, 1993), 465; David Grimsted, "Rioting in Its Jacksonian Setting," *Am. Hist. Rev.* 77 (1972): 361–97, 365.

4. Jürgen Habermas, *The Structural Transformation of the Public Sphere* (Cambridge: MIT Press, 1993). See also Chapter 4.

5. E.g., the Alien and Sedition Acts. See Elkins and McKitrick, *Age of Federalism,* 691–711.

6. See, e.g., Norman Cohen, "The Philadelphia Election Riot of 1742," *Penn. Mag. of History and Biography* 92 (1968): 306–19; Russell Weigley, ed., *Philadelphia: A 300-Year History* (New York: W. W. Norton, 1982), 60; Ellis Oberholtzer, *Philadelphia: A History of the City and Its People,* 4 vols. (Philadelphia: S. J. Clarke, 1912) 1:148. The following account of the riot is drawn largely from Cohen.

7. Cohen, "The Philadelphia Election Riot of 1742," 310–15.

8. *Pennsylvania Archives,* 8th ser. (n.p., 1931), 4:2828–31, 2843–51.

9. Cohen, "The Philadelphia Election Riot of 1742," 315–19. On riot control tactics, see the discussion later in this chapter.

10. *Pennsylvania Gazette,* Sept. 16, 1742, in *The Papers of Benjamin Franklin,* ed. Leonard Labarree, 31 vols. (New Haven, Conn.: Yale Univ. Press, 1961), 2:363–64; "To the Freeholders and Other Electors for the City and County of Philadelphia" [1764], in ibid., 11:377.

11. Cohen, "The Philadelphia Election Riot of 1742"; Weigley, *Philadelphia: A 300-Year History,* 60; Oberholtzer, *Philadelphia: A History of the City and Its People,* 1:148.

12. Joseph Kelley, Jr., *Pennsylvania: The Colonial Years* (New York: Doubleday, 1980), 140, 169.

13. Weigley, *Philadelphia: A 300-Year History,* 60.

14. Kelley, *Pennsylvania: The Colonial Years,* 209–19.

15. On the tradition of mob action, see Charles Tilly, *From Mobilization to Revolution* (Reading, Mass.: Addison-Wesley, 1978); George Rudé, *The Crowd in History* (New York: John Wiley & Sons, 1964), 31, 33–34; E. J. Hobsbawm, *Primitive Rebels* (New York: W. W. Norton, 1959); and later in this chapter. Norman Cohen suggests, but does not explore, this interpretation of the riot as an example of popular dissatisfaction with the Quaker party. Cohen, "The Philadelphia Election Riot of 1742," 317.

16. *Pennsylvania Archives,* 8th ser., 4:2830.

17. E.g., Gilje, *The Road to Mobocracy,* 5, 17; Maier, "Popular Uprisings," 16–17, 24.

18. *By the Honourable Patrick Gordon, Esq.; A Proclamation* (Philadelphia: Printed by Andrew Bradford, 1726).

19. Thomas Ellwood, *A Discourse Concerning Riots* (London: Thomas Hawkins, 1683); Minutes of the Provincial Council of Pennsylvania (n.p., 1852), 9:268–69 (referring to the Paxton rebels as rioters); "Petition to the Pennsylvania Assembly Regarding Fairs" [1731], in Labarree, *The Papers of Benjamin Franklin,* 1:211–12 (referring to late-night carousing as "riotous"). In practice, all that is required for an occurrence to be a riot is that there be many people involved (the crowd) and that it be "disorderly." Therefore, "riot" and "mob action" were essentially synonomous in eighteenth-century discourse and are used synonomously in this study.

20. Acts and Resolves of the Province of Massachusetts Bay, 3:647 (chap. 18 of province laws, 1752–1753), quoted in Maier, "Popular Uprisings," 27; Gouverneur Morris to Mr. Penn, May 20, 1774, in *American Archives,* ed. Peter Force, 4th ser., 6 vols. (Washington, D.C.: M. St. Clair Clarke & Peter Force, 1839), 1:342; *By the Honourable James Delancey, Esq., A Proclamation* (Apr. 2, 1755).

3

21. William Burnham, "God's Providence in Placing Men in the Respective Stations and Conditions" (New London, Conn.: T. Green, 1722), 43–44, in *Connecticut and Massachusetts Election Sermons,* ed. Ronald Bosco (Delmar, N.Y.: Scholars' Facsimiles and Reprints, 1978).

22. John Winthrop, "A Modell of Christian Charity" [1630], in *The American Intellectual Tradition,* ed. David Hollinger and Charles Capper, 2 vols. (Oxford: Oxford Univ. Press, 1989), 1:7. I have modernized the spelling in the original text.

23. Timothy Cutler, *The Firm Union of a People Represented* (New London, Conn., 1717), 48. See also Samuel Whittelsey, *A Publick Spirit Recommended* (New London, Conn., 1731); Andrew Eliot, *A Sermon Preached before His Excellency Francis Bernard, Esq.* (Boston, 1765).

24. Eliot, *A Sermon Preached before his Excellency Francis Bernard,* 7.

25. J. G. A. Pocock, "The Classical Theory of Deference," *Am. Hist. Rev.* 81 (1976): 516–23.

26. See John Kirby, "Early American Politics—The Search for Ideology: An Historiographical Analysis and Critique of the Concept of 'Deference'," *J. of Politics* 32 (1970): 808–38, 822–23; John K. Alexander, "Deference in Colonial Pennsylvania and that Man from New Jersey," *Penn. Mag. of History and Biography* 102 (1978): 422–36 (discussing a 1776 letter to the *Pennsylvania Evening Post* complaining that "the poorer commonalty, having hitherto had little or no hand in government, seem to think it does not belong to them to have any").

27. John Trenchard and Thomas Gordon, *Cato's Letters* [1720–1723], 4 vols. (Indianapolis: Liberty Fund, 1995), 2:607–8. On the influence of *Cato's Letters* in America, see Bernard Bailyn, *The Ideological Origins of the American Revolution* (Cambridge, Mass.: Belknap Press, 1967), 35–37.

28. David Spring, "Walter Bagehot and Deference," *Am. Hist. Rev.* 81 (1976): 524–31, 529 (quoting Walter Bagehot, *The English Constitution* [London: World's Classics ed., 1928], 236–37).

29. See, e.g., Michael Zuckerman, *Peaceable Kingdoms* (New York: Alfred A. Knopf, 1970). Tendentious or not, however, the point is well taken. See Alan Taylor, *Liberty Men and Great Proprietors* (Chapel Hill: Univ. of North Carolina Press, 1990), 4–9, detailing the extent of "backcountry resistance" to rule by the gentry throughout the eighteenth century.

30. John Winthrop, *The History of New England from 1630–1649* [1825–1826], 2 vols. (Boston: Little, Brown, 1853), 279–80; William Penn, "Preface to the First Frame of Government" [1682], in William Penn Tercentenary Committee, *Remember William Penn, 1644–1944* (Harrisburg: Commonwealth of Pennsylvania William Penn Tercentenary Committee, 1944), 80–82.

31. I am indebted to Carey McWilliams for pointing this out.

32. See Vernon Parrington, *The Colonial Mind, 1620–1800* (New York: Harcourt, Brace, 1927), 38–75, for a survey of egalitarian ideas in colonial New England (and Winthrop's resistance to them). For Franklin's democratic sentiments, see *Pennsylvania Gazette,* Mar. 21–30, 1738 (defending Pennsylvania's democratic constitution).

33. Caroline Robbins, *The Eighteenth-Century Commonwealthmen* (Cambridge: Harvard Univ. Press, 1959), 7–16; Gordon Wood, *The Creation of the American Republic, 1776–1787* (New York: W. W. Norton, 1969), 70–75; Gary Nash, "The Transformation of Urban Politics, 1700–1765," *J. Am. Hist.* 60 (1973): 605–32; Alan Taylor, "From Fathers to Friends of the People," *J. Early Republic* 11 (1991): 465–91. The relative egalitarianism of seventeenth- and eighteenth-century colonial America continues to be debated. Much of this debate is fueled by the failure to define precisely what counts as "democracy." See, e.g., Joshua Miller, *The Rise and Fall of Democracy in Early America, 1630–1789* (University Park: Pennsylvania State Univ. Press, 1991); Zuckerman, *Peaceable Kingdoms,* 187–88. Zuckerman argues that New England communities were democratic because there generally was no stable oligarchy and the franchise was broad; but politics may be structured by deference even if the elite is not a stable group. See Taylor, "From Fathers to Friends," and "The Art of Hook and Snivey," *J. Am. Hist.* 79 (1993): 1371–96 (arguing that social mobility coexisted with deference politics even after the Revolution; the nouveaux riches were expected to gain social acceptance by the established elite before they sought political power).

34. For the debate on the reality of deferential attitudes in the lower class, see Alexander, "Deference in Colonial Pennsylvania"; Kirby, "Early American Politics—The Search for Ideology."

35. Carl Bridenbaugh, *Cities in Revolt* (Oxford: Oxford Univ. Press, 1955), 148; Kirby, "Early American Politics," 816–17; Wood, *Creation of the American Republic,* 74; R. Eugene Harper, *The Transformation of Western Pennsylvania, 1770–1800* (Pittsburgh: Univ. of Pittsburgh Press, 1991), 40–41, 141. Ellis Oberholtzer attributes the increasing attention to public appearance to Governor Gordon's attention to formal public ceremony after taking office in 1726 (*Philadelphia: A History of the City and Its People,* 1:136–37). The emerging social hierarchy was challenged to some extent by the religious revivalism that we call the Great Awakening, but revivalism failed to seriously undermine the development of hierarchy in the church and society in general. Susan Juster, *Disorderly Women* (Ithaca, N.Y.: Cornell Univ. Press, 1994); Jon Butler, *Awash in a Sea of Faith* (Cambridge: Harvard Univ. Press, 1990).

36. Richard Bushman, *King and People in Provincial Massachusetts*

(Chapel Hill: Univ. of North Carolina Press, 1985); Taylor, "From Fathers to Friends."

37. Alfred Young, "English Plebeian Culture and Eighteenth-Century American Radicalism," in *Origins of Anglo-American Radicalism,* ed. Margaret Jacobs and James Jacobs (London: George Allen & Unwin, 1984); Bushman, *King and People;* Wood, *Creation of the American Republic.*

38. On elites, see Bushman, *King and People,* 55–87; on the poor, see Alexander, "Deference in Colonial Pennsylvania" and Steven Rosswurm, *Arms, Country and Class* (New Brunswick, N.J.: Rutgers Univ. Press, 1987), 24–29. Gary Nash locates the beginnings of an egalitarian ethos in Philadelphia in the 1760s. ("Artisans and Politics in Eighteenth-Century Philadelphia," in Jacobs and Jacobs, *Origins of Anglo-American Radicalism*). His chief evidence, however, is the increase in rioting and voting, which is not inconsistent with acceptance of social hierarchy. See n. 26.

39. Gurdon Saltonstall, "A Sermon Preached before the General Assembly of the Colony of Connecticut" [1697], in Sacvan Bercovitch, *Election Day Sermons: Plymouth and Connecticut* (New York: AMS Press, 1983), 74.

40. Jacob Duche, "The Duty of Standing Fast in Our Spiritual and Temporal Liberties" [1775], in *The Patriot Preachers of the American Revolution,* ed. Frank Moore (New York: Charles T. Evans, 1862), 79.

41. Minutes of the Provincial Council of Pennsylvania, 9:276 (1852); *By the Honourable Patrick Gordon, Esq; A Proclamation* (Philadelphia: Printed by Andrew Bradford, 1726); *By the Honourable Patrick Gordon, Esq; A Proclamation* (Philadelphia: Printed by Andrew Bradford, 1729); *To the Honourable Patrick Gordon . . .* (Philadelphia, 1729) (address by the General Assembly). For other examples of antiriot rhetoric, see *An Act for Preventing Tumults and Riotous Assemblies* (Philadelphia, 1764); *An Act for Preventing Tumults and Riotous Assemblies* (Philadelphia, 1771); *By the President and the Supreme Executive Council of the Commonwealth of Pennsylvania, A Proclamation* (1787); Pennsylvania Archives, 8th ser., 4:2828–30, 2843–50 (selections from legislative action concerning the Philadelphia election riots of 1742); *Pennsylvania Gazette,* May 3, 1738; "Poor Richard, 1747," in Labarree, *The Papers of Benjamin Franklin,* 3:106.

42. Bushman, *King and People,* 177; Joyce Appleby, Margaret Jacobs, and James Jacobs, "Introduction," in Jacobs and Jacobs, *Origins of Anglo-American Radicalism,* 7; Nash, "Artisans and Politics in Eighteenth-Century Philadelphia," 170.

43. Tilly, *From Mobilization to Revolution;* Rudé, *The Crowd in History,* 31, 33–34; Hobsbawm, *Primitive Rebels.*

44. Barbara Clark Smith, "Food Rioters and the American Revolution,"

William & Mary Quart., 3d ser., 51 (1994): 3–34; Rudé, *The Crowd in History,* 19–65.

45. J. C. D. Clark, *The Language of Liberty* (Cambridge: Cambridge Univ. Press, 1994), 240–82, especially 268–71; Rosswurm, *Arms, Country and Class;* Eric Foner, *Tom Paine and Revolutionary America* (Oxford: Oxford Univ. Press, 1976); Rudé, *The Crowd in History,* 33–45.

46. On the carnival, see Mikhail Bakhtin, *Rabelais and His World* (Cambridge: MIT Press, 1968), 5–11.

47. For an account of the mobbings, see Rosswurm, *Arms, Country and Class,* 30–33. Pauline Maier, commenting on the relative nonviolence of American mobs, notes that attacks on customs officials were an exception to this rule. She speculates that this may have been due to the presence of foreigners among the rioting sailors ("Popular Uprisings," 17).

48. See Young, "English Plebeian Culture," for descriptions of ritual punishments borrowed from English plebeian culture. The ritual element of mob action is commonly recognized. See Peter Burke, *Popular Culture in Early Modern Europe* (London: Temple & Smith, 1978); Tilly, *From Mobilization to Revolution;* Hobsbawm, *Primitive Rebels.* Studies such as these usually characterize eighteenth-century riots as ritualized types of political action aimed at enforcing the moral economy but fail to note their relation to the rituals of deference. Of course, not all riots were directed at government officials, but even the occurrence of a riot indicated a troublesome lack of deference to the authorities.

49. John Adams to Abigail Adams, July 6, 1774, in *Adams Family Correspondence,* ed. L. H. Butterfield, 6 vols. (Cambridge, Mass.: Belknap Press, 1963), 1:126; Minutes of the Provincial Council of Pennsylvania, 9:268–69, 271 (1852).

50. *The Proceedings of the Governor, Council and House of Representatives of the Province of Massachusetts-Bay, Concerning an Indemnification for the Sufferers by the Rioters in Boston, from August 27, 1765, to June 28, 1766.*

51. Maier, "Popular Uprisings," 19, 29–30; Wood, "A Note on Mobs," 639. See Kelley, *Pennsylvania: The Colonial Years,* 494–95, on Governor Penn's reluctance to use the militia against the Paxton rebels. George Washington expressed a similar reluctance to use force in response to the Whiskey Insurrection, fearing that it would undermine the legitimacy of the regime (Elkins and McKitrick, *Age of Federalism,* 465).

52. *An Act for Preventing Tumults and Riotous Assemblies . . .* (Philadelphia, 1764).

53. Kelley, *Pennsylvania: The Colonial Years,* 495.

54. *Pennsylvania Archives,* 8th ser. (n.p., 1931), 4:2847.

55. Samuel Cooke, "A Sermon Preached at Cambridge" [1770], in *The Pulpit of the American Revolution,* ed. John Thornton (Boston: Gould & Lincoln, 1860), 172.

56. *Pennsylvania Packet,* June 1, 1772.

57. Ibid., Nov. 11, 1771. See also Maier, "Popular Uprisings," 25.

58. E.g., Maier, "Popular Uprisings," 24–26; Wood, "A Note on Mobs," 10; Gilje, *The Road to Mobocracy,* 6–9.

59. John Locke, *Two Treatises of Government* [1690] (New York: Hafner Press, 1947), 233. Locke's influence on revolutionary rhetoric continues to be hotly debated. See, e.g., Jerome Huyler, *Locke in America* (Lawrence: Univ. Press of Kansas, 1995); Michael Zuckert, *Natural Rights and the New Republicanism* (New Haven, Conn.: Yale Univ. Press, 1994). Fortunately, we needn't resolve the issue here; I am interested less in the sources of revolutionary doctrine than in what the revolutionary leaders actually said.

60. Cooke, "A Sermon Preached at Cambridge," 163.

61. Locke is often cited as authority for an individual right of resistance, but he is better interpreted as justifying the community's right to dissolve and reform the government, while preserving to individuals *at most* the right to use violence to protect their lives from illegal uses of force by magistrates (*Two Treatises of Government,* 225). In any case, the founders did not need to assert an individual right of resistance, since they were ostensibly acting in the name of the community.

62. Jonathan Mayhew, "A Discourse Concerning Unlimited Submission and Non-Resistance to the Higher Powers" [1750], in Thornton, *The Pulpit of the American Revolution,* 69.

63. John Adams, "Novanglus" [1774], in *The Works of John Adams,* ed. Charles F. Adams, 10 vols. (Boston: Charles C. Little & James Brown, 1851), 4:81.

64. Ibid. Other examples of this rhetoric can be found in Maier, *From Resistance to Revolution,* 28–42.

65. Adams, "Novanglus," 4:84 (quoting Locke; the emphasis is Adams's).

66. Cooke, "A Sermon Preached in Cambridge," 167.

67. See Maier, *From Resistance to Revolution,* 33–34, for a collection of Whig objections to mobs.

68. Adams, "Novanglus," 4:82.

69. The comments on the Stamp Act mobs are quoted in Rosswurm, *Arms, Country and Class,* 34; comments on impressment gangs are quoted in Maier, "Popular Uprisings," 9.

70. *The Proceedings of the Governor, Council and House of Representatives of the Province of Massachusetts-Bay, Concerning an Indemnification for the Sufferers by the Rioters in Boston.* See also J. A. W. Gunn, *Beyond Liberty and*

Property (Kingston, Canada: McGill-Queen's Univ. Press, 1983), 81, for examples of the equation of the mob with the people in eighteenth-century English politics.

71. Maier, "Popular Uprisings," 8–13; Smith, "Food Rioters and the American Revolution," 3.

72. See Maier, "Popular Uprisings," 21; Gilje, *The Road to Mobocracy,* 273. On the posse, see Sir Robert Chambers, *A Course of Lectures on the English Law, 1767–1773,* 2 vols. (Madison: Univ. of Wisconsin Press, 1986), 1:238; Sir Frederick Pollock and Frederic Maitland, *The History of English Law before the Time of Edward I,* 2d ed., 2 vols. (Cambridge: Cambridge Univ. Press, 1968), 2:578–79.

73. Hutchinson to Grant, July 27, 1768, quoted in Maier, "Popular Uprisings," 27. Hutchinson, however, fell back on the language of governance to condemn the 1765 mob that attacked him and his family: "The laws of our country are open to punish those who have offended. This destroying of all peace and order of the community—*all will feel its effects.*" Francis Bernard to Lords of Trade, Nov. 30, 1765, quoted in Bernard Bailyn, *The Ordeal of Thomas Hutchinson* (Cambridge: Harvard Univ. Press, 1974), 36.

74. John Dunbar, ed., *The Paxton Papers* (The Hague: Martinus Nijhoff, 1957), 96; Maier, "Popular Uprisings," 9; Minutes of the Provincial Council of Pennsylvania, 9:274.

75. Anon., *An Address to the Inhabitants of the Province of the Massachusetts-Bay, by a Lover of His Country* (Boston: Rogers & Fowles, 1747).

76. Ibid.

77. Thomas Reid, "Essays on the Active Powers of Man" [1788], in *The Works of Thomas Reid,* ed. Sir William Hamilton, 2 vols. (Bristol: Thoemmes Press, 1994), 2:571. See Herbert Hovenkamp, *Science and Religion in America 1800–1860* (Philadelphia: Univ. of Pennsylvania Press, 1978), 5–20, on the influence of Reid and his followers in eighteenth-century America.

78. David Hume, *A Treatise of Human Nature* [1740] (Oxford: Clarendon Press, 1978), 413. See also Reid, "Essay on the Active Powers," 2:511, 570–72. See Ann Douglas, *The Feminization of American Culture* (New York: Alfred A. Knopf, 1977), on the pervasive influence of the reason-passion dichotomy well into the nineteenth century.

79. Samuel West, "A Sermon Preached" [1776], in Thornton, *Pulpit of the American Revolution,* 273.

80. *The Diary and Letters of Gouverneur Morris,* ed. Anne Morris, 2 vols. (New York: Da Capo Press, 1970), 2:468; "Poor Richard, 1747," in Labarree, *The Papers of Benjamin Franklin,* 3:106.

81. Jefferson to W. S. Smith, Nov. 13, 1787, in Ford, *Works of Thomas Jefferson,* 5:362; Jefferson to Ezra Stiles, Dec. 24, 1786, in *The Writings of*

Thomas Jefferson, ed. H. A. Washington, 9 vols. (Washington, D.C.: Taylor & Maury, 1853), 2:77.

82. West, "A Sermon Preached," 307; Jonathan Mayhew, "The Snare Broken" [1766], in Moore, *Patriot Preachers of the American Revolution,* 40; John Hurt, "The Love of Country" [1777], in ibid., 145.

83. Anon., *To the Delaware Pilots* (Philadelphia, 1773).

84. Phillips Payson, "A Sermon Preached before the Honorable Council . . . " [1778], in Thornton, *Pulpit of the American Revolution,* 333; Hurt, "The Love of Country," 149–50.

85. William Smith, "A Sermon on the Present Situation of American Affairs" [1775], in Moore, *Patriot Preachers of the American Revolution,* 110; John Zubly, "The Law of Liberty" [1775], in ibid., 139–40; Nathaniel Whitaker, "An Antidote Against Toryism" [1777], in ibid., 213–14.

86. John Adams to Abigail Adams, July 6, 1774, in Butterfield, *Adams Family Correspondence,* 1:126.

87. Reid, "Essay on the Active Powers," 2:534.

88. John Dickinson, "Speech to the House of Assembly" [1764], in *The Political Writings of John Dickinson,* 2 vols. (Wilmington, Del.: Bonsal & Niles, 1801), 1:3.

89. Mayhew, "The Snare Broken," 23.

90. Trenchard and Gordon, *Cato's Letters,* 1:103.

91. John Dickinson, "The Farmer's Letters," in *The Political Writings of John Dickinson,* 1:148; Adams, "Novanglus," 4:84.

92. *To the Honourable Patrick Gordon etc., The humble Address of the Representatives,* Mar. 29, 1729; Washington to James Madison, Nov. 5, 1786, in *Writings of George Washington,* ed. John Fitzpatrick, 39 vols. (Washington, D.C.: U.S. Government Printing Office, 1939), 29:51.

93. Adams, "Novanglus," 4:82–84; Cooke, "A Sermon Preached in Cambridge," 167 (emphasis added).

94. Eliot, *A Sermon Preached before His Excellency Francis Bernard,* 45; Adams, "Novanglus," 4:82 (quoting Locke).

95. Robert Schomburgk, *The History of Barbados* (London: Frank Cass, 1971), 331.

96. John Dickinson, "An Address to the Committee of Correspondence in Barbadoes" [1766], in *The Political Writings of John Dickinson,* 1:101–2.

97. Ibid., 102–5.

98. Ibid., 99–100. "Two of three mobs" was, of course, an understatement; mob action was either threatened or actually took place throughout the colonies. See Maier, *Resistance to Revolution,* 53–57.

99. Dickinson, "An Address to the Committee of Correspondence in Barbadoes," 1:107–8.

100. Ibid., 108, 113 (emphasis in original).

101. Ibid., 118, 120.

102. Maier, *Resistance to Revolution,* 53–57.

103. Dickinson, "An Address to the Committee of Correspondence in Barbadoes," 1:128.

104. *Pennsylvania Packet,* Oct. 31, 1781, Dec. 8, 1781.

105. Dickinson, "The Farmer's Letters," 1:167 (emphasis in original).

106. Ibid., 167–70.

107. Ibid., 168.

108. William Smith, "A Sermon on the Present Situation of American Affairs" [1775], in Moore, *Patriot Preachers of the American Revolution,* 109; West, "A Sermon Preached," 302.

109. *Pennsylvania Packet,* Mar. 25, 1777.

110. Mayhew, "The Snare Broken," 43.

111. Maier, *From Resistance to Revolution,* 67.

112. Ibid., 69.

113. The incident is recounted in C. H. Lincoln, *The Revolutionary Movement in Pennsylvania 1760–1776,* Univ. of Pennsylvania Series in History I (Philadelphia: For the University, 1901), 199–200.

114. *The Complete Writings of Thomas Paine,* ed. Philip Foner, 2 vols. (New York: Citadel Press, 1945), 4:289. The quotation is from an address published in Philadelphia in December 1778.

115. James Logan, quoted in Kelley, *Pennsylvania: The Colonial Years,* 157 ("The last two elections for Assembly . . . were very mobbish, and carried by a Levelling spirit").

116. *Pennsylvania Packet,* Mar. 25, 1777.

117. Regina Morantz, " 'Democracy' and 'Republic' in American Ideology, 1787–1840," Ph.D. diss., Columbia Univ., 1971.

118. Ibid., 29–30.

119. Anti-Federalists, of course, worried that restrictions on participation could create a de facto aristocracy, a problem that the Federalists were never quite able to resolve. But their debate turned more on what constituted adequate representation than on the principle that sovereignty lay with "the people." See Terence Ball, " 'A Republic—If You Can Keep It,' " in *Conceptual Change and the Constitution,* ed. Terence Ball and J. G. A. Pocock (Lawrence: Univ. Press of Kansas, 1988), 147–49.

120. Morantz, " 'Democracy' and 'Republic' in American Ideology," 18–25; R. R. Palmer, "Notes on the Use of the Word 'Democracy' 1789–1799," *Pol. Sci. Quart.* 68 (1953): 203–26.

121. Quoted in Wood, *Creation of the American Republic,* 230.

122. Fisher Ames, "Dangers of American Liberty" [1805], in *The Works*

of Fisher Ames, ed. W. B. Allen, 2 vols. (Indianapolis: Liberty Classics, 1983), 1:125.

123. Ibid., 1:126 (emphasis added).

124. *Federal Gazette,* Feb. 10, 1789.

125. Wood, *Creation of the American Republic,* 319–26; *Proceedings of the General Town-Meeting* (Philadelphia: F. Bailey, 1779); James Wright to Governour Gage, June 27, 1775, in Force, *American Archives,* 4th ser., 2:1109; Gouverneur Morris to Mr. Penn, May 20, 1774, in Force, *American Archives,* 4th ser., 1:343.

126. Adams, "Novanglus," 4:74; Gouverneur Morris to Mr. Penn, May 20, 1774, in Force, *American Archives,* 4th ser., 1:342.

127. Quoted in Wood, *Creation of the American Republic,* 233.

128. Quoted in John Alexander, "Poverty, Fear, and Continuity," in *The Peoples of Philadelphia,* ed. Allen Davis and Mark Haller (Philadelphia: Temple Univ. Press, 1973), 24.

129. Harry Tinkcum, *The Republicans and Federalists in Pennsylvania* (Harrisburg: Pennsylvania Historical & Museum Commission, 1950), 177. The fact that Israel was not, in fact, Jewish apparently escaped his detractors. Edwin Wolf and Maxwell Whiteman, *The History of the Jews in Philadelphia from Colonial Times to the Age of Jackson* (Philadelphia: Jewish Publication Society of America, 1956), 31.

130. William Cobbett, *A History of the American Jacobins, Commonly Denominated Democrats* (Philadelphia: William Cobbett, 1796), 12–15.

131. John Robison, *Proofs of a Conspiracy against All Religions and Governments of Europe Carried on in the Secret Meetings of the Free Masons, Illuminati, and Reading Societies* (Philadelphia: Dobson & Cobbett, 1798), 12; Howard Mumford Jones, *American and French Culture* (Chapel Hill: Univ. of North Carolina Press, 1927), 396–400, 530–50; Russel Nye, *The Cultural Life of the New Nation* (New York: Harper & Row, 1960), 212, 238–39.

132. John Adams to Richard Cranch, Aug. 2, 1776, quoted in Wood, *Creation of the American Republic,* 92.

133. Isaac Kramnick, ed., *Federalist Papers* [1787] (London: Penguin Books, 1987), 126.

134. Thomas Paine, "Rights of Man, Part II" [1792], in Foner, *The Complete Writings of Thomas Paine,* 1:369.

135. Ibid., 372.

136. Maier, "Popular Uprisings", 34; *Philadelphia Gazette,* Feb. 19, 1798.

137. Fisher Ames, "Camillus II" [1787], in Allen, *The Works of Fisher Ames,* 1:65; Benjamin Rush, "On the Defects of the Confederation" [1787], in *The Selected Writings of Benjamin Rush,* ed. Dagobert Runes (New York: Philosophical Library, 1947), 28.

138. Ames, "Camillus II," 1:65–68. Ames also referred to the protection of rights afforded by an independent judiciary, but this argument is subject to the obvious complaint that the enforcement of judicial decisions depends on the executive branch, which is the branch commonly thought to be most liable to abuse its power.

139. This focus on voting was a new element in American political thought; as Gordon Wood has pointed out, at the time of the Revolution, the act of voting was not central to the concept of free government (Wood, *Creation of the American Republic,* 168).

140. Noah Webster, *A Collection of Essays and Fugitiv Writings* (n.p., 1790), 72.

141. Ibid., 55, 53.

142. Adams to Noah Webster, Apr. 30, 1784, in *Writings of Samuel Adams,* ed. Harry Cushing, 4 vols. (New York: Octagon Books, 1968), 4:305; Paine, "Rights of Man, Part II," 1:369.

143. Webster, *Fugitiv Writings,* 55, 72.

144. Fisher Ames, "The Republican XI" [1804], in Allen, *The Works of Fisher Ames,* 1:117.

145. Fisher Ames, "Lucius Junius Brutus I" [1786], in Allen, *The Works of Fisher Ames,* 1:42; "The Republican XI" [1804], in ibid., 1:117–18 (emphasis added).

146. Cope, *Philadelphia Merchant,* 52; *Philadelphia Gazette,* Feb. 17, 1798.

147. Fisher Ames, "Speech on the Jay Treaty" [1796], in Allen, *The Works of Fisher Ames,* 2:1145.

148. Fisher Ames, "Camillus IV" [1787], in Allen, *The Works of Fisher Ames,* 1:83.

149. See Maier, *From Resistance to Revolution,* passim. William Gordon, "A Discourse Preached" [1774], in Thornton, *Pulpit of the American Revolution,* 203; Nathaniel Whitaker, "An Antidote against Toryism" [1777], in Moore, *Patriot Preachers of the American Revolution,* 214–15 (praising prudence, but warning against "overprudence" that diminishes zeal).

150. *Philadelphia Gazette,* Feb. 20, 1798.

151. "The Address and Reasons of Dissent" [1787], in *The Anti-Federalist,* ed. Herbert Storing (Chicago: Univ. of Chicago Press, 1981), 204.

152. Kramnick, *The Federalist Papers,* 88–89.

153. Ibid., 92, 156; "Centinel I" [1787], in Storing, *The Anti-Federalist,* 13–14; "Brutus X" [1788], in ibid., 160; Kramnick, *The Federalist Papers,* 314.

154. Kramnick, *The Federalist Papers,* 122, 126.

155. Ibid., 92, 198, 199, 241, 242, 265, 317; "Centinel I," 14; "Federal

Farmer VI" [1788], in Storing, *The Anti-Federalist,* 66; "Brutus I" [1788], in ibid., 108.

156. Thomas Tucker, *Conciliatory Hints, Attempting by a Fair State of Matters, to Remove Party Prejudice* (Charleston, 1784), quoted in Wood, *Creation of the American Republic,* 343.

2. Rioting in the Antebellum Era

1. *Mechanics' Free Press,* Jan. 31, 1829.
2. Charles Godfrey Leland, *Memoirs* (London: William Heineman, 1894), 216.
3. Michael Feldberg, *The Turbulent Era* (Oxford: Oxford Univ. Press, 1980), 5.
4. Leonard Richards, *"Gentlemen of Property and Standing"* (Oxford: Oxford Univ. Press, 1970), 10–13; David Grimsted, "Rioting in Its Jacksonian Setting," *Am. Hist. Rev.* 77 (1972): 362; John Runcie, " 'Hunting the Nigs' in Philadelphia: The Race Riot of August 1834," *Pennsylvania History* 39 (1972): 189; Hugh Davis Graham and Ted Gurr, *Violence in America* (New York: Bantam Books, 1969), 53–54.
5. Paul Gilje, *The Road to Mobocracy* (Chapel Hill: Univ. of North Carolina Press, 1987), 285–88. Gilje attributes the increasingly violent character of rioting after the Civil War to the antebellum developments discussed in this section, such as the loss of the nonviolent conventions of traditional mob action.
6. See Roger Lane, *Policing the City: Boston 1822–1885* (Cambridge: Harvard Univ. Press, 1967), 29; Gilje, *The Road to Mobocracy,* 205–32; Feldberg, *The Turbulent Era,* 104–8.
7. On the social composition of mobs, see Richards, *"Gentlemen of Property and Standing,"* passim; Grimsted, "Rioting in Its Jacksonian Setting," 385–89. On the values of working-class communities, see Teresa Murphy, *Ten Hours' Labor* (Ithaca, N.Y.: Cornell Univ. Press, 1992); Bruce Laurie, *Working Peoples of Philadelphia, 1800–1850* (Philadelphia: Temple Univ. Press, 1980). Laurie identifies three separate value-systems among working people in Philadelphia; only "the traditionalists" regularly engaged in rioting (ibid., 33–83).
8. Robert Collyer, *Lights and Shadows of American Life* (Boston: Brainard & Co., [1838?]), 39.
9. John M. Werner, *Reaping the Bloody Harvest* (New York and London: Garland, 1986), 19–20; Edward Abdy, *Journal of a Residence and Tour in the United States* (London: J. Murray, 1835), 388–92; Charles Dickens, *American*

Notes [1857] (Gloucester: Peter Smith, 1968), 262–63; Thomas Brothers, *The United States as They Are* (London: Longman, Orme, Brown, Green & Longmans, 1840).

10. *Niles' Register,* Sept. 5, 1835, p. 1; Oct. 17, 1835, p. 99; May 24, 1834, p. 210 (quoting a New York grand jury); Nov. 28, 1835, p. 211 (quoting the *Arkansas Advocate*).

11. Ibid., Jan. 2, 1836, p. 299.

12. Alexis de Tocqueville, *Democracy in America* [1848] (Garden City, N.Y.: Anchor Press Books, 1969), 50–51.

13. *The Friend,* Oct. 23, 1828.

14. Murphy, *Ten Hours' Labor,* 9–12.

15. Hierarchical relationships in the workplace and the family continued to be contested in the 1830s and 1840s. See Murphy, *Ten Hours' Labor;* Paul Johnson, *A Shopkeeper's Millennium* (New York: Hill & Wang, 1978); Philip Scranton, "Varieties of Paternalism: Industrial Structures and the Social Relations of Production in American Textiles," *Am. Quart.* 36 (1984): 235–75.

16. See Paula Baker, "The Domestication of Politics: Women and American Political Society, 1780–1920," *Am. Hist. Rev.* 89 (1984): 620–47.

17. Ibid.; Alexander Saxton, *The Rise and Fall of the White Republic* (London: Verso, 1990); David Roediger, *The Wages of Whiteness* (London: Verso, 1991). I don't mean to suggest that race and gender were irrelevant to citizenship before this period, but the research of Baker, Saxton, and Roediger indicates that it was during the early nineteenth century that citizenship began to be defined primarily in terms of whiteness and maleness rather than class.

18. *Niles' Register,* Aug. 8, 1835, p. 393; Charge of King, President, to the Grand Jury, 4 *Penn. L. J.* 29, 30 (1844); *Pennsylvanian,* Aug. 3, 1835; *Niles' Register,* Sept. 5, 1838, p. 1.

19. For a more recent statement of the principle, see Michael Walzer, *Spheres of Justice* (New York: Basic Books, 1983).

20. Ronald Formisano, *The Transformation of Political Culture* (Oxford: Oxford Univ. Press, 1983); Mary P. Ryan, *Civic Wars* (Berkeley: Univ. of California Press, 1997), 108–9, 113.

21. This dynamic is illustrated in Ronald Formisano, *The Birth of Mass Political Parties: Michigan, 1827–1861* (Princeton, N.J.: Princeton Univ. Press, 1971).

22. On the withdrawal of the upper class from politics, especially in Philadelphia, see Sam Bass Warner, *The Private City* (Philadelphia: Univ. of Pennsylvania Press, 1968); E. Digby Baltzell, *Philadelphia Gentlemen* (Glencoe, Ill.: Free Press, 1958).

23. Sidney George Fisher, *A Philadelphia Perspective: The Diary of Sidney*

George Fisher Covering the Years 1834–1871, ed. Nicholas Wainwright (Philadelphia: Historical Society of Pennsylvania, 1967), 34, 51 (hereafter *Diary of Sidney George Fisher*).

24. Ibid., 7–8.

25. *Niles' Register,* May 24, 1834, p. 203.

26. *National Enquirer and Constitutional Advocate of Universal Liberty,* Aug. 3, 1836; *National Gazette and Literary Register,* Mar. 15 and 26, 1831. See also *Pennsylvania Freeman,* Mar. 15, 1838.

27. *Diary of Sidney George Fisher,* 22, 64, 104.

28. Ibid., 7, 22.

29. Anon., *The Life and Adventures of Charles Anderson Chester, Notorious Leader of the Philadelphia "Killers"* (Philadephia: Published for the Printers, 1850).

30. *Pennsylvania Packet,* Nov. 11, 1771.

31. *The Life and Adventures of Charles Anderson Chester,* 36.

32. The development of this gender-based ideology of social order is detailed in Baker, "The Domestication of Politics"; Barbara Berg, *The Remembered Gate* (Oxford: Oxford Univ. Press, 1978); Mary Ryan, *Women in Public* (Baltimore: Johns Hopkins Univ. Press, 1990).

33. *Niles' Register,* Aug. 23, 1834, p. 435 (quoting an excerpt from the *Philadelphia Intelligencer,* Aug. 15, 1834); July 19, 1834, p. 357 (quoting an excerpt from the *New York Commercial Advertiser,* July 10, 1834).

34. *Niles' Register,* Aug. 23, 1834, p. 426.

35. *Mechanics' Free Press,* July 19, 1828.

36. Gordon Wood, *Creation of the American Republic, 1776–1787* (New York: W. W. Norton, 1969), 52. See also Thomas Pangle, *The Spirit of Modern Republicanism* (Chicago: Univ. of Chicago Press, 1988), 74–111; Lance Banning, "Some Second Thought on Virtue and the Course of Revolutionary Thinking," in *Conceptual Change and the Constitution,* ed. Terence Ball and J. G. A. Pocock (Lawrence: Univ. Press of Kansas, 1988).

37. George Simmons, *Public Spirit and Mobs* (Springfield, Mass.: Merriam, Chapin & Co; Boston: Wm. Crosby & H. P. Nichols, 1851), 21–23.

38. Accounts of the riot can be found in *Niles' Register,* July 13, 1844, pp. 308–10; *Commonwealth v. Daley,* 4 *Penn. L. J.* 150 (1844).

39. Anon., *The Truth Unveiled, A Calm and Impartial Exposition of the Origin and Immediate Cause of the Terrible Riots and Rebellion in Philadelphia in May and July,* AD *1844* (Baltimore: Metropolitan Tract Society, 1844). "Inflammatory works" probably referred to the spate of anti-Catholic literature, such as Maria Monk's *Awful Disclosures of . . . the Hotel Dieu Nunnery at Montreal* (1836). See David Reynolds, *Beneath the American Renaissance* (New York: Alfred A. Knopf, 1988), 64–65.

40. John Hancock Lee, *The Origin and Progress of the American Party in Politics* (Philadelphia: Elliott & Gihon, 1855), 16.

41. Abraham Lincoln, "Address before the Young Men's Lyceum of Springfield, Illinois" [1838], in *The Collected Works of Abraham Lincoln,* ed. Roy Basler (New Brunswick, N.J.: Rutgers Univ. Press, 1953), 115.

42. *Niles' Register,* Apr. 5, 1835, p. 85.

43. David Grimsted, *American Mobbing, 1826–1861: Toward Civil War* (New York: Oxford Univ. Press, 1998), 4. Grimsted notes that the meaning of "mob" changed during Andrew Jackson's presidency. By the 1830s, it was being used to refer not to the lower orders generally but only to actual rioters.

44. Ibid., May 24, 1834, p. 210.

45. *The Diary of Philip Hone,* ed. Allan Nevins, 2 vols. (New York: Dodd, Mead, 1927), 1:508.

46. Gilje, *The Road to Mobocracy,* 127–42.

47. "Immigration," *North Am. Rev.* 40 (1835): 462, 464, 466.

48. *Christian Chronicle,* Sept. 9, 1846.

49. Quoted in Roy Akagi, "The Pennsylvania Constitution of 1838," *Penn. Mag. of Hist. and Bio.* 48 (1924): 318.

50. *Pennsylvania Freeman,* March 29, 1838.

51. Akagi, "The Pennsylvania Constitution of 1838," 319. Blacks and immigrants were frequently compared; one delegate even proposed that freed slaves be naturalized like immigrants were. *Proceedings and Debates of the Pennsylvania Convention* (Harrisburg: Packer, Barrett, & Parke, 1838), 9:351.

52. *Mechanics' Free Press,* July 19, 1828.

53. "Immigration," 462.

54. Ibid., 463, 467. See also Lee, *Origin and Progress of the American Party in Politics,* 22.

55. *Pennsylvanian,* Aug. 3, 1835.

56. Samuel Whelpley, "A Compend of History from the Earliest Times; Comprehending a General View of the Present State of the World," 8th ed. [1825], in Edith Abbot, *Historical Aspects of the Immigration Problem* (Chicago: Univ. of Chicago Press, 1926), 730–31.

57. Ibid., 731.

58. Samuel Morse, "Imminent Dangers to the Free Institutions of the United States through Foreign Immigration, and the Present State of the Naturalization Laws" [1854], in Abbott, *Historical Aspects of the Immigration Problem,* 449–51.

59. From the Irish *Newry Examiner,* in Abbott, *Historical Aspects of the Immigration Problem,* 75.

60. Whelpley, "A Compend of History from the Earliest Times," 729.

61. "Immigration," (1835): 463, 459 (emphasis added).

62. *Niles' Register,* Sept. 19, 1835, p. 33; *Commonwealth v. Daley,* 4 *Penn. L. J.* 150, 161 (1844); *Niles' Register,* Jan. 2, 1836, p. 299; *Pennsylvanian,* July 31, 1834.

63. *Niles' Register,* Sept. 26, 1829, pp. 68–69.

64. *Pennsylvanian,* July 10, 1835.

65. Hone, *Diary of Philip Hone,* 40–41; *United States Gazette,* Apr. 17, 1837 (quoted in Runcie, " 'Hunting the Nigs'," 188.)

66. Michael Schudson, *Discovering the News* (New York: Basic Books, 1978), 16; Runcie, " 'Hunting the Nigs'," 187–88.

67. *Pennsylvania Freeman,* May 31, 1838 (quoting the *Pennsylvanian*).

68. Phyllis Japp attributes the Grimkés' retirement in part to this riot. See "Esther or Isaiah?: The Abolitionist-Feminist Rhetoric of Angelina Grimké," *Quart. J. of Speech* 71 (1985): 335–48, 344.

69. *Pennsylvania Freeman,* May 24, 1838.

70. The Philadelphia riots are described in Werner, *Reaping the Bloody Harvest,* 166–212. See also Richards, *"Gentlemen of Property and Standing"* (detailing anti-abolitionist riots directed at printing presses, etc.); *The Friend,* Oct. 18, 1828 (account of riot among Ohio Quakers, targeting a meetinghouse).

71. *Niles' Register,* Apr. 26, 1834, p. 130.

72. Ibid., July 19, 1834, p. 358. For other negative evaluations of Tappan, see the *Pennsylvanian,* July 8, 9, and 10, 1834.

73. Abdy, *Journal of a Residence and Tour in the United States,* 389, 391. Similar rhetoric is found in *Commonwealth v. Daley,* 4 *Penn. L. J.* 150, 154 (1844).

74. George Simmons, *Public Spirit and Mobs,* 19–20 (emphasis in original).

75. Ibid., 20. He goes on to assert, oddly, that "all who will invade other men's privileges, and abridge their rights, attack their persons, and endanger their liberty, should do it by the processes of law."

76. *Pennsylvanian,* July 11, 1834.

77. David Smiley, *The Lion of White Hall* (Madison: Univ. of Wisconsin Press, 1962), 96–99. The degree to which Clay resisted the mob was the subject of some debate after the event. Some abolitionists accused Clay of instigating the attack by arming his office; Clay responded that the mob didn't know that the office was armed. He also pointed out that no one was present to defend the building—all the while, however, insisting that he would have been justified in defending it and would have done so if not weakened by typhoid. *Pennsylvania Freeman,* Jan. 29, 1846, p. 3.

78. Simmons, *Public Spirit and Mobs,* 21.

79. *National Enquirer,* Nov. 26, 1836; *National Gazette,* Feb. 26, 1831; *Niles' Register,* Sept. 26, 1829, p. 65.

80. *Niles' Register* Feb. 8, 1834, p. 399.

81. Lee, *Origin and Progress of the American Party in Politics,* 40.

82. Feldberg, *The Turbulent Era,* 9–23.

83. Charge of King, President, to the Grand Jury, 4 *Penn. L. J.* 29, 31 (1844).

84. *Commonwealth v. Daley,* 4 *Penn. L. J.* 150, 154 (1844).

85. Ibid., 154.

86. Julie Winch, *Philadelphia's Black Elite* (Philadelphia: Temple Univ. Press, 1988), 149–50. See also Ryan, *Civic Wars,* 131 (noting the blurry line between riots and meetings).

87. Richards, *"Gentlemen of Property and Standing,"* 51–52.

88. *Niles' Register,* Oct. 3, 1835, p. 73 (quoting the *Southern Patriot*) and 64 (quoting *Columbia Telescope*).

89. Ibid., Oct. 3, 1835, p. 72, and Aug. 8, 1835, pp. 402–3 (collecting reactions to the postal campaign).

90. Grimsted, "Rioting in Its Jacksonian Setting," 375; Thomas Slaughter, *Bloody Dawn* (Oxford: Oxford Univ. Press, 1991), (quoting the *Pennsylvanian,* Sept. 13, 1851).

91. *Pennsylvania Freeman,* May 24, 1838.

92. For a more detailed analysis of abolitionism and mobs, see Grimsted, *American Mobbing.* Grimsted explores in depth the integral role of mob action in abolition and antiabolition politics.

93. Ibid., Feb. 5, 1846 (quoting Act of Assembly, 1835, ch. 325).

94. *Pennsylvania Freeman,* Mar. 22, 1838.

95. See Adin Ballou, *Christian Non-Resistance, in All its Important Bearings, Illustrated and Defended* (Philadelphia: J. M. M'Kim, 1846).

96. See Gilje, *The Road to Mobocracy,* 205–32 (attributing the rejection of mob action to the increasing hegemony of a new middle-class value system).

97. Asa Earl Martin, *Pennsylvania History Told by Contemporaries* (New York: Macmillan, 1925), 195.

98. *Pennsylvanian,* July 10, 1834.

99. Grimsted, "Rioting in Its Jacksonian Setting," 380–81 (quoting a handbill circulated in Baltimore in 1836).

100. Charge of King, President, to the Grand Jury, 4 *Penn. L. J.* 29, 35 (1844).

101. Ibid., 29, 31.

102. Ibid., 40. See also *Niles' Register,* Apr. 5, 1834, p. 85 (every citizen should consider himself a "special constable to preserve the public peace"); *Commonwealth v. Daley,* 4 *Penn. L. J.* 150 (1844).

103. *Pennsylvanian,* July 15, 1835.

104. *Hazard's Register,* July 3, 1830, pp. 6–9, and Nov. 2, 1833, pp. 281–85; Werner, *Reaping the Bloody Harvest,* 210–12, 7–8.

105. Gilje, *The Road to Mobocracy*, 285–88; Grimsted, "Rioting in Its Jacksonian Setting," 396; Werner, *Reaping the Bloody Harvest*, 7–8; Lane, *Policing the City*, 29; James Richardson, *The New York Police* (New York: Oxford Univ. Press, 1970), 25. But see Michael Feldberg, "Urbanization as a Cause of Violence," in *The Peoples of Philadelphia*, ed. Allen Davis and Mark Haller, (Philadelphia: Temple Univ. Press, 1973), 53–69 (criticizing this hypothesis).

106. See note 103. These sources do not offer any substantial evidence that eighteenth-century riot control tactics actually controlled riots.

107. *Niles' Register*, July 19, 1834, p. 346; *Pennsylvanian*, July 14, 1834.

108. See Chapter 1.

109. Examples of police responses to riots can be found in Werner, *Reaping the Bloody Harvest*, 50–212. See also *Niles' Register*, July 13, 1844, 308–10 (riot of 1844); *Niles' Register*, Aug. 23, 1834, pp. 435–36 (riot of 1834); Lane, *Policing the City*, 30 (Boston's response to the burning of a convent); Richardson, *The New York Police*, 28–29 (New York's response to an 1834 race riot); *Pennsylvanian*, July 15, 1834.

110. Charge of King, President, to the Grand Jury, 4 *Penn. L. J.* 29, 31 (1844); *Pennsylvanian*, July 29, 1835 (quoting the *New York Evening Post*).

111. Quotations are from *Hazard's Register*, Nov. 2, 1833, pp. 281–85. See also *Hazard's Register*, July 3, 1830, pp. 6–9; Lane, *Policing the City*, 31.

112. *Hazard's Register*, Nov. 2, 1833, p. 282.

113. *Niles' Register*, Aug. 23, 1834, p. 426.

114. Ibid., July 13, 1844, p. 308; Oct. 18, 1834, p. 104; *Pennsylvania Freeman*, May 31, 1838.

115. *Diary of Sidney George Fisher*, 165.

116. Angelina Grimké, "Christian Heroism" [1835], in *The Public Years of Sarah and Angelina Grimké*, ed. Larry Ceplair (New York: Columbia Univ. Press, 1989), 26.

117. *Pennsylvania Freeman*, May 24, 1838.

118. *National Enquirer*, Aug. 17, 1836.

3. Neoclassical Rhetoric and Political Oratory

1. John Hancock Lee, *The Origin and Progress of the American Party* (Philadelphia: Elliott & Gihon, 1855), 34.

2. Charles Brockden Brown, *Wieland, or The Transformation* [1798] (Port Washington, N.Y.: Kennikat Press, 1963), 44.

3. This reading is based on Jane Tompkins, *Sensational Design* (New York: Oxford Univ. Press, 1985), 40–61.

4. Brown, *Wieland,* p. 63.

5. Ibid., 71–72.

6. Frances Trollope, *Domestic Manners of the Americans* [1832] (New York: Alfred A. Knopf, 1949), 262–63. Trollope did not estimate how large Wright's audience was, but she regularly drew crowds of 3,000 or more; in fact, she canceled a series of lectures in Philadelphia the previous summer because they were attended by only "about eleven or twelve hundred persons" (*Free Enquirer,* July 8, 1829, p. 292).

7. *Saturday Bulletin,* June 25, 1830, quoted in Trollope, *Domestic Manners,* 263, n. 5.

8. Kathleen Kendall and Jeanne Fisher, "Frances Wright on Women's Rights: Eloquence versus Ethos," *Quart. J. of Speech* 60 (1974): 62; Trollope, *Domestic Manners,* 73.

9. Trollope, *Domestic Manners,* 70.

10. Kendall and Fisher, "Frances Wright on Women's Rights," 62 (quoting Orestes Brownson and the *New York Commercial Advertiser*).

11. Lyman Beecher, "Lectures on Political Atheism and Kindred Subjects," in *Works,* 3 vols. (Boston: John P. Jewett, 1852), 1:94, 92.

12. Frances Wright D'Arusmont, "Course of Popular Lectures" [1834], in *Life, Letters and Lectures,* ed. Annette Baxter and Leon Stein (New York: Arno Press, 1972), 184–97.

13. *Saturday Bulletin,* June 25, 1830, quoted in Trollope, *Domestic Manners,* 263, n. 5.

14. Celia Eckhardt, *Fanny Wright: Rebel in America* (Cambridge: Harvard Univ. Press, 1984), 186–87.

15. D'Arusmont, "Course of Popular Lectures," 189–90.

16. Trollope, *Domestic Manners,* 263, n. 5.

17. D'Arusmont, "Course of Popular Lectures," 101–16.

18. *E.g., The Free Enquirer,* July 22, 1829, pp. 308, 311.

19. Eckhardt, *Fanny Wright,* 204.

20. Mary Cayton, "The Making of an American Prophet: Emerson, His Audience, and the Rise of the Culture Industry in Nineteenth-Century America," *Am. Hist. Rev.* 92 (1987): 601. Since newspapers did not begin covering lectures in detail until the late 1830s, the level of coverage given to Wright was unusual.

21. Eckhardt, *Fanny Wright,* 186–88.

22. Kendall and Fisher, "Frances Wright on Women's Rights," 65.

23. Eckhardt, *Fanny Wright,* 3; Sean Wilentz, *Chants Democratic* (Oxford: Oxford Univ. Press, 1984), 182; Eckhardt, *Fanny Wright,* 195.

24. *Free Enquirer,* June 19, 1830, p. 268.

25. Carl Bode, *The American Lyceum* (New York: Oxford Univ. Press, 1956), 6–12; Frederick Antczak, *Thought and Character* (Ames: Iowa State Univ. Press, 1985), 61–63.

26. Antczak, *Thought and Character,* 63–64; Donald Scott, "The Popular Lecture and the Creation of a Public in Mid-Nineteenth-Century America," *J. Am. Hist.* 66 (1980): 800. Scott found that more than 3,000 lectures were advertised in New York between 1840 and 1860 (ibid., 791).

27. Sidney George Fisher, *A Philadelphia Perspective: Diary of Sidney George Fisher Covering the Years 1834–1871,* ed. Nicholas Wainwright (Philadelphia: Historical Society of Pennsylvania, 1967), 35, 85, 117, 109 (hereafter *Diary of Sidney George Fisher*). See also *Public Ledger,* Sept. 11, 1840 (advertising a course of lectures offered by the William Wirt Literary Institute, which "engaged several of our most eminent orators").

28. Bruce Laurie, *Working People of Philadelphia, 1800–1850* (Philadelphia: Temple Univ. Press, 1980), 70–71, 95 (on working men's societies); Julie Winch, *Philadelphia's Black Elite* (Philadelphia: Temple Univ. Press, 1988), 84–87. *Philadelphia Evening Bulletin,* Oct. 25, 1848 (speech by Daniel Webster at Faneuil Hall). Apparently, the only Philadelphians who resisted the impulse to establish societies were the Irish Catholics, for whom the church already provided a comprehensive organizational framework for the community. Dennis Clark, *The Irish in Philadelphia* (Philadelphia: Temple Univ. Press, 1973), 91, 95–105.

29. *National Laborer,* Nov. 26, 1836, reprinted in John R. Commons, ed., *Documentary History of American Industrial Society,* 10 vols. (New York: Russell & Russell, 1958), 5:61.

30. On the increasing use of conventions and stump speaking in the 1830s, see Richard McCormick, *The Presidential Game* (Oxford: Oxford Univ. Press, 1982), 200–202.

31. Scott, "The Popular Lecture," 798 (Lincoln); Antczak, *Thought and Character,* 73–74 (Crockett).

32. *Diary of Sidney George Fisher,* 2–5.

33. *United States Gazette,* Jan. 12, 1830; *National Gazette and Literary Register,* Jan. 14, 1830. For other examples, see *National Gazette and Literary Register,* May 16, 1837 (meeting on the suspension of specie payments); *United States Gazette,* Jan. 6, 1830 (on a New York City Council meeting); *Pennsylvania Freeman,* May 17, 1838 (on speeches given at the opening of Pennsylvania Hall); *Pennsylvania Freeman,* Apr. 26, 1838 (a speech by Daniel O'Connell to the British Parliament).

34. *Public Ledger,* July 25, 1840. That politicians frequently spoke for the newspapers, rather than for their immediate audiences, was also a subject of

complaint. See "Glances at Congress," *U.S. Democratic Rev.* 1 (1837–1838): 71–72; "Congressional Eloquence," *North Am. Rev.* 52 (1841): 115.

35. *Public Ledger,* Sept. 11, 1840.

36. *National Gazette and Literary Register,* Jan. 23, 28, 25, Feb. 5, and Jan. 27, 1830. Similar language is used in the *United States Gazette,* Jan. 28, 29, 30, and Feb. 1, 1830. Such criticism was common in the periodical literature as well. Christine Oravec, "The Democratic Critics: An Alternative American Rhetorical Tradition of the Nineteenth Century," *Rhetorica* 4 (1986): 395–421.

37. Letter from Sarah and Angelina Grimké to Jane Smith, Jan. 20, 1837, in *The Public Years of Sarah and Angelina Grimké,* ed. Larry Ceplair (New York: Columbia Univ. Press, 1989), 115–16.

38. *Pennsylvanian,* July 14, 1834.

39. *Pennsylvania Freeman,* Sept. 17, 1840; Blanche Hersh, *The Slavery of Sex* (Urbana: Univ. of Illinois Press, 1978), 27–28. Hersh notes that the Philadelphia Female Anti-Slavery Society called on a black man to chair their first meeting (ibid., 14).

40. C. Peter Ripley, ed., *The Black Abolitionist Papers,* 5 vols. (Chapel Hill: Univ. of North Carolina Press, 1991), 3:252; *National Enquirer and Constitutional Advocate,* Jan. 25, 1838. See also *Pennsylvania Freeman,* Jan. 22, 1846, on the New Bedford Lyceum's exclusion of blacks.

41. *Pennsylvanian,* July 8, 1834.

42. Leonard Richards, *"Gentlemen of Property and Standing"* (New York: Oxford Univ. Press, 1970), 43. Richards connects the violence directed at promiscuous audiences to fears of amalgamation (ibid., pp. 31–43). See also Winch, *Philadelphia's Black Elite,* 87.

43. Ebenezer Porter, *Analysis of the Principles of Rhetoric and Delivery* (New York: Leavitt, 1827), 13. See later in this chapter for further discussion of this point.

44. I do not mean to contest the considerable scholarship demonstrating that early female activists developed a variety of political activities, from organizing fund-raising fairs to assuming quasi-governmental positions, that allowed them to participate in politics without taking the podium. Paula Baker, "The Domestication of Politics: Women and American Political Society, 1780–1920," *Am. Hist. Rev.* 89 (1984): 632–35; Keith Melder, *Beginnings of Sisterhood* (New York: Schocken Books, 1977), 70–71. But those concerned with enhancing the political status of women, such as the Grimké sisters, Maria West Chapman, and Abby Kelley, continued to emphasize public speaking, so that the propriety of women speaking in public became the first focal point for the American debate over women's rights. See Melder,

Beginnings of Sisterhood, 95–112; Blanche Hersh, "Am I Not a Woman and a Sister?" in *Anti-Slavery Reconsidered,* ed. Lewis Perry and Michael Fellman (Baton Rouge: Louisiana State Univ. Press, 1979).

45. Barbara Clark Smith, "Food Rioters and the American Revolution," *William & Mary Quart.,* 3d ser., 51 (1994): 16 (reports were vague about the social composition of mobs, referring to them simply as "the people"). Smith argues that by participating in mobs, women "cast themselves as competent actors in a political context" (ibid., 29). But she provides no evidence that participating in mobs improved the political status of women. On the contrary, she recognizes that rioting was not a form of "proto-citizenship"— women could participate in riots precisely because it was a crowd action in which individual traits were not important determinants of agency (ibid., 30–31). Of course, by the middle of the antebellum period, the racial and class dimensions of mob action had become pronounced. But by that point, mob action was no longer considered political action at all, but the very opposite of political action. See Chapter 1.

46. Laurie, *Working People of Philadelphia,* 95; *Pennsylvania Freeman,* Mar. 15, 1838. On reactions to Lucretia Mott, see *National Enquirer and Constitutional Advocate,* Aug. 31, 1836.

47. Mary Ryan in *Civic Wars* (Berkeley: Univ. of California Press, 1997) makes a similar point regarding the public pageantry of the antebellum era, particularly parades. She maintains that antebellum street culture accommodated differences with a festive sociability, thus allowing "the people" to come together without losing their ethnic and class identities. The point is well-taken, but I suspect that Ryan underestimates the amount of conflict these activities engendered.

48. William Heighton, "An Address to the Members of Trade Societies and the Working Classes Generally" [1827], in *William Heighton: Pioneer Labor Leader of Jacksonian Philadelphia,* ed. Philip Foner (New York: International Publishers, 1991), 63.

49. Ibid., 64.

50. Ibid.

51. Kenneth Cmiel, *Democratic Eloquence* (New York: William Morrow, 1990), 47; Gordon Wood, *Creation of the American Republic, 1776–1787* (New York: W. W. Norton, 1969), 486–87.

52. *Mechanics' Free Press,* June 28, 1828.

53. *Pennsylvanian,* Jan. 7, 1833.

54. See Cmiel, *Democratic Eloquence,* 41–46.

55. Foner, *William Heighton,* 20.

56. *Mechanics' Free Press,* Aug. 29, 1829, in Foner, *William Heighton,* 28.

57. Melder, *Beginnings of Sisterhood,* 83–84; Phyllis Japp, "Esther or

Isaiah? The Abolitionist-Feminist Rhetoric of Angelina Grimké," *Quart. J. of Speech* 71 (1985): 337–39 (summarizing negative reactions to Grimké's lectures).

58. Catharine Beecher, *An Essay on Slavery and Abolitionism, with Reference to the Duty of American Females* [1837] (Freeport, N.Y.: Books for Libraries Press, 1970), 103. See also Melder, *Beginnings of Sisterhood,* 77–94 (detailing reactions to Grimké's activities).

59. Beecher, *An Essay on Slavery and Abolitionism,* 94, 46.

60. Ibid., 48.

61. Ibid., 97–102.

62. Melder, *Beginnings of Sisterhood,* 79–93.

63. "Letters to Catherine [*sic*] E. Beecher" [1838], in Ceplair, *The Public Years,* 166.

64. Ibid., 161.

65. Ibid., 180.

66. Ibid., 195.

67. This phrase appears in Grimké's "Appeal to the Women of the Nominally Free States" [1837], in Ceplair, *The Public Years,* 132.

68. "Letters to Catherine [*sic*] E. Beecher" [1838], 193.

69. On Cornish, see Ripley, *Black Abolitionist Papers,* 3:95–96.

70. *Colored American,* Mar. 4, 1837, in Ripley, *Black Abolitionist Papers,* 3:217.

71. Ibid.

72. Ibid., 219.

73. See Chapter 1.

74. Cornish's argument is not the only or even the most interesting defense of an independent black press, but the belief that the oppressed must "vindicate their character" was a common theme. See, e.g., "Essay by 'Sydney,'" *Colored American,* Mar. 6, 1841, in Ripley, *Black Abolitionist Papers,* 3:356–59. See also the editorial by Frederick Douglass in *North Star,* Dec. 3, 1847, in *Frederick Douglass: The Narrative and Selected Writings,* ed. Michael Meyer (New York: Random House, 1984), 263.

75. In a similar vein, black activists also tried to discourage parades, a common political practice, on the grounds that they "increase the prejudice and contempt of whites." See "Minutes of the Fourth Annual Conventions for the Improvement of the Free People of Color" [1834], in *Minutes of the Proceedings of the National Negro Conventions,* ed. Howard Bell (New York: Arno Press and New York Times, 1969), 14–16.

76. Cmiel, *Democratic Eloquence.*

77. See Michael Kramer, *Imagining Language in America* (Princeton, N.J.: Princeton Univ. Press, 1992), 35–63.

78. Beecher, *Essay on Slavery and Abolitionism*, 102–3.

79. George Campbell, *The Philosophy of Rhetoric* [1776] (Carbondale and Edwardsville: Southern Illinois Univ. Press, 1963), 1; Richard Whately, *Elements of Rhetoric* [1828] (Carbondale and Edwardsville: Southern Illinois Univ. Press, 1963), 2, 175. See also Hugh Blair, *Lectures on Rhetoric and Belles Lettres* [1783] (London: Baynes & Sons, 1823), 252.

80. Sharon Crowley, *The Methodical Memory* (Carbondale and Edwardsville: Southern Illinois Univ. Press, 1990), 56–57; Gregory Clark and S. Michael Halloran, eds., *Oratorical Culture in Nineteenth-Century America* (Carbondale and Edwardsville: Southern Illinois Univ. Press, 1993), 6–8, 15–17; Nan Johnson, *Nineteenth-Century Rhetoric in North America* (Carbondale and Edwardsville: Southern Illinois Univ. Press, 1991), 19; Warren Guthrie, "The Development of Rhetorical Theory in America: 1635–1850," *Speech Monographs* 16 (1949): 98–113; Terence Martin, *The Instructed Vision* (Bloomington: Indiana Univ. Press, 1961), 24. See Daniel Howe, *Political Culture of the American Whigs* (Chicago: Univ. of Chicago Press, 1979), on the centrality of oratory to politics in the antebellum era.

81. Campbell, *Philosophy of Rhetoric*, 104; Blair, *Lectures*, 98.

82. John Quincy Adams, *Lectures on Rhetoric and Oratory* [1810] (New York: Russell & Russell, 1962), 46, 36; Blair, *Lectures*, 36; Adams, *Lectures*, 30, 62. See also Campbell, *Philosophy of Rhetoric*, 7.

83. Adams, *Lectures*, 30.

84. George Gregory, *Letters on Literature, Taste, and Composition, Addressed to His Son* (Philadelphia: Bradford & Inskeep, 1809), 149.

85. Whately, *Elements of Rhetoric*, 10.

86. Adams, *Lectures*, 30–31.

87. Ethos also included the delineation of the character of others and how the speaker should adapt his speech to the character of the audience. See William Sattler, "Conceptions of Ethos in Ancient Rhetoric," *Speech Monographs* 14 (1947): 55–65.

88. Blair, *Lectures*, 368; Whately, *Elements of Rhetoric*, 207.

89. Campbell, *Philosophy of Rhetoric*, 96. This understanding of the role of sympathy was based on the theories of Adam Smith and David Hume. See James Golden and Edward Corbett, *The Rhetoric of Blair, Campbell, and Whately* (New York: Holt, Rinehart & Winston, 1968), 15; Campbell, *Philosophy of Rhetoric*, xliii–xliv.

90. Campbell, *Philosophy of Rhetoric*, 98.

91. Blair, *Lectures*, 368; Campbell, *Philosophy of Rhetoric*, 97.

92. Whately, *Elements of Rhetoric*, 219.

93. Ibid., 220.

94. Campbell also considered this use of ethos but could not quite explain how it worked: "[T]he speaker's conviction of the truth of what he advanceth, adds to all his other arguments as evidence, *though not precisely the same,* yet near akin to that of his own testimony" (*Philosophy of Rhetoric,* 96 [emphasis added]). He also asserted that this type of evidence carries the most weight with "the vulgar," which implies that its influence is not entirely rational (ibid).

95. Whately, *Elements of Rhetoric,* 219–21.

96. See Chapter 1.

97. Samuel Whittelsey, *A Publick Spirit Recommended* (New London, Conn., 1731), 1.

98. Ibid., 34.

99. Jonathan Boucher, *A View of the Causes and Consequences of the American Revolution* (London: G. G. & J. Robinson, 1797) (the quotation appears in the dedication). See Golden and Corbett, *The Rhetoric of Blair, Campbell, and Whately,* 16, on the influence of Protestantism on neoclassical rhetoric.

100. Blair, *Lectures,* 130.

101. Campbell, *Philosophy of Rhetoric,* 225–26.

102. See Cmiel, *Democratic Eloquence,* 28; Howe, *Political Culture of the American Whigs,* 31; Clark and Halloran, *Oratorical Culture in Nineteenth-Century America,* 16.

103. Blair, *Lectures,* 254.

104. Daniel Howe, "The Political Psychology of The Federalist," *William & Mary Quart.,* 3d ser., 44 (1987): 485–509; Martin, *The Instructed Vision,* 27–53; Johnson, *Nineteenth-Century Rhetoric in North America,* 21–23.

105. Thomas Reid, "Essays on the Intellectual Powers of Man" [1785], in *The Works of Thomas Reid,* ed. Sir William Hamilton, 2 vols. (Bristol: Thoemmes Press, 1994), 1:242.

106. Adams, *Lectures,* 31.

107. Blair, *Lectures,* 348.

108. Campbell, *Philosophy of Rhetoric,* 77.

109. Ibid., 2, 72.

110. Ibid., 2.

111. Blair, *Lectures,* 348.

112. Campbell, *Philosophy of Rhetoric,* 148; Adams, *Lectures,* 41, 47.

113. Blair, *Lectures,* 4.

114. Ibid., 33.

115. Ibid., 37.

116. Campbell, *Philosophy of Rhetoric,* 103, 78.

117. Ibid., 78.

118. "Congressional Eloquence," *North Am. Rev.* 52 (1841): 109–48. See also "Orations and Speeches on Various Occasions, by Edward Everett," *North Am. Rev.* 44 (1837): 138–53 (review); *National Gazette and Literary Register,* Mar. 19, 1831 (reviewing Daniel Webster's *Speeches and Forensic Arguments*).

119. "Calhoun's Speech against the Conquest of Mexico," *Am. Rev.* 7 (1848): 225.

120. *Niles' Register,* May 24, 1834.

121. Oravec, "The Democratic Critics," 415–17.

122. "Congressional Eloquence," 144, 135.

123. "Mr. Forrest's Ovation," *Democratic Rev.* 3 (1838): 56.

124. *The Friend,* Oct. 18, 1828; *Pennsylvania Freeman,* Mar. 15, 1838.

125. *Public Ledger,* Sept. 30, 1840.

126. Beecher, *Essay on Slavery and Abolitionism,* 101–2; James Forten, "Speech Delivered before the Philadelphia Female Anti-Slavery Society" [1836], in Ripley, *Black Abolitionist Papers,* 3:154–55. A related aspect of this devaluation of politics was an anti-institutionalist argument that human government (because it is based on force) is inherently sinful. But even Frances Wright, who did not share this anti-institutionalism, devalued politics because (she said) it had become a field of display, power, and contention. D'Arusmont, "Course of Popular Lectures," 152.

127. *Pennsylvania Freeman,* Apr. 26, 1838.

128. Robert Fuller, *Mesmerism and the American Cure of Souls* (Philadelphia: Univ. of Pennsylvania Press, 1982), 1–47.

129. Charles Caldwell, *Facts in Mesmerism* (Louisville: Prentice & Weissinger, 1842), xxi, 60.

130. E.g., Fuller, *Mesmerism and the American Cure of Souls,* 39, 44 (mesmerists LaRoy Sunderland and Joseph Buchanan attributed its power to mental sympathy).

131. Caldwell, *Facts in Mesmerism,* 58. See also David Reese, *Humbugs of New-York* (New York: John S. Taylor, 1838), 34.

132. Nathaniel Hawthorne, *The Blithedale Romance* [1852] (Oxford: Oxford Univ. Press, 1991), 198; Ralph Waldo Emerson, *Journals and Miscellaneous Notebooks,* ed. William Gilman, 15 vols. (Cambridge, Mass.: Belknap Press, 1965), 5:147; A Gentleman of Philadelphia, *The Philosophy of Animal Magnetism* [1837] (Philadelphia: Patterson & White Co., 1928), 38.

133. Fuller, *Mesmerism and the American Cure of Souls,* 31–38; Reese, *Humbugs of New-York.*

134. E.g., Clark and Halloran, *Oratorical Culture in Nineteenth-Century America,* 15–17; Antczak, *Thought and Character,* Johnson, *Nineteenth-*

Century Rhetoric in North America, 161–68; Cmiel, *Democratic Eloquence.* For an attempt to reformulate rhetoric to make it more compatible with democracy, see Edward Channing, *Lectures Read to the Seniors in Harvard College* [1856] (Carbondale and Edwardsville: Southern Illinois Univ. Press, 1968).

135. "Address to the Journeymen Cordwainers of the City and County of Philadelphia" [1835], in Commons, *Documentary History of American Industrial Society,* 6:26.

136. Adam Smith, *The Theory of Moral Sentiments* [1759] (Indianapolis: Liberty Fund, 1984), 52–53. Smith was cagey about whether deference relations are desirable; he asserted that social order is best supported by deference, but the tone of his analysis is hostile to the pretensions of the great and the obsequiousness of the humble. The view that deference stems from sympathy was shared by Thomas Reid and David Hume. See Thomas Reid, "Essay on the Active Powers of Man" [1788], in Hamilton, *The Works of Thomas Reid,* 2:592–93; David Hume, *A Treatise of Human Nature* [1740] (Oxford: Clarendon Press, 1978), 357–58.

137. On sympathy, see Chapter 6.

138. Heighton, "An Address to the Members of Trade Societies," 65.

139. D'Arusmont, "Course of Popular Lectures," 117.

140. Heighton, "An Address to the Members of Trade Societies," 69–74. Enlightenment rhetoric was most prevalent in, but was not confined to, working class politics. For example, most people used Enlightenment rhetoric when talking about the press. See Chapter 4.

141. Of course, rational independence was also an important component of the republican tradition, but in that tradition it was conceived in more materialist terms as stemming from economic independence—hence the virtue of the yeoman farmer, whose economic independence was the foundation of his ability to act as a free, equal citizen in the political arena.

142. See, e.g., *Public Ledger,* Mar. 7, 1840 (criticizing the "crouching, shrinking, slavish submission" and the "surrender of dignity, decency, opinion, thought, and conduct" to party that marks a true politician). The Philadelphia trade unions were particularly defensive about the charge that they demanded conformity. See, e.g., *Pennsylvanian,* Feb. 9, 1836, in Commons, *Documentary History of American Industrial Society,* 5:392.

143. William E. Channing, "Remarks on Associations" [1829], in *Works,* 6 vols. (Boston: Crosby, Nichols & Co., 1853), 1:303–4.

144. *American Banner,* July 12, 1851 (emphasis added).

145. "How Stands the Case?" *Democratic Rev.* 1838 (Sept.): 13, quoted in Oravec, "The Democratic Critics," 410; Heighton, "Address to the Members of Trade Societies," 85.

146. *Diary of Sidney George Fisher,* 7.

147. Beecher, "Lectures on Political Atheism," 1:92, 94.

4. Enlightenment Rationalism and Political Debate

1. Richard John, *Spreading the News* (Cambridge: Harvard Univ. Press, 1995), 56–7.

2. Henry Tappan, *An Essay on the Expression of Passion in Oratory* (New York: C. W. Benedict, 1848), 7, 14–15.

3. Hinton Helper, *The Impending Crisis of the South* [1857] (New York: Collier Books, 1963), 237.

4. John, *Spreading the News,* 57.

5. Richard Whately, *Elements of Rhetoric* [1828] (Carbondale and Edwardsville: Southern Illinois Univ. Press, 1963), 3, 5–6.

6. *Pennsylvanian,* Jan. 7, 1833.

7. James Golden and Edward Corbett, *The Rhetoric of Blair, Campbell, and Whately* (New York: Holt, Rinehart & Winston, 1968), 9–11.

8. George Campbell, *The Philosophy of Rhetoric* [1776] (Carbondale and Edwardsville: Southern Illinois Univ. Press, 1963), 2, 72. See Chapter 3.

9. Charles G. Leland, *Memoirs* (London: William Heineman, 1894), 221.

10. Horace Greeley, introduction to *The Writings of Cassius Marcellus Clay* [1848] (New York: Arno Press, 1969), v.

11. Jürgen Habermas, *The Structural Transformation of the Public Sphere* (Cambridge: MIT Press, 1993), 31–43.

12. Charles Brockden Brown, *Alcuin: A Dialogue* [1798] (New York: Grossman Publishers, 1970), 8.

13. Ibid., 13.

14. Habermas, *Structural Transformation,* 54.

15. Habermas acknowledges that this ideal may not have been realized but insists that "as an idea it had become institutionalized and thereby stated as an objective claim. If not realized, it was at least consequential" (ibid., 36). See Geoff Eley, "Nations, Publics, and Political Cultures: Placing Habermas in the Nineteenth Century," in *Habermas and the Public Sphere,* ed. Craig Calhoun (Cambridge: MIT Press, 1992), on the extent to which the public sphere was realized in practice.

16. Brown, *Alcuin,* 14–28.

17. Habermas maintains that "intrinsic to the idea of a public opinion born of the power of the better argument was the claim to that morally pretentious rationality that strove to discover what was at once just and right"

(*Structural Transformation,* 54). Much of his later work is aimed at supporting this claim. For my purposes, it is enough to note that public opinion was conceptualized as the expression of the type of reason—universal, abstract, and permanent—that law was supposed to be based on (ibid., 53).

18. Ibid., 28, 53.

19. J. A. W. Gunn, *Beyond Liberty and Property* (Kingston, Canada: McGill-Queen's Univ. Press, 1983), 43–95, 260–315; Habermas, *Structural Transformation,* 59–67.

20. Habermas, *Structural Transformation,* 60–61, 63.

21. Ibid., 25.

22. *New York Gazette,* Oct. 28, 1734, quoted in Stephen Botein, " 'Meer Mechanics' and an Open Press," *Perspectives in American History* 9 (1975): 179; John Camm, *A Single and Distinct View of the Act . . .* (Annapolis, Md., 1763), appendix, quoted in ibid., 169. Botein points out that a free press could mean either a press that was open to all political positions or a press that was open only to those who opposed the government (ibid., 205).

23. *Boston Evening-Post,* Mar. 30, 1741, quoted in Botein, " 'Meer Mechanics' and an Open Press," 181.

24. Thomas Leonard, *The Power of the Press* (Oxford: Oxford Univ. Press 1986), 65; Michael Schudson, "Was There Ever a Public Sphere? If So, When? Reflections on the American Case," in Calhoun, *Habermas and the Public Sphere,* 154–55.

25. *Christian Chronicle,* Sept. 23, 1846.

26. Robert Collyer, *Lights and Shadows of American Life* (Boston: Brainard & Co., [1838?]), 9.

27. Alfred McClung Lee, *The Daily Newspaper in America* (New York: Macmillan, 1937), 718, 725, 728; John, *Spreading the News,* 38. Lee's study compiles data from a variety of sources, including the U.S. Census and C. S. Brigham's "Bibliography of American Newspapers, 1690–1820" in *Proceedings of the American Antiquarian Society* (1913–1927). The difficulties of gathering data on this subject are legion, so the figures quoted should be taken as approximations. On the one hand, the number of newspapers is probably too low; many newspapers had brief and unrecorded careers. The circulation figures, on the other hand, may be too high, since the primary sources for these figures are the publishers' own reports, which were probably inflated.

The population figure is taken directly from *Seventh Census of the United States—1850* (New York: Arno Press, 1976), ix. The comparable figure for 1820 is 8,095,461, which means that there was about one newspaper for every 15,800 free persons in 1820.

28. Lee, *The Daily Newspaper,* 258. For example, *The Friend,* the *Chris-*

tian Chronicle, the *National Enquirer and Constitutional Advocate of Universal Liberty,* and the *Pennsylvania Freeman* were $2 per year; the *American Advocate* was $4 per year; and the *National Gazette and Literary Register* and the *Philadelphia Evening Bulletin* were $5 per year.

29. Carl Wittke, *The German-Language Press in America* (Lexington: Univ. of Kentucky Press, 1957), 28 (describing the practice of pooling resources among Pennsylvania Germans). On taverns and reading rooms, see Lee, *The Daily Newspaper,* 265.

30. *National Gazette and Literary Register,* Mar. 24, 1831.

31. Robert Rutland, *The Newsmongers* (New York: Dial Press, 1973), 113.

32. Frank L. Mott, *American Journalism,* 3d ed. (New York: Macmillan, 1962), 216.

33. *Philadelphia Evening Bulletin,* Apr. 10, 1847. Its editor, Charles Leland, noted in his memoirs that the paper also supported Native Americanism and temperance (Leland, *Memoirs,* 216).

34. See *Christian Chronicle,* Aug. 5, Sept. 9, and Oct. 28, 1846, for discussions of political issues such as immigration and citizenship.

35. Schudson, "Was There Ever a Public Sphere?" 157. See also Richard Hofstadter, *The Idea of a Party System* (Berkeley: Univ. of California Press, 1969), 246–48; Richard McCormick, *The Presidential Game* (Oxford: Oxford Univ. Press, 1982), 197–99. But see Daniel Howe, *Political Culture of the American Whigs* (Chicago: Univ. of Chicago Press, 1979), 7–8 (arguing correctly that campaign hoopla did not preclude rational discourse).

36. *United States Gazette,* Jan. 1, 2, and 5, 1830.

37. Ibid., Jan. 1, 2, 5, and 27, 1830.

38. *American Banner,* Apr. 26, 1851. Reading competitors' newspapers was also necessary for the more mundane purpose of stealing news. See Leland, *Memoirs,* 221, on this practice.

39. Lewis Saum, *The Popular Mood of Pre–Civil War America* (Westport, Conn.: Greenwood Press, 1980), 143–74; William Gienap, " 'Politics Seem to Enter in to Everything,' " in *Essays on American Antebellum Politics, 1840–1860,* ed. Stephen Maizlish and John Kushman (College Station: Texas A&M Univ. Press, 1982), 32–35. (Saum's conclusion is based on the discovery that the diaries and letters he examined seldom referred to politics. But the fact that politics was not considered a suitable topic for intimate conversation does not mean that it did not attract much public interest.)

40. John Cannon, ed., *The Letters of Junius* (Oxford: Clarendon Press, 1978); see esp. xvii–xix, xxi–xxix. As Cannon points out, Junius was criticized for his lack of civility, provocative style, and failure to engage readers' critical faculties—precisely the charges typically leveled at antebellum political journalism.

41. *Pennsylvania Freeman,* Mar. 12, 1846.

42. Although I refer throughout this chapter to "the Enlightenment model" and more generally to "Enlightenment rationalism," I am not suggesting that the model I describe is the only understanding of political debate that is compatible with Enlightenment thought. The Enlightenment did not speak with a single voice or produce a single, coherent philosophy; many of the criticisms that could be leveled at this model—for example, its rejection of interest as a positive force in politics—derive from the Enlightenment tradition as well. Here I am simply exploring one strain of Enlightenment thought that had a significant influence on American discourse about political action.

43. Steven Shapin, *A Social History of Truth* (Chicago: Univ. of Chicago Press, 1994), 124.

44. Obadiah Walker, *Of Education, Especially of Young Gentlemen* (Oxford, 1673), 226, quoted in Shapin, *Social History of Truth,* 117.

45. *The Friend,* Oct. 25, 1828; *Pennsylvania Freeman,* Feb. 5, 1846; *American Banner,* Apr. 26, 1851.

46. *Public Ledger,* Sept. 2, 1840.

47. *Mechanics' Free Press,* Apr. 16, 1831.

48. *Public Ledger,* Sept. 2, 1840. In emphasizing the importance of scientific debate as a model for political argument, I do not mean to deny that the norms of civil conversation may have had an independent influence of the norms of political debate. For example, Catharine Beecher emphasized the importance of civility in her attack on Angelina Grimké, without referring in any way to the Enlightenment understanding of scientific inquiry (Catharine Beecher, *Essay on Slavery and Abolitionism with Reference to the Duty of American Females* [1837] [Freeport, N.Y.: Books for Libraries Press, 1970]). But the emphasis on civility was more commonly associated with an emphasis on an Enlightenment conception of debate as truth seeking.

49. *Mechanics' Free Press,* Apr. 26, 1828.

50. Frances Wright D'Arusmont, "Course of Popular Lectures," [1834], in *Life, Letters and Lectures,* ed. Annette Baxter and Leon Stein (New York: Arno Press, 1972), vii, ix.

51. Ibid., 8.

52. Ibid., 50.

53. *National Gazette and Literary Register,* Jan. 4, 1830.

54. Ibid. See also Edward Channing, *Lectures Read to Seniors in Harvard College* [1856] (Carbondale and Edwardsville: Southern Illinois Univ. Press, 1968), 81 (political truth consists in "connections in events, perpetuity in the action of political causes, identity in the nature of man, under all governments and in all climates"). Other examples of such rhetoric is collected in

L. L. Bernard and Jessie Bernard, *Origins of American Sociology* (New York: Thomas Y. Crowell, 1943), 50–51.

55. Matthew Carey, *Essays on Political Economy* [1822] (New York: Augustus M. Kelley, 1968).

56. Ibid., 17–18.

57. Ibid.

58. Louis Gerteis, *Morality and Utility in American Antislavery Reform* (Chapel Hill: Univ. of North Carolina Press, 1987), 64–83; Eric Foner, *Free Soil, Free Labor, Free Men* (New York: Oxford Univ. Press, 1970), 41–44.

59. Quoted in Bernard and Bernard, *Origins of American Sociology*, 788. See ibid., 33–55 on the growing hegemony of scientific accounts of social phenomena during the antebellum era.

60. L. A. Hine, "A General Statistical Society for the United States," *Merchants' Magazine* 18 (1848): 398. Tucker's proposal appears under the same title in *Merchants' Magazine* 17 (1847): 571–77.

61. Hine, "A General Statistical Society for the United States," 398.

62. Ibid., 399.

63. D'Arusmont, "Course of Popular Lectures," 10, 8. Shapin's *A Social History of Truth* highlights this theme of distrust of testimony, arguing that it was aimed at persuading people to stop relying on ancient authority. But another element of the denigration of testimony is this distrust of language as a reliable vehicle for conveying information.

64. Ibid., 144 (emphasis added).

65. John Locke, *An Essay Concerning Human Understanding* [1690] (London: J. M. Dent & Sons, 1961), xxxix.

66. Ibid., 24. See ibid., 6, for similar language. Descartes had little use for the arts of rhetoric either. René Descartes, *Discourse on Method* [1637] (Indianapolis: Bobbs-Merrill Educational Publishing, 1960), 7.

67. *American Advocate*, July 30, 1844.

68. *The Friend*, Oct. 18, 1828; Apr. 18, 1829.

69. Cornish to Garrison, Dec. 31, 1830, in *The Black Abolitionist Papers*, ed. C. Peter Ripley, 5 vols. (Chapel Hill: Univ. of North Carolina Press, 1991), 3:85; *Colored American*, Mar. 4, 1837, in ibid., 217. Abolitionists typically mixed the language of Enlightenment rationalism with Christian rhetoric, so that the language of revelation had religious as well as rationalist overtones.

70. Biddle to Joseph Gales, Mar. 2, 1831, *Correspondence of Nicholas Biddle Dealing with National Affairs*, ed. Reginald McGrane (Boston and New York: Houghton Mifflin, 1919), 126; Biddle to William Bucknor, July 13, 1832, in ibid., 195.

71. *American Banner,* July 19, 1851; "The Supreme Court of the United States," *U.S. Democratic Rev.* 1 (1838): 143–44.

72. *Philadelphia Evening Bulletin,* Apr. 10, 1847; William Heighton, "An Address to the Members of Trade Societies and to the Working Classes Generally" [1827], in *William Heighton: Pioneer Labor Leader of Jacksonian Philadelphia,* ed. Philip Foner (New York: International Publishers, 1991), 91–92.

73. *Christian Chronicle,* Sept. 2, 1846.

74. *Public Ledger,* Sept. 28, 1840.

75. *Mechanics' Free Press,* Apr. 16, 1831.

76. Carey, *Essays on Political Economy,* 19; "The Supreme Court of the United States," 143–44.

77. Carey, *Essays on Political Economy,* 19.

78. *American Banner,* June 28, 1851.

79. *Public Ledger,* Sept. 28, 1840.

80. *Philadelphia Evening Bulletin,* Apr. 10, 1847. See also *American Banner,* July 26, 1851 (quoting Winfield Scott: "Democratic Americans would include all good native citizens devoted to our country and its institutions").

81. Heighton, "An Address to the Members of Trade Societies," 79.

82. *Mechanics' Free Press,* July 19, 1828; *United States Gazette,* Jan. 1, 1830; *Philadelphia Evening Bulletin,* Apr. 10, 1847. See also Hofstadter, *The Idea of a Party System,* 196–98, on the pervasive belief that American republicanism is, "at least in principle, perfect."

83. *Pennsylvanian,* July 4, 1835.

84. *Niles' Register,* Apr. 26, 1834, p. 131.

85. *New York Evening Post,* Jan. 12, 1829, quoted in Celia Eckhardt, *Fanny Wright: Rebel in America* (Cambridge: Harvard Univ. Press, 1984), 188.

86. D'Arusmont, "Course of Popular Lectures," 192.

87. Ibid., v.

88. Ibid., v–vi.

89. *Pennsylvania Freeman,* Apr. 5, 1838.

90. *National Gazette and Literary Register,* Mar. 12, 1831. See also *New York Statesman,* Nov. 18, 1823, quoted in Michael Wallace, "Changing Concepts of Party in the United States: New York, 1815–1828," *Am. Hist. Rev.* 74 (1968): 469 ("any system which tends to . . . effect reconciliation and a submission to the will of the majority, and a relinquishment of private attachments, such a system we call a cardinal principle in the administration of a representative government").

91. *National Gazette and Literary Register,* May 16, 1837.

92. *United States Gazette,* Jan 1, 1830.

93. Beecher, *Essay on Slavery and Abolitionism,* 97–102; Angelina Grimké, "Letters to Catherine [*sic*] Beecher" [1838], in *The Public Years of Sarah and Angelina Grimké,* ed. Larry Ceplair (New York: Columbia Univ. Press, 1989), 180; see Chapter 3. It's beyond the scope of this book to examine in detail the arguments used to support race, gender, and class exclusions. My impression is that the exclusion of women and blacks was typically supported by the claim that allowing them to participate would disrupt the private sphere; Beecher's argument about the effect of Grimké's lectures on the abolition debate was somewhat idiosyncratic in this respect. Exclusion of immigrants, however, was generally justified by fears that they would degrade public rationality. See Chapter 2.

94. Habermas, *Structural Transformation,* 58–59.

95. Botein, " 'Meer Mechanics' and an Open Press," 182.

96. Biddle to Joseph Gales, Mar. 2, 1831, in McGrane, *Correspondence,* 125; D'Arusmont, "Course of Popular Lectures," 20, viii.

97. "To the Journeymen Cordwainers of the City and County of Philadelphia" [1835], in *A Documentary History of American Industrial Society,* ed. John R. Commons, 10 vols. (New York: Russell & Russell, 1958), 6:42. See John R. Commons et al., *History of Labor in the United States,* 4 vols. (New York: Macmillan, 1918), 1:387–93, for details of the strike.

98. "To the Journeymen Cordwainers of the City and County of Philadelphia," 6:70.

99. Ibid., 75.

100. See, e.g., *American Banner,* July 12, 1851.

101. *Mechanics' Free Press,* July 19 1828.

102. D'Arusmont, "Course of Popular Lectures," vii.

103. Ibid., 146.

104. Ibid., 36, 43, 16.

105. Shapin, *Social History of Truth,* 224.

106. D'Arusmont, "Course of Popular Lectures," 143.

107. William Whipper, "Speech Delivered before the Colored Temperance Society of Philadelphia" [1834], in Ripley, *Black Abolitionist Papers,* 3:126.

108. *Mechanics' Free Press,* June 21, 1828.

109. Ibid., June 21, 1828.

110. Ibid., May 3, 1828.

111. Albert O. Hirschman, *The Passions and the Interests* (Princeton, N.J.: Princeton Univ. Press, 1977), 32–48.

112. William Elder, *Third Parties* (Philadelphia: Merrihew & Thompson, 1851), 12.

113. Ibid., 13, 5.

114. Ibid., 22, 1–2.

115. Lucretia Mott, "The Truth of God . . . The Righteousness of God" [1841], in *Lucretia Mott: Her Complete Speeches and Sermons,* ed. Dana Green (New York: Edwin Mellen Press, 1980), 30–31.

116. Angelina Grimké, "An Appeal to the Women of the Nominally Free States" [1837], in Ceplair, *The Public Years,* 131; Angelina Grimké, "Appeal to the Christian Women of the South" [1836], in ibid., 67.

117. *Pennsylvanian,* July 8, 1835; July 19, 1834; July 2, 1835.

118. *The Man,* June 29, 1835, in Commons, *A Documentary History,* 6:41–42.

119. Quoted in Lance Banning, "Some Second Thoughts on Virtue and the Course of Revolutionary Thinking," in *Conceptual Change and the Constitution,* ed. Terence Ball and J. G. A. Pocock (Lawrence: Univ. of Kansas, 1988), 195, n. 4.

120. *Pennsylvanian,* Aug. 3, 1835; *Philadelphia Evening Bulletin,* May 4, 1847; *Public Ledger,* Oct. 10, 1840. Niles made the same complaint about the abolitionists; See *Niles' Register,* July 19, 1834, p. 346. But see Wallace, "Changing Concepts of Party," 489 (quoting Martin Van Buren's speech to the U.S. Senate, in which he defended party spirit as preventing "that apathy which has proved the ruin of Republics"; this was, however, an idiosyncratic interpretation of ancient history).

121. John Hancock Lee, *The Origin and Progress of the American Party in Politics* (Philadelphia: Elliott & Gihon, 1855), 20.

122. Assuming, of course, that political truth is objective and easily accessible to everyone.

123. Biddle to James Hunter, May 4, 1831, in McGrane, *Correspondence,* 127.

124. Thomas Govan, *Nicholas Biddle: Nationalist and Public Banker* (Chicago: Univ. of Chicago Press, 1959), 153–55.

125. Ibid., 189–96.

126. Biddle to Joseph Hemphill, Feb. 10, 1831, in McGrane, *Correspondence,* 124.

127. Michael Schudson, *Discovering the News* (New York: Basic Books, 1978), 15–18; Mott, *American Journalism,* 215; *United States Gazette,* Feb. 1, 1830; *National Gazette and Literary Register,* Mar. 24, 1831.

128. *United States Gazette,* Jan. 29, 1830.

129. *National Gazette and Literary Register,* Jan. 8, 1830.

130. Ibid., Jan. 11, 1830.

131. Habermas, *Structural Transformation,* 58–59.

132. *National Gazette and Literary Register,* Jan. 8, 1830.

133. Ibid., Jan. 22, 1830.

134. *Niles' Register,* Sept. 15, 1832, p. 39.

135. Biddle to Monroe, July 6, 1807, in McGrane, *Correspondence,* 3; *Philadelphia Evening Bulletin,* Sept. 13, 1848.

136. *Mechanics' Free Press,* Apr. 16, 1831; *National Gazette and Literary Register,* Mar. 24, 1831.

137. *Philadelphia Evening Bulletin,* Oct. 24, 1848; *American Banner,* Aug. 9, 1851. See also *National Gazette and Literary Register,* Feb. 19, 1831 ("It is well, when we are about to enter into battle, to calculate the probable issue"); Wallace, "Changing Concepts of Party," 470.

138. See Chapter 1.

139. *Pennsylvanian,* July 30, 1835.

140. Gerald Leonard, "Partisan Political Theory and the Unwritten Constitution," Ph.D. diss., Univ. of Michigan, 1992, pp. 15–29. See also Wallace, "Changing Concepts of Party"; Hofstadter, *The Idea of a Party System.* Wallace and Hofstadter make the point that this eighteenth-century conception of party was gradually being undermined by Martin Van Buren and the Albany Regency.

141. *American Banner,* July 26, 1851.

142. *Niles' Register,* Sept. 26, 1829.

143. Throughout the antebellum era, policy issues were typically framed as having deep constitutional significance. See Leonard, "Partisan Political Theory," 2–3.

144. *Albany Argus,* Feb. 17, 1827, quoted in Wallace, "Changing Concepts of Party," 461.

145. *American Banner,* June 7, 1851.

146. *National Gazette and Literary Register,* Feb. 17, 1831.

147. *Philadelphia Evening Bulletin,* June 1, 1847.

148. Ibid., Sept. 16, 1848.

149. Ibid., June 1, 1847.

150. "Charles Jared Ingersoll," *U.S. Democratic Rev.* 6 (1839): 349.

151. *Public Ledger,* Sept. 8, 1840. For similar language, see *National Advocate,* Sept. 6, 1824, quoted in Wallace, "Changing Concepts of Party," 464 ("[The proprietor of a party journal] should never possess . . . the right of governing. . . . To the political opinions and views of his party, he should ever be subservient.").

152. *National Gazette and Literary Register,* Jan. 21, 1830.

153. Schudson, *Discovering the News,* 22. See ibid., 18–23, for details of the development of the penny press.

154. Habermas, *Structural Transformation,* 185.

155. Quoted in Schudson, *Discovering the News,* 22.

156. Ibid., 22–30, 50–57. See the earlier discussion of colonial printers' avoidance of politics.

157. Habermas, *Structural Transformation,* 184–85.

5. Storytelling

1. *Pennsylvania Freeman,* Oct. 8, 1840.

2. Ibid.

3. Ibid.

4. Frederick Douglass, *Narrative of the Life of Frederick Douglass, an American Slave* [1845], in *Frederick Douglass: Autobiographies* (New York: Library of America, 1994), xviii (hereafter *Narrative of Frederick Douglass*).

5. Frances Smith Foster, *Witnessing Slavery,* 2d ed. (Madison: Univ. of Wisconsin Press, 1994), 64, xxx.

6. Ibid., 22–23.

7. Mary Wilson Starling, *The Slave Narrative: Its Place in American History* (Boston: G. K. Hill, 1981), 84–97.

8. Ibid., 106–30.

9. William Andrews, *To Tell a Free Story* (Urbana: Univ. of Illinois Press, 1986), xi; Foster, *Witnessing Slavery,* 4; Charles T. Davis and Henry Louis Gates, *The Slave's Narrative* (Oxford: Oxford Univ. Press, 1985), xxiii.

10. See, e.g., Jean Yellin's introduction to the recently authenticated narrative of Harriet Jacobs, *Incidents in the Life of a Slave Girl* [1861] (Cambridge: Harvard Univ. Press, 1987). Most studies of slave narratives either exclude fictional narratives altogether or treat them separately (see, e.g., Davis and Gates, *The Slave's Narrative;* Starling, *The Slave Narrative*).

11. James M'Cune Smith, introduction to *My Bondage and My Freedom* [1855], in *Frederick Douglass: Autobiographies,* 126 (hereafter *My Bondage and My Freedom*).

12. Ibid., 143.

13. *Narrative of Frederick Douglass,* 15–24.

14. Ibid., 37–38; *My Bondage and My Freedom,* 218.

15. *My Bondage and My Freedom,* 209.

16. Ibid., 224.

17. Ibid., p. 226. The 1797 edition of the *Columbian Orator* contained a speech by Sheridan, but it did not concern Catholic emancipation. Douglass may have been thinking of a speech by O'Connor on the topic, which immediately followed the dialogue between master and slave. Caleb Bingham, ed., *Columbian Orator* (Boston: Manning & Loring, 1797), 240, 243.

18. *Narrative of Frederick Douglass,* 42.

19. Geoffrey Clive, *The Romantic Enlightenment* (New York: Meridian Books, 1960), 20.

20. Herbert Hovenkamp, *Science and Religion in America 1800–1860* (Philadelphia: Univ. of Pennsylvania Press, 1978), 20.

21. Earl of Shaftesbury, "Inquiry Concerning Virtue or Merit" [1699], in *British Moralists*, ed. L. A. Selby-Bigge, 2 vols. (Oxford: Clarendon Press, 1897), 1:12–13, 20–21; Frances Hutcheson, "Inquiry Concerning the Original of Our Ideas of Virtue or Moral Good" [1725], in ibid., 1:77–78; Shaftesbury, ibid., 1:20–21.

22. Thomas Reid, "Essays on the Active Powers of Man" [1788], in *Works*, ed. Sir William Hamilton, 2 vols. (Bristol: Thoemmes Press, 1994), 2:637–43.

23. This language of interiority harmonizes with a similar theme in Protestant theology: the belief that the indwelling Holy Spirit provides the believer with an internal touchstone of truth, so that moral truth could be discovered through a process of introspection. See Geoffrey Nuttall, *The Holy Spirit in Puritan Faith and Experience* (Oxford: Basil Blackwell, 1946), for an extensive analysis of this concept. But Douglass does not put his enlightenment in a religious context at all; on the contrary, he makes only the briefest references to his own religious convictions in both his *Narrative* and *My Bondage and My Freedom.* This is not to suggest that Protestant theology had no influence on his story, however; I consider the relationship between the theology and moral philosophy of the slave narratives in Chapter 6.

24. *My Bondage and My Freedom*, 230–31.

25. See Chapter 4.

26. Reid, "Essays on the Active Powers," 2:637–38, 641, 1:438.

27. *Narrative of Frederick Douglass*, 66.

28. Ibid., 241–42; Reid, *Works*, 1:439.

29. Bingham, *Columbian Orator*, 240–42.

30. Genesis 9:25; A Southern Clergyman, "A Defense of Southern Slavery" [1851], in *A Defense of Southern Slavery and Other Pamphlets* (New York: Negro Universities Press, 1969), ii.

31. *Narrative of Frederick Douglass*, 83–84.

32. Ibid., 46.

33. Ibid., 47. For similar discussions of auctions, see Olive Gilbert, *Narrative of Sojourner Truth* [1850], ed. William Katz (New York: Arno Press and New York Times, 1968) 26; Jacobs, *Incidents in the Life of a Slave Girl*, 11.

34. *Narrative of Frederick Douglass*, 86.

35. Ibid., 44.

36. Ibid., 60.

37. Ibid., 65. See also James Pennington, "The Fugitive Blacksmith"

[1849], in *Great Slave Narratives,* ed. Arna Bontemps (Boston: Beacon Press, 1969), 216.

38. The phrase was coined by Richard Slotkin in *Regeneration through Violence* (Middleton, Conn.: Wesleyan Univ. Press, 1973).

39. *My Bondage and My Freedom,* 286. See also Pennington, "The Fugitive Blacksmith," 60.

40. Jacobs, *Incidents in the Life of a Slave Girl,* 17; William Craft, "Running a Thousand Miles for Freedom" [1860], in Bontemps, *Great Slave Narratives,* 293.

41. Gilbert, *Narrative of Sojourner Truth,* 30, 33, 41.

42. *Narrative of Frederick Douglass,* 73–74.

43. Mattie Griffiths, *Autobiography of a Female Slave* (New York: Redfield, 1857), 21; Pennington, "The Fugitive Blacksmith," 245; Josiah Henson, *Father Henson's Story* [1858] (Boston: Gregg Press, 1970), 22–23.

44. *My Bondage and My Freedom,* 288. See also Jacobs, *Incidents in the Life of a Slave Girl,* 43–44; Henry Brown, *Narrative* [1849] (Philadelphia: Rhistoric Publications, 1969), 16; Gilbert, *Narrative of Sojourner Truth,* 16.

45. *Narrative of Frederick Douglass,* 36.

46. Ibid., 7.

47. Ibid., 96, 4.

48. See Terence Martin, *The Instructed Vision* (Bloomington: Indiana Univ. Press, 1961), on the relationship between Enlightenment thought and the case against fiction.

49. *Pennsylvania Freeman,* Oct. 8, 1840.

50. *Philadelphia Evening Bulletin,* Apr. 20, 1847. See also *Pennsylvanian,* July 2, 1834. Martin points out that most novelists shared these attitudes; in fact, he argues that antebellum novelists seemed to have "no viable concept of fiction" (*The Instructed Vision,* 129–30, 135).

51. *Pennsylvanian,* July 2, 1834; Martin, *The Instructed Vision,* 135.

52. Martin, *The Instructed Vision,* 82–83.

53. Charles Ball, *Slavery in the United States* (New York: John S. Taylor, 1837), xi.

54. Ibid., 284.

55. Harriet Beecher Stowe, *Uncle Tom's Cabin* [1852], 2 vols. (New York: AMS Press, 1967), 2:253–54.

56. Martin, *The Instructed Vision,* 79–81.

57. William G. Hawkins, *Lunsford Lane* (Boston: Crosby & Nichols, 1863), viii, vii.

58. Ibid., 13.

59. Ibid., 15.

60. Ball, *Slavery in the United States,* 390–91.

61. "Narratives of Fugitive Slaves," *Christian Examiner* 48 (July 1849): 62; *Pennsylvanian,* July 31, 1834; Angelina Grimké to Theodore Weld, Jan. 21, 1838, *Letters of Theodore Dwight Weld, Angelina Grimké and Sarah Grimké 1822–1844,* ed. Gilbert Barnes and Dwight Dumond, 2 vols. (New York: D. Appleton-Century, 1934), 2:523.

62. W. L. G. Smith, *Life at the South* (Buffalo: Geo. H. Derby, 1852), 17.

63. Mary Eastman, *Aunt Phillis's Cabin* (Philadelphia: Lippincott, Grambo, 1852), 266–78, 271. See also "Black Letters; or Uncle Tom-Foolery in Literature," *Graham's Magazine* 42 (1853): 209–15.

64. Eastman, *Aunt Phillis's Cabin,* 271.

65. Ibid., 278.

66. *My Bondage and My Freedom,* 367.

67. Quoted in *The Frederick Douglass Papers,* ed. John W. Blassingame, vol. 1 (New Haven, Conn.: Yale Univ. Press, 1979), l–li.

68. *North Am. Rev.* 77 (1853): 487.

69. William Wells Brown, *The Narrative* [1848] (Reading, Mass.: Addison-Wesley, 1969), 82.

70. Ibid.

71. Theodore Weld, *American Slavery as It Is* (New York: American Anti-Slavery Society, 1839), 7–9.

72. Moses Roper, *A Narrative of the Adventures and Escape of Moses Roper* [1838] (New York: Negro Universities Press, 1970), xii; Hawkins, *Lunsford Lane,* vii; Jacobs, *Incidents in the Life of a Slave Girl,* 2.

73. Ball, *Slavery in the United States,* 2, 15. See also Jacobs, *Incidents in the Life of a Slave Girl,* xxiv–v.

74. See Chapter 4.

75. Ball, *Slavery in the United States,* 288–89.

76. Jacobs, *Incidents in the Life of a Slave Girl,* 74.

77. Weld, *American Slavery as It Is,* 129.

78. "Narratives of Fugitive Slaves," 471 (emphasis added). See also Weld, *American Slavery as It Is,* 53, 11.

79. Weld, *American Slavery as It Is,* 48–49.

80. Eastman, *Aunt Phillis's Cabin,* 277.

81. A Citizen of Georgia, "Remarks upon Slavery" [1835], in *A Defense of Southern Slavery and Other Pamphlets,* 19.

82. Henson, *Father Henson's Story,* 15.

83. Ibid.

84. Weld, *American Slavery as It Is,* 9–10.

85. Jacobs, *Incidents in the Life of a Slave Girl,* 28.

86. Weld, *American Slavery as It Is,* 52.

87. Hawkins, *Lunsford Lane,* v–vi.

88. Henry Box Brown, *Narrative,* 11.

89. Ibid., 13.

90. *Narrative of Frederick Douglass,* 12.

91. Henry Brown, *Narrative,* 31; William Wells Brown, *The Narrative,* 45.

92. See Foster, *Witnessing Slavery,* 5, 65, on the fugitive's dual status as exemplary and representative.

93. Jacobs, *Incidents in the Life of a Slave Girl,* 43–44.

94. Weld, *American Slavery as It Is,* 110.

95. Starling, *The Slave Narrative,* 226–27; Jacobs, *Incidents in the Life of a Slave Girl,* xv–xxv.

96. Griffiths, *Autobiography of a Female Slave,* 249, 86.

97. Hawkins, *Lunsford Lane,* 137.

98. Sarah Joseph Hale, *Northwood; or, Life North and South,* 2d ed. (New York: H. Long & Brother, 1852), 22.

99. "Review," *North Am. Rev.* 77 (1853): 467.

100. Emily Pearson, *Cousin Franck's Household, or, Scenes in the Old Dominion,* 3d ed. (Boston: Upham, Ford & Olmstead, 1853), vii.

101. See Martin, *The Instructed Vision,* 126–27, on novelists' claim to moral truth.

102. Southern Clergyman, "A Defense of Southern Slavery," 9.

103. Citizen of Georgia, "Remarks upon Slavery," 23–24 (emphasis added).

104. Eastman, *Aunt Phillis's Cabin,* 118, 271.

105. "Black Letters; or Uncle Tom-Foolery in Literature," 211.

106. Southern Clergyman, "A Defense of Southern Slavery," 30. See also Smith, *Life at the South,* 22.

107. "Narratives of Fugitive Slaves," 69–70.

108. George M. Frederickson, *The Black Image in the White Mind* (New York: Harper & Row, 1971), 4.

109. Andrews, *To Tell a Free Story,* 3 (quoting *The Emancipator,* Jan. 3, 1839, p. 146).

110. Griffiths, *Autobiography of a Female Slave,* 249.

111. "Review," 473 (emphasis added).

112. Weld, *American Slavery as It Is,* 9.

113. Ibid., 156.

114. Ibid., 77.

115. Ibid., 64.

116. This practice was not unique to slave narratives; for example, the

1807 romance novel *Lucinda; or, the Mountain Mourner* began with a letter
signed by a number of respectable persons testifying to the authenticity of
the story. Martin, *The Instructed Vision*, 80–81.

117. Starling, *The Slave Narrative*, 253 (quoting the *Liberator* 16:35).

118. Pennington, "The Fugitive Blacksmith," 222.

119. Ibid.

120. Ibid., 224–25; 227–28. For similar language, see Gilbert, *Narrative
of Sojourner Truth*, 33.

121. William Wells Brown, *The Narrative*, 22–23.

122. See Lawrence W. Levine, " 'Some Go Up and Some Go Down': The
Meaning of the Slave Trickster," in *The Hofstadter Aegis: A Memorial*, ed.
Stanley Elkins and Eric McKitrick (New York: Alfred A. Knopf, 1974), 94–
124.

123. Andrews, *To Tell a Free Story*, 3 (quoting Samuel Howe, *The Refugees
from Slavery in Canada West* [Boston: Wright and Potter, 1864], 3).

124. *Narrative of Frederick Douglass*, 27. See also Ball, *Slavery in the
United States*, 102.

125. Weld, *American Slavery as It Is*, 122.

126. Eastman, *Aunt Phillis's Cabin*, 93–94 (referring to the money they
made on their books and speeches).

127. See Chapter 4.

128. Hinton Helper, *The Impending Crisis of the South* [1857] (New York:
Collier Books, 1963), 19; Louis Gerteis, *Morality and Utility in American Anti-
slavery Reform* (Chapel Hill: Univ. of North Carolina Press, 1987), 64–85.

129. Helper, *The Impending Crisis*, 81–82.

130. Ibid., 37, 40, 39, 38 (quoting Wm. C. Taylor).

131. Samuel Wolfe, *Helper's Impending Crisis Dissected* [1860] (New York:
Negro Universities Press, 1969), 41.

132. Ibid., 49.

133. Stowe, *Uncle Tom's Cabin*, 1:xxxix.

134. See Starling, *The Slave Narrative*, 307.

135. Ibid., 308.

6. Sympathy

1. *Five Hundred Thousand Strokes for Freedom* (London: W&F Cash,
1853), preface, 3; Harriet Jacobs, *Incidents in the Life of a Slave Girl* [1861],
ed. Jean Yellin (Cambridge: Harvard Univ. Press, 1987), 1; James Pennington, "The Fugitive Blacksmith" [1849], in *Great Slave Narratives*, ed. Arna

Bontemps (Boston: Beacon Press, 1969), 246; Theodore Weld, *American Slavery as It Is* (New York: American Anti-Slavery Society, 1839), 11.

2. Jacobs, *Incidents in the Life of a Slave Girl,* title page; Henry Brown, *Narrative* [1849] (Philadelphia: Rhistoric Publications, 1969), 16.

3. William Elder, *Third Parties* (Philadelphia: Merrihew & Thompson, 1851), 12.

4. Louis Gerteis, *Morality and Utility in American Antislavery Reform* (Chapel Hill: Univ. of North Carolina Press, 1987), 64–75.

5. *Five Hundred Thousand Strokes for Freedom,* preface, 3; Josiah Henson, *Father Henson's Story* [1858] (Boston: Gregg Press, 1970), 212.

6. William Hill Brown, *The Power of Sympathy* [1789] (Columbus: Ohio State University Press, 1969), 153.

7. Robert Fuller, *Mesmerism and the American Cure of Souls* (Philadelphia: Univ. of Pennsylvania Press, 1982), 39 (on "mental sympathy"); Edgar Allen Poe "A Tale of the Ragged Mountains" [1844], in *The Complete Works of Edgar Allen Poe,* ed. James A. Harrison, 2d ed., 17 vols. (New York: AMS Press, 1979), 4:163–76.

8. Adam Smith, *The Theory of Moral Sentiments* [1759] (Indianapolis: Liberty Fund, 1984), 9–10.

9. Susanna Rowson, *Charlotte Temple* [1794] (New York: Funk & Wagnalls, 1905), 82; Hannah W. Foster, *The Coquette* [1797] (Oxford: Oxford Univ. Press, 1986), 11, 141; Fanny Fern, *Ruth Hall* [1855] (New York: Penguin Books, 1997), 112.

10. Nathaniel Hawthorne, *The Blithedale Romance* [1852] (Oxford: Oxford Univ. Press, 1991), 222. This is only one of the many varieties of sympathy Hawthorne explores in the novel. Contrast, for example, the less emotional and less praiseworthy sympathy that the middle-class narrator shares with the laborers he condescends to eat lunch with: "[I]f ever I did deserve to be soundly cuffed by a fellow-mortal, for secretly putting weight upon some imaginary social advantage, it must have been while I was striving to prove myself ostentatiously his equal, and no more. . . . The poor, proud man should look at both sides of sympathy like this" (ibid., 25).

11. Sarah Grimké to William Lloyd Garrison, Aug. 30, 1835, in *The Public Years of Sarah and Angelina Grimké,* ed. Larry Ceplair (New York: Columbia Univ. Press, 1989), 25; Sarah Grimké, "Epistle to the Clergy of the Southern States" [1836], in ibid., 104.

12. See Chapter 5.

13. Hawthorne, *The Blithedale Romance;* Poe, "A Tale of the Ragged Mountains."

14. See Chapter 1.

15. Hinton Helper, *The Impending Crisis of the South* [1857] (New York: Collier Books, 1963), 36; A Southern Clergyman, "A Defence of Southern Slavery" [1851], in *A Defense of Southern Slavery and Other Pamphlets* (New York: Negro Universities Press, 1969), i.

16. "Black Letters; or Uncle Tom-Foolery in Literature," *Graham's Magazine* 42 (1853): 212.

17. *Pennsylvania Freeman*, Mar. 5, 1846.

18. Frederick Douglass, *The Narrative of the Life of Frederick Douglass, an American Slave* [1845], in *Frederick Douglass: Autobiographies* (New York: Library of America, 1994), 8 (hereafter *Narrative of Frederick Douglass*).

19. Quoted in Helper, *The Impending Crisis,* 308.

20. Mattie Griffiths, *Autobiography of a Female Slave* (New York: Redfield, 1857), 193, 260–77; Frederick Douglass, "What to the Slave Is the Fourth of July?" [1852], in *The Frederick Douglass Papers,* ed. John W. Blassingame, 2 vols. (New Haven, Conn.: Yale Univ. Press, 1979), 2:370.

21. *Narrative of Frederick Douglass,* 9.

22. Charles Ball, *Slavery in the United States* (New York: John S. Taylor, 1837), v; Jacobs, *Incidents in the Life of a Slave Girl,* 36; Weld, *American Slavery as It Is,* 52.

23. Weld, *American Slavery as It Is,* 51–52.

24. William G. Hawkins, *Lunsford Lane* (Boston: Crosby & Nichols, 1863), 28–29.

25. Griffiths, *Autobiography of a Female Slave,* 75; Harriet Beecher Stowe, *Uncle Tom's Cabin* [1852], 2 vols. (New York: AMS Press, 1967), 1:160–63.

26. Weld, *American Slavery as It Is,* 110; Hawkins, *Lunsford Lane,* 189–90; Weld, ibid., 57.

27. Stowe, *Uncle Tom's Cabin,* 1:113.

28. See Martha Nussbaum, *Love's Knowledge* (New York: Oxford Univ. Press, 1990), 79, for a lucid discussion of this question.

29. Smith, *The Theory of Moral Sentiments,* 161–62.

30. This idea is captured by the concept of the "judgment of charity." See Baird Tipson, "Invisible Saints: The 'Judgment of Charity' in the Early New England Churches," *Church History* 44 (Mar. 1975): 460–71.

31. Frances Hutcheson, "Inquiry Concerning the Original of Our Ideas of Virtue or Moral Good" [1725], in *British Moralists,* ed. L. A. Selby-Biggs, 2 vols. (Oxford: Clarendon Press, 1897), 1:156; Jeremy Bentham, "Introduction to the Principles of Morals and Legislation" [1780], in ibid., 1:410.

32. Hutcheson, "Inquiry Concerning the Original of Our Ideas of Virtue or Moral Good," 1:116.

33. Stowe, *Uncle Tom's Cabin,* 1:46.

34. Matthew 20:1–16 is the basis for this reasoning.

35. Stowe, *Uncle Tom's Cabin*, 1:11.

36. Ibid., 1:104, 113.

37. Ibid., 1:105.

38. Ibid., 1:304, 289.

39. Ibid., 1:304.

40. Stowe herself suggests this interpretation of Ophelia's fault and reformation in her "Key to Uncle Tom's Cabin" (ibid., 2:278).

41. Ibid., 1:296, 302.

42. Ibid., 1:86–87.

43. Ibid., 1:299.

44. Ibid., 1:300.

45. Ibid., 2:12–13, 20.

46. Angelina Grimké, "Appeal to the Christian Women of the South" [1836], in Ceplair, *The Public Years*, 64.

47. "Review," *North Am. Rev.* 77 (1853): 472.

48. *Five Hundred Thousand Strokes for Freedom*, 12 (emphasis added).

49. Perry Miller, *The Life of the Mind in America* (New York: Harcourt, Brace & World, 1965), 26–27.

50. William Craft, "Running a Thousand Miles for Freedom" [1860], in Bontemps, *Great Slave Narratives*, 270; William Wells Brown, *The Narrative* [1848] (Reading, Mass.: Addison-Wesley, 1969), xxvii–xxviii; Frederick Douglass, *My Bondage and My Freedom* [1855], in *Frederick Douglass: Autobiographies*, 125; Stowe, *Uncle Tom's Cabin*, 2:245.

51. Henry Brown, *Narrative*, v.

52. Ibid., vi.

53. *Five Hundred Thousand Strokes for Freedom*, preface, 9; Henson, *Father Henson's Story*, 22.

54. *Pennsylvania Freeman*, Oct. 8, 1840; Brown, *The Power of Sympathy*, 31–33. See Terence Martin, *The Instructed Vision* (Bloomington: Indiana Univ. Press, 1961), 61–76, on the case against novels.

55. William Lloyd Garrison, introduction to *Narrative of Frederick Douglass*, 3; Stowe, *Uncle Tom's Cabin*, 245.

56. See, e.g., Hawkins, *Lunsford Lane*, vii. ("It is hoped . . . that the example and industry and of patient endurance of trials, and the integrity of character unfolded in the life of Lunsford Lane, may inspire [our colored fellow citizens] to the imitation of virtues, without which they can never secure the respect and sympathy of the good.")

57. See Herbert Ross Brown, *The Sentimental Novel in America 1789–1860* (New York: Pageant Books, 1959), 74–99.

58. Jean Baker, *Affairs of Party* (Ithaca, N.Y.: Cornell Univ. Press, 1983), 270; Ronald Formisano, *The Birth of Mass Political Parties:* Michigan, 1827–1861 (Princeton, N.J.: Princeton Univ. Press, 1971), 133.

59. Formisano, *The Birth of Mass Political Parties,* 133–34; Baker, *Affairs of Party,* 270. See Perry Miller, *The Life of the Mind in America,* 12–13, and Sacvan Bercovitch, *American Jeremiad* (Madison: Univ. of Wisconsin Press, 1978), on the view that Christianity is the foundation of American political institutions.

60. James Forten, "Speech Delivered before the Philadelphia Female Anti-Slavery Society" [1836], in *Black Abolitionist Papers,* ed. C. Peter Ripley, 5 vols. (Chapel Hill: Univ. of North Carolina Press, 1991), 3:163; Angelina Grimké to Sarah Grimké, Sept. 27, 1835, in Ceplair, *The Public Years,* 28–29; Grimké, "Appeal to the Christian Women of the South," 67.

61. Grimké, "Appeal to the Christian Women of the South," 66.

62. William Andrews, *To Tell a Free Story* (Urbana: Univ. of Illinois Press, 1986), 62; Pennington, "The Fugitive Blacksmith," 243; Craft, "Running a Thousand Miles," 313; Hawkins, *Lunsford Lane,* 15.

63. Frances Smith Foster, *Witnessing Slavery,* 2d ed. (Madison: Univ. of Wisconsin Press, 1994), 77; Pennington, "The Fugitive Blacksmith," 242–45; Henson, *Father Henson's Story,* 27–29. Douglass does give his conversion a couple of paragraphs in his 1893 autobiography. See Frederick Douglass, *Life and Times of Frederick Douglass* [1881], in *Frederick Douglass: Autobiographies,* 538–39.

64. Pennington, "The Fugitive Blacksmith," 242; Ball, *Slavery in the United States,* 164; Henson, *Father Henson's Story,* 27–28.

65. Owen Watkins, *The Puritan Experience* (London: Routledge & Kegan Paul, 1972), 6; Perry Miller, *The New England Mind: The Seventeenth Century* (Cambridge: Harvard Univ. Press, 1967), 284; Wilson Carey McWilliams, *The Idea of Fraternity in America* (Berkeley: Univ. of California Press, 1973), 114–22; Sheldon Wolin, *Politics and Vision* (Boston: Little, Brown, 1960), 183–85.

66. See John G. West, *The Politics of Revelation and Reason* (Lawrence: Univ. Press of Kansas, 1996).

67. Miller, *The New England Mind,* 251–52, 258–59.

68. Ann Douglas, *The Feminization of American Culture* (New York: Alfred A. Knopf, 1977), 121–64.

69. Charles Finney, *Lectures on Revivals of Religion* [1835], ed. William McLoughlin (Cambridge, Mass.: Belknap Press, 1960), 17, 50; Miller, *The New England Mind,* 280.

70. Miller, *The New England Mind,* 300–301; Watkins, *The Puritan Experience,* 6.

71. Edward Park, *The Theology of the Intellect and of the Feelings* (Andover, Mass.: Warren F. Draper, 1850), 9–10, 15.

72. *Narrative of Frederick Douglass,* 3–4; Geoffrey Nuttall, *The Holy Spirit in Puritan Faith and Experience* (Oxford: Basil Blackwell, 1946), 40 (quoting W. Cradock, "Gospel-Holinesse," 'To the Reader' and p. 32 [1651]).

73. Finney, *Lectures on Revivals,* 18.

74. Miller, *The New England Mind,* 287–88; Watkins, *The Puritan Experience,* 39–40.

75. Watkins, *The Puritan Experience,* 31; Patricia Caldwell, *The Puritan Conversion Narrative* (Cambridge: Harvard Univ. Press, 1983), 107. Perry Miller makes the point that God might use any experience as a means of conversion (*The New England Mind,* 289).

76. Caldwell, *The Puritan Conversion Narrative,* 91–96; Daniel Shea, *Spiritual Autobiography in Early America,* 2d ed. (Madison: Univ. of Wisconsin Press, 1988), xiv–xv.

77. Jarena Lee, "Religious Experience and Journal of Mrs. Jarena Lee, Giving an Account of Her Call to Preach the Gospel" [1849], in *Spiritual Narratives,* ed. Sue E. Houchins (Oxford: Oxford Univ. Press, 1988), 97. This understanding of the role of conversion narratives was more common in England, but Americans also recognized their didactic potential. As one defender of the practice insisted, the narrative could be "desired of the people of God, for the increase of their owne joy to see God glorified, and Christs name professed, and his vertues held forth, and for the increase of their love to those that joyne with them" (Caldwell, *The Puritan Conversion Narrative,* 76, (quoting John Allin and Thomas Shepard, *A Defence of the Answer . . .* [London, 1648], 194)).

78. Another way to evaluate the authenticity of personal testimony is to test it against scripture; the written word of God is supposed to be an infallible guide to His will. But the truth contained in the scriptures could be apprehended only through the agency of the Holy Spirit; thus the Word must be tested by the Spirit even while the Spirit leads one's interpretation of the Word. See Nuttall, *The Holy Spirit,* 22–23. There was an ongoing debate about whether the Word or the Spirit should have priority; thus it seems that scripture reading is governed by the same hermeneutic process as listening to conversion narratives.

79. Lee, "Religious Experience," 3, 17.

80. Calvin Pease, *Import and Value of the Popular Lecturing of the Day* (Burlington, Vt.: Chauncey Goodrich, 1842), 22, 34–35.

81. *Narrative of Frederick Douglass,* 7.

82. Olive Gilbert, *Narrative of Sojourner Truth* [1850], ed. William Katz (New York: Arno Press and *New York Times,* 1968), 16.

83. Andrews, *To Tell a Free Story*, 99–100.

84. *Narrative of Frederick Douglass*, 74, 12; Henry Brown, *Narrative*, 69, 63; "Narratives of Fugitive Slaves," *Christian Examiner* 48 (July 1849): 68; William Wells Brown, *The Narrative*, 45. See also Hawkins, *Lunsford Lane*, 51.

85. See West, *The Politics of Revelation and Reason*.

86. *The Liberator*, Oct. 21, 1859.

Conclusion

1. Frederick Douglass, "What to the Slave Is the Fourth of July?" [1852], in *The Frederick Douglass Papers*, ed. John W. Blassingame, 2 vols. (New Haven, Conn.: Yale Univ. Press, 1982), 2:358–59.

2. Ibid., 2:362–65.

3. Ibid., 2:368–69.

4. Ibid., 2:374. 376, 378, 371.

5. Ibid., 2:387.

6. This was the defendant's (unsuccessful) argument in *United States v. O'Brien*, 391 US 367 (1968). The strategy was more successful in other First Amendment cases. See *Stromberg v. California*, 283 US 359 (1931) (displaying a Communist flag was protected as "political discussion"); *Brown v. Louisiana*, 383 US 131 (1966) (First Amendment rights include the right to protest "by silent and reproachful presence" in a restricted area).

7. See Amy Guttmann and Dennis Thompson, *Democracy and Disagreement* (Cambridge, Mass.: Belknap Press, 1996), 135–37, on the deliberative ends served by "impassioned and immoderate speech" and storytelling. But see Benjamin Barber, *Strong Democracy* (Berkeley: Univ. of California Press, 1984), 178–98, on the nondeliberative ends served by deliberation.

8. Jane Mansbridge, *Beyond Adversary Democracy* (New York: Basic Books, 1980).

9. E.g., Guttman and Thompson, *Democracy and Disagreement*, 135–37.

10. Richard Rorty, "Feminism and Pragmatism," *Mich. Quart. Rev.* 30 (spring 1991): 232.

BIBLIOGRAPHY

Newspapers and Periodicals

American Advocate (Philadelphia)
American Banner (Philadelphia)
American Review (Philadelphia)
Christian Chronicle (Philadelphia)
Christian Examiner
Federal Gazette
The Free Enquirer
The Friend (Philadelphia)
Graham's Magazine
Hazard's Register
The Liberator
Mechanics' Free Press (Philadelphia)
The Merchants' Magazine
National Enquirer and Constitutional Advocate of Universal Liberty (Philadelphia)
National Gazette and Literary Register (Philadelphia)
Niles' Weekly Register
North American Review
Pennsylvania Freeman (Philadelphia)
Pennsylvania Gazette (Philadelphia)
Pennsylvania (Philadelphia)
Pennsylvania Packet (Philadelphia)
Philadelphia Evening Bulletin
Philadelphia Gazette
Public Ledger (Philadelphia)
United States Democratic Review
United States Gazette (Philadelphia)

Government Documents

An Act for Preventing Tumults and Riotous Assemblies, and for the More Speedy and Effectual Punishing the Rioters. Philadelphia, 1764.

An Act for Preventing Tumults and Riotous Assemblies, and for the More Speedy and Effectual Punishing the Rioters. Philadelphia, 1771.

Brown v. Louisiana, 383 US 131 (1966).

By the Honourable James Delancey, Esq., A Proclamation. April 2, 1755.

By the Honourable Patrick Gordon, Esq.; A Proclamation. Philadelphia: Printed by Andrew Bradford, 1726.

By the Honourable Patrick Gordon, Esq.; A Proclamation. Philadelphia: Printed by Andrew Bradford, 1729.

By the President and the Supreme Executive Council of the Commonwealth of Pennsylvania, A Proclamation. November 12, 1787.

Charge of King, President, to the Grand Jury, 4 *Pennsylvania Law Journal* 29 (1844).

Commonwealth v. Daley, 4 *Pennsylvania Law Journal* 150 (1844).

Minutes of the Provincial Council of Pennsylvania. N.p., 1852.

Pennsylvania Archives. 8th series. N.p., 1931.

Proceedings and Debates of the Pennsylvania Convention. Harrisburg: Packer, Barrett, & Parke, 1838.

Proceedings of the General Town-Meeting. Philadelphia: F. Bailey, 1779.

The Proceedings of the Governor, Council and House of Representatives of the Province of Massachusetts-Bay, Concerning an Indemnification for the Sufferers by the Rioters in Boston, from August 27, 1765, to June 28, 1766.

Seventh Census of the United States—1850. New York: Arno Press, 1976.

Stromberg v. California, 283 US 359 (1931).

To the Honourable Patrick Gordon, Esq.; Governour of the Province of Pennsylvania, etc. The Humble Address of the Representatives. . . . Philadelphia, March 29, 1729.

United States v. O'Brien, 391 US 367 (1968).

Books, Pamphlets, and Collected Works

Abbot, Edith. *Historical Aspects of the Immigration Problem.* Chicago: University of Chicago Press, 1926.

Abdy, Edward. *Journal of a Residence and Tour in the United States.* London: J. Murray, 1835.

Adams, John. *The Works of John Adams.* Edited by Charles F. Adams. 10 vols. Boston: Charles C. Little & James Brown, 1851.

Adams, John Quincy. *Lectures on Rhetoric and Oratory* [1810]. New York: Russell & Russell, 1962.

Adams, Samuel. *The Writings of Samuel Adams.* Edited by Harry Cushing. 4 vols. New York: Octagon Books, 1968.

Adams Family Correspondence. Edited by L. H. Butterfield. 6 vols. Cambridge, Mass.: Belknap Press, 1963.

Ames, Fisher. *The Works of Fisher Ames*. Edited by W. B. Allen. 2 vols. Indianapolis: Liberty Classics, 1983.

Anon. *An Address to the Inhabitants of the Province of the Massachusetts-Bay, by a Lover of His Country.* Boston: Rogers & Fowles, 1747.

Anon. *The Life and Adventures of Charles Anderson Chester, Notorious Leader of the Philadelphia "Killers."* Philadelphia: Published for the Printers, 1850.

Anon. *The Truth Unveiled, A Calm and Impartial Exposition of the Origin and Immediate Cause of the Terrible Riots and Rebellion in Philadelphia in May and July, AD 1844.* Baltimore: Metropolitan Tract Society, 1844.

Anon. *To the Delaware Pilots.* Philadelphia, 1773.

Ball, Charles. *Slavery in the United States.* New York: John S. Taylor, 1837.

Ballou, Adin. *Christian Non-Resistance, in All Its Important Bearings, Illustrated and Defended.* Philadelphia: J. M. M'Kim, 1846.

Barnes, Gilbert, and Dwight Dumond, eds. *Letters of Theodore Dwight Weld, Angelina Grimké and Sarah Grimké 1822–1844.* 2 vols. New York: D. Appleton-Century, 1934.

Beecher, Catharine. *An Essay on Slavery and Abolitionism, with Reference to the Duty of American Females* [1837]. Freeport, N.Y.: Books for Libraries Press, 1970.

Beecher, Lyman. *Works.* 3 vols. Boston: John P. Jewett, 1852.

Bell, Howard, ed. *Minutes of the Proceedings of the National Negro Conventions.* New York: Arno Press and *New York Times,* 1969.

Bercovitch, Sacvan. *Election Day Sermons: Plymouth and Connecticut.* New York: AMS Press, 1983.

Biddle, Nicholas. *Correspondence of Nicholas Biddle Dealing with National Affairs.* Edited by Reginald McGrane. Boston and New York: Houghton Mifflin, 1919.

Bingham, Caleb, ed. *Columbian Orator.* Boston: Manning & Loring, 1797.

Blair, Hugh. *Lectures on Rhetoric and Belles Lettres* [1783]. London: Baynes & Sons, 1823.

Bontemps, Arna, ed. *Great Slave Narratives.* Boston: Beacon Press, 1969.

Bosco, Ronald, ed. *Connecticut and Massachusetts Election Sermons.* Delmar, N.Y.: Scholars' Facsimiles and Reprints, 1978.

Boucher, Jonathan. *A View of the Causes and Consequences of the American Revolution.* London: G. G. & J. Robinson, 1797.

Brothers, Thomas. *The United States As They Are.* London: Longman, Orme, Brown, Green & Longmans, 1840.

Brown, Charles Brockden. *Alcuin: A Dialogue* [1798]. New York: Grossman Publishers, 1970.

———. *Wieland, or The Transformation* [1789]. Port Washington, N.Y.: Kennikat Press, 1963.

Brown, Henry. *Narrative* [1849]. Philadelphia: Rhistoric Publications, 1969.

Brown, William Hill. *The Power of Sympathy* [1789]. Columbus: Ohio State University Press, 1969.

Brown, William Wells. *The Narrative* [1848]. Reading, Mass.: Addison-Wesley, 1969.

Caldwell, Charles. *Facts in Mesmerism.* Louisville: Prentice & Weissinger, 1842.

Campbell, George. *The Philosophy of Rhetoric* [1776]. Carbondale and Edwardsville: Southern Illinois University Press, 1963.

Carey, Matthew. *Essays on Political Economy* [1822]. New York: Augustus M. Kelley, 1968.

Chambers, Robert. *A Course of Lectures on the English Law, 1767–1773.* 2 vols. Madison: University of Wisconsin Press, 1986.

Channing, Edward. *Lectures Read to the Seniors in Harvard College* [1856]. Carbondale and Edwardsville: Southern Illinois University Press, 1968.

Channing, William E. *Works.* 6 vols. Boston: Crosby, Nichols, 1853.

Cobbett, William. *A History of the American Jacobins, Commonly Denominated Democrats.* Philadelphia: William Cobbett, 1796.

Collyer, Robert. *Lights and Shadows of American Life.* Boston: Brainard & Co. [1838?].

Commons, John R., ed. *Documentary History of American Industrial Society.* 10 vols. New York: Russell & Russell, 1958.

Cope, Thomas. *Philadelphia Merchant: The Diary of Thomas Cope, 1800–1851.* Edited by Eliza Harrison. South Bend, Ind.: Gateway Editions, 1978.

Cutler, Timothy. *The Firm Union of a People Represented.* New London, Conn., 1717.

D'Arusmont, Frances Wright. *Life, Letters and Lectures.* Edited by Annette Baxter and Leon Stein. New York: Arno Press, 1972.

A Defense of Southern Slavery and Other Pamphlets. New York: Negro Universities Press, 1969.

Descartes, René. *Discourse on Method* [1637]. Indianapolis: Bobbs-Merrill Educational Publishing, 1960.

Dickens, Charles. *American Notes* [1857]. Gloucester: Peter Smith, 1968.

Dickinson, John. *The Political Writings of John Dickinson.* 2 vols. Wilmington, Del.: Bonsal & Niles, 1801.

Douglass, Frederick. *Frederick Douglass: Autobiographies.* New York: Library of America, 1994.

——. *Frederick Douglass: The Narrative and Selected Writings.* Edited by Michael Meyer. New York: Random House, 1984.

——. *The Frederick Douglass Papers.* Edited by John W. Blassingame. 5 vols. New Haven, Conn.: Yale University Press, 1979–92.

Dunbar, John, ed. *The Paxton Papers.* The Hague: Martinus Nijhoff, 1957.

Eastman, Mary. *Aunt Phillis's Cabin.* Philadelphia: Lippincott, Grambo, 1852.

Elder, William. *Third Parties.* Philadelphia: Merrihew & Thompson, 1851.

Eliot, Andrew. *A Sermon Preached before His Excellency Francis Bernard, Esq.* Boston, 1765.

Ellwood, Thomas. *A Discourse Concerning Riots.* London: Thomas Hawkins, 1683.

Emerson, Ralph Waldo. *Journals and Miscellaneous Notebooks.* Edited by William Gilman. 15 vols. Cambridge, Mass.: Belknap Press, 1965.

Fern, Fanny. *Ruth Hall* [1855]. New York: Penguin Books, 1997.

Finney, Charles. *Lectures on Revivals of Religion* [1835]. Edited by William McLoughlin. Cambridge, Mass.: Belknap Press, 1960.

Fisher, Sidney George. *A Philadelphia Perspective: The Diary of Sidney George Fisher Covering the Years 1834–1871.* Edited by Nicholas Wainwright. Philadelphia: Historical Society of Pennsylvania, 1967.

Five Hundred Thousand Strokes for Freedom. London: W&F Cash, 1853.

Force, Peter. *American Archives.* 4th series. 6 vols. Washington, D.C.: M. St. Clair Clarke & Peter Force, 1839.

Foster, Hannah W. *The Coquette* [1797]. Oxford: Oxford University Press, 1986.

Franklin, Benjamin. *The Papers of Benjamin Franklin.* Edited by Leonard Labarree. 31 vols. New Haven, Conn.: Yale University Press, 1961.

A Gentleman of Philadelphia. *The Philosophy of Animal Magnetism* [1837]. Philadelphia: Patterson & White Co., 1928.

Gilbert, Olive. *Narrative of Sojourner Truth* [1850]. Edited by William Katz. New York: Arno Press and *New York Times,* 1968.

Greeley, Horace, ed. *The Writings of Cassius Marcellus Clay* [1848]. New York: Arno Press, 1969.

Gregory, George. *Letters on Literature, Taste, and Composition, Addressed to His Son.* Philadelphia: Bradford & Inskeep, 1809.

Griffiths, Mattie. *Autobiography of a Female Slave.* New York: Redfield, 1857.

Grimké, Sarah, and Angelina Grimké. *The Public Years of Sarah and Angelina Grimké.* Edited by Larry Ceplair. New York: Columbia University Press, 1989.

Hale, Sarah Joseph. *Northwood; or, Life North and South.* 2d ed. New York: H. Long & Brother, 1852.

Hawkins, William G. *Lunsford Lane*. Boston: Crosby & Nichols, 1863.

Hawthorne, Nathaniel. *The Blithedale Romance* [1852]. Oxford: Oxford University Press, 1991.

Helper, Hinton. *The Impending Crisis of the South* [1857]. New York: Collier Books, 1963.

Henson, Josiah. *Father Henson's Story* [1858]. Boston: Gregg Press, 1970.

Hollinger, David, and Charles Capper, eds. *The American Intellectual Tradition*. 2 vols. Oxford: Oxford University Press, 1989.

Hone, Philip. *The Diary of Philip Hone*. Edited by Allan Nevins. 2 vols. New York: Dodd, Mead, 1927.

Houchins, Sue E., ed. *Spiritual Narratives*. Oxford: Oxford University Press, 1988.

Hume, David. *A Treatise of Human Nature* [1740]. Oxford: Clarendon Press, 1978.

Jacobs, Harriet. *Incidents in the Life of a Slave Girl* [1861]. Edited by Jean Yellin. Cambridge: Harvard University Press, 1987.

Jefferson, Thomas. *The Works of Thomas Jefferson*. Edited by Paul Ford. 12 vols. New York and London: G. P. Putnam's Sons, 1904.

———. *The Writings of Thomas Jefferson*. Edited by H. A. Washington. 9 vols. Washington, D.C.: Taylor & Maury, 1853.

Junius. *The Letters of Junius*. Edited by John Cannon. Oxford: Clarendon Press, 1978.

Kramnick, Isaac, ed. *The Federalist Papers* [1787]. London: Penguin Books, 1987.

Lee, John Hancock. *The Origin and Progress of the American Party in Politics*. Philadelphia: Elliott & Gihon, 1855.

Leland, Charles Godfrey. *Memoirs*. London: William Heineman, 1894.

Lincoln, Abraham. *The Collected Works of Abraham Lincoln*. Edited by Roy Basler. New Brunswick, N.J.: Rutgers University Press, 1953.

Locke, John. *An Essay Concerning Human Understanding* [1690]. London: J. M. Dent & Sons, 1961.

———. *Two Treatises of Government* [1690]. New York: Hafner Press, 1947.

Martin, Asa Earl. *Pennsylvania History Told by Contemporaries*. New York: Macmillan, 1925.

Moore, Frank, ed. *The Patriot Preachers of the American Revolution*. New York: Charles T. Evans, 1862.

Morris, Gouverneur. *The Diary and Letters of Gouverneur Morris*. Edited by Anne Morris. 2 vols. New York: Da Capo Press, 1970.

Mott, Lucretia. *Lucretia Mott: Her Complete Speeches and Sermons*. Edited by Dana Green. New York: Edwin Mellen Press, 1980.

Paine, Thomas. *The Complete Writings of Thomas Paine.* Edited by Philip Foner. 2 vols. New York: Citadel Press, 1945.

Park, Edward. *The Theology of the Intellect and of the Feelings.* Andover, Mass.: Warren F. Draper, 1850.

Pearson, Emily. *Cousin Franck's Household, or, Scenes in the Old Dominion.* 3d ed. Boston: Upham, Ford & Olmstead, 1853.

Pease, Calvin. *Import and Value of the Popular Lecturing of the Day.* Burlington, Vt.: Chauncey Goodrich, 1842.

Poe, Edgar Allen. *The Complete Works of Edgar Allen Poe.* Edited by James A. Harrison. 2d ed. 17 vols. New York: AMS Press, 1979.

Pollock, Sir Frederick, and Frederic Maitland. *The History of English Law before the Time of Edward I.* 2d ed. 2 vols. Cambridge: Cambridge University Press, 1968.

Porter, Ebenezer. *Analysis of the Principles of Rhetoric and Delivery.* New York: Leavitt, 1827.

Reese, David. *Humbugs of New-York.* New York: John S. Taylor, 1838.

Reid, Thomas. *The Works of Thomas Reid.* Edited by Sir William Hamilton. 2 vols. Bristol: Thoemmes Press, 1994.

Ripley, C. Peter, ed. *The Black Abolitionist Papers.* 5 vols. Chapel Hill: University of North Carolina Press, 1991.

Robison, John. *Proofs of a Conspiracy against All Religions and Governments of Europe Carried on in the Secret Meetings of the Free Masons, Illuminati, and Reading Societies.* Philadelphia: Dobson & Cobbett, 1798.

Roper, Moses. *A Narrative of the Adventures and Escape of Moses Roper* [1838]. New York: Negro Universities Press, 1970.

Rowson, Susanna. *Charlotte Temple* [1794]. New York: Funk and Wagnalls, 1905.

Rush, Benjamin. *The Selected Writings of Benjamin Rush.* Edited by Dagobert Runes. New York: Philosophical Library, 1947.

Selby-Bigge, L. A., ed. *British Moralists.* 2 vols. Oxford: Clarendon Press, 1897.

Simmons, George. *Public Spirit and Mobs.* Springfield, Mass.: Merriam, Chapin; Boston: Wm. Crosby & H. P. Nichols, 1851.

Smith, Adam. *The Theory of Moral Sentiments* [1759]. Indianapolis: Liberty Fund, 1984.

Smith, W. L. G. *Life at the South.* Buffalo, N.Y.: Geo. H. Derby, 1852.

Storing, Herbert, ed. *The Anti-Federalist.* Chicago: University of Chicago Press, 1981.

Stowe, Harriet Beecher. *Uncle Tom's Cabin* [1852]. 2 vols. New York: AMS Press, 1967.

Tappan, Henry. *An Essay on the Expression of Passion in Oratory.* New York: C. W. Benedict, 1848.

Thornton, John, ed. *The Pulpit of the American Revolution.* Boston: Gould & Lincoln, 1860.

Tocqueville, Alexis de. *Democracy in America* [1848]. Garden City, N.Y.: Anchor Press Books, 1969.

Trenchard, John, and Thomas Gordon. *Cato's Letters* [1720–1723]. 4 vols. Indianapolis: Liberty Fund, 1995.

Trollope, Frances. *Domestic Manners of the Americans* [1832]. New York: Alfred A. Knopf, 1949.

Washington, George. *Writings of George Washington.* Edited by John Fitzpatrick. 39 vols. Washington, D.C.: U.S. Government Printing Office, 1939.

Webster, Noah. *A Collection of Essays and Fugitiv Writings.* N.p., 1790.

Weld, Theodore. *American Slavery as It Is.* New York: American Anti-Slavery Society, 1839.

Whately, Richard. *Elements of Rhetoric* [1828]. Carbondale and Edwardsville: Southern Illinois University Press, 1963.

Whittelsey, Samuel. *A Publick Spirit Recommended.* New London, Conn., 1731.

William Penn Tercentenary Committee. *Remember William Penn, 1644–1944.* Harrisburg: Commonwealth of Pennsylvania William Penn Tercentenary Committee, 1944.

Winthrop, John. *The History of New England, from 1630–1649* [1825–1826]. 2 vols. Boston: Little, Brown, 1853.

Wolfe, Samuel. *Helper's Impending Crisis Dissected* [1860]. New York: Negro Universities Press, 1969.

Secondary Sources

Akagi, Roy. "The Pennsylvania Constitution of 1838." *Pennsylvania Magazine of History and Biography* 48 (1924): 301–33.

Alexander, John K. "Deference in Colonial Pennsylvania and that Man from New Jersey." *Pennsylvania Magazine of History and Biography* 102 (1978): 422–36.

Andrews, William. *To Tell a Free Story.* Urbana: University of Illinois Press, 1986.

Antczak, Frederick. *Thought and Character.* Ames: Iowa State University Press, 1985.

Bailyn, Bernard. *The Ideological Origins of the American Revolution.* Cambridge, Mass.: Belknap Press, 1967.

——. *The Ordeal of Thomas Hutchinson.* Cambridge: Harvard University Press, 1974.

Baker, Jean. *Affairs of Party.* Ithaca, N.Y.: Cornell University Press, 1983.

Baker, Paula. "The Domestication of Politics: Women and American Political Society, 1780–1920." *American Historical Review* 89 (1984): 620–47.

Bakhtin, Mikhail. *Rabelais and His World.* Cambridge: MIT Press, 1968.

Ball, Terence, and J. G. A. Pocock. *Conceptual Change and the Constitution.* Lawrence: University Press of Kansas, 1988.

Baltzell, E. Digby. *Philadelphia Gentlemen.* Glencoe, Ill.: Free Press, 1958.

Barber, Benjamin. *Strong Democracy.* Berkeley: University of California Press, 1984.

Bercovitch, Sacvan. *American Jeremiad.* Madison: University of Wisconsin Press, 1978.

Berg, Barbara. *The Remembered Gate.* Oxford: Oxford University Press, 1978.

Bernard, L. L., and Jessie Bernard. *Origins of American Sociology.* New York: Thomas Y. Crowell, 1943.

Bode, Carl. *The American Lyceum.* New York: Oxford University Press, 1956.

Botein, Stephen. " 'Meer Mechanics' and an Open Press." *Perspectives in American History* 9 (1975): 127–225.

Bridenbaugh, Carl. *Cities in Revolt.* Oxford: Oxford University Press, 1955.

Brown, Herbert Ross. *The Sentimental Novel in American 1789–1860.* New York: Pageant Books, 1959.

Burke, Peter. *Popular Culture in Early Modern Europe.* London: Temple & Smith, 1978.

Bushman, Richard. *King and People in Provincial Massachusetts.* Chapel Hill: University of North Carolina Press, 1985.

Butler, Jon. *Awash in a Sea of Faith.* Cambridge: Harvard University Press, 1990.

Caldwell, Patricia. *The Puritan Conversion Narrative.* Cambridge: Harvard University Press, 1983.

Calhoun, Craig, ed. *Habermas and the Public Sphere.* Cambridge: MIT Press, 1992.

Cayton, Mary. "The Making of an American Prophet: Emerson, His Audience, and the Rise of the Culture Industry in Nineteenth-Century America." *American Historical Review* 92 (1987): 597–620.

Clark, Dennis. *The Irish in Philadelphia.* Philadelphia: Temple University Press, 1973.

Clark, Gregory, and S. Michael Halloran, eds. *Oratorical Culture in Nineteenth-Century America.* Carbondale and Edwardsville: Southern Illinois University Press, 1993.

Clark, J. C. D. *The Language of Liberty.* Cambridge: Cambridge University Press, 1994.

Clive, Geoffrey. *The Romantic Enlightenment.* New York: Meridian Books, 1960.

Cmiel, Kenneth. *Democratic Eloquence.* New York: William Morrow, 1990.

Cohen, Norman. "The Philadelphia Election Riot of 1742." *Pennsylvania Magazine of History and Biography* 92 (1968): 306–19.

Commons, John R., et al. *History of Labor in the United States.* 4 vols. New York: Macillan, 1918.

Crowley, Sharon. *The Methodical Memory.* Carbondale and Edwardsville: Southern Illinois University Press, 1990.

Davis, Allen, and Mark Haller. *The Peoples of Philadelphia.* Philadelphia: Temple University Press, 1973.

Davis, Charles T., and Henry Louis Gates. *The Slave's Narrative.* Oxford: Oxford University Press, 1985.

Douglas, Ann. *The Feminization of American Culture.* New York: Alfred A. Knopf, 1977.

Dryzek, John. *Discursive Democracy.* Cambridge: Cambridge University Press, 1990.

Eckhardt, Celia. *Fanny Wright: Rebel in America.* Cambridge: Harvard University Press, 1984.

Elkins, Stanley, and Eric McKitrick. *The Age of Federalism.* Oxford: Oxford University Press, 1993.

———, eds. *The Hofstadter Aegis: A Memorial.* New York: Alfred A. Knopf, 1974.

Feldberg, Michael. *The Turbulent Era.* Oxford: Oxford University Press, 1980.

Fishkin, James. *Democracy and Deliberation.* New Haven, Conn.: Yale University Press, 1991.

Foner, Eric. *Free Soil, Free Labor, Free Men.* New York: Oxford University Press, 1970.

———. *Tom Paine and Revolutionary America.* Oxford: Oxford University Press, 1976.

Foner, Philip. *William Heighton: Pioneer Labor Leader of Jacksonian Philadelphia.* New York: International Publishers, 1991.

Formisano, Ronald. *The Birth of Mass Political Parties: Michigan, 1827–1861.* Princeton, N.J.: Princeton University Press, 1971.

———. *The Transformation of Political Culture.* Oxford: Oxford University Press, 1983.

Foster, Frances Smith. *Witnessing Slavery.* 2d ed. Madison: University of Wisconsin Press, 1994.

Frederickson, George M. *The Black Image in the White Mind*. New York: Harper & Row, 1971.

Fuller, Robert. *Mesmerism and the American Cure of Souls*. Philadelphia: University of Pennsylvania Press, 1982.

Gerteis, Louis. *Morality and Utility in American Antislavery Reform*. Chapel Hill: University of North Carolina Press, 1987.

Gilje, Paul. *The Road to Mobocracy*. Chapel Hill: University of North Carolina Press, 1987.

Golden, James, and Edward Corbett. *The Rhetoric of Blair, Campbell, and Whately*. New York: Holt, Rinehart & Winston, 1968.

Govan, Thomas. *Nicholas Biddle: Nationalist and Public Banker*. Chicago: University of Chicago Press, 1959.

Graham, Hugh Davis, and Ted Gurr. *Violence in America*. New York: Bantam Books, 1969.

Grimsted, David. *American Mobbing, 1826–1861*. New York: Oxford University Press, 1998.

——. "Rioting in Its Jacksonian Setting." *American Historical Review* 77 (1972): 361–97.

Gunn, J. A. W. *Beyond Liberty and Property*. Kingston, Canada: McGill-Queen's University Press, 1983.

Guthrie, Warren. "The Development of Rhetorical Theory in America: 1635–1850." *Speech Monographs* 16 (1949): 98–113.

Guttman, Amy, and Dennis Thompson. *Democracy and Disagreement*. Cambridge, Mass.: Belknap Press, 1996.

Habermas, Jürgen. *The Structural Tranformation of the Public Sphere*. Cambridge: MIT Press, 1993.

Hamilton, Alan, and Philip Pettit, eds. *The Good Polity*. Oxford: Basil Blackwell, 1989.

Harper, R. Eugene. *The Transformation of Western Pennsylvania, 1770–1800*. Pittsburgh: University of Pittsburgh Press, 1991.

Hersh, Blanche. *The Slavery of Sex*. Urbana: University of Illinois Press, 1978.

Herzog, Don. *Happy Slaves*. Chicago: University of Chicago Press, 1989.

Hirschman, Albert O. *The Passions and the Interests*. Princeton, N.J.: Princeton University Press, 1977.

Hobsbawm, E. J. *Primitive Rebels*. New York: W. W. Norton, 1959.

Hofstadter, Richard. *The Idea of a Party System*. Berkeley: University of California Press, 1969.

Hovenkamp, Herbert. *Science and Religion in America 1800–1860*. Philadelphia: University of Pennsylvania Press, 1978.

Howe, Daniel. *Political Culture of the American Whigs*. Chicago: University of Chicago Press, 1979.

————. "The Political Psychology of The Federalist." *William & Mary Quarterly*, 3d ser., 44 (1987): 485–509.

Huyler, Jerome. *Locke in America*. Lawrence: University Press of Kansas, 1995.

Jacobs, Margaret, and James Jacobs, eds. *Origins of Anglo-American Radicalism*. London: George Allen & Unwin, 1984.

Japp, Phyllis. "Esther or Isaiah? The Abolitionist-Feminist Rhetoric of Angelina Grimké." *Quarterly Journal of Speech* 71 (1985): 335–48.

John, Richard. *Spreading the News*. Cambridge: Harvard University Press, 1995.

Johnson, Nan. *Nineteenth-Century Rhetoric in North America*. Carbondale and Edwardsville: Southern Illinois University Press, 1991.

Johnson, Paul. *A Shopkeeper's Millennium*. New York: Hill & Wang, 1978.

Jones, Howard Mumford. *American and French Culture*. Chapel Hill: University of North Carolina Press, 1927.

Juster, Susan. *Disorderly Women*. Ithaca, N.Y.: Cornell University Press, 1994.

Kelley, Joseph. *Pennsylvania: The Colonial Years*. New York: Doubleday, 1980.

Kendall, Kathleen, and Jeanne Fisher. "Frances Wright on Women's Rights: Eloquence versus Ethos." *Quarterly Journal of Speech* 60 (1974): 58–68.

Kirby, John. "Early American Politics—The Search for Ideology: An Historiographical Analysis and Critique of the Concept of 'Deference.' " *Journal of Politics* 32 (1970): 808–38.

Kramer, Michael. *Imagining Language in America*. Princeton, N.J.: Princeton University Press, 1992.

Lane, Roger. *Policing the City: Boston 1822–1885*. Cambridge: Harvard University Press, 1967.

Laurie, Bruce. *Working People of Philadelphia, 1800–1850*. Philadelphia: Temple University Press, 1980.

Lee, Alfred McClung. *The Daily Newspaper in America*. New York: Macmillan, 1937.

Leonard, Gerald. "Partisan Political Theory and the Unwritten Constitution." Ph.D. diss., University of Michigan, 1992.

Leonard, Thomas. *The Power of the Press*. Oxford: Oxford University Press, 1986.

Lincoln, C. H. *The Revolutionary Movement in Pennsylvania 1760–1776*. University of Pennsylvania Series in History I. Philadelphia: For the University, 1901.

Maier, Pauline. *From Resistance to Revolution*. New York: Alfred A. Knopf, 1972.

————. "Popular Uprisings and Civil Authority in Eighteenth-Century America." *William & Mary Quarterly*, 3d ser., 27 (1970): 3–35.

Maizlish, Stephen, and John Kushman, eds. *Essays on American Antebellum Politics, 1840–1860.* College Station: Texas A&M University Press, 1982.

Manin, Bernard. "On Legitimacy and Political Deliberation." *Political Theory* 15 (August 1987): 338–68.

Mansbridge, Jane. *Beyond Adversary Democracy.* New York: Basic Books, 1980.

Martin, Terence. *The Instructed Vision.* Bloomington: Indiana University Press, 1961.

McCormick, Richard. *The Presidential Game.* Oxford: Oxford University Press, 1982.

McWilliams, Wilson Carey. *The Idea of Fraternity in America.* Berkeley: University of California Press, 1973.

Melder, Keith. *Beginnings of Sisterhood.* New York: Schocken Books, 1977.

Miller, Joshua. *The Rise and Fall of Democracy in Early America, 1630–1789.* University Park: Pennsylvania State University Press, 1991.

Miller, Perry. *The Life of the Mind in America.* New York: Harcourt, Brace & World, 1965.

———. *The New England Mind: The Seventeenth Century.* Cambridge: Harvard University Press, 1967.

Morantz, Regina. " 'Democracy' and 'Republic' in American Ideology, 1787–1840." Ph.D. diss., Columbia University, 1971.

Mott, Frank L. *American Journalism,* 3d ed. New York: Macmillan, 1962.

Murphy, Teresa. *Ten Hours' Labor.* Ithaca, N.Y.: Cornell University Press, 1992.

Nash, Gary. "The Transformation of Urban Politics, 1700–1765." *Journal of American History* 60 (1973): 605–32.

Nussbaum, Martha. *Love's Knowledge.* Oxford: Oxford University Press, 1990.

———. *Poetic Justice.* Boston: Beacon Press, 1995.

Nuttall, Geoffrey. *The Holy Spirit in Puritan Faith and Experience.* Oxford: Basil Blackwell, 1946.

Nye, Russell. *The Cultural Life of the New Nation.* New York: Harper & Row, 1960.

Oberholtzer, Ellis. *Philadelphia: A History of the City and Its People.* 4 vols. Philadelphia: S. J. Clarke, 1912.

Oravec, Christine. "The Democratic Critics: An Alternative American Rhetorical Tradition of the Nineteenth Century." *Rhetorica* 4 (1986): 395–421.

Palmer, R. R. "Notes on the Use of the Word 'Democracy' 1789–1799." *Political Science Quarterly* 68 (1953): 203–26.

Pangle, Thomas. *The Spirit of Modern Republicanism.* Chicago: University of Chicago Press, 1988.

Parrington, Vernon. *The Colonial Mind, 1620–1800.* New York: Harcourt, Brace, 1927.

Perry, Lewis, and Michael Fellman. *Anti-Slavery Reconsidered.* Baton Rouge: Louisiana State University Press, 1979.

Pocock, J. G. A. "The Classical Theory of Deference." *American Historical Review* 81 (1976): 516–23.

Reynolds, David. *Beneath the American Renaissance.* New York: Alfred A. Knopf, 1988.

Richards, Leonard. *"Gentlemen of Property and Standing."* Oxford: Oxford University Press, 1970.

Richardson, James. *The New York Police.* New York: Oxford University Press, 1970.

Robbins, Caroline. *The Eighteenth-Century Commonwealthmen.* Cambridge: Harvard University Press, 1959.

Roediger, David. *The Wages of Whiteness.* London: Verso, 1991.

Rorty, Richard. *Contingency, Irony, and Solidarity.* Cambridge: Cambridge University Press, 1989.

———. "Feminism and Pragmatism." *Michigan Quarterly Review* 30 (spring 1991): 231–58.

Rosswurm, Steven. *Arms, Country and Class.* New Brunswick, N.J.: Rutgers University Press, 1987.

Rudé, George. *The Crowd in History.* New York: John Wiley & Sons, 1964.

Runcie, John. " 'Hunting the Nigs' in Philadelphia: The Race Riot of August 1834." *Pennsylvania History* 39 (1972): 187–218.

Rutland, Robert. *The Newsmongers.* New York: Dial Press, 1973.

Ryan, Mary P. *Civic Wars.* Berkeley: University of California Press, 1997.

———. *Women in Public.* Baltimore: Johns Hopkins University Press, 1990.

Sanders, Lynn. "Against Deliberation." *Political Theory* 25 (June 1997): 347–76.

Sattler, William. "Conceptions of Ethos in Ancient Rhetoric." *Speech Monographs* 14 (1947): 55–65.

Saum, Lewis. *The Popular Mood of Pre–Civil War America.* Westport, Conn.: Greenwood Press, 1980.

Saxton, Alexander. *The Rise and Fall of the White Republic.* London: Verso, 1990.

Schomburgk, Robert. *The History of Barbados.* London: Frank Cass, 1971.

Schudson, Michael. *Discovering the News.* New York: Basic Books, 1978.

Scott, Donald. "The Popular Lecture and the Creation of a Public in Mid-Nineteenth-Century America." *Journal of American History* 66 (1980): 791–809.

Scranton, Philip. "Varieties of Paternalism: Industrial Structures and the

Social Relations of Production in American Textiles." *American Quarterly* 36 (1984): 235–75.

Shapin, Steven. *A Social History of Truth.* Chicago: University of Chicago Press, 1994.

Shea, Daniel. *Spiritual Autobiography in Early America.* 2d ed. Madison: University of Wisconsin Press, 1988.

Slaughter, Thomas. *Bloody Dawn.* Oxford: Oxford University Press, 1991.

Slotkin, Richard. *Regeneration through Violence.* Middleton, Conn.: Wesleyan University Press, 1973.

Smiley, David. *The Lion of White Hall.* Madison: University of Wisconsin Press, 1962.

Smith, Barbara Clark. "Food Rioters and the American Revolution." *William & Mary Quarterly,* 3d ser., 51 (1994): 3–34.

Spring, David. "Walter Bagehot and Deference." *American Historical Review* 81 (1976): 524–31.

Starling, Mary Wilson. *The Slave Narrative: Its Place in American History.* Boston: G. K. Hill, 1981.

Sunstein, Cass. "Beyond the Republican Revival." *Yale Law Journal* 97 (1988): 1539–90.

Taylor, Alan. "The Art of Hook and Snivey." *Journal of American History* 79 (1993): 1371–96.

———. "From Fathers to Friends of the People." *Journal of the Early Republic* 11 (1991): 465–91.

———. *Liberty Men and Great Proprietors.* Chapel Hill: University of North Carolina Press, 1990.

Tilly, Charles. *From Mobilization to Revolution.* Reading, Mass.: Addison-Wesley, 1978.

Tinkcum, Harry. *The Republicans and Federalists in Pennsylvania.* Harrisburg: Pennsylvania Historical & Museum Commission, 1950.

Tipson, Baird. "Invisible Saints: The 'Judgment of Charity' in the Early New England Churches." *Church History* 44 (March 1975): 460–71.

Tompkins, Jane. *Sensational Design.* New York: Oxford University Press, 1985.

Wallace, Michael. "Changing Concepts of Party in the United States: New York, 1815–1828." *American Historical Review* 74 (1968): 453–91.

Walzer, Michael. *Spheres of Justice.* New York: Basic Books, 1983.

Warner, Sam Bass. *The Private City.* Philadelphia: University of Pennsylvania Press, 1968.

Watkins, Owen. *The Puritan Experience.* London: Routledge & Kegan Paul, 1972.

Weigley, Russell, ed. *Philadelphia: A 300-Year History.* New York: W. W. Norton, 1982.

Werner, John M. *Reaping the Bloody Harvest.* New York and London: Garland, 1986.

West, John G. *The Politics of Revelation and Reason.* Lawrence: University Press of Kansas, 1996.

Wilentz, Sean. *Chants Democratic.* Oxford: Oxford University Press, 1984.

Winch, Julie. *Philadelphia's Black Elite.* Philadelphia: Temple University Press, 1988.

Wittke, Carl. *The German-Language Press in America.* Lexington: University of Kentucky Press, 1957.

Wolf, Edwin, and Maxwell Whitemen. *The History of the Jews in Philadelphia from Colonial Times to the Age of Jackson.* Philadelphia: Jewish Publication Society of America, 1956.

Wolin, Sheldon. *Politics and Vision.* Boston: Little, Brown, 1960.

Wood, Gordon. *The Creation of the American Republic, 1776–1787.* New York: W. W. Norton, 1969.

———. "A Note on Mobs in the American Revolution." William & Mary Quarterly, 3d ser., 23 (1963): 635–42.

Yankelovich, David. *Coming to Public Judgment.* Syracuse, N.Y.: Syracuse University Press, 1991.

Zuckerman, Michael. *Peaceable Kingdoms.* New York: Alfred A. Knopf, 1970.

Zuckert, Michael. *Natural Rights and the New Republicanism.* New Haven, Conn.: Yale University Press, 1994.

INDEX